Philip's
School Atlas

| world maps | thematic maps | study maps |

CHANCELLOR
PRESS

CONTENTS

Note: Each section is colour-coded on this contents page and on the heading of each page for ease of reference.

This edition published by Chancellor Press, an imprint of Bounty Books a division of Octopus Publishing Group Ltd, 2-4 Heron Quays, London E14 4JP

Reprinted 2002

© 2000 George Philip Limited (reprinted 2001)

Published in Great Britain in 2000 as Philip's Modern School Atlas 93rd edition by George Philip Limited

Cartography by Philip's

ISBN 0 7537 0490 0

BRITISH ISLES MAPS

A separate map key is provided on the first page of the World Maps section.

SETTLEMENTS

■ **LONDON**　　■ **GLASGOW**　　▣ **BRADFORD**　　▣ Brighton　　● Gateshead

◉ *Aylesbury*　　◎ *Sligo*　　⊙ *Selkirk*　　○ *Burford*　　○ *Lampeter*

Settlement symbols and type styles vary according to the population and importance of towns

　Built up areas　　　　　□ London Boroughs

ADMINISTRATION

────── International boundaries　　　**W A L E S**　Country names

────── National boundaries　　　　　KENT　Administrative area names

─ ─ ─ Administrative boundaries　　　*EXMOOR*　National park names

COMMUNICATIONS

══ Motorways　　　　　　　　　　　　──── Main passenger railways
═══ *under construction*　　　　　　 ─ ─ ─. *under construction*
　　　　　　　　　　　　　　　　　　　 ⊣──⊢ *in tunnels*

──── Major roads　　　　　　　　　　 ──── Other passenger railways
─ ─ ─. *under construction*　　　　　 ─ ─ ─. *under construction*
⊣──⊢ *in tunnels*　　　　　　　　　　 ⊣──⊢ *in tunnels*

──── Other important roads　　　　　 ········· Canals
─ ─ ─. *under construction*　　　　　 ·········· *in tunnels*
⊣──⊢ *in tunnels*

　　　⊕　Major airports　　　　　⊕　Other airports

PHYSICAL FEATURES

〜 Perennial rivers　　　　　　　▲ 444　Elevations in metres

▨ Tidal flats　　　　　　　　　　▾ 38　Depths below sea level
　　　　　　　　　　　　　　　　　　　　in metres

◗ Lakes or reservoirs

⬭ Reservoirs under
　construction

ELEVATION AND DEPTH TINTS

Height of Land above Sea Level　　**Land below Sea Level**　　**Depth of Sea**

in metres	1000	750	500	400	200	100	0							
								150	300	600	1500	3000	6000	in feet
in feet	3000	2250	1500	1200	600	300								
							0	20	50	100	200	500	1000	2000
														in metres

SHETLAND
ISLANDS
on same scale

West from Greenwich

Projection : Conical with two standard parallels

ORKNEY ISLANDS
on same scale

CARTOGRAPHY BY PHILIP'S.

1:1 000 000

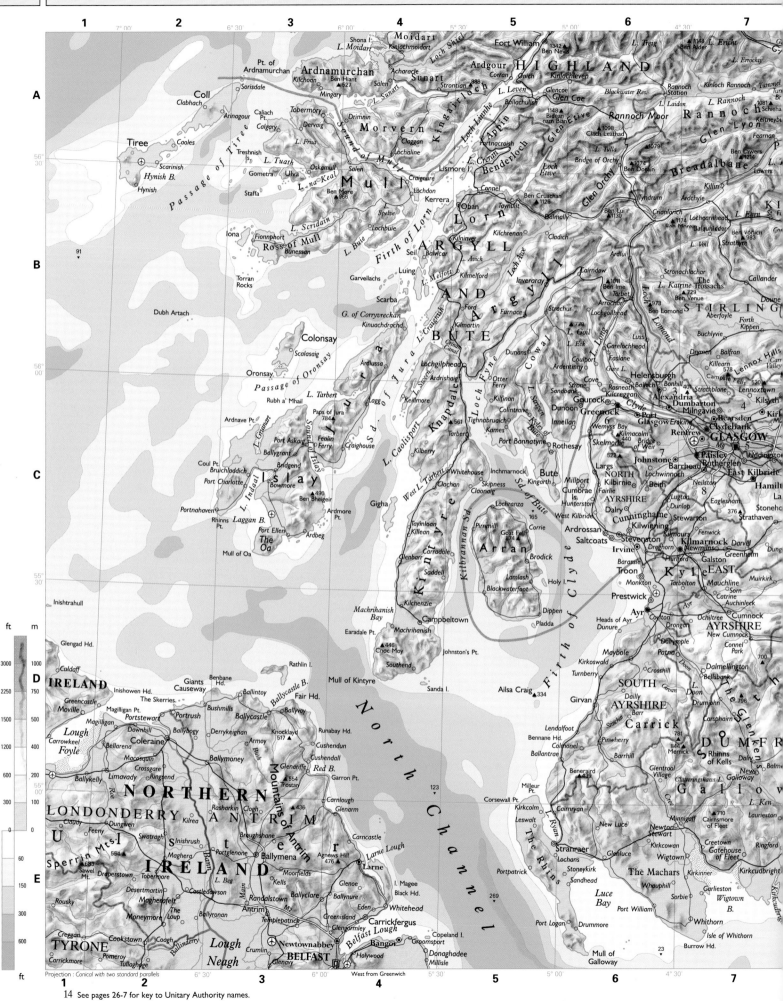

Projection : Conical with two standard parallels

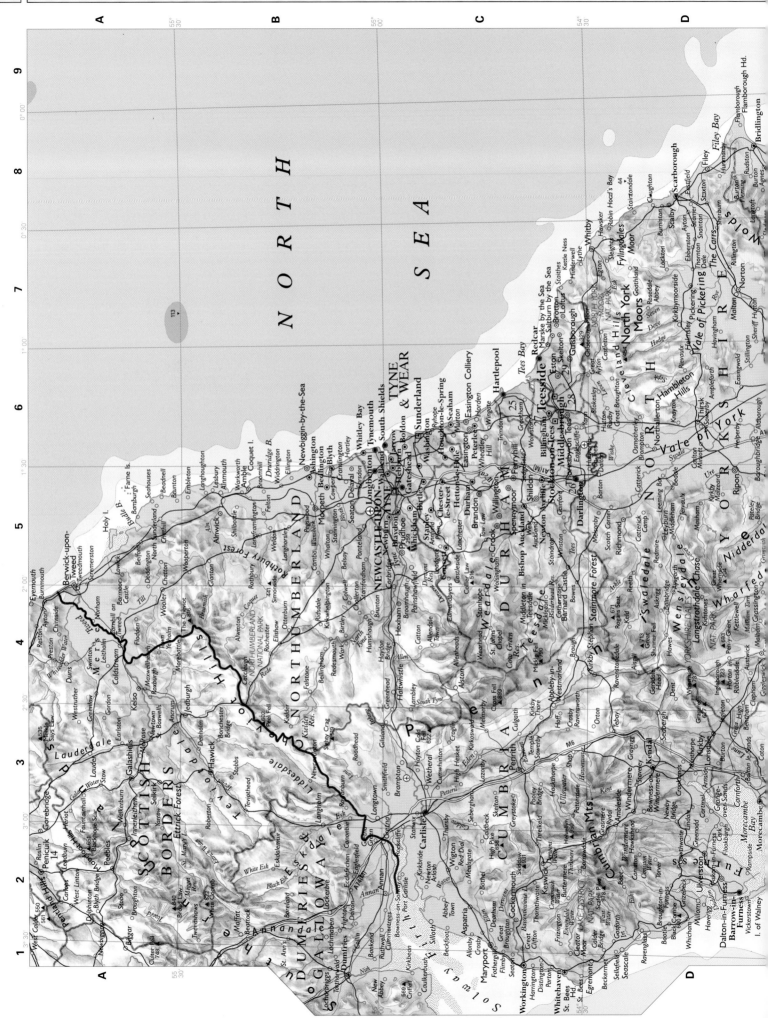

See pages 26-7 for key to Unitary Authority names.

Projection : Conical with two standard parallels

1:1 000 000

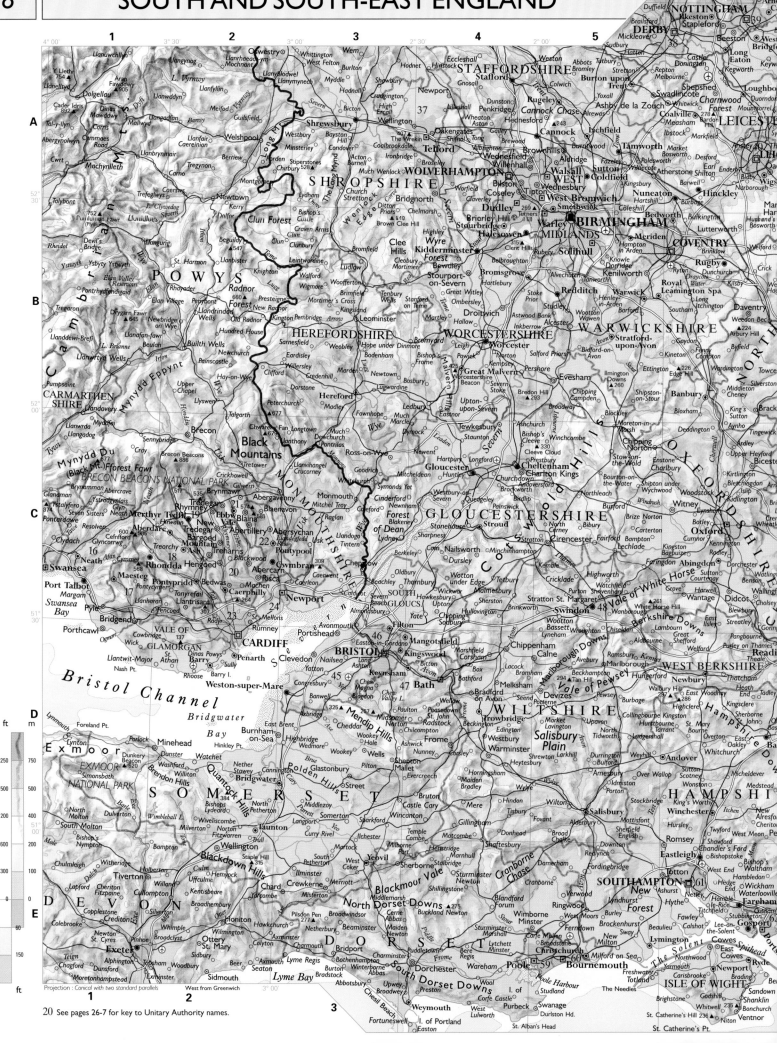

Projection : Conical with two standard parallels   West from Greenwich

20 See pages 26-7 for key to Unitary Authority names.

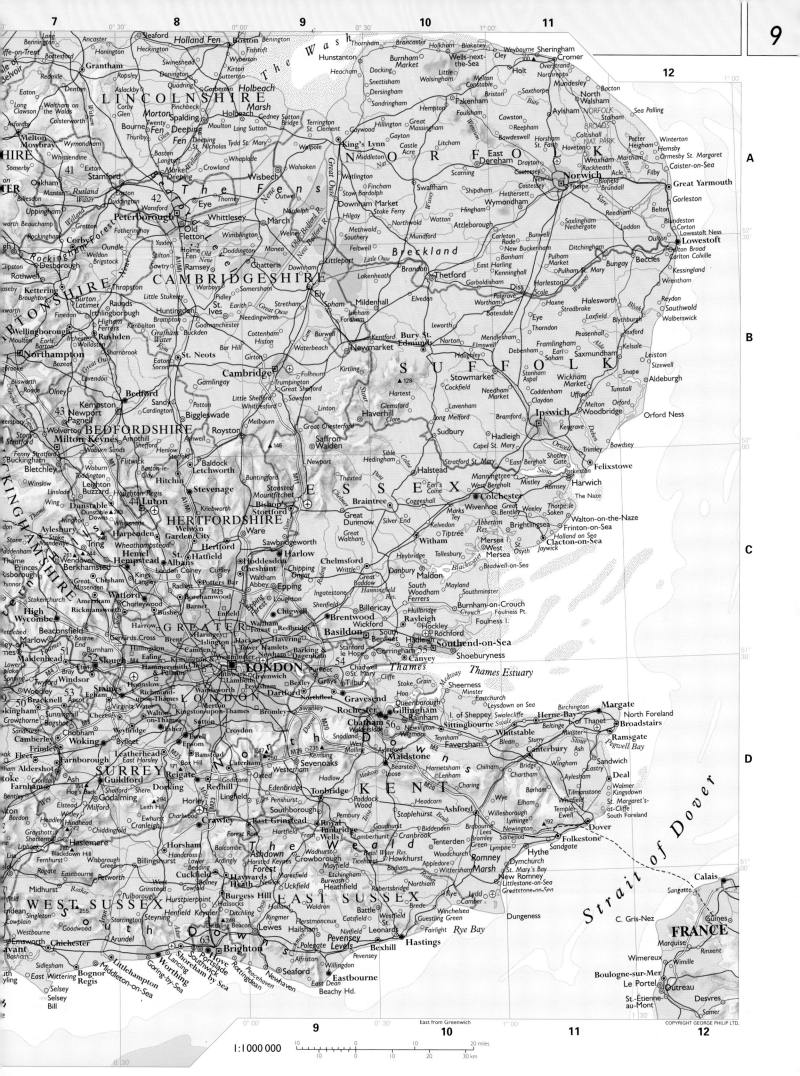

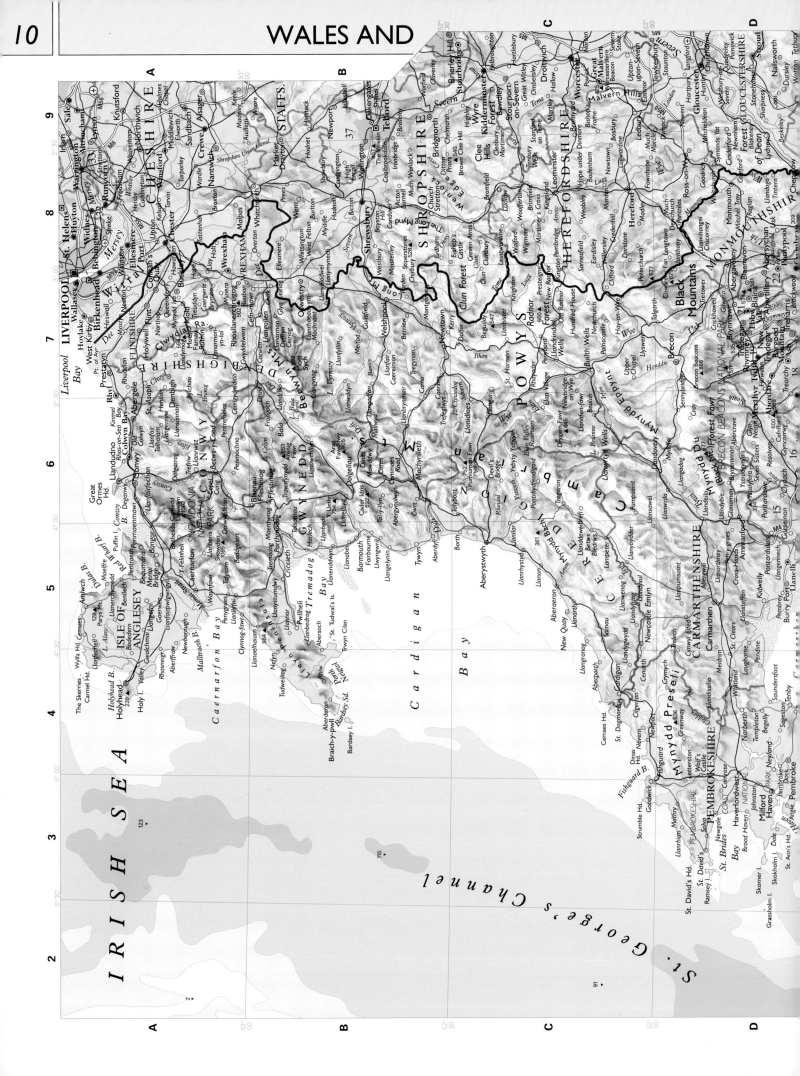

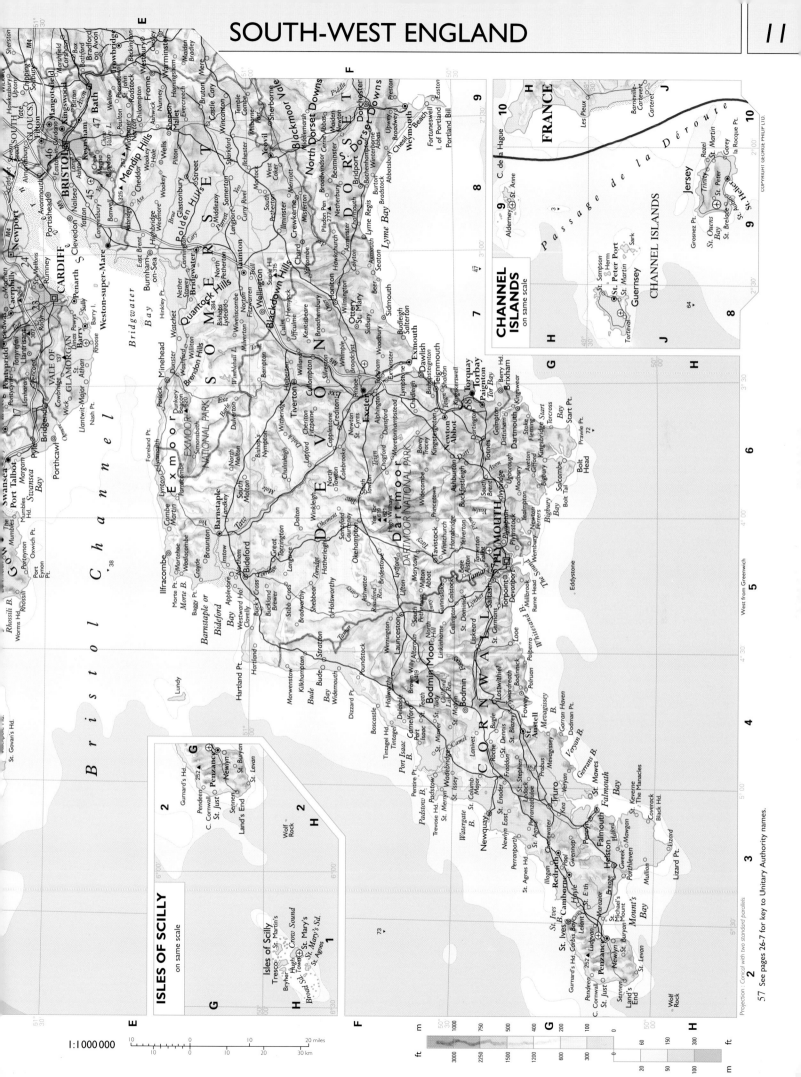

A T L A N T I C

O C E A N

MALIN HD.

Projection : Conical with two standard parallels

West from Greenwich

1:1 000 000

10   0   10   20 miles

10   0   10   20   30 km

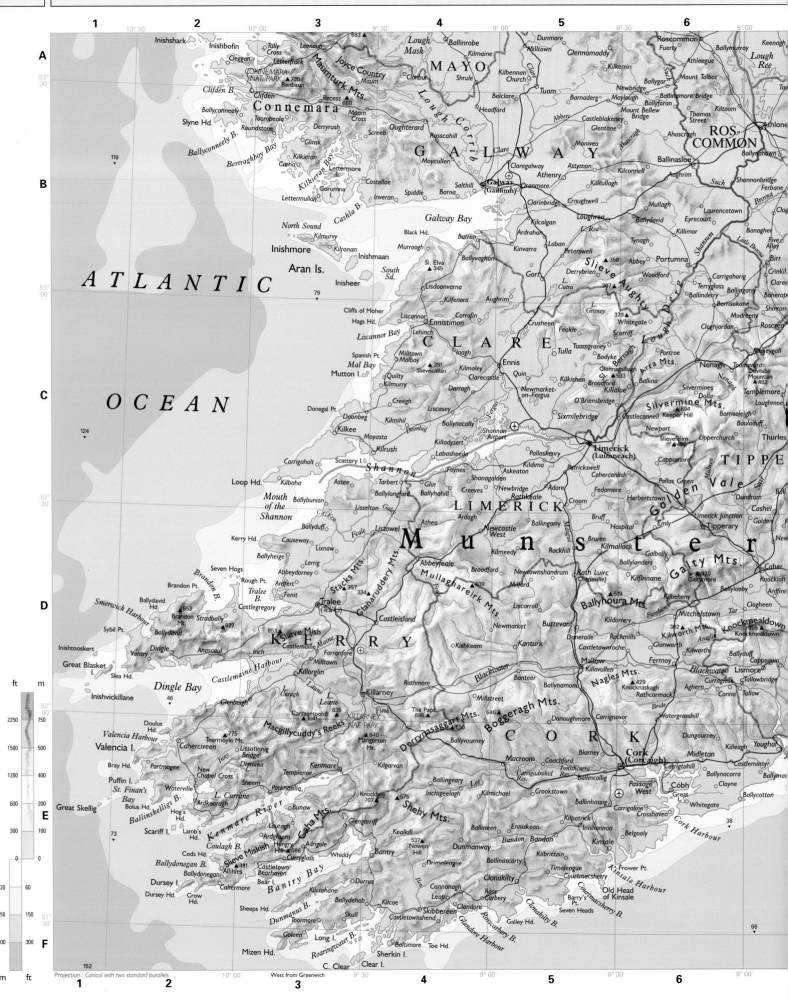

A

B

C

D

E

F

7   7° 30'   8   7° 00'   9   6° 30'   10   6° 00'   11   5° 30'   12   5° 00'   13

53° 30'

53° 00'

52° 30'

52° 00'

51° 30'

WESTMEATH

Carrickboy
Ballinalack
L. Derravaragh
Delvin
Ballynacarrigy
mahon
L. Iron
L. Owel
Rathconrath
Mullingar
Killucan
Ballivor
Ballymore
The Downs
Cloghan
Killucan
Royal Canal
Castletown
Geoghegan
L. Ennell
Kinnegad
Clonard
Horseleap
Ballynagore
Rochfortbridge
Moyvally
Johnstown
Bridge
Clara
Kilbeggan
Tyrrellspass
Edenderry
Durrow
Abbey
Derrygrogan
Killane
Clodiagh
Daingean
Scregган
Tullamore
Ballinagar

OFFALY **Bog of Allen**

Killeigh
Geashill
Rathangan
Kilcormac
Portarlington
Cushina
Barrow
amstown
Rosenallis
Mountmellick
Port Laoise
(Maryborough)
Vicarstown

MEATH

Athboy
Templetogher
Boyne
Trim
Stamford
Dunshaughlin
Rathmolyon
Summerhill
Ianfield
Dunboyne
Moyvally
Donadea
Cloncurry
Kilcock
Maynooth
Clonee
Leixlip
Lucan
Celbridge
Clane
Robertstown
Allenwood
Naas
Droichead Nua
(Newbridge)
Kilcullen
Ballymore
Eustace
Hollywood

Ardcath
Ratoath
Ballyboghil
Ward
Finglas
Glasnevin
Clontarf

Naul
Lusk
Rush
Lambay I.
Donabate
Malahide
Portmarnock
Baldoyle
Ireland's Eye
Howth
Howth Hd.

Balbriggan
Skerries

DUBLIN
DUBLIN
(Baile Atha Cliath)
Blackrock
Dun Laoghaire (Dúnleary)
Dalkey
Killiney

Clondalkin
Rathcoole
Tallaght
Capidstown
Hill
Brittas
Kill
Rathmore
▲380

KILDARE

Kildare
Monasterevin
New Inn

Poulaphouca
Res.

▲754
Kippure
506 ▲
Great
Sugar
Loaf
Bray Hd.
Greystones

Enniskerry
Bray
2
Newtown Mount Kennedy
Newcastle

IRISH

SEA

L E I N S T E R

529 ▲
Arderin
Slieve Bloom
Mountrath
Castletown
Mountmellick

LAOIS

Borris-in-Ossory
naghmore
Erril
Ballycolla
Durrow
Rathdowney

Stradbally
Abbeyleix
Ballyroan
Clogh
Castlecomer
Ballyragget
Johnstown
Freshford
Moyne
Urlingford

Fontstown
Athy
Kilkea
Timolin
Moone
Baltinglass
Ballylynan
Arless
Ballickmoyler
Graigue
Carlow
Nurney
Leighlinbridge
Oldleighlin
Paulstown

Vicarstown
Stradbally

Dunlavin
Donard
Greese
Rathvilly
Hacketstown
Kiltegan
Knockananna
Clonmore
Shillelagh
Ballon
Fennagh
Kildavin

Roundwood
Laragh
Glenealy
Kilbride
Rathdrum
Aghavannagh
Aughrim
Woodenbridge
Avoca
Croghan Mt.
▲607
Coolgreany

Vartry
Res.
Ballinalea
Rathnew
Wicklow
Wicklow Hd.

Mizen Hd.

Arklow
Arklow Hd.
Kilmichael Pt.

W I C K L O W
Lugnaquilla
926 ▲

Wicklow Mountains
Mt. Leinster
▲796

CARLOW

Tullow
Tinahely
Derry
Carnew
Craanford
Gorey
Camolin
Ballycanew
Courtown
Riverchapel

Braich-y-pwll
Bardsey I.

123
▼

115
▼

S E A

Kilkenny
(Cill Chainnigh)
Gowran
Bennettsbridge
Muine Bheag
(Bagenalstown)
Goresbridge
Borris

KILKENNY

Kilmanagh
Ballymurphy
Kells
Thomastown
Graiguenamanagh
Kilmagany
Inistioge

Blackstairs Mts.
Kilealy
Blackstairs
Mt.
519 ▲
Brandon
Glynn
Ballywilliam
Clonroche

Ballycarney
Ballindaggan
Ford
Enniscorthy
Blackwater

WEXFORD

New
Birmingham
Ballingarry
Killenaule
Drangan
Mullinahone
Windgap
Callan
Kilmaganny
Tullaghought

Oilgate

Castlebridge

Fethard
Cloneen
Ninemilehouse
▲722
Slievenamon
Kilsheelan
Carrick-on-Suir
Piltown
Fiddown
Mullinavat
Killinaspick

Kilkenny
Ballynabola
Foulkesmill
Taghmon

Wexford Harbour
Wexford (Loch Garman)
Rosslare
Rosslare Harbour
Greenore Pt.

Tuskar Rock

91
▼

St. George's Channel

llyclerahan
nmel
755 ▲
Comeragh Mts.
Carrickbeg
Portlaw
Fiddown
Mooncoin
onavullagh Mts.
792 ▲
727 ▲
Kilbrien
Kilmeadan
illstreet
Ballylaneen
Kilmacthomas
Tramore
Waterford
(Port Laírge)
Passage
East
Arthurstown
Tintern
Abbey
Duncormick
Bridgetown
Bannow
Kilmore
Fethard
Bannow
B.
Baginbun
Hd.
Crossfarnoge
Pt.
Saltee Is.
Hook
Hd.
Kilmore
Quay
Lady's
I. Lake
Tacumshin
L.
Broadway
Churchtown
Carnsore Pt.

TERFORD

ngarvan
Ringville
Dungarvan Harbour
Helvick Hd.

Mine Hd.

Ardmore
Ardmore Hd.
B.

Stradbally
Bunmahon
Annestown
Tramore B.
Dunmore
East
Waterford Harbour

51
▼

115
▼

Strumble Hd.
Goodwick
Fishguard B.
Dinas
Hd.
Newport

Fishguard
Greenway
Mathry
Letterston
Llanrhian
St. David's Hd.
St. David's
Solva
Ramsey I.
Newgale
COAST
Wolf's
Castle
Carnrose

PEMBROKESHIRE

Haverfordwest
NATIONAL
Broad Haven
Johnston
St. Brides
Bay
Skomer I.
Milford
Haven
Skokholm I.
Dale
PARK
Neyland
Grassholm I.
St. Ann's Hd.
Pembroke
Dock
Angle
Pembroke
Milford Haven
Linney Hd.
St. Govan's Hd.

C E L T I C

S E A

CARTOGRAPHY BY PHILIP'S.

1:1 000 000

10   0   10   20 miles
10   0   10   20   30 km

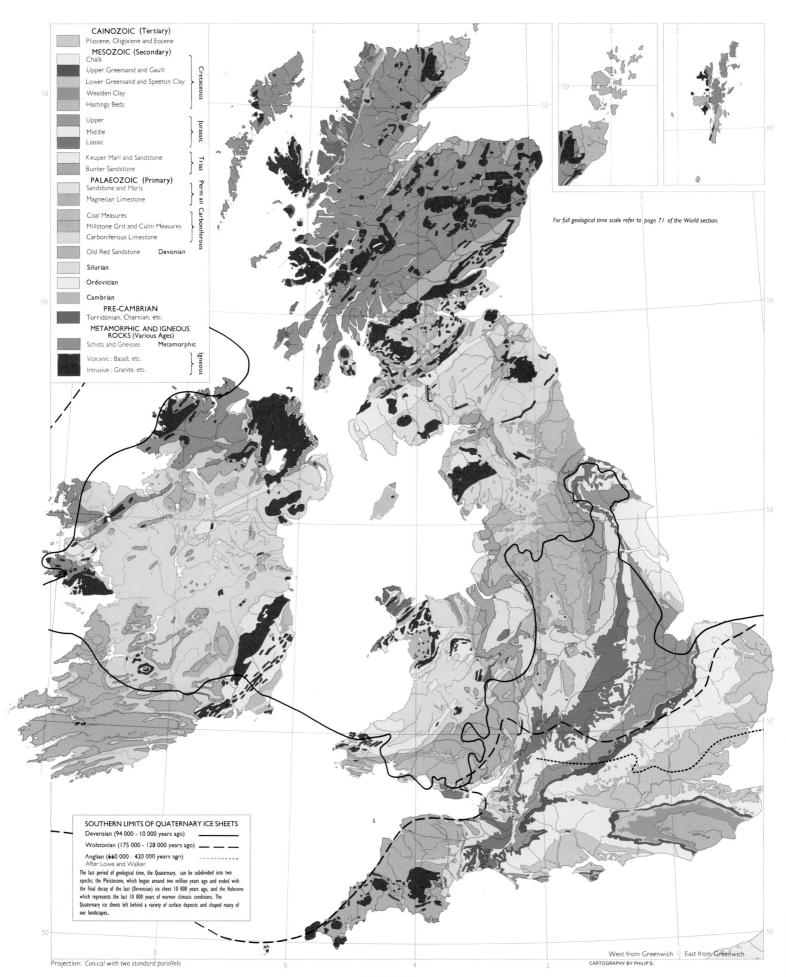

CAINOZOIC (Tertiary)
Pliocene, Oligocene and Eocene

MESOZOIC (Secondary)
Chalk — Cretaceous
Upper Greensand and Gault
Lower Greensand and Speeton Clay
Wealden Clay
Hastings Beds

Upper — Jurassic
Middle
Liassic

Keuper Marl and Sandstone — Trias
Bunter Sandstone

PALAEOZOIC (Primary)
Sandstone and Marls — Permian
Magnesian Limestone

Coal Measures — Carboniferous
Millstone Grit and Culm Measures
Carboniferous Limestone

Old Red Sandstone — Devonian

Silurian

Ordovician

Cambrian

PRE-CAMBRIAN
Torridonian, Charnian, etc.

METAMORPHIC AND IGNEOUS ROCKS (Various Ages)
Schists and Gneisses — Metamorphic

Volcanic : Basalt, etc. — Igneous
Intrusive : Granite, etc.

For full geological time scale refer to page 71 of the World section.

SOUTHERN LIMITS OF QUATERNARY ICE SHEETS
Devensian (94 000 - 10 000 years ago) ————
Wolstonian (175 000 - 128 000 years ago) – – – –
Anglian (660 000 - 420 000 years ago) ············
After Lowe and Walker

The last period of geological time, the Quaternary, can be subdivided into two epochs; the Pleistocene, which began around two million years ago and ended with the final decay of the last (Devensian) ice sheet 10 000 years ago, and the Holocene which represents the last 10 000 years of warmer climatic conditions. The Quaternary ice sheets left behind a variety of surface deposits and shaped many of our landscapes.

Projection: *Conical with two standard parallels*

West from Greenwich 0 East from Greenwich

CARTOGRAPHY BY PHILIP'S.

1:4 000 000

20   0   20   40   60 miles
20 0 20 40 60 80 km

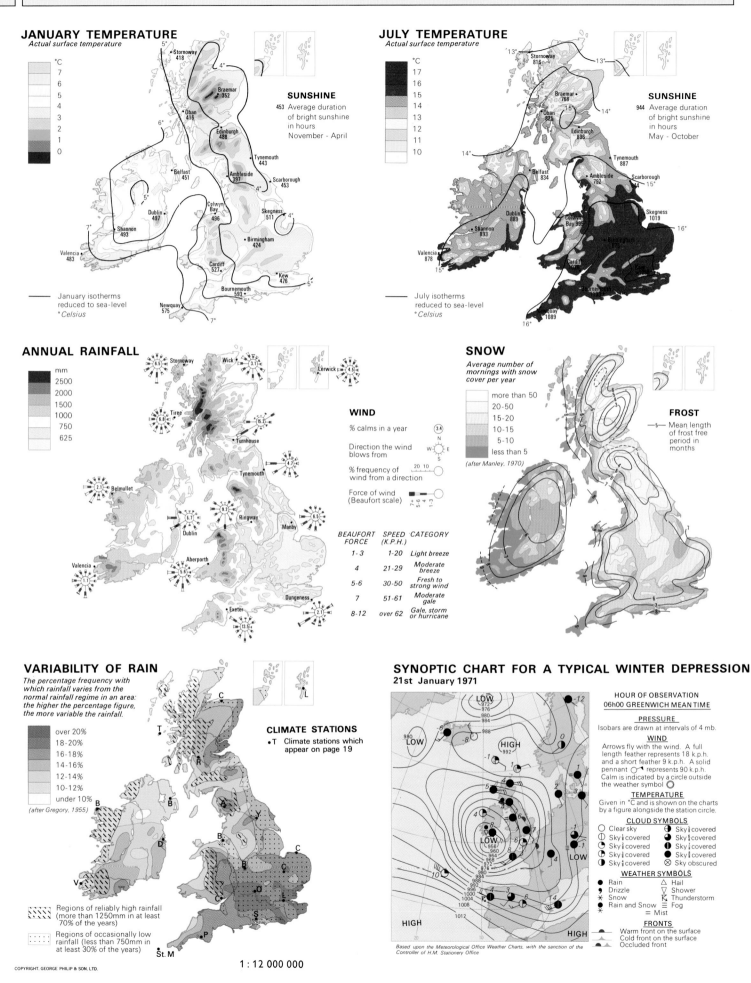

JANUARY TEMPERATURE
Actual surface temperature

°C
7
6
5
4
3
2
1
0

SUNSHINE

453 Average duration of bright sunshine in hours November - April

Stornoway 418
Braemar 352
Oban 416
Edinburgh 488
Tynemouth 443
Belfast 451
Ambleside 397
Scarborough 453
Colwyn Bay 496
Skegness 511
Dublin 497
Shannon 493
Birmingham 424
Valencia 483
Cardiff 527
Kew 476
Bournemouth 593
Newquay 575

—— January isotherms reduced to sea-level °Celsius

JULY TEMPERATURE
Actual surface temperature

°C
17
16
15
14
13
12
11
10

SUNSHINE

944 Average duration of bright sunshine in hours May - October

Stornoway 816
Braemar 768
Oban 825
Edinburgh 896
Tynemouth 887
Belfast 834
Ambleside 792
Scarborough
Colwyn Bay 995
Skegness 1019
Dublin 889
Shannon 893
Birmingham
Valencia 878
Cardiff
Kew
Bournemouth
Newquay 1089

—— July isotherms reduced to sea-level °Celsius

ANNUAL RAINFALL

mm
2500
2000
1500
1000
750
625

Stornoway Wick
Lerwick
Tiree
Turnhouse
Belmullet
Tynemouth
Dublin
Ringway
Manby
Valencia
Aberporth
Dungeness
Exeter

WIND

% calms in a year (3.4)

Direction the wind blows from

% frequency of wind from a direction 20 10

Force of wind (Beaufort scale)

BEAUFORT FORCE	SPEED (K.P.H.)	CATEGORY
1-3	1-20	Light breeze
4	21-29	Moderate breeze
5-6	30-50	Fresh to strong wind
7	51-61	Moderate gale
8-12	over 62	Gale, storm or hurricane

SNOW
Average number of mornings with snow cover per year

more than 50
20-50
15-20
10-15
5-10
less than 5

(after Manley, 1970)

FROST

—5— Mean length of frost free period in months

VARIABILITY OF RAIN

The percentage frequency with which rainfall varies from the normal rainfall regime in an area: the higher the percentage figure, the more variable the rainfall.

over 20%
18-20%
16-18%
14-16%
12-14%
10-12%
under 10%

(after Gregory, 1955)

CLIMATE STATIONS

•T Climate stations which appear on page 19

Regions of reliably high rainfall (more than 1250mm in at least 70% of the years)

Regions of occasionally low rainfall (less than 750mm in at least 30% of the years)

SYNOPTIC CHART FOR A TYPICAL WINTER DEPRESSION
21st January 1971

HOUR OF OBSERVATION 06h00 GREENWICH MEAN TIME

PRESSURE
Isobars are drawn at intervals of 4 mb.

WIND
Arrows fly with the wind. A full length feather represents 18 k.p.h. and a short feather 9 k.p.h. A solid pennant represents 90 k.p.h. Calm is indicated by a circle outside the weather symbol ◯

TEMPERATURE
Given in °C and is shown on the charts by a figure alongside the station circle.

CLOUD SYMBOLS

◯ Clear sky	◑ Sky ⅗ covered
◔ Sky ⅒ covered	◑ Sky ⅘ covered
◑ Sky ⅕ covered	◕ Sky ⅞ covered
◑ Sky ¼ covered	⬤ Sky fully covered
◑ Sky ½ covered	⊗ Sky obscured

WEATHER SYMBOLS

● Rain	△ Hail		
⁹ Drizzle	▽ Shower		
✳ Snow	⚡ Thunderstorm		
✳ Rain and Snow	≡ Fog		
	= Mist		

FRONTS

—●— Warm front on the surface
—▲— Cold front on the surface
—▲— Occluded front

Based upon the Meteorological Office Weather Charts, with the sanction of the Controller of H.M. Stationery Office

COPYRIGHT. GEORGE PHILIP & SON, LTD.

1 : 12 000 000

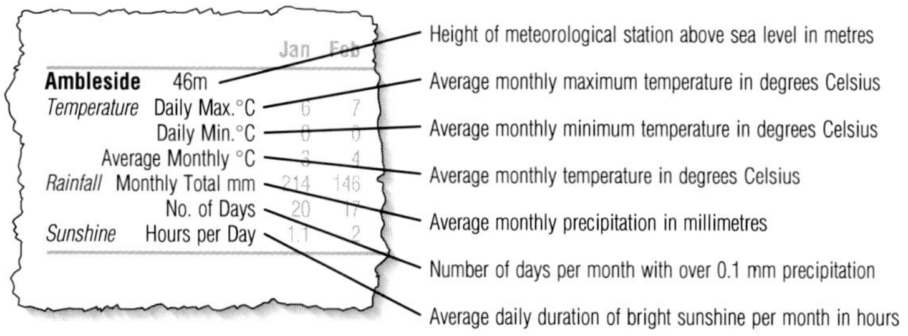

Jan Feb
Ambleside 46m
Temperature Daily Max.°C 6 7
Daily Min.°C 0 0
Average Monthly °C 3 4
Rainfall Monthly Total mm 214 146
No. of Days 20 17
Sunshine Hours per Day 1.1 2
Height of meteorological station above sea level in metres
Average monthly maximum temperature in degrees Celsius
Average monthly minimum temperature in degrees Celsius
Average monthly temperature in degrees Celsius
Average monthly precipitation in millimetres
Number of days per month with over 0.1 mm precipitation
Average daily duration of bright sunshine per month in hours

		Jan	Feb	Mar	Apr	May	June	July	Aug	Sep	Oct	Nov	Dec	Year
Ambleside	46m													
Temperature	Daily Max.°C	6	7	9	12	16	19	20	19	17	13	9	7	13
	Daily Min.°C	0	0	2	4	6	9	11	11	9	6	3	1	5
	Average Monthly °C	3	4	6	8	11	14	15	15	13	10	6	4	9
Rainfall	Monthly Total mm	214	146	112	101	90	111	134	139	184	196	209	215	1851
	No. of Days	20	17	15	15	14	15	18	17	18	19	19	21	208
Sunshine	Hours per Day	1.1	2	3.2	4.5	6	5.7	4.5	4.2	3.3	2.2	1.4	1	3.3
Belfast	4m													
Temperature	Daily Max.°C	6	7	9	12	15	18	18	18	16	13	9	7	12
	Daily Min.°C	2	2	3	4	6	9	11	11	9	7	4	3	6
	Average Monthly °C	4	4	6	8	11	13	15	15	13	10	7	5	9
Rainfall	Monthly Total mm	80	52	50	48	52	68	94	77	80	83	72	90	845
	No. of Days	20	17	16	16	15	16	19	17	18	19	19	21	213
Sunshine	Hours per Day	1.5	2.3	3.4	5	6.3	6	4.4	4.4	3.6	2.6	1.8	1.1	3.5
Belmullet	9m													
Temperature	Daily Max.°C	8	9	10	12	14	16	17	17	16	14	10	9	12
	Daily Min.°C	3	4	4	6	8	10	11	11	10	8	5	4	7
	Average Monthly °C	5	6	7	9	11	13	14	14	13	11	8	6	10
Rainfall	Monthly Total mm	108	64	82	70	75	80	76	95	108	116	127	131	1132
	No. of Days	18	13	16	15	14	12	14	17	16	18	20	22	195
Sunshine	Hours per Day	1.9	2.5	3.4	5.2	7	6	4.6	5.1	3.9	2.9	1.9	1.3	3.8
Birkenhead	60m													
Temperature	Daily Max.°C	6	6	9	11	15	17	19	19	16	13	9	7	12
	Daily Min.°C	2	2	3	5	8	11	13	13	11	8	5	3	7
	Average Monthly °C	4	4	6	8	11	14	16	16	14	10	7	5	10
Rainfall	Monthly Total mm	64	46	40	41	55	55	67	80	66	71	76	65	726
	No. of Days	18	13	13	13	13	13	15	15	15	17	17	19	181
Sunshine	Hours per Day	1.6	2.4	3.5	5.3	6.3	6.7	5.7	5.4	4.2	2.9	1.8	1.3	3.9
Birmingham	163m													
Temperature	Daily Max.°C	5	6	9	12	16	19	20	20	17	13	9	6	13
	Daily Min.°C	2	2	3	5	7	10	12	12	10	7	5	3	7
	Average Monthly °C	3	4	6	8	11	15	16	16	14	10	7	5	10
Rainfall	Monthly Total mm	74	54	50	53	64	50	69	69	61	69	84	67	764
	No. of Days	17	15	13	13	14	13	15	14	14	15	17	18	178
Sunshine	Hours per Day	1.4	2.1	3.2	4.6	5.4	6	5.4	5.1	3.9	2.8	1.6	1.2	3.6
Cambridge	12m													
Temperature	Daily Max.°C	6	7	11	14	17	21	22	22	19	15	10	7	14
	Daily Min.°C	1	1	2	4	7	10	12	12	10	6	4	2	6
	Average Monthly °C	3	4	6	9	12	15	17	17	14	10	7	5	10
Rainfall	Monthly Total mm	49	35	36	37	45	45	58	55	51	51	54	41	558
	No. of Days	15	13	10	11	11	11	12	12	11	13	14	14	147
Sunshine	Hours per Day	1.7	2.5	3.8	5.1	6.2	6.7	6	5.7	4.6	3.4	1.9	1.4	4.1
Cardiff	62m													
Temperature	Daily Max.°C	7	7	10	13	16	19	20	21	18	14	10	8	14
	Daily Min.°C	2	2	3	5	8	11	12	13	11	8	5	3	7
	Average Monthly °C	4	5	7	9	12	15	16	17	14	11	8	6	10
Rainfall	Monthly Total mm	108	72	63	65	76	63	89	97	99	109	116	108	1065
	No. of Days	18	14	13	13	13	13	14	15	16	16	17	18	180
Sunshine	Hours per Day	1.7	2.7	4	5.6	6.4	6.9	6.2	6	4.7	3.4	1.9	1.5	4.3
Craibstone	91m													
Temperature	Daily Max.°C	5	6	8	10	13	16	18	17	15	12	8	6	11
	Daily Min.°C	0	0	2	3	5	8	10	10	8	6	3	1	5
	Average Monthly °C	3	3	5	7	9	12	14	13	12	9	6	4	8
Rainfall	Monthly Total mm	78	55	53	51	63	54	95	75	67	92	93	80	856
	No. of Days	19	16	15	15	14	14	18	15	16	18	19	18	197
Sunshine	Hours per Day	1.8	2.9	3.5	4.9	5.9	6.1	5.1	4.8	4.3	3.1	2	1.5	3.8
Cromer	54m													
Temperature	Daily Max.°C	6	7	9	12	15	18	21	20	18	14	10	8	13
	Daily Min.°C	1	1	3	5	7	10	12	13	11	8	5	3	7
	Average Monthly °C	4	4	6	8	11	14	16	16	15	11	7	5	10
Rainfall	Monthly Total mm	58	46	37	39	48	39	63	56	54	61	64	53	618
	No. of Days	18	16	13	13	11	11	13	12	14	16	18	18	173
Sunshine	Hours per Day	1.8	2.6	4	5.4	6.4	6.8	6.3	5.8	5	3.6	2	1.9	4.3
Dublin	47m													
Temperature	Daily Max.°C	8	8	10	13	15	18	20	19	17	14	10	8	14
	Daily Min.°C	1	2	3	4	6	9	11	11	9	6	4	3	6
	Average Monthly °C	4	5	7	8	11	14	15	15	13	10	7	6	10
Rainfall	Monthly Total mm	67	55	51	45	60	57	70	74	72	70	67	74	762
	No. of Days	13	10	10	11	10	11	13	12	12	11	12	14	139
Sunshine	Hours per Day	1.9	2.5	3.4	5	6.2	6	4.8	4.9	3.9	3.2	2.1	1.6	3.8

		Jan	Feb	Mar	Apr	May	June	July	Aug	Sep	Oct	Nov	Dec	Year
Durham	102m													
Temperature	Daily Max.°C	6	6	9	12	15	18	20	19	17	13	9	7	13
	Daily Min.°C	0	0	1	3	6	9	11	10	9	6	3	2	5
	Average Monthly °C	3	3	5	7	10	13	15	15	13	9	6	4	9
Rainfall	Monthly Total mm	59	51	38	38	51	49	61	67	60	63	66	55	658
	No. of Days	17	15	14	13	13	14	15	14	14	16	17	17	179
Sunshine	Hours per Day	1.7	2.5	3.3	4.6	5.4	6	5.1	4.8	4.1	3	1.9	1.4	3.6
Lerwick	82m													
Temperature	Daily Max.°C	5	5	6	8	11	13	14	14	13	10	8	6	9
	Daily Min.°C	1	1	2	3	5	7	10	10	8	6	4	3	5
	Average Monthly °C	3	3	4	5	8	10	12	12	11	8	6	4	7
Rainfall	Monthly Total mm	109	87	69	68	52	55	72	71	87	104	111	118	1003
	No. of Days	25	22	20	21	15	15	17	17	19	23	24	25	243
Sunshine	Hours per Day	0.8	1.8	2.9	4.4	5.3	5.3	4	3.8	3.5	2.2	2.2	0.5	3
London (Kew)	5m													
Temperature	Daily Max.°C	6	7	10	13	17	20	22	21	19	14	10	7	14
	Daily Min.°C	2	2	3	6	8	12	14	13	11	8	5	4	7
	Average Monthly °C	4	5	7	9	12	16	18	17	15	11	8	5	11
Rainfall	Monthly Total mm	54	40	37	37	46	45	57	59	49	57	64	48	593
	No. of Days	15	13	11	12	12	11	12	11	13	13	15	15	153
Sunshine	Hours per Day	1.5	2.3	3.6	5.3	6.4	7.1	6.4	6.1	4.7	3.2	1.8	1.3	4.1
Oxford	63m													
Temperature	Daily Max.°C	7	7	11	14	17	20	22	22	19	14	10	8	14
	Daily Min.°C	1	1	2	5	7	10	12	12	10	7	4	2	6
	Average Monthly °C	4	4	6	9	12	15	17	17	14	11	7	5	10
Rainfall	Monthly Total mm	61	44	43	41	55	52	55	60	59	64	69	57	660
	No. of Days	13	10	9	9	10	9	10	10	10	11	12	13	126
Sunshine	Hours per Day	1.7	2.6	3.9	5.3	6.1	6.6	5.9	5.7	4.4	3.2	2.1	1.6	4.1
Plymouth	27m													
Temperature	Daily Max.°C	8	8	10	12	15	18	19	19	18	15	11	9	14
	Daily Min.°C	4	4	5	6	8	11	13	13	12	9	7	5	8
	Average Monthly °C	6	6	7	9	12	15	16	16	15	12	9	7	11
Rainfall	Monthly Total mm	99	74	69	53	63	53	70	77	78	91	113	110	950
	No. of Days	19	15	14	12	12	12	14	14	15	16	17	18	178
Sunshine	Hours per Day	1.9	2.9	4.3	6.1	7.1	7.4	6.4	6.4	5.1	3.7	2.2	1.7	4.6
Renfrew	6m													
Temperature	Daily Max.°C	5	7	9	12	15	18	19	19	16	13	9	7	12
	Daily Min.°C	1	1	2	4	6	9	11	11	9	6	4	2	6
	Average Monthly °C	3	4	6	8	11	14	15	15	13	9	7	4	9
Rainfall	Monthly Total mm	111	85	69	67	63	70	97	93	102	119	106	127	1109
	No. of Days	19	16	15	15	14	15	17	17	17	18	18	20	201
Sunshine	Hours per Day	1.1	2.1	2.9	4.7	6	6.1	5.1	4.4	3.7	2.3	1.4	0.8	3.4
St Helier	9m													
Temperature	Daily Max.°C	9	8	11	13	16	19	21	21	19	16	12	10	15
	Daily Min.°C	5	4	6	7	10	13	15	15	14	11	8	6	9
	Average Monthly °C	7	6	8	10	13	16	18	18	17	13	10	8	12
Rainfall	Monthly Total mm	89	68	57	43	44	39	48	67	69	77	101	99	801
	No. of Days	19	15	13	12	11	10	11	12	15	15	17	19	169
Sunshine	Hours per Day	2.3	3.1	5	6.7	7.8	8.5	7.8	7.6	5.6	4.1	2.5	1.8	5.3
St Mary's	50m													
Temperature	Daily Max.°C	9	9	11	12	14	17	19	19	18	15	12	10	14
	Daily Min.°C	6	6	7	7	9	12	13	14	13	11	9	7	9
	Average Monthly °C	8	7	9	10	12	14	16	16	15	13	10	9	12
Rainfall	Monthly Total mm	91	71	69	46	56	49	61	64	67	80	96	94	844
	No. of Days	22	17	16	13	14	14	16	15	16	17	19	21	200
Sunshine	Hours per Day	2	2.9	4.2	6.4	7.6	7.6	6.7	6.7	5.2	3.9	2.5	1.8	4.8
Southampton	20m													
Temperature	Daily Max.°C	7	8	11	14	17	20	22	22	19	15	11	8	15
	Daily Min.°C	2	2	3	5	8	11	13	13	11	7	5	3	7
	Average Monthly °C	5	5	7	10	13	16	17	17	15	11	8	6	11
Rainfall	Monthly Total mm	83	56	52	45	56	49	60	69	70	86	94	84	804
	No. of Days	17	13	13	12	12	12	13	13	14	14	16	17	166
Sunshine	Hours per Day	1.8	2.6	4	5.7	6.7	7.2	6.5	6.4	4.9	3.6	2.2	1.6	4.5
Tiree	9m													
Temperature	Daily Max.°C	7	7	9	10	13	15	16	16	15	12	10	8	12
	Daily Min.°C	4	3	4	5	7	10	11	11	10	8	6	5	7
	Average Monthly °C	5	5	6	8	10	12	14	14	13	10	8	6	9
Rainfall	Monthly Total mm	117	77	67	64	55	70	91	90	118	129	122	128	1128
	No. of Days	23	19	17	17	15	16	20	18	20	23	22	24	234
Sunshine	Hours per Day	1.3	2.6	3.7	5.7	7.5	6.8	5.2	5.3	4.2	2.6	1.6	0.9	4
Valencia	9m													
Temperature	Daily Max.°C	9	9	11	13	15	17	18	18	17	14	12	10	14
	Daily Min.°C	5	4	5	6	8	11	12	13	11	9	7	6	8
	Average Monthly °C	7	7	8	9	11	0	15	15	14	12	9	8	11
Rainfall	Monthly Total mm	105	107	103	75	80	81	107	95	122	140	151	168	1400
	No. of Days	20	15	14	13	13	13	15	15	16	17	18	21	190
Sunshine	Hours per Day	1.6	2.5	3.5	5.2	6.5	5.9	4.7	4.9	3.8	2.8	2	1.3	3.7
York	17m													
Temperature	Daily Max.°C	6	7	10	13	16	19	21	21	18	14	10	7	13
	Daily Min.°C	1	1	2	4	7	10	12	12	10	7	4	2	6
	Average Monthly °C	3	4	6	9	12	15	17	16	14	10	7	5	10
Rainfall	Monthly Total mm	59	46	37	41	50	50	62	68	55	56	65	50	639
	No. of Days	17	15	13	13	13	14	15	14	14	15	17	17	177
Sunshine	Hours per Day	1.3	2.1	3.2	4.7	6.1	6.4	5.6	5.1	4.1	2.8	1.6	1.1	3.7

WATER SUPPLY

- Regions of reliably high rainfall (more than 1250 mm in at least 70% of the years)
- ③ Major reservoirs (capacity over 20 million cubic metres, see list opposite for details)
- Existing inter-regional transfers of water (by pipeline and river)
- Proposed inter-regional transfers of water (by pipeline and river)
- □ Proposed estuary storage site
- ▽ Proposed groundwater storage site
- Principal sources of groundwater (porous and jointed aquifers)

1 : 7 000 000

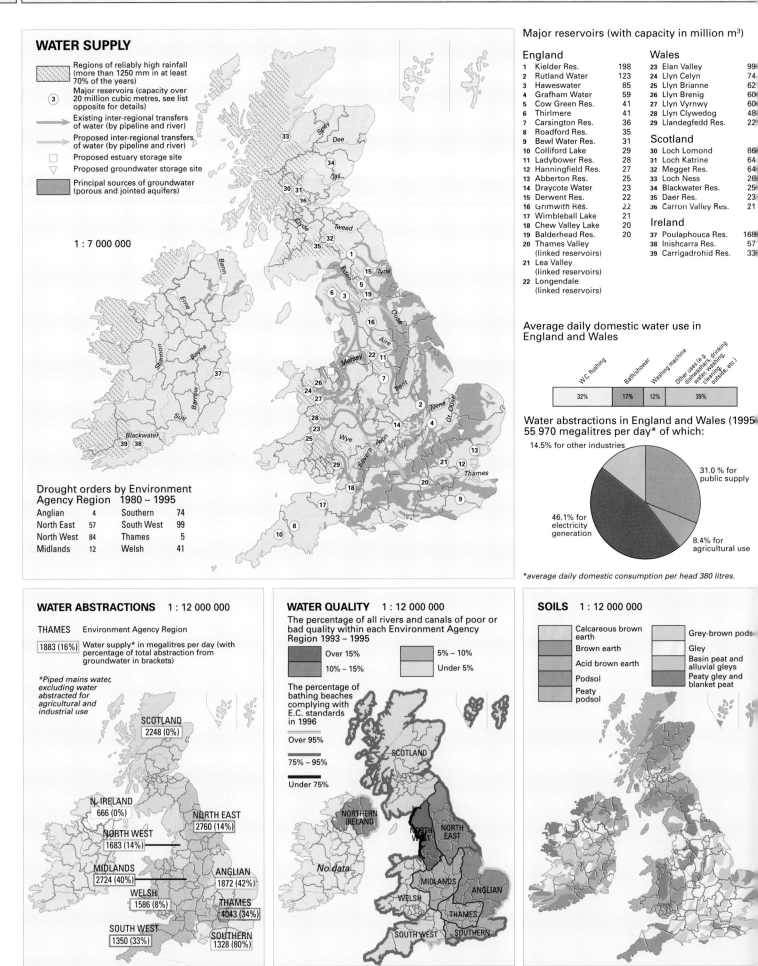

Drought orders by Environment Agency Region 1980 – 1995

Anglian	4	Southern	74
North East	57	South West	99
North West	84	Thames	5
Midlands	12	Welsh	41

Major reservoirs (with capacity in million m³)

England
1	Kielder Res.	198
2	Rutland Water	123
3	Haweswater	85
4	Grafham Water	59
5	Cow Green Res.	41
6	Thirlmere	41
7	Carsington Res.	36
8	Roadford Res.	35
9	Bewl Water Res.	31
10	Colliford Lake	29
11	Ladybower Res.	28
12	Hanningfield Res.	27
13	Abberton Res.	25
14	Draycote Water	23
15	Derwent Res.	22
16	Grimwith Res.	22
17	Wimbleball Lake	21
18	Chew Valley Lake	20
19	Balderhead Res.	20
20	Thames Valley (linked reservoirs)	
21	Lea Valley (linked reservoirs)	
22	Longendale (linked reservoirs)	

Wales
23	Elan Valley	99
24	Llyn Celyn	74
25	Llyn Brianne	62
26	Llyn Brenig	60
27	Llyn Vyrnwy	60
28	Llyn Clywedog	48
29	Llandegfedd Res.	22

Scotland
30	Loch Lomond	86
31	Loch Katrine	64
32	Megget Res.	64
33	Loch Ness	26
34	Blackwater Res.	25
35	Daer Res.	23
36	Carron Valley Res.	21

Ireland
37	Poulaphouca Res.	168
38	Inishcarra Res.	57
39	Carrigadrohid Res.	33

Average daily domestic water use in England and Wales

W.C. flushing	Bath/shower	Washing machine	Other uses (e.g. dishwashers, drinking water, washing, cleaning, outside, etc.)
32%	17%	12%	39%

Water abstractions in England and Wales (1995) 55 970 megalitres per day* of which:

- 14.5% for other industries
- 31.0 % for public supply
- 8.4% for agricultural use
- 46.1% for electricity generation

*average daily domestic consumption per head 380 litres.

WATER ABSTRACTIONS   1 : 12 000 000

THAMES   Environment Agency Region

1883 (16%)   Water supply* in megalitres per day (with percentage of total abstraction from groundwater in brackets)

*Piped mains water, excluding water abstracted for agricultural and industrial use

- SCOTLAND 2248 (0%)
- N. IRELAND 666 (0%)
- NORTH EAST 2760 (14%)
- NORTH WEST 1683 (14%)
- MIDLANDS 2724 (40%)
- ANGLIAN 1872 (42%)
- WELSH 1586 (8%)
- THAMES 4043 (34%)
- SOUTH WEST 1350 (33%)
- SOUTHERN 1328 (80%)

WATER QUALITY   1 : 12 000 000

The percentage of all rivers and canals of poor or bad quality within each Environment Agency Region 1993 – 1995

- Over 15%
- 10% – 15%
- 5% – 10%
- Under 5%

The percentage of bathing beaches complying with E.C. standards in 1996

- Over 95%
- 75% – 95%
- Under 75%

SCOTLAND

NORTHERN IRELAND

No data

NORTH WEST

NORTH EAST

MIDLANDS

ANGLIAN

WELSH

THAMES

SOUTH WEST

SOUTHERN

SOILS   1 : 12 000 000

- Calcareous brown earth
- Brown earth
- Acid brown earth
- Podsol
- Peaty podsol
- Grey-brown pods
- Gley
- Basin peat and alluvial gleys
- Peaty gley and blanket peat

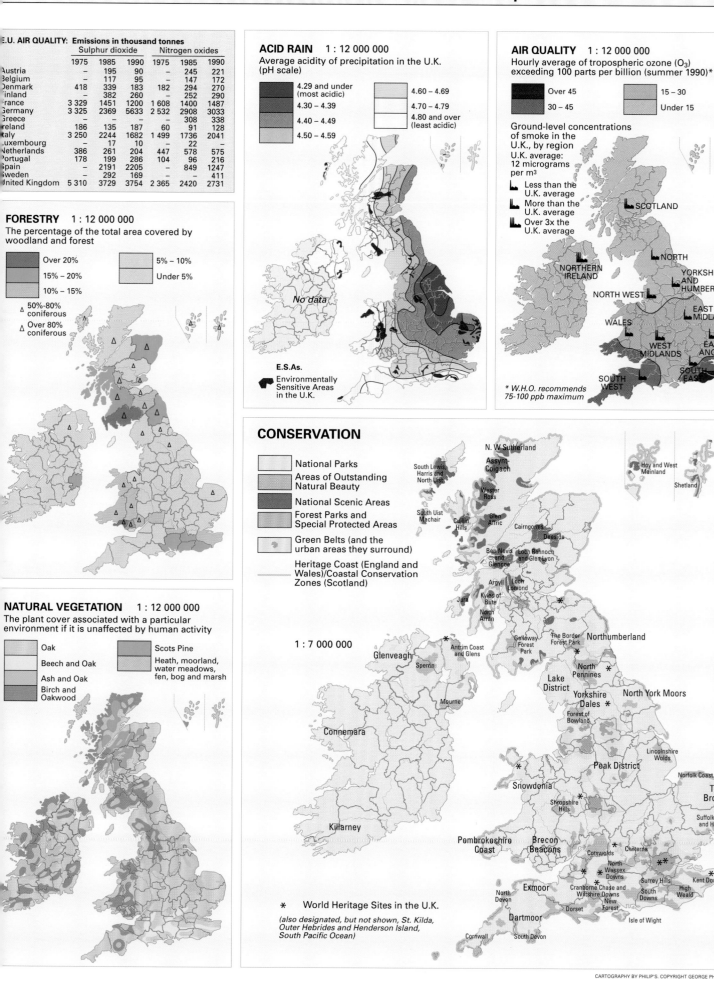

E.U. AIR QUALITY: Emissions in thousand tonnes

	Sulphur dioxide			Nitrogen oxides		
	1975	1985	1990	1975	1985	1990
Austria	–	195	90	–	245	221
Belgium	–	117	95	–	147	172
Denmark	418	339	183	182	294	270
Finland	–	382	260	–	252	290
France	3 329	1451	1200	1 608	1400	1487
Germany	3 325	2369	5633	2 532	2908	3033
Greece	–	–	–	–	308	338
Ireland	186	135	187	60	91	128
Italy	3 250	2244	1682	1 499	1736	2041
Luxembourg	–	17	10	–	22	–
Netherlands	386	261	204	447	578	575
Portugal	178	199	286	104	96	216
Spain	–	2191	2205	–	849	1247
Sweden	–	292	169	–	–	411
United Kingdom	5 310	3729	3754	2 365	2420	2731

FORESTRY   1 : 12 000 000

The percentage of the total area covered by woodland and forest

- Over 20%
- 15% – 20%
- 10% – 15%
- 5% – 10%
- Under 5%

△ 50%-80% coniferous
△ Over 80% coniferous

NATURAL VEGETATION   1 : 12 000 000

The plant cover associated with a particular environment if it is unaffected by human activity

- Oak
- Beech and Oak
- Ash and Oak
- Birch and Oakwood
- Scots Pine
- Heath, moorland, water meadows, fen, bog and marsh

ACID RAIN   1 : 12 000 000

Average acidity of precipitation in the U.K. (pH scale)

- 4.29 and under (most acidic)
- 4.30 – 4.39
- 4.40 – 4.49
- 4.50 – 4.59
- 4.60 – 4.69
- 4.70 – 4.79
- 4.80 and over (least acidic)

No data

E.S.As.
Environmentally Sensitive Areas in the U.K.

AIR QUALITY   1 : 12 000 000

Hourly average of tropospheric ozone (O$_3$) exceeding 100 parts per billion (summer 1990)*

- Over 45
- 30 – 45
- 15 – 30
- Under 15

Ground-level concentrations of smoke in the U.K., by region
U.K. average: 12 micrograms per m^3

- Less than the U.K. average
- More than the U.K. average
- Over 3x the U.K. average

SCOTLAND
NORTHERN IRELAND
NORTH
YORKSHIRE AND HUMBERSIDE
NORTH WEST
EAST MIDLANDS
WALES
WEST MIDLANDS
EAST ANGLIA
SOUTH WEST
SOUTH EAST

* W.H.O. recommends 75-100 ppb maximum

CONSERVATION

- National Parks
- Areas of Outstanding Natural Beauty
- National Scenic Areas
- Forest Parks and Special Protected Areas
- Green Belts (and the urban areas they surround)
- Heritage Coast (England and Wales)/Coastal Conservation Zones (Scotland)

1 : 7 000 000

N. W. Sutherland
South Lewis, Harris and North Uist
Assynt-Coigach
Hoy and West Mainland
Shetland
Wester Ross
South Uist Machair
Glen Affric
Cairngorms
Cuillin Hills
Deeside
Ben Nevis and Glencoe
Loch Rannoch and Glen Lyon
Argyll
Loch Lomond
Jura
Kyles of Bute
North Arran
Galloway Forest Park
The Border Forest Park
Northumberland
Glenveagh
Antrim Coast and Glens
Sperrin
North Pennines
Lake District
Yorkshire Dales
North York Moors
Mourne
Forest of Bowland
Connemara
Lincolnshire Wolds
Peak District
Norfolk Coast
Snowdonia
The Broads
Shropshire Hills
Suffolk Coast and Heaths
Killarney
Pembrokeshire Coast
Brecon Beacons
Cotswolds
Chilterns
North Wessex Downs
Surrey Hills
Kent Downs
Exmoor
Cranborne Chase and Wiltshire Downs
South Downs
High Weald
North Devon
Dorset
New Forest
Isle of Wight
Dartmoor
Cornwall
South Devon

✳ World Heritage Sites in the U.K.

(also designated, but not shown, St. Kilda, Outer Hebrides and Henderson Island, South Pacific Ocean)

CARTOGRAPHY BY PHILIP'S. COPYRIGHT GEORGE PHILIP LTD

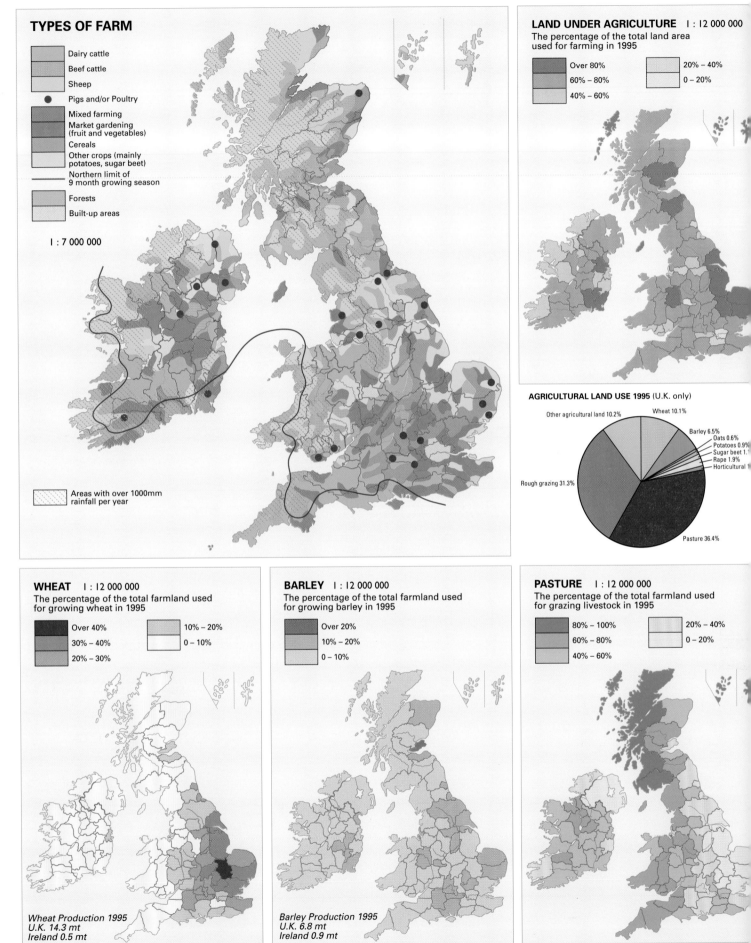

TYPES OF FARM

Dairy cattle
Beef cattle
Sheep
● Pigs and/or Poultry
Mixed farming
Market gardening (fruit and vegetables)
Cereals
Other crops (mainly potatoes, sugar beet)
Northern limit of 9 month growing season
Forests
Built-up areas

1 : 7 000 000

Areas with over 1000mm rainfall per year

LAND UNDER AGRICULTURE   1 : 12 000 000

The percentage of the total land area used for farming in 1995

Over 80%
60% – 80%
40% – 60%
20% – 40%
0 – 20%

AGRICULTURAL LAND USE 1995 (U.K. only)

Other agricultural land 10.2%
Wheat 10.1%
Barley 6.5%
Oats 0.6%
Potatoes 0.9%
Sugar beet 1.1%
Rape 1.9%
Horticultural
Rough grazing 31.3%
Pasture 36.4%

WHEAT   1 : 12 000 000

The percentage of the total farmland used for growing wheat in 1995

Over 40%
30% – 40%
20% – 30%
10% – 20%
0 – 10%

Wheat Production 1995
U.K. 14.3 mt
Ireland 0.5 mt

BARLEY   1 : 12 000 000

The percentage of the total farmland used for growing barley in 1995

Over 20%
10% – 20%
0 – 10%

Barley Production 1995
U.K. 6.8 mt
Ireland 0.9 mt

PASTURE   1 : 12 000 000

The percentage of the total farmland used for grazing livestock in 1995

80% – 100%
60% – 80%
40% – 60%
20% – 40%
0 – 20%

CARTOGRAPHY BY PHILIP'S. COPYRIGHT GEORGE PHI

NUMBER AND SIZE OF AGRICULTURAL HOLDINGS IN THE U.K.

Average size of holdings (hectares)

	1940	1980	1995
England & Wales	33.8	60.2	61.7
Scotland	81.8	96.2	160.2
Northern Ireland	13.7	24.2	35.9

500 000 holdings
400 000 holdings
300 000 holdings
200 000 holdings
100 000 holdings

Over 100 hectares
50 – 100 hectares
40 – 50 hectares
20 – 40 hectares
5 – 20 hectares
2 – 5 hectares
Under 2 hectares

1940 1950 1960 1970 1980 1995

POTATOES 1 : 12 000 000

The percentage of the total farmland used for growing potatoes in 1995

Over 3%
2% – 3%
1% – 2%
Under 1%

MARKET GARDENING 1 : 12 000 000

The percentage of the total farmland used for market gardening in 1995

Over 4%
3% – 4%
2% – 3%
1% – 2%
Under 1%

FISHING

Quantities of fish landed at major ports (port districts in Scotland) in 1995

('000 tonnes)
100
50
25
10
5

Type of fish landed

Demersal (Deep Sea Fish)
Pelagic (Shallow Water Fish)
Shellfish

Fishing Regions
IV   North Sea
VIa   West Scotland
VIIa   Irish Sea
VIIb/h/j W. Ireland & Sole Bank
VIId/e   English Channel
VIIf/g   Bristol Ch. & S. E. Ireland

Fish landed according to region of capture (1995)

Demersal
Pelagic
1 fish represents 10 000 tonnes caught

Region boundary

VIa
Shetland
Kinlochbervie
Wick
Stornoway
Fraserburgh
Ullapool
Mallaig
Aberdeen
Peterhead
IV
Killybegs
Greencastle
Amble
Ayr
Blyth
North Shields
VIIa
Hartlepool
Whitby
Rossaveal
Fleetwood
Scarborough
Bridlington
Howth
Hull
Grimsby
Castletownbere
Dunmore East
Cobh
Lowestoft
Milford Haven
VIIf/g
Weymouth
Padstow
Shoreham
Plymouth
Poole
Newlyn
Looe
VIIb/h/j
Falmouth
Brixham
VIId/e

1 : 10 000 000

Average annual value of fish (£/tonne)
700
600
500
400
300
200
100
0

Fishermen in thousands
50
40
30
20
10

permanently employed fishermen
Annual average value of fish (£/tonne)
part-time

1938 1940 1950 1960 1970 1980 1990 1995

1000 500 200 100 50 m

VALUE OF AGRICULTURAL OUTPUT (U.K. only)

£ billion
12
10
8
6
4
2
0
1970 1980 1990

Farm crops
Horticulture
Livestock
Livestock Products

AGRICULTURAL LAND & LIVESTOCK, 1970-90 (U.K. only)

Agricultural land (thousand ha)
Livestock (thousands)

1970 (19 123)
26.7%
41.1%
32.2%

1970 (46 749)
26.7%
17.2%
56.1%

1980 (18 953)
28.3%
40.6%
31.1%

1980 (52 687)
25.6%
15.0%
59.4%

1990 (18 542)
30.0%
40.0%
30.0%

1990 (63 307)
18.9%
11.7%
69.4%

Crops
Pasture
Rough grazing

Cattle and calves
Pigs
Sheep and Lambs

CARTOGRAPHY BY PHILIP'S. COPYRIGHT GEORGE PHILIP LTD

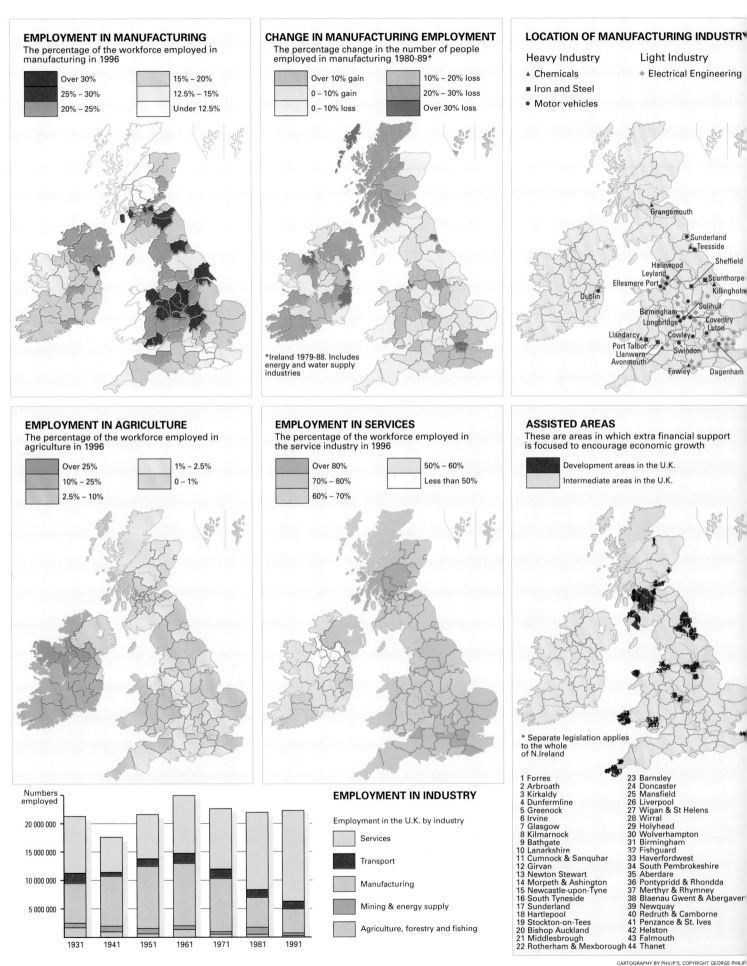

EMPLOYMENT IN MANUFACTURING
The percentage of the workforce employed in manufacturing in 1996

- Over 30%
- 25% – 30%
- 20% – 25%
- 15% – 20%
- 12.5% – 15%
- Under 12.5%

CHANGE IN MANUFACTURING EMPLOYMENT
The percentage change in the number of people employed in manufacturing 1980-89*

- Over 10% gain
- 0 – 10% gain
- 0 – 10% loss
- 10% – 20% loss
- 20% – 30% loss
- Over 30% loss

*Ireland 1979-88. Includes energy and water supply industries

LOCATION OF MANUFACTURING INDUSTRY

Heavy Industry
- ▲ Chemicals
- ■ Iron and Steel
- ● Motor vehicles

Light Industry
- ◆ Electrical Engineering

Grangemouth
Sunderland
Teesside
Sheffield
Halewood
Leyland
Ellesmere Port
Scunthorpe
Killingholm
Dublin
Birmingham
Solihull
Longbridge
Coventry
Luton
Llandarcy
Cowley
Port Talbot
Llanwern
Swindon
Avonmouth
Fawley
Dagenham

EMPLOYMENT IN AGRICULTURE
The percentage of the workforce employed in agriculture in 1996

- Over 25%
- 10% – 25%
- 2.5% – 10%
- 1% – 2.5%
- 0 – 1%

EMPLOYMENT IN SERVICES
The percentage of the workforce employed in the service industry in 1996

- Over 80%
- 70% – 80%
- 60% – 70%
- 50% – 60%
- Less than 50%

ASSISTED AREAS
These are areas in which extra financial support is focused to encourage economic growth

- Development areas in the U.K.
- Intermediate areas in the U.K.

* Separate legislation applies to the whole of N.Ireland

1 Forres	23 Barnsley
2 Arbroath	24 Doncaster
3 Kirkaldy	25 Mansfield
4 Dunfermline	26 Liverpool
5 Greenock	27 Wigan & St Helens
6 Irvine	28 Wirral
7 Glasgow	29 Holyhead
8 Kilmarnock	30 Wolverhampton
9 Bathgate	31 Birmingham
10 Lanarkshire	32 Fishguard
11 Cumnock & Sanquhar	33 Haverfordwest
12 Girvan	34 South Pembrokeshire
13 Newton Stewart	35 Aberdare
14 Morpeth & Ashington	36 Pontypridd & Rhondda
15 Newcastle-upon-Tyne	37 Merthyr & Rhymney
16 South Tyneside	38 Blaenau Gwent & Abergaven
17 Sunderland	39 Newquay
18 Hartlepool	40 Redruth & Camborne
19 Stockton-on-Tees	41 Penzance & St. Ives
20 Bishop Auckland	42 Helston
21 Middlesbrough	43 Falmouth
22 Rotherham & Mexborough	44 Thanet

EMPLOYMENT IN INDUSTRY

Numbers employed

Employment in the U.K. by industry

- Services
- Transport
- Manufacturing
- Mining & energy supply
- Agriculture, forestry and fishing

20 000 000
15 000 000
10 000 000
5 000 000

1931 1941 1951 1961 1971 1981 1991

CARTOGRAPHY BY PHILIP'S. COPYRIGHT GEORGE PHILIP

1 : 12 000 000

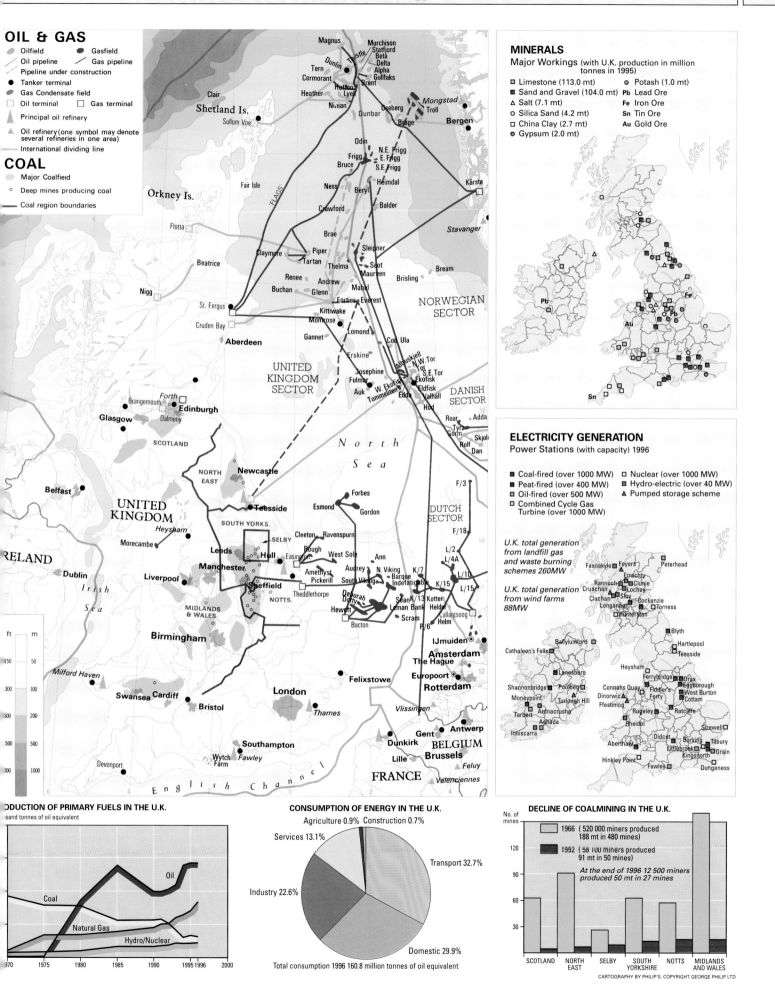

OIL & GAS

- Oilfield
- Gasfield
- Oil pipeline
- Gas pipeline
- Pipeline under construction
- Tanker terminal
- Gas Condensate field
- Oil terminal
- Gas terminal
- Principal oil refinery
- Oil refinery (one symbol may denote several refineries in one area)
- International dividing line

COAL

- Major Coalfield
- Deep mines producing coal
- Coal region boundaries

MINERALS

Major Workings (with U.K. production in million tonnes in 1995)

- Limestone (113.0 mt)
- Potash (1.0 mt)
- Sand and Gravel (104.0 mt)
- Pb Lead Ore
- Salt (7.1 mt)
- Fe Iron Ore
- Silica Sand (4.2 mt)
- Sn Tin Ore
- China Clay (2.7 mt)
- Au Gold Ore
- Gypsum (2.0 mt)

ELECTRICITY GENERATION

Power Stations (with capacity) 1996

- Coal-fired (over 1000 MW)
- Nuclear (over 1000 MW)
- Peat-fired (over 400 MW)
- Hydro-electric (over 40 MW)
- Oil-fired (over 500 MW)
- Pumped storage scheme
- Combined Cycle Gas Turbine (over 1000 MW)

U.K. total generation from landfill gas and waste burning schemes 260MW

U.K. total generation from wind farms 88MW

PRODUCTION OF PRIMARY FUELS IN THE U.K.
thousand tonnes of oil equivalent

CONSUMPTION OF ENERGY IN THE U.K.

- Agriculture 0.9%
- Construction 0.7%
- Services 13.1%
- Transport 32.7%
- Industry 22.6%
- Domestic 29.9%

Total consumption 1996 160.8 million tonnes of oil equivalent

DECLINE OF COALMINING IN THE U.K.

- 1966 (520 000 miners produced 188 mt in 480 mines)
- 1992 (58 100 miners produced 91 mt in 50 mines)

At the end of 1996 12 500 miners produced 50 mt in 27 mines

SCOTLAND, NORTH EAST, SELBY, SOUTH YORKSHIRE, NOTTS, MIDLANDS AND WALES

CARTOGRAPHY BY PHILIP'S. COPYRIGHT GEORGE PHILIP LTD

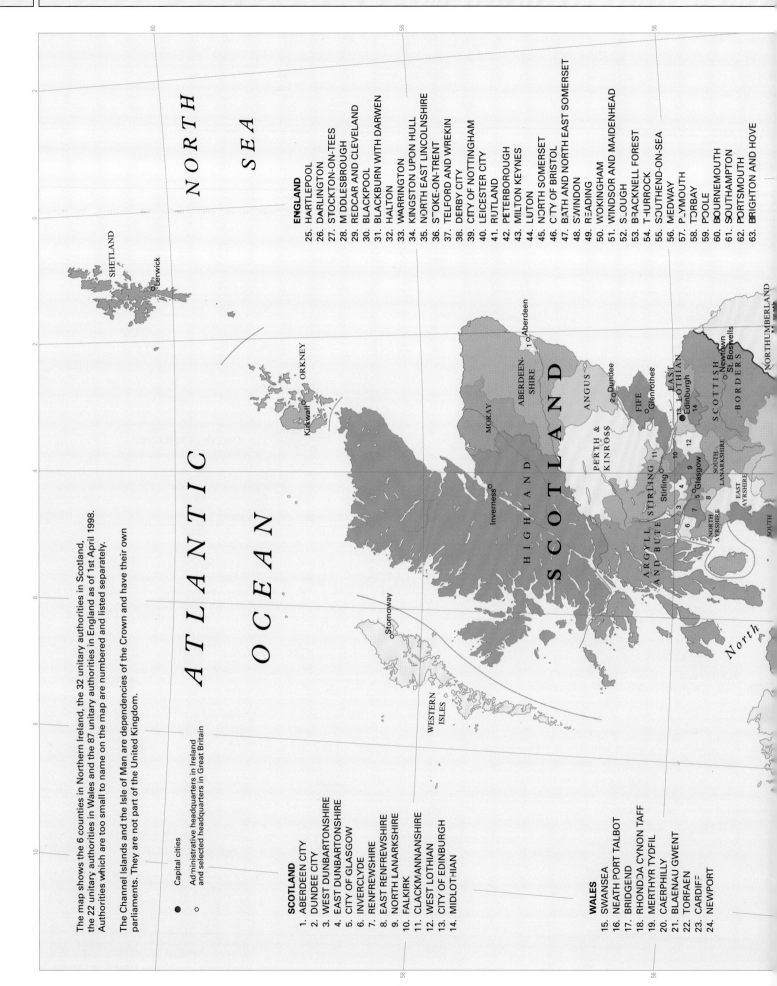

The map shows the 6 counties in Northern Ireland, the 32 unitary authorities in Scotland, the 22 unitary authorities in Wales and the 87 unitary authorities in England as of 1st April 1998. Authorities which are too small to name on the map are numbered and listed separately.

The Channel Islands and the Isle of Man are dependencies of the Crown and have their own parliaments. They are not part of the United Kingdom.

● Capital cities

○ Administrative headquarters in Ireland and selected headquarters in Great Britain

NORTH SEA

ATLANTIC OCEAN

SHETLAND
Lerwick

ORKNEY
Kirkwall

WESTERN ISLES
Stornoway

HIGHLAND
Inverness

MORAY

ABERDEEN-SHIRE
Aberdeen

SCOTLAND

ANGUS
Dundee

PERTH & KINROSS

FIFE
Glenrothes

EAST LOTHIAN
Edinburgh

SCOTTISH BORDERS
Newtown St. Boswells

Stirling
Glasgow

NORTH AYRSHIRE

SOUTH LANARKSHIRE

EAST AYRSHIRE

SOUTH

NORTHUMBERLAND

North

SCOTLAND
1. ABERDEEN CITY
2. DUNDEE CITY
3. WEST DUNBARTONSHIRE
4. EAST DUNBARTONSHIRE
5. CITY OF GLASGOW
6. INVERCLYDE
7. RENFREWSHIRE
8. EAST RENFREWSHIRE
9. NORTH LANARKSHIRE
10. FALKIRK
11. CLACKMANNANSHIRE
12. WEST LOTHIAN
13. CITY OF EDINBURGH
14. MIDLOTHIAN

WALES
15. SWANSEA
16. NEATH PORT TALBOT
17. BRIDGEND
18. RHONDDA CYNON TAFF
19. MERTHYR TYDFIL
20. CAERPHILLY
21. BLAENAU GWENT
22. TORFAEN
23. CARDIFF
24. NEWPORT

ENGLAND
25. HARTLEPOOL
26. DARLINGTON
27. STOCKTON-ON-TEES
28. MIDDLESBROUGH
29. REDCAR AND CLEVELAND
30. BLACKPOOL
31. BLACKBURN WITH DARWEN
32. HALTON
33. WARRINGTON
34. KINGSTON UPON HULL
35. NORTH EAST LINCOLNSHIRE
36. STOKE-ON-TRENT
37. TELFORD AND WREKIN
38. DERBY CITY
39. CITY OF NOTTINGHAM
40. LEICESTER CITY
41. RUTLAND
42. PETERBOROUGH
43. MILTON KEYNES
44. LUTON
45. NORTH SOMERSET
46. CITY OF BRISTOL
47. BATH AND NORTH EAST SOMERSET
48. SWINDON
49. READING
50. WOKINGHAM
51. WINDSOR AND MAIDENHEAD
52. SLOUGH
53. BRACKNELL FOREST
54. THURROCK
55. SOUTHEND-ON-SEA
56. MEDWAY
57. PLYMOUTH
58. TORBAY
59. POOLE
60. BOURNEMOUTH
61. SOUTHAMPTON
62. PORTSMOUTH
63. BRIGHTON AND HOVE

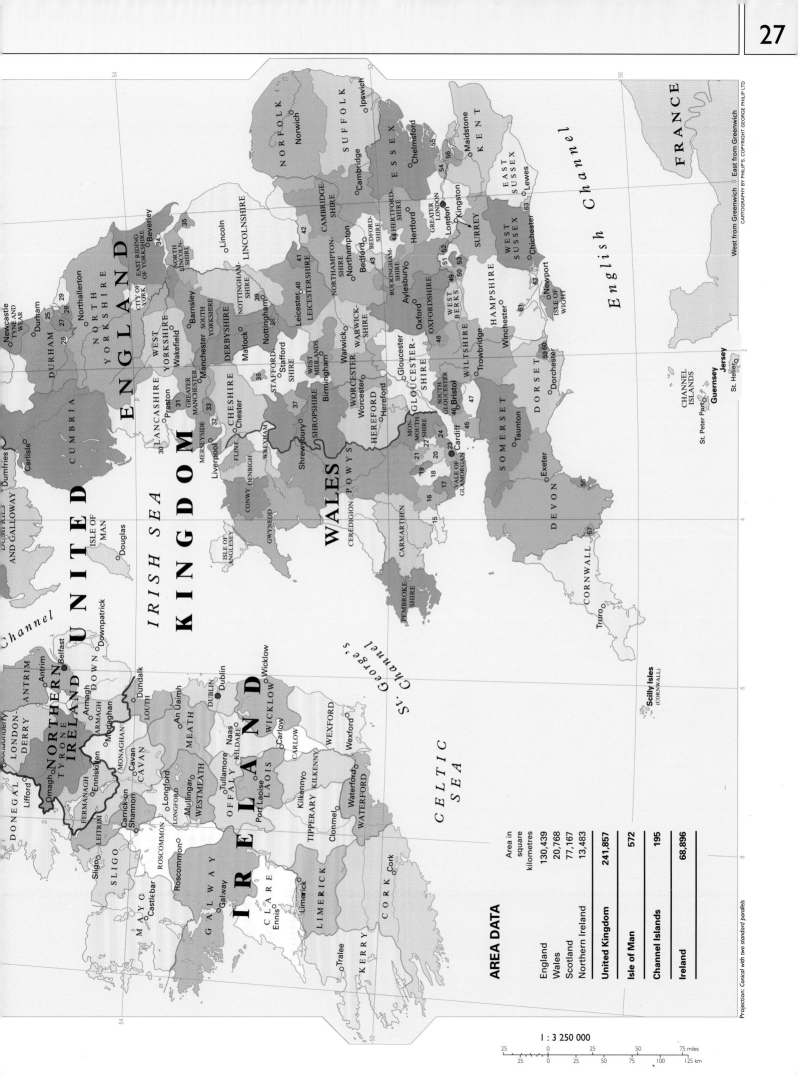

FRANCE

English Channel

West from Greenwich | East from Greenwich
CARTOGRAPHY BY PHILIP'S. COPYRIGHT GEORGE PHILIP LTD

ENGLAND

Newcastle
TYNE AND WEAR
Durham
DURHAM
Carlisle
CUMBRIA
Northallerton
NORTH YORKSHIRE
Beverley
EAST RIDING OF YORKSHIRE
CITY OF YORK
NORTH LINCOLNSHIRE
Lincoln
LINCOLNSHIRE

WEST YORKSHIRE
Wakefield
Barnsley
SOUTH YORKSHIRE
Manchester
GREATER MANCHESTER
Preston
LANCASHIRE
Chester
CHESHIRE
DERBYSHIRE
Matlock
NOTTINGHAM-SHIRE
Nottingham

Liverpool
MERSEYSIDE
FLINT
DENBIGH
CONWY
WREXHAM
Shrewsbury
SHROPSHIRE
STAFFORD-SHIRE
Stafford
WEST MIDLANDS
Birmingham
Leicester
LEICESTERSHIRE

WALES

GWYNEDD
ISLE OF ANGLESEY
CEREDIGION
POWYS
HEREFORD
Hereford
WORCESTER
Worcester
WARWICK-SHIRE
Warwick
MON-MOUTH-SHIRE
GLOUCESTER-SHIRE
Gloucester

CARMARTHEN
PEMBROKE-SHIRE
VALE OF GLAMORGAN
Cardiff
SOUTH GLOUCESTER
Bristol

NORTHAMPTON-SHIRE
Northampton
BEDFORD-SHIRE
Bedford
BUCKINGHAM-SHIRE
Aylesbury
Oxford
OXFORDSHIRE
WEST BERKS
HAMPSHIRE
Winchester
WILTSHIRE
Trowbridge
SOMERSET
Taunton
DORSET
Dorchester
DEVON
Exeter
CORNWALL
Truro

CAMBRIDGE-SHIRE
Cambridge
NORFOLK
Norwich
SUFFOLK
Ipswich
ESSEX
Chelmsford
HERTFORD-SHIRE
Hertford
GREATER LONDON
London
Kingston
SURREY
KENT
Maidstone
EAST SUSSEX
Lewes
WEST SUSSEX
Chichester
Newport
ISLE OF WIGHT

Scilly Isles
(CORNWALL)

St. George's Channel

CELTIC SEA

CHANNEL ISLANDS
St. Peter Port
Guernsey
Jersey
St. Helier

IRELAND

DONEGAL
Lifford
Sligo
SLIGO
LEITRIM
Carrick-on-Shannon
Castlebar
MAYO
ROSCOMMON
Roscommon
LONGFORD
Longford
CAVAN
Cavan
MONAGHAN
Monaghan

Galway
GALWAY
CLARE
Ennis
LIMERICK
Limerick
KERRY
Tralee
CORK
Cork
WATERFORD
Waterford
TIPPERARY
Clonmel
KILKENNY
Kilkenny
LAOIS
Port Laoise
OFFALY
Tullamore
WESTMEATH
Mullingar
An Uaimh
MEATH
LOUTH
Dundalk
DUBLIN
Dublin
KILDARE
Naas
CARLOW
Carlow
WEXFORD
Wexford
WICKLOW
Wicklow

NORTHERN IRELAND

Belfast
ANTRIM
Antrim
DOWN
Downpatrick
ARMAGH
Armagh
TYRONE
Omagh
FERMANAGH
Enniskillen
LONDON-DERRY

Channel

UNITED KINGDOM

IRISH SEA

ISLE OF MAN
Douglas

DUMFRIES AND GALLOWAY
Dumfries

AREA DATA

	Area in square kilometres
England	130,439
Wales	20,768
Scotland	77,167
Northern Ireland	13,483
United Kingdom	**241,857**
Isle of Man	**572**
Channel Islands	**195**
Ireland	**68,896**

Projection: Conical with two standard parallels

1 : 3 250 000

25 0 25 50 75 miles
25 0 25 50 75 100 125 km

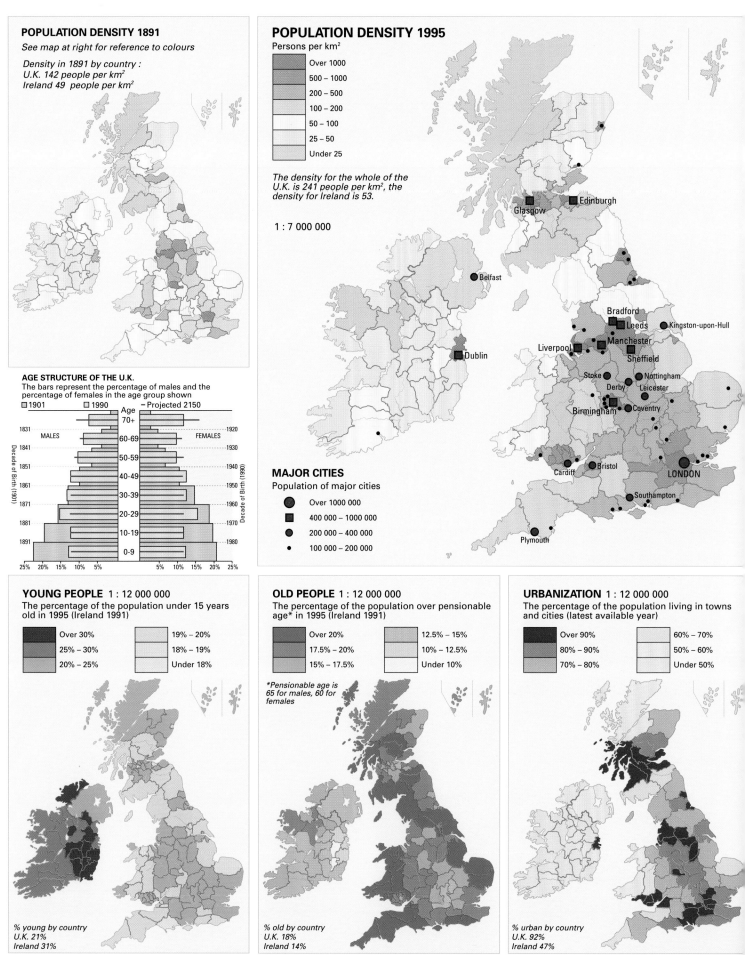

POPULATION DENSITY 1891

See map at right for reference to colours

Density in 1891 by country :
U.K. 142 people per km²
Ireland 49 people per km²

POPULATION DENSITY 1995

Persons per km²

- Over 1000
- 500 – 1000
- 200 – 500
- 100 – 200
- 50 – 100
- 25 – 50
- Under 25

The density for the whole of the U.K. is 241 people per km², the density for Ireland is 53.

1 : 7 000 000

Glasgow Edinburgh

Belfast

Dublin

Bradford
Leeds Kingston-upon-Hull
Liverpool Manchester
Sheffield
Stoke Nottingham
Derby Leicester
Birmingham Coventry

Cardiff Bristol LONDON
Southampton

Plymouth

MAJOR CITIES

Population of major cities

- Over 1 000 000
- 400 000 – 1 000 000
- 200 000 – 400 000
- 100 000 – 200 000

AGE STRUCTURE OF THE U.K.

The bars represent the percentage of males and the percentage of females in the age group shown

□ 1901   □ 1990   — Projected 2150

Age

Decade of Birth (1901)		Age		Decade of Birth (1990)
1831		70+		1920
1841	MALES	60-69	FEMALES	1930
1851		50-59		1940
1861		40-49		1950
1871		30-39		1960
1881		20-29		1970
1891		10-19		1980
		0-9		

25% 20% 15% 10% 5%   5% 10% 15% 20% 25%

YOUNG PEOPLE 1 : 12 000 000

The percentage of the population under 15 years old in 1995 (Ireland 1991)

- Over 30%
- 25% – 30%
- 20% – 25%
- 19% – 20%
- 18% – 19%
- Under 18%

% young by country
U.K. 21%
Ireland 31%

OLD PEOPLE 1 : 12 000 000

The percentage of the population over pensionable age* in 1995 (Ireland 1991)

- Over 20%
- 17.5% – 20%
- 15% – 17.5%
- 12.5% – 15%
- 10% – 12.5%
- Under 10%

*Pensionable age is 65 for males, 60 for females

% old by country
U.K. 18%
Ireland 14%

URBANIZATION 1 : 12 000 000

The percentage of the population living in towns and cities (latest available year)

- Over 90%
- 80% – 90%
- 70% – 80%
- 60% – 70%
- 50% – 60%
- Under 50%

% urban by country
U.K. 92%
Ireland 47%

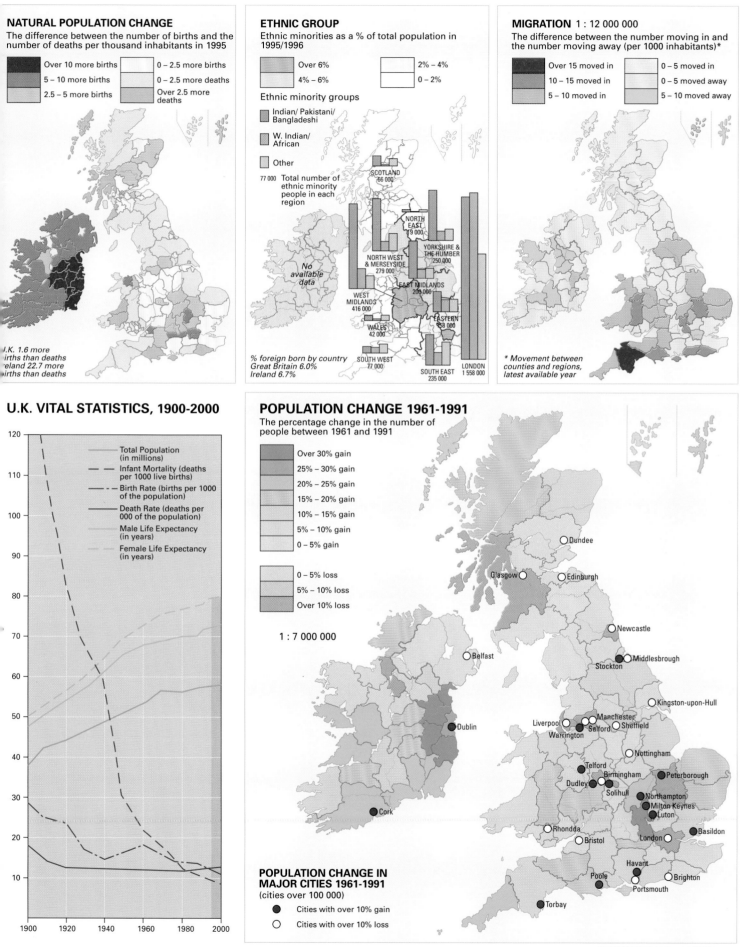

NATURAL POPULATION CHANGE

The difference between the number of births and the number of deaths per thousand inhabitants in 1995

- Over 10 more births
- 5 – 10 more births
- 2.5 – 5 more births
- 0 – 2.5 more births
- 0 – 2.5 more deaths
- Over 2.5 more deaths

U.K. 1.6 more births than deaths
Ireland 22.7 more births than deaths

ETHNIC GROUP

Ethnic minorities as a % of total population in 1995/1996

- Over 6%
- 4% – 6%
- 2% – 4%
- 0 – 2%

Ethnic minority groups

- Indian/ Pakistani/ Bangladeshi
- W. Indian/ African
- Other

77 000 Total number of ethnic minority people in each region

SCOTLAND 56 000
NORTH EAST 19 000
NORTH WEST & MERSEYSIDE 279 000
YORKSHIRE & THE HUMBER 250 000
No available data
EAST MIDLANDS 200 000
WEST MIDLANDS 416 000
WALES 42 000
EASTERN 158 000
SOUTH WEST 77 000
SOUTH EAST 235 000
LONDON 1 558 000

% foreign born by country
Great Britain 6.0%
Ireland 6.7%

MIGRATION 1 : 12 000 000

The difference between the number moving in and the number moving away (per 1000 inhabitants)*

- Over 15 moved in
- 10 – 15 moved in
- 5 – 10 moved in
- 0 – 5 moved in
- 0 – 5 moved away
- 5 – 10 moved away

* Movement between counties and regions, latest available year

U.K. VITAL STATISTICS, 1900-2000

- Total Population (in millions)
- Infant Mortality (deaths per 1000 live births)
- Birth Rate (births per 1000 of the population)
- Death Rate (deaths per 000 of the population)
- Male Life Expectancy (in years)
- Female Life Expectancy (in years)

POPULATION CHANGE 1961-1991

The percentage change in the number of people between 1961 and 1991

- Over 30% gain
- 25% – 30% gain
- 20% – 25% gain
- 15% – 20% gain
- 10% – 15% gain
- 5% – 10% gain
- 0 – 5% gain
- 0 – 5% loss
- 5% – 10% loss
- Over 10% loss

1 : 7 000 000

Dundee
Glasgow
Edinburgh
Newcastle
Belfast
Middlesbrough
Stockton
Kingston-upon-Hull
Manchester
Liverpool
Salford
Sheffield
Warrington
Nottingham
Dublin
Telford
Birmingham
Peterborough
Dudley
Solihull
Northampton
Milton Keynes
Luton
Cork
Rhondda
London
Basildon
Bristol
Havant
Poole
Brighton
Portsmouth
Torbay

POPULATION CHANGE IN MAJOR CITIES 1961-1991
(cities over 100 000)

- ● Cities with over 10% gain
- ○ Cities with over 10% loss

CARTOGRAPHY BY PHILIP'S. COPYRIGHT GEORGE PHILIP LTD

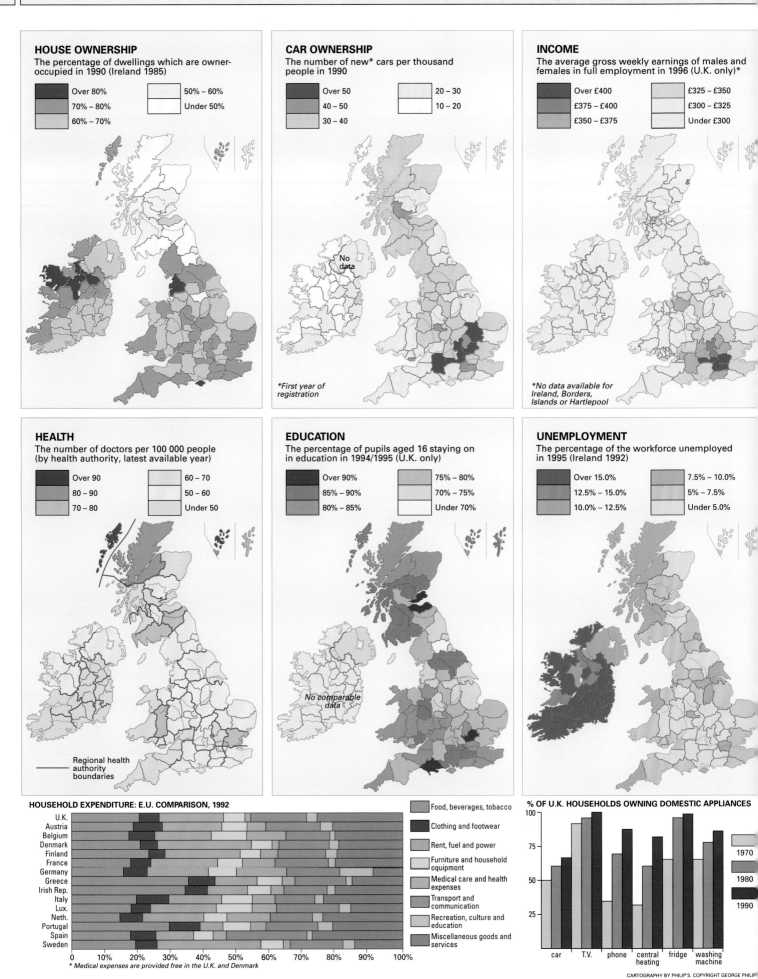

HOUSE OWNERSHIP
The percentage of dwellings which are owner-occupied in 1990 (Ireland 1985)

- Over 80%
- 70% – 80%
- 60% – 70%
- 50% – 60%
- Under 50%

CAR OWNERSHIP
The number of new* cars per thousand people in 1990

- Over 50
- 40 – 50
- 30 – 40
- 20 – 30
- 10 – 20

No data

*First year of registration

INCOME
The average gross weekly earnings of males and females in full employment in 1996 (U.K. only)*

- Over £400
- £375 – £400
- £350 – £375
- £325 – £350
- £300 – £325
- Under £300

*No data available for Ireland, Borders, Islands or Hartlepool

HEALTH
The number of doctors per 100 000 people (by health authority, latest available year)

- Over 90
- 80 – 90
- 70 – 80
- 60 – 70
- 50 – 60
- Under 50

— Regional health authority boundaries

EDUCATION
The percentage of pupils aged 16 staying on in education in 1994/1995 (U.K. only)

- Over 90%
- 85% – 90%
- 80% – 85%
- 75% – 80%
- 70% – 75%
- Under 70%

No comparable data

UNEMPLOYMENT
The percentage of the workforce unemployed in 1995 (Ireland 1992)

- Over 15.0%
- 12.5% – 15.0%
- 10.0% – 12.5%
- 7.5% – 10.0%
- 5% – 7.5%
- Under 5.0%

HOUSEHOLD EXPENDITURE: E.U. COMPARISON, 1992

U.K.
Austria
Belgium
Denmark
Finland
France
Germany
Greece
Irish Rep.
Italy
Lux.
Neth.
Portugal
Spain
Sweden

0   10%   20%   30%   40%   50%   60%   70%   80%   90%   100%

* Medical expenses are provided free in the U.K. and Denmark

- Food, beverages, tobacco
- Clothing and footwear
- Rent, fuel and power
- Furniture and household equipment
- Medical care and health expenses
- Transport and communication
- Recreation, culture and education
- Miscellaneous goods and services

% OF U.K. HOUSEHOLDS OWNING DOMESTIC APPLIANCES

100
75
50
25

car   T.V.   phone   central heating   fridge   washing machine

1970
1980
1990

CARTOGRAPHY BY PHILIP'S. COPYRIGHT GEORGE PHILIP

U.K. TRADE

TOP TEN TRADING PARTNERS 1996

One container represents 1% of the total value of imports or 1% of the total value of exports

IMPORTS

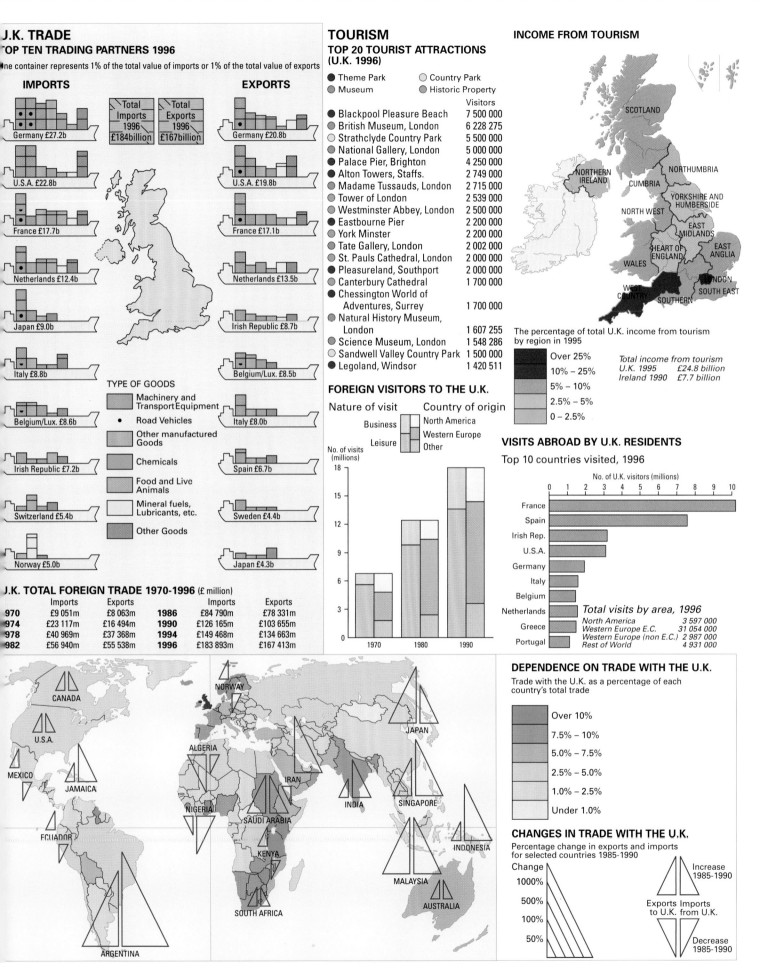

Germany £27.2b
U.S.A. £22.8b
France £17.7b
Netherlands £12.4b
Japan £9.0b
Italy £8.8b
Belgium/Lux. £8.6b
Irish Republic £7.2b
Switzerland £5.4b
Norway £5.0b

Total Imports 1996 £184billion	Total Exports 1996 £167billion

EXPORTS

Germany £20.8b
U.S.A. £19.8b
France £17.1b
Netherlands £13.5b
Irish Republic £8.7b
Belgium/Lux. £8.5b
Italy £8.0b
Spain £6.7b
Sweden £4.4b
Japan £4.3b

TYPE OF GOODS

- Machinery and Transport Equipment
- • Road Vehicles
- Other manufactured Goods
- Chemicals
- Food and Live Animals
- Mineral fuels, Lubricants, etc.
- Other Goods

U.K. TOTAL FOREIGN TRADE 1970-1996 (£ million)

	Imports	Exports		Imports	Exports
1970	£9 051m	£8 063m	1986	£84 790m	£78 331m
1974	£23 117m	£16 494m	1990	£126 165m	£103 655m
1978	£40 969m	£37 368m	1994	£149 468m	£134 663m
1982	£56 940m	£55 538m	1996	£183 893m	£167 413m

TOURISM

TOP 20 TOURIST ATTRACTIONS (U.K. 1996)

- ● Theme Park
- ○ Country Park
- ● Museum
- ○ Historic Property

	Visitors
● Blackpool Pleasure Beach	7 500 000
● British Museum, London	6 228 275
○ Strathclyde Country Park	5 500 000
● National Gallery, London	5 000 000
● Palace Pier, Brighton	4 250 000
● Alton Towers, Staffs.	2 749 000
● Madame Tussauds, London	2 715 000
○ Tower of London	2 539 000
○ Westminster Abbey, London	2 500 000
● Eastbourne Pier	2 200 000
○ York Minster	2 200 000
● Tate Gallery, London	2 002 000
○ St. Pauls Cathedral, London	2 000 000
● Pleasureland, Southport	2 000 000
● Canterbury Cathedral	1 700 000
● Chessington World of Adventures, Surrey	1 700 000
● Natural History Museum, London	1 607 255
● Science Museum, London	1 548 286
○ Sandwell Valley Country Park	1 500 000
● Legoland, Windsor	1 420 511

FOREIGN VISITORS TO THE U.K.

Nature of visit
- Business
- Leisure

Country of origin
- North America
- Western Europe
- Other

No. of visits (millions)

1970 1980 1990

INCOME FROM TOURISM

SCOTLAND
NORTHERN IRELAND
NORTHUMBRIA
CUMBRIA
NORTH WEST
YORKSHIRE AND HUMBERSIDE
EAST MIDLANDS
HEART OF ENGLAND
WALES
EAST ANGLIA
WEST COUNTRY
SOUTHERN
LONDON
SOUTH EAST

The percentage of total U.K. income from tourism by region in 1995

- Over 25%
- 10% – 25%
- 5% – 10%
- 2.5% – 5%
- 0 – 2.5%

Total income from tourism
U.K. 1995   £24.8 billion
Ireland 1990   £7.7 billion

VISITS ABROAD BY U.K. RESIDENTS

Top 10 countries visited, 1996

No. of U.K. visitors (millions)
0 1 2 3 4 5 6 7 8 9 10

France
Spain
Irish Rep.
U.S.A.
Germany
Italy
Belgium
Netherlands
Greece
Portugal

Total visits by area, 1996
North America   3 597 000
Western Europe E.C.   31 054 000
Western Europe (non E.C.) 2 987 000
Rest of World   4 931 000

DEPENDENCE ON TRADE WITH THE U.K.

Trade with the U.K. as a percentage of each country's total trade

- Over 10%
- 7.5% – 10%
- 5.0% – 7.5%
- 2.5% – 5.0%
- 1.0% – 2.5%
- Under 1.0%

CHANGES IN TRADE WITH THE U.K.

Percentage change in exports and imports for selected countries 1985-1990

Change
1000%
500%
100%
50%

Increase 1985-1990

Exports to U.K.   Imports from U.K.

Decrease 1985-1990

CANADA
NORWAY
U.S.A.
MEXICO
JAMAICA
ALGERIA
NIGERIA
ECUADOR
SAUDI ARABIA
KENYA
SOUTH AFRICA
IRAN
INDIA
SINGAPORE
JAPAN
MALAYSIA
INDONESIA
AUSTRALIA
ARGENTINA

ROADS AND FERRIES

— M6 — Motorways

—— Main primary routes

(56) Average 24 hour flow of vehicles at a selected point on a motorway. Figures are given in thousands for 1996

········· Principal car ferry routes

Long haul sea ferry destinations

RAILWAYS

—— Electrified lines

—— Other main lines

Furthest distances from London reached within a journey time of

	3 hours	6 hours
1950	▲	●
1995	▲	●

Channel Tunnel

- - - - Channel Tunnel

—— Proposed high speed rail link

CHANNEL TUNNEL

Estimated journey times between London–Brussels and London–Paris

Hours

	1990/1	Best time achievable using existing networks
	1993	Opening of Channel Tunnel
	1998	Completion of new line in Belgium

MEANS OF TRANSPORTATION WITHIN THE U.K.

'000 million tonne km 200 175 150 125 100 75 50 25 0

0 100 200 300 400 500 600 700 '000 million passenger km

GOODS

PASSENGERS

1975
1980
1985
1990
1995

■ Road
■ Rail
□ Private Transport
□ Rail
■ Water
□ Pipelines
■ Public Transport

Air transport accounted for 2200 million passenger km in 1975, 4000 million in 1985 and 6000 million in 1995

SEAPORTS

Goods traffic by port (thousand tonnes) 1995

50 000
25 000
10 000
5 000

% imports — Foreign Traffic
% exports
% imports — Domestic Traffic
% exports

AIRPORTS

Passenger traffic 1996 (thousands)

50 000
5 000
1 000
250

International

Domestic

• Selected airports with less than 200 000 passengers

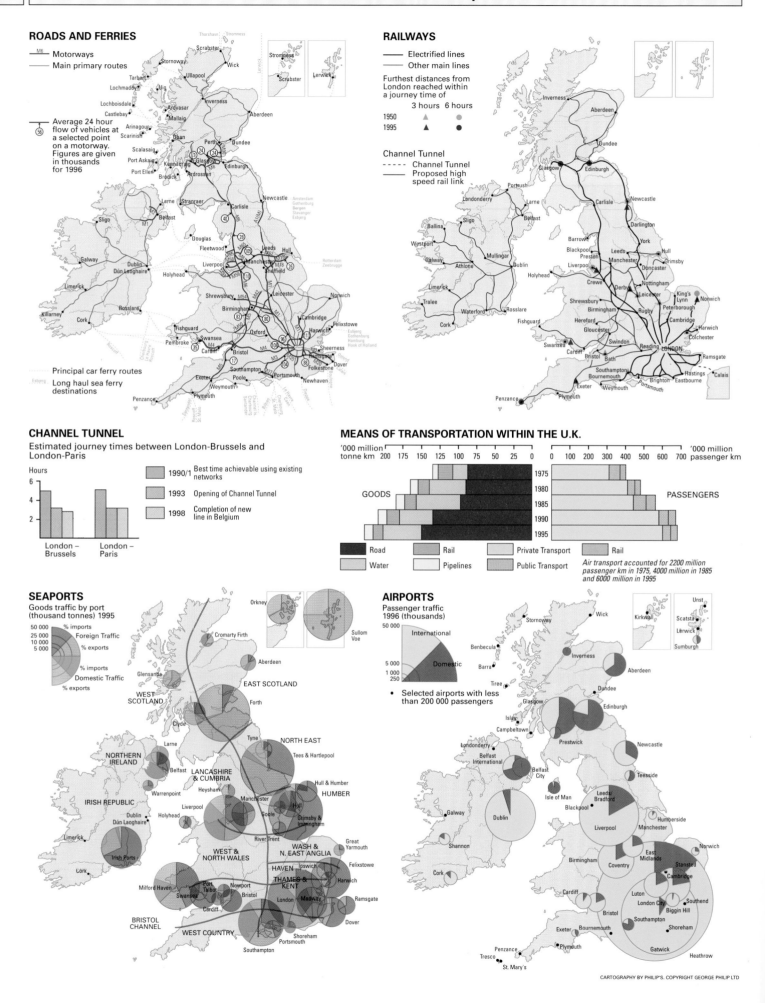

CARTOGRAPHY BY PHILIP'S. COPYRIGHT GEORGE PHILIP LTD

INDEX TO
BRITISH ISLES MAPS

This index lists the major placenames which appear on the large-scale maps of the British Isles (pages *2–15* with the yellow band). Placenames for the rest of the world can be found in the World Index, with the turquoise band.

The first number beside each name in the index gives the map page on which that feature or place will be found. The letter and figure immediately after the page number give the grid square within which the feature is situated. The letter represents the latitude and the figure the longitude. In some cases the feature may fall within the specified square, while the name is outside. This is usually the case only with very large features. Rivers are indexed to their mouths or confluence.

The 'geographical co-ordinates' which follow the letter-figure references give the latitude and longitude of each place. The first co-ordinate indicates latitude – the distance north of the Equator. The second co-ordinate indicates longitude – the distance east or west of the Greenwich Meridian. Both latitude and longitude are measured in degrees and minutes (there are 60 minutes in a degree).

Thus the entry in the index for Runcorn reads:

Runcorn............. **7 F3**   53 20N   2 44W

This indicates that Runcorn appears on map page 7 in grid square F3 at latitude 53 degrees, 20 minutes north and at longitude 2 degrees, 44 minutes west. To find Runcorn by using the geographical co-ordinates, look at the edges of the map. The degrees of latitude are indicated by blue figures on the left-hand edge of the map and the degrees of longitude are marked on the bottom edge of the map. Runcorn will be found where lines extended from the two points on the map edge would cross on the map.

An open square □ indicates that the name refers to an administrative unit such as a county or region; rivers are indicated by an arrow ➝. Names composed of a proper name (Wight) and a description (Isle of) are positioned alphabetically by the proper name. All names beginning St. are alphabetized under Saint. A list of abbreviations used can be found in the World Index at the end of the atlas.

Place names on the turquoise-coded World Map section are to be found in the index at the rear of the book.

Ben Klibreck   **Darton**

Place names on the turquoise-coded World Map section are to be found in the index at the rear of the book.

Narrows   **Slieve Elva**

Place names on the turquoise-coded World Map section are to be found in the index at the rear of the book.

Slieve Foye · **Youghal**

WORLD MAPS

SETTLEMENTS

◌ PARIS　　　■ Berne　　　◉ Livorno　　　◉ Brugge　　　◎ Algeciras　　　⊙ Frejus　　　○ Oberammergau　　　○ Thira

Settlement symbols and type styles vary according to the scale of each map and indicate the importance
of towns on the map rather than specific population figures

∴ Ruins or Archæological Sites　　　　　　˅ Wells in Desert

ADMINISTRATION

——— International Boundaries

– – – International Boundaries
(Undefined or Disputed)

········ Internal Boundaries

National Parks

Country Names

NICARAGUA

Administrative
Area Names

KENT

CALABRIA

International boundaries show the *de facto* situation where there are rival claims to territory

COMMUNICATIONS

——— Principal Roads

⌒ Other Roads

⌁ Trails and Seasonal Roads

≍ Passes

✧ Airfields

⌒ Principal Railways

⌒ Railways
Under Construction

⌒ Other Railways

⊣---⊢ Railway Tunnels

············· Principal Canals

PHYSICAL FEATURES

⌁ Perennial Streams

········ Intermittent Streams

◯ Perennial Lakes

⬭ Intermittent Lakes

Swamps and Marshes

Permanent Ice
and Glaciers

▲ 8848 Elevations in metres

▼ 8050 Sea Depths in metres

1134 Height of Lake Surface
Above Sea Level
in metres

ELEVATION AND DEPTH TINTS

Height of Land Above Sea Level　　　　Land Below Sea Level　　　Depth of Sea

in metres　6000　4000　3000　2000　1500　1000　400　200　0

in feet　18 000　12 000　9000　6000　4500　3000　1200　600

　　　　　　　　　　　　　　　　　　6000　12 000　15 000　18 000　24 000　in feet

　　　　　　　　　　　　　　　　0　200　2000　4000　5000　6000　8000　in metres

Some of the maps have different contours to highlight and clarify the principal relief features

Projection: Hammer Equal Area

Hanoi ● Capital Cities

CARTOGRAPHY BY PHILIP'S.

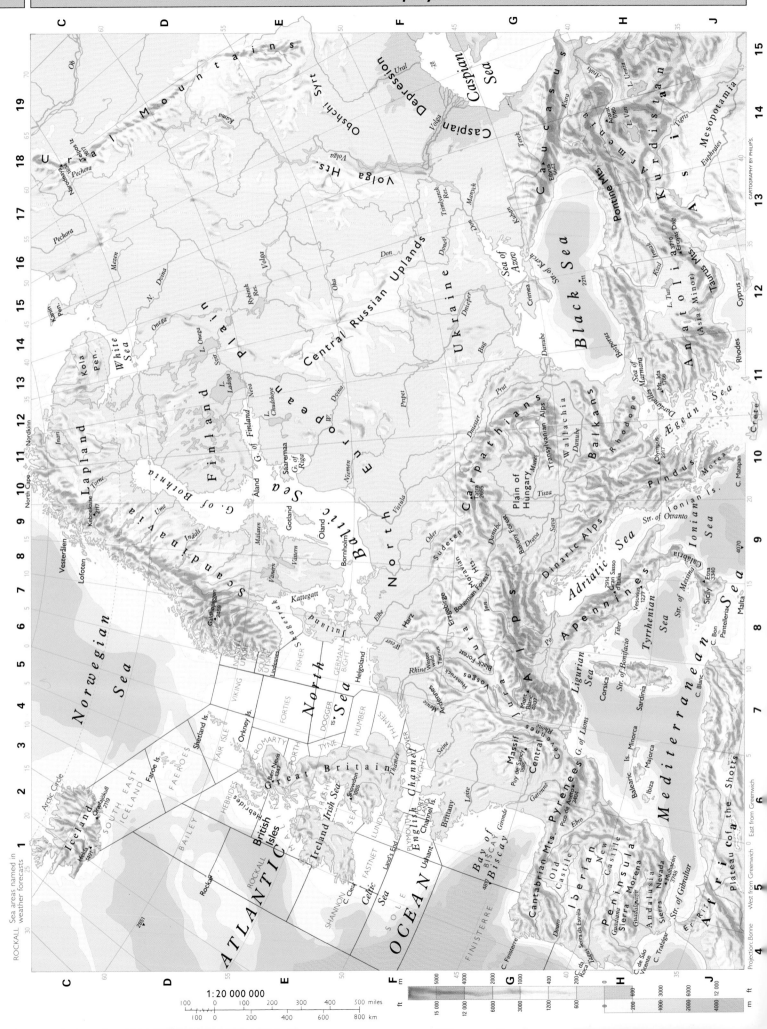

1:20 000 000

100   0   100   200   300   400   500 miles

100   0   200   400   600   800 km

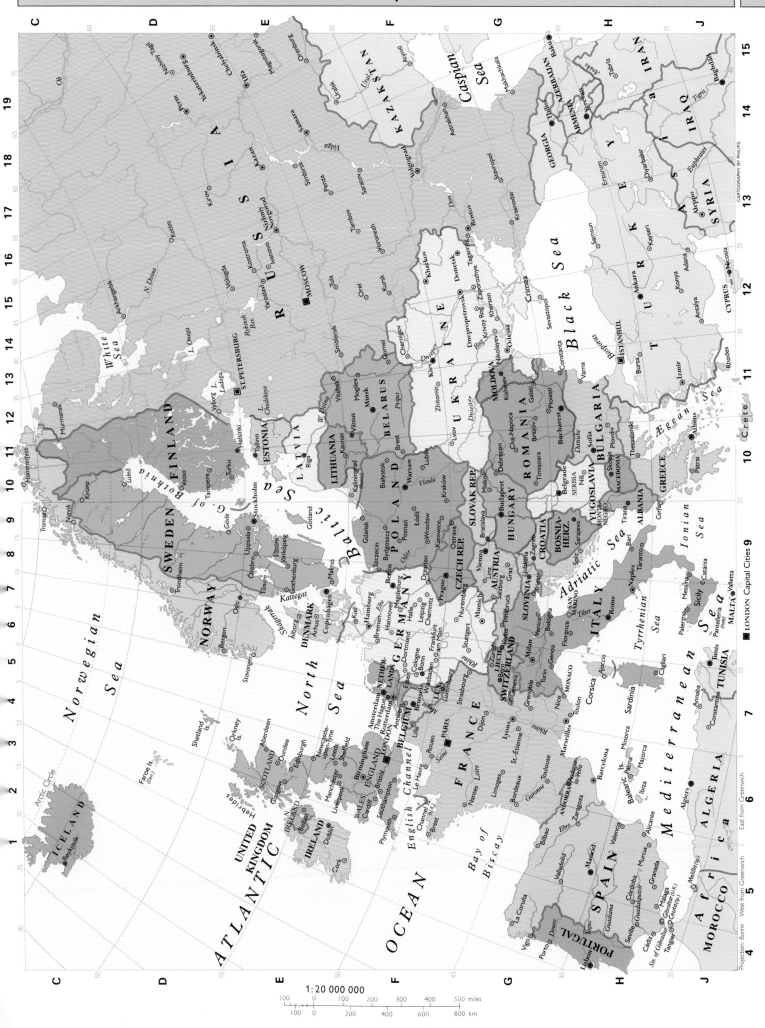

Projection: Bonne   West from Greenwich   C   East from Greenwich

CARTOGRAPHY BY PHILIP'S

■ LONDON Capital Cities

1:20 000 000

```
100   0    100   200   300   400   500 miles

100   0        200       400       600       800 km
```

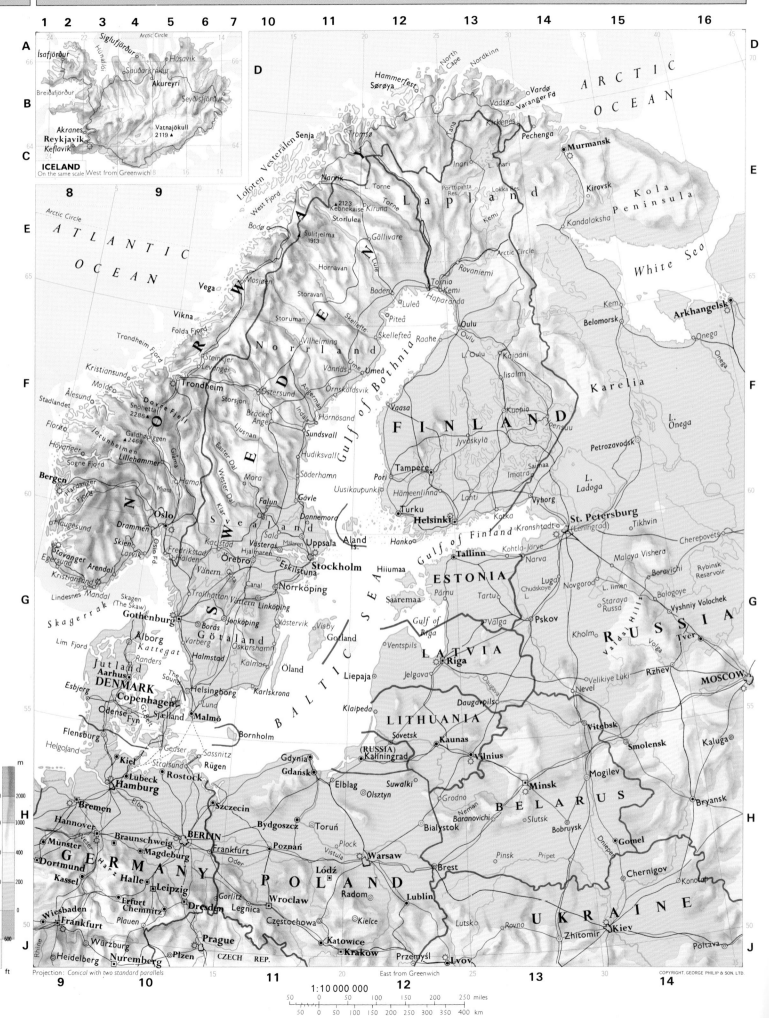

ICELAND
On the same scale. West from Greenwich

Projection: Conical with two standard parallels

1:10 000 000

BRITISH ISLES

8

A
1 2 3 4 5 6 7 8 9

Shetland Is.
Yell
Unst
Fetlar
Askøy
Bergen
Osøyri

Foula
Mainland
Lerwick

NORWAY
Stord
Bømlo
Leirvik
Haugesund

A T L A N T I C   O C E A N

1224

Fair Isle
Kopervik
Åkrahamn

Boknafjorden

B
316
Westray
Sanday
Stronsay
Stavanger
Sandnes
Bryne
Nærbø

Orkney Is.
Mainland
Hoy
Kirkwall
South
Ronaldsay

Pentland Firth

C. Wrath
Thurso
Wick

Outer Hebrides
Lewis
Stornoway
North Minch
Helmsdale

St. Kilda
789
Lairg
Golspie

North
Uist
Harris
Tain
Invergordon
Dingwall
Moray Firth
Buckie
Banff
Fraserburgh

Benbecula
Portree
L. Ness
Inverness
Nairn
Elgin
Spey
Huntly
Peterhead

C
South Uist
Skye
1182
Aviemore
Don
Inverurie
Aberdeen

Barra
Rhum
Elgg
Ben Nevis
1342
Fort William
1214
Ballater
Stonehaven

Coll
Tobermory
Forfar
Montrose
Arbroath

Tiree
Mull
Oban
Dundee
St. Andrews
N O R T H

Colonsay
L. Lomond
973
Perth
Glenrothes
238

Jura
Greenock
Stirling
Dunfermline
Kirkcaldy
Dunbar
S E A

D
Islay
Paisley
Glasgow
Edinburgh
Berwick-upon-Tweed

Arran
East Kilbride
Hamilton
Galashiels
Alnwick

Campbeltown
Irvine
Kilmarnock
640
Jedburgh
816
Cheviot Hills

Malin Hd.
Buncrana
Ayr
Hawick

Aran I.
Letterkenny
Coleraine
Girvan
Dumfries
Hexham
Newcastle-upon-Tyne
South Shields

Donegal
Londonderry
Ballymena
Larne
Kirkcudbright
Annan
Gateshead
Sunderland

U
NORTHERN IRELAND
Antrim
Bangor
Mull of Galloway
Whitehaven
Carlisle
Durham
Hartlepool
Redcar

Lifford
Omagh
Lough
Neagh
Belfast
Lisburn
893
Darlington
Middlesbrough

Bundoran
Lower L.
Erne
Enniskillen
Portadown
Lurgan
Workington
Cumbrian
Mts.
978
Stockton-on-Tees
Scarborough

Ballina
Sligo
Clones
Armagh
Newry
Douglas
Barrow-in-Furness
Bridlington

L. Conn
Leitrim
Cavan
Castleblayney
I. of Man
Lancaster

UNITED
Castlebar
Roscommon
Longford
Ceanannus Mor
Dundalk
Harrogate
York
Beverley

Westport
Lough
Ree
Mullingar
Boyne
Drogheda
Blackpool
Keighley
Leeds
Kingston upon Hull

KINGDOM
Lough
Mask
Lough
Corrib
Athlone
Dublin
Preston
Burnley
636
Bradford
Scunthorpe

Connemara
Galway
Ballinasloe
Tullamore
Dun Laoghaire
Blackburn
Halifax
Huddersfield
Barnsley
Doncaster
Grimsby

Galway B.
Birr
Liffey
Bray
Holyhead
Bangor
Bolton
Manchester
Oldham
Rotherham
Lincoln

E
Aran Is.
IRELAND
Lough
Derg
Port Laoise
Athy
Anglesey
Colwyn Bay
Chester
Liverpool
Warrington
Stockport
Sheffield
Louth

I R I S H
Ennis
Nenagh
Thurles
Carlow
Kilkenny
926
Arklow
Snowdon
1085
Wrexham
Crewe
Chesterfield
Mansfield
Skegness

Texel
Den Helder

Kilrush
Limerick
Tipperary
Pwllheli
Cambrian
Mts.
Stoke-on-Trent
Derby
Nottingham
The Wash
Cromer

953
Listowel
Clonmel
Carrick-on-Suir
Wexford
Cardigan
Bay
Shrewsbury
Welshpool
Stafford
Leicester
Grantham
King's Lynn
Norwich
Great Yarmouth
Lowestoft

Tralee
Mallow
Blackwater
Waterford
Rosslare
Aberystwyth
Telford
Nuneaton
Corby
Peterborough
Thetford

S E A
Dingle
Killarney
Dungarvan
Fishguard
BIRMINGHAM
Wolverhampton
Coventry
Rugby
Northampton
Ely
Bury St. Edmunds
Ipswich

NETHERLANDS
Haarlem
The Hague

Carrauntoohill
1041
Macgillycuddy's Reeks
Cork
Bandon
Youghal
St. George's Channel
Cardiff
Redditch
Worcester
Hereford
Royal
Leamington Spa
Bedford
Cambridge
Felixstowe
Harwich
Colchester

Hoek van Holland
ROTTERDAM
Dordrecht

C. Clear
Bantry
Kinsale
Cóbh
99
Fishguard
WALES
Brecon
886
Cheltenham
Gloucester
Oxford
Milton Keynes
Stevenage
Luton
Harlow
Chelmsford

Vlissingen

Haverfordwest
Milford Haven
Pembroke
Merthyr Tydfil
Neath
Cwmbran
High Wycombe
Watford
Basildon
Southend-on-Sea

Margate
Zeebrugge
Oostende
Antwerp

F
Llanelli
Rhondda
Newport
Swindon
Slough
LONDON
Reigate
Chatham
Canterbury
Dover

Brugge
Gent
Mechelen
BELGIUM

Swansea
Port Talbot
Barry
Cardiff
Bristol
Bath
Newbury
Reading
Maidstone
Ashford
Folkestone
Str. of Dover
Calais
Dunkerque

BRUSSELS

Bristol Channel
Weston-super-Mare
Basingstoke
Guildford
Crawley
Hastings
C.
Gris-Nez
Boulogne-sur-Mer
St.-Omer
Tournai

Lille
Roubaix

C E L T I C
Barnstaple
Exmoor
Taunton
Salisbury
Winchester
Fareham
Eastbourne
Worthing
Brighton
Le Touquet-Paris-Plage
33
Béthune
Bruay-en-Artois
Lens
Valenciennes

Bude
Yeovil
Southampton
Bournemouth
Poole
Portsmouth
Isle of Wight
Newport
Weymouth
English Channel

S E A
618
Dartmoor
Exeter
Exmouth
Torbay
E n g l i s h   C h a n n e l
Abbeville
Le Tréport
Dieppe
Fécamp
St. Quentin

P i c a r d i e

G
Newquay
Truro
St. Austell
Plymouth
Penzance
Land's End
Falmouth
Le Havre
Rouen
FRANCE
Amiens

Isles of Scilly
C. de la Hague
Pte. de
Barfleur
Bolbec

West from Greenwich
Alderney
St. Peter
Port
Cherbourg
Valognes
East from Greenwich
CARTOGRAPHY BY PHILIP'S.

Projection: _Conical with two standard parallels_
2
3
Guernsey
Sark
Cotentin
Trouville-sur-Mer
Caen
Seine
Elbeuf
Lisieux

50
1 : 5 000 000
50
100 miles
Channel Is.
(U.K.)
Jersey
St. Helier
Bayeux

50
0
50
100
150
km

Elevation scale
ft   m
3000   1000
1500   500
600   200
0   0
50   150
100   300
200   600
500   1500
1000   3000
2000   6000
m ft

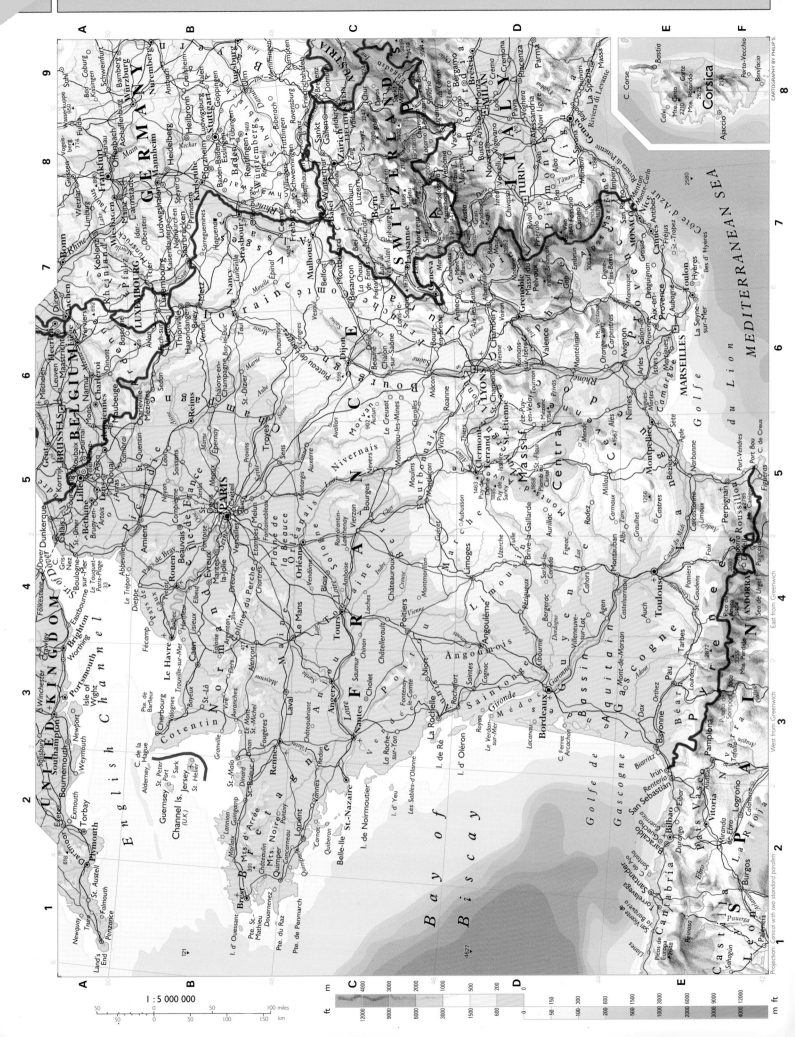

Corsica

1 : 5 000 000

Projection: Conical with two standard parallels

CARTOGRAPHY BY PHILIP'S

Projection: Conical with two standard parallels

1 : 5 000 000

Projection: Conical with two standard parallels

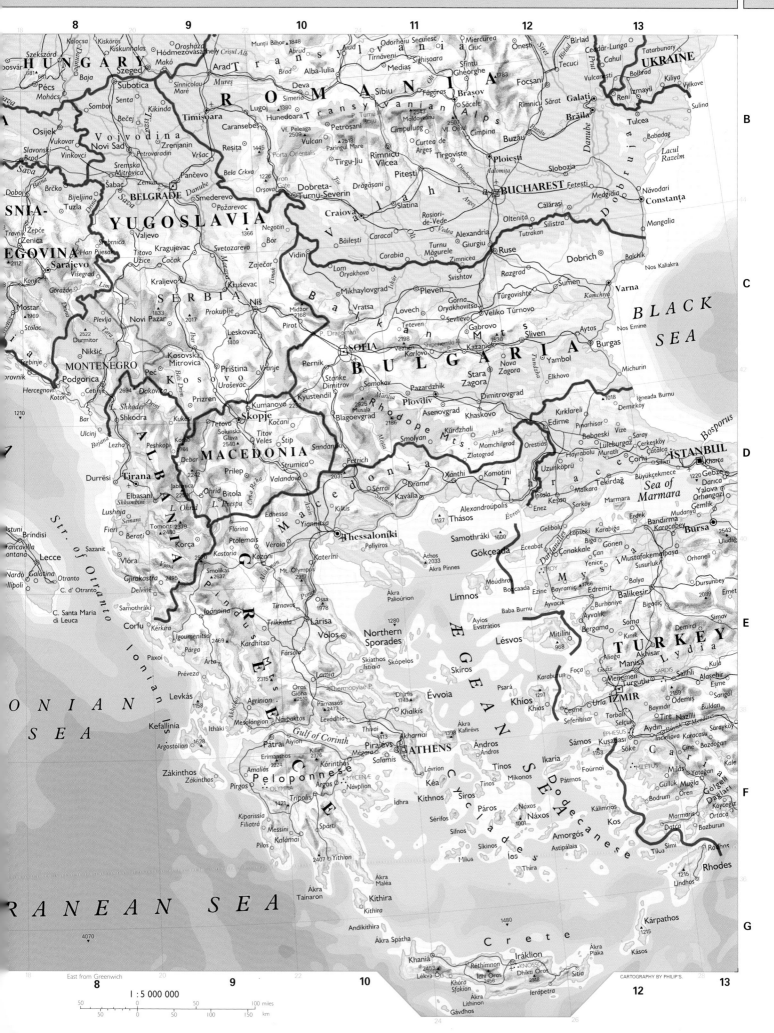

East from Greenwich

1 : 5 000 000

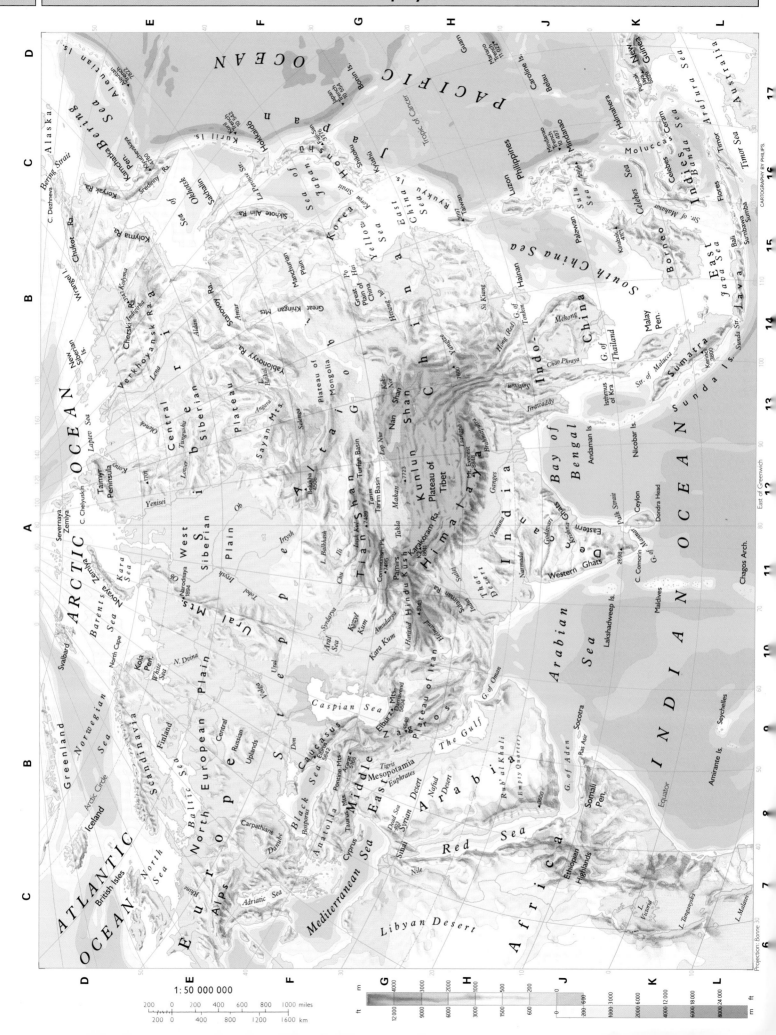

1:50 000 000

200   0   200   400   600   800   1000 miles
200 0   400   800   1200   1600 km

Projection Bonne

East of Greenwich

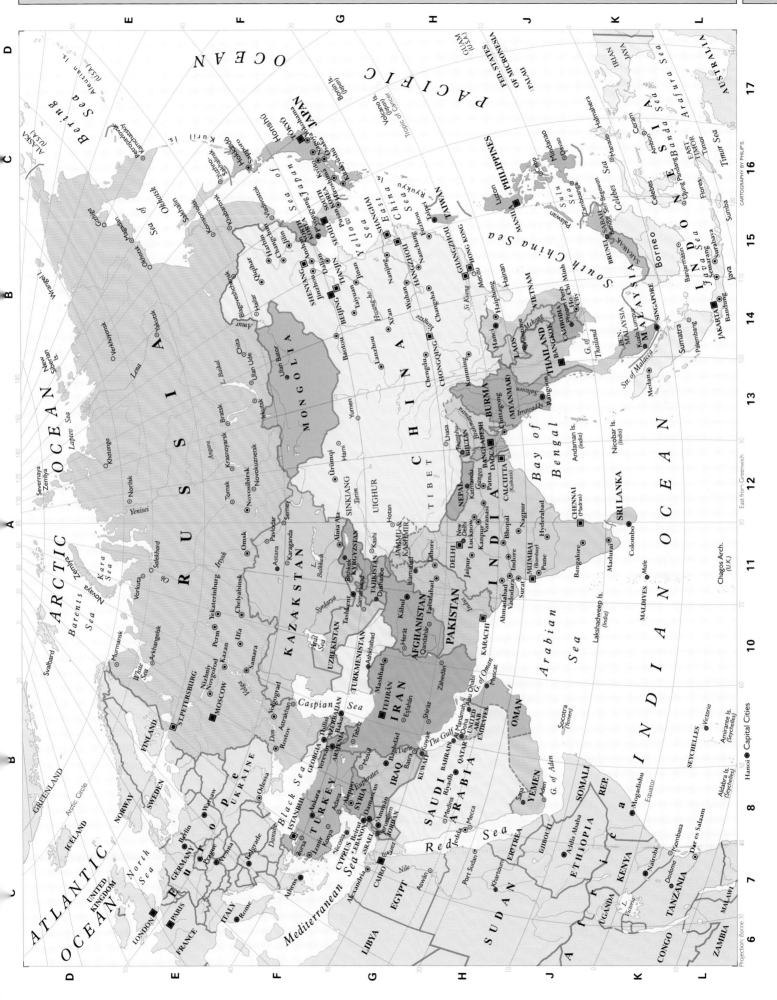

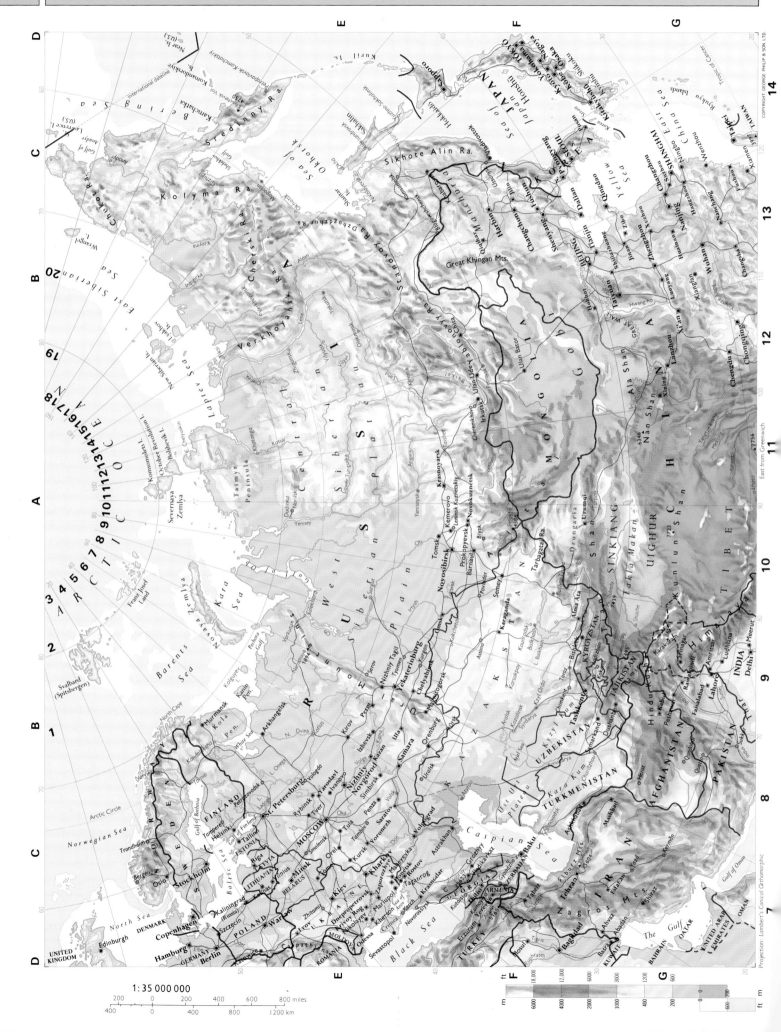

1:35 000 000

SOUTHERN HONSHU,
KYUSHU AND SHIKOKU

1 2 3 4 5 6 7

A

SEA OF JAPAN

Suzu-Misaki
Wajima
Nanao
Himi
Toyama Bay
Takaoka
Toyama
Nagano
Kanazawa
Tōkamachi
2578
Komatsu
Shinano-Gawa
Kanuma
Utsunomiya
Hitachi
Fukui
Matsumoto
Ueda Maebashi
Takasaki
Kiryu
Tochigi
Mito
Takefu
3190
Kantō-Sanchi
Chichibu
Ashikaga
Kumagaya
Ōmiya
Tsuchiura
Tsuruga
2702 Takayama
Ina
Kōnosu
Kawagoe
Urawa
Kawaguchi
Ichikawa
Chōshi
Matsue
Kyō-ga-Saki
Wakasa-Wan
Ōgaki
Gifu
Ichinomiya
3063
Iida 3192
TŌKYŌ
Funabashi
Izumo
Jizō-Zaki
Yonago
1712
Tottori
Toyooka
Maizuru
Ayabe
Seto
NAGOYA
Fuji-no-miya
KAWASAKI
Chiba
Ichihara

B

Hamada
Masuda
Tsuyama
Fukuchiyama
KYOTO
Hikone
Ōtsu Kuwana
Yokkaichi
Toyota
Okazaki
3776 Hiratsuka
YOKOHAMA
Odawara
Yokosuka
Tateyama
Hagi
HIROSHIMA
Fukuyama
Himeji
Amagasaki
KOBE
Nishinomiya
Nara
Ise Toyohashi
Shimizu
Shizuoka
Hamamatsu
Atami
Ito
Nojima-Zaki
Onoda
Otake
Mihara
Akashi
Okayama
ŌSAKA
Higashiōsaka
Tse-Wan
Ise
Numazu
Suruga-Wan
Irō-Zaki
Ō-Shima
Yamaguchi Iwakuni
Kurashiki
Shōdo-Shima
Takamatsu
Sakai
Matsuzaka
Shimada
Nii-Jima
Shimonoseki
Tokuyama
Imabari
Marugame
Sakaide Naruto
Izumi-sano
Kishiwada
Awaji-Shima
Daiō-Misaki
Miyake-Jima
Izu-Shotō

KITAKYŪSHŪ
Nōgata Yukuhashi Buzen
SHIKOKU
Niihama
1955
Saijō
Wakayama
1915 *Kii-Sanchi*
Owase
Fukuoka
Karatsu
Iki
Iizuka
Hita
Matsuyama
Shikoku-Sanchi
Kōchi
Anan
Kii Channel
Tanabe
Shingū

C

Tosu
Saga
Kurume
Beppu
Yawatahama
Tosa-Wan
Muroto
Muroto-Misaki
Sasebo
Ōmura
Ōita
Usuki
1787
Uwajima
Nakamura
Ashizuri-Zaki
Bungo Channel
Isahaya
Ōmuta
Kumamoto
Saiki

D

Nagasaki
Yatsushiro
Nobeoka
Hyūga
makusa-Shotō
Minamata
Miyazaki
Sendai
Kokubu
Miyakonojō
Nichinan
Kagoshima
Makurazaki
Kanoya

Sata-Misaki
Ōsumi Channel
Nishin'omote
Osumi Islands
Tane-ga-Shima
1935
Yaku-Shima

PACIFIC OCEAN

3
East from Greenwich
1:5 000 000
Projection: Conical with two standard parallels

E
Rebun-Tō
Sōya-Misaki
Wakkanai
Sea of Okhotsk
13
Rishiri-Tō
45
Shiretoko-Misaki
Ishikari-Gawa
Rumoi
Mashike
Abashiri
2290
Danisu-San-Zan
Nemuro Str.
Kamui-Misaki
Ishikari-Wan
Asahigawa
HOKKAIDŌ
Nemuro

F
Otaru
SAPPORO
Obihiro
Kushiro
Okushiri-Tō
Uchiura-Wan
Muroran
Poroshiri-Dake
2052
Hakodate
Tsugaru Str.
Erimo-Misaki
Shiragami-Misaki
Shiriya-Zaki
Aomori
Hirosaki
Hachinohe
11
Oga-Hantō
Iwate-San
2041
Morioka
32
Akita
Miyako
Takami-Sanchi
Kamaishi
7756

SEA OF JAPAN

D
40
Sakata
Ishinomaki
Sado
Yamagata
Azuma-San
Sendai
Niigata
2024
Fukushima
Nagaoka
Kōriyama
Iwaki

G
Suzu-Misaki
Wajima
Noto-Hantō
Toyama
Utsunomiya
Mito
Kanazawa
3190
Maebashi
8412
Chōshi
Inubō-Zaki
TŌKYŌ
Fuji-San
3776
YOKOHAMA
NAGOYA
Yokosuka
Bōsō-Hantō
KYOTO
KOBE
ŌSAKA
Sakai
Shizuoka
Hamamatsu
Toyohashi
Nojima-Zaki
Wakayama
Sanchi
Ise-Wan
Nii-Jima
Ō-Shima
Miyake-Jima

SOUTH KOREA
Suwŏn
Chungju
Taejŏn
Pohang
Kunsan Iri
Chŏnju
Taegu
Kwangju
1915 Chinju
Masan
PUSAN
Mokpo
Sunchon
Yŏsu
Korea Str.
Tsushima

G
Matsue
Tottori
Oki-Shotō
Wakasa-Wan
Biwa-Ko
35
HIROSHIMA
Okayama
Inland Sea
Shimonoseki
Kure
KITAKYŪSHŪ
Takamatsu
Tokushima
FUKUOKA
Matsuyama
SHIKOKU
Kōchi
Tosa-Wan
Muroto-Misaki
Shio-no-Misaki

H
Cheju Do
1950
Sasebo
Gotō-Rettō
Ōmuta
Kumamoto
Nagasaki
Nomo-Zaki
Miyazaki
Ashizuri-Zaki
KYUSHU
Kagoshima
Hachijō-Jima

EAST CHINA SEA

PACIFIC OCEAN

Kagoshima-Wan
Ōsumi Channel
1935
Ōsumi-Shotō
Tane-ga-Shima
Yaku-Shima

11
12
East from Greenwich
1:10 000 000
Projection: Bonne

JAPAN

COPYRIGHT. GEORGE. PHILIP & SON. LTD.

ft	m
9000	3000
6000	1500
4500	1000
3000	400
1200	200
600	
200	600
	2000 6000
	4000 12,000
	6000 18,000
	8000 24,000

m ft

8 9 10

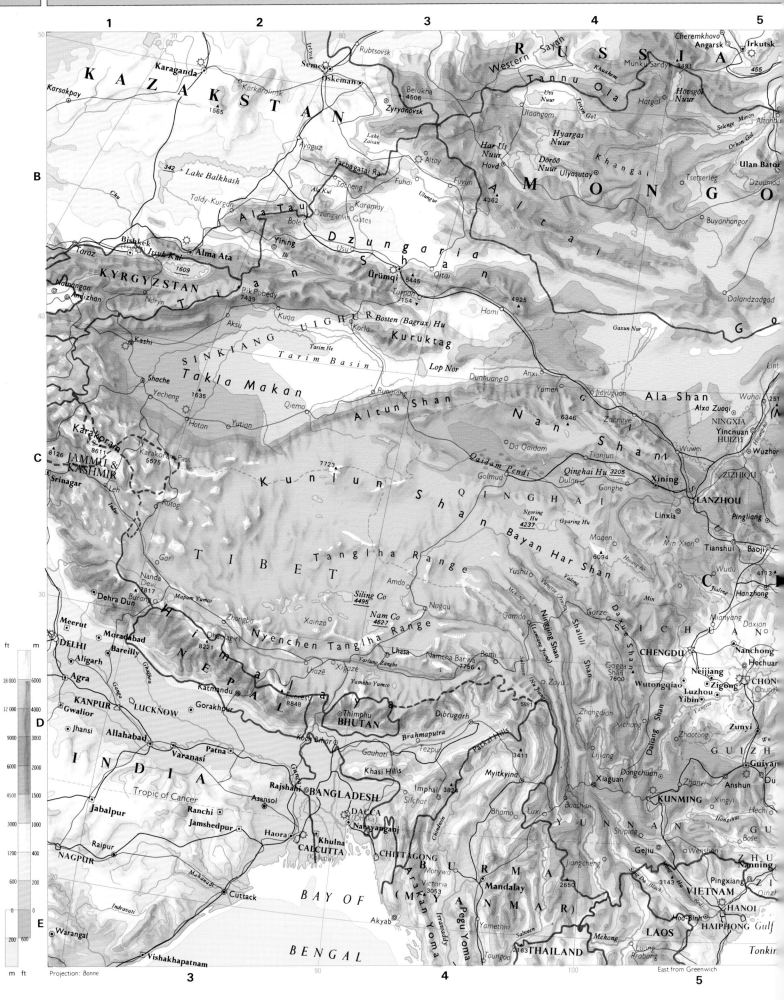

1:15 000 000

100   0   100   200   300   400 miles

100   0   100   200   300   400   500   600 km

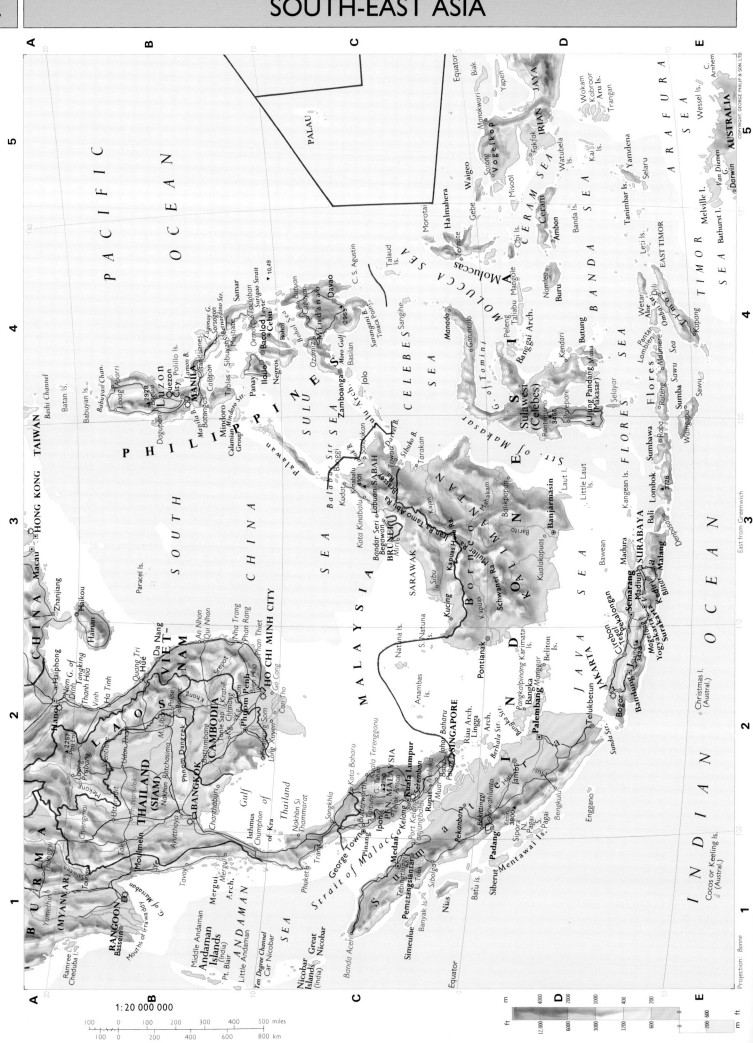

Projection: Bonne

1:20 000 000

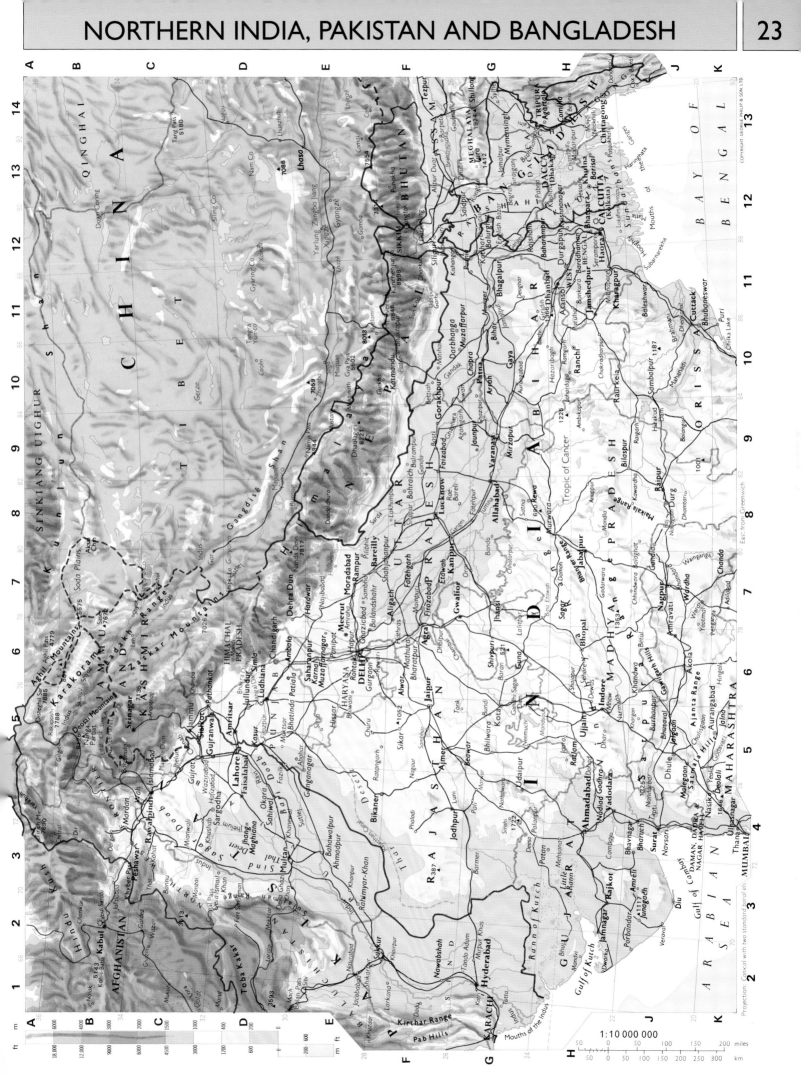

1:10 000 000

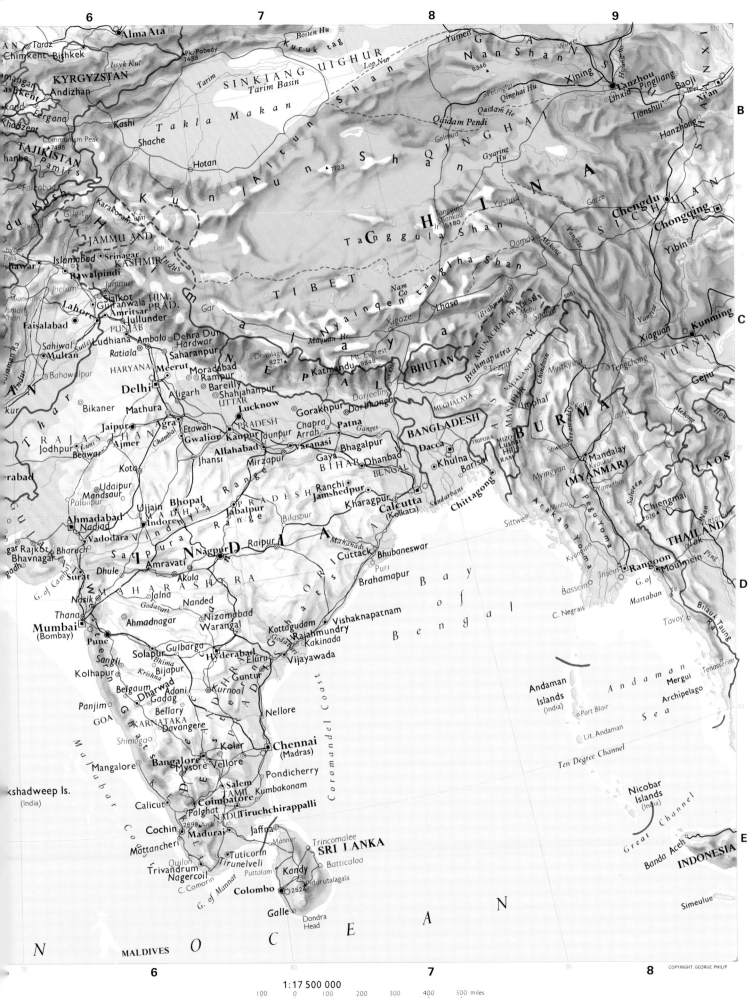

1:17 500 000

100   0   100   200   300   400   500 miles
100   0 100 200 300 400 500 600 700 800 km

AFRICA : *physical*

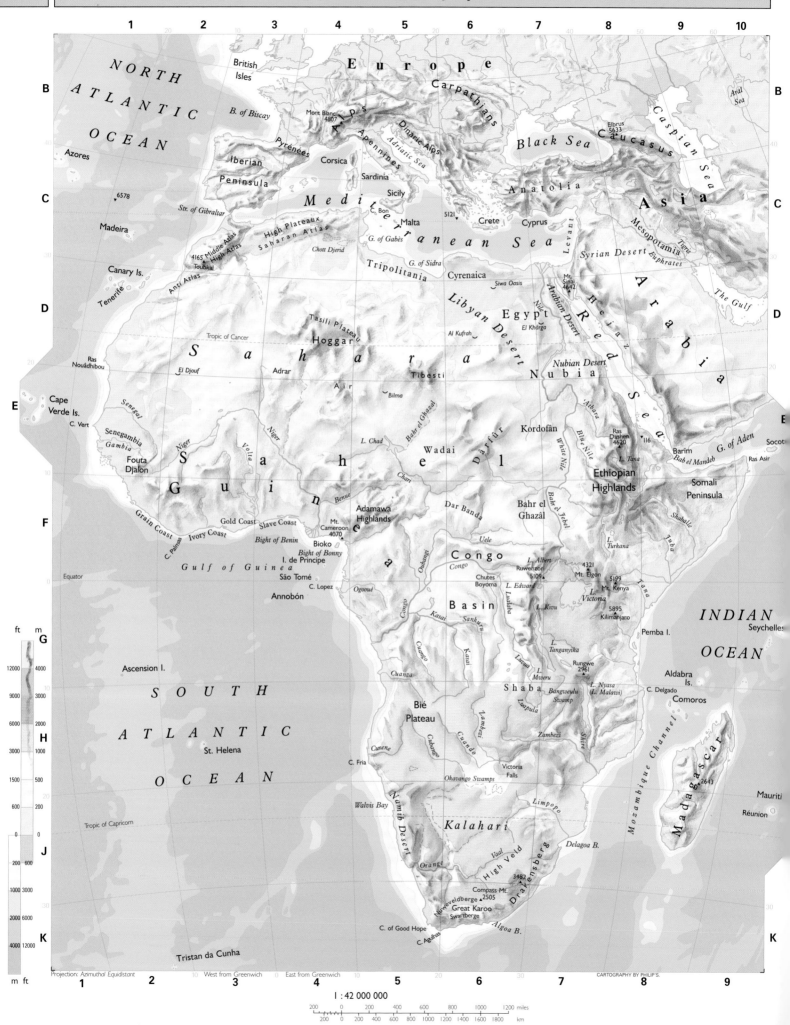

NORTH ATLANTIC OCEAN

British Isles

Europe

Carpathians

B. of Biscay

Mont Blanc 4807
A l p s
Pyrénées
Dinaric Alps
Apennines
Adriatic Sea
Black Sea
Caucasus
Elbrus 5633
Caspian Sea
Aral Sea

Azores

Iberian Peninsula
Corsica
Sardinia
Sicily
Anatolia
A s i a

6578

Madeira

Str. of Gibraltar
High Plateaux
Saharan Atlas
Middle Atlas
4165 High Atlas
Toubkal
C. Bon
Malta
5121
Crete
Cyprus
Mesopotamia
Tigris
The Gulf

Canary Is.
Tenerife
Anti Atlas
Chott Djerid
G. of Gabès
M e d i t e r r a n e a n   S e a
Levant
Syrian Desert
Euphrates

A r a b i a

Ras Nouâdhibou

Tropic of Cancer
G. of Sidra
Tripolitania
Cyrenaica
Siwa Oasis
Libyan Desert
Egypt
El Kharga
Arabian Desert
Mt. Sinai 4642
Hejaz
Red Sea

Tasili Plateau
Hoggar
S a h a r a
Al Kufrah
Nubian Desert
Nubia
Ras Dashen 4620
116

El Djouf
Adrar
Air
Tibesti
Bilma

Cape Verde Is.
C. Vert
Senegal
Senegambia
Gambia
Fouta Djalon
Niger
Volta
Niger
L. Chad
Bahr el Ghazal
Wadai
Darfur
Kordofàn
Albara
White Nile
Blue Nile
L. Tana
Barim
Bab el Mandeb
Ras Asir
Socot

S a h
G u i n
Grain Coast
Gold Coast
Ivory Coast
Slave Coast
C. Palmas
Bight of Benin
Benue
Adamawa Highlands
Mt. Cameroon 4070
Dar Banda
Bahr el Ghazâl
Ethiopian Highlands
Somali Peninsula
Shabelle

e l

Bioko
Bight of Bonny
I. de Principe
São Tomé
Gulf of Guinea
Uele
Ubangi
C o n g o
Congo
Chutes Boyoma
L. Albert
Ruwenzori 5109
Mt. Elgon
4321
Juba

Equator
C. Lopez
Annobón
Ogooué
B a s i n
Kasai
Sankuru
L. Edward
Lualaba
L. Kivu
L. Victoria
Mt. Kenya 5199
Kilimanjaro 5895
Tana

INDIAN OCEAN
Seychelles

Ascension I.
Cuango
Cuanza
Congo
Kasai
L. Tanganyika
L. Mweru
Rungwe 2961
Pemba I.

S O U T H
A T L A N T I C
St. Helena
Bié Plateau
Shaba
Bangweulu Swamp
L. Nyasa (L. Malawi)
C. Delgado
Comoros
Aldabra Is.

O C E A N
Lualaba
Zambezi
Cuanza
Luapula
Zambezi
Shire
Madagascar
Mozambique Channel

C. Fria
Cunene
Cubango
Victoria Falls
2643
Mauriti
Réunion

Walvis Bay
Cuando
Limpopo

Tropic of Capricorn
K a l a h a r i
Okavango Swamps

Namib Desert
Orange
Vaal
High Veld
Drakensberg
3482
Delagoa B.

Muweveldberge 2505
Compass Mt.
Great Karoo
Swartberge
Algoa B.
C. of Good Hope
C. Agulhas

Tristan da Cunha

Projection: *Azimuthal Equidistant*
West from Greenwich
East from Greenwich
CARTOGRAPHY BY PHILIP'S.

1 : 42 000 000

200   0   200   400   600   800   1000   1200 miles
200   0   200   400   600   800   1000   1200   1400   1600   1800
km

ft   m
G
12000 4000
9000   3000
H
6000   2000
3000   1000
1500   500
J
600   200
0   0
200   600
K
1000   3000
2000   6000
4000   12000
m ft

AFRICA : *political*

1 2 3 4 5 6 7 8 9 10

NORTH
ATLANTIC
OCEAN

UNITED KINGDOM
LONDON
NETH.
BELG.
PARIS
FRANCE
SWITZ.
B. of Biscay

GERMANY POLAND
Warsaw
CZECH REP.
Prague
Vienna SLOVAK REP.
AUSTRIA
HUNGARY
CROATIA
BOS.-
HERZ.
YUG.
ROMANIA

Kiev
UKRAINE

RUSSIA
Volgograd
KAZAKSTAN
Aral Sea

Caspian Sea

Azores
(Port.)

Madrid
PORTUGAL
SPAIN
Lisbon

Corsica
Rome
Sardinia
ITALY

Adriatic Sea
ALB. MAC.
BULGARIA
Black Sea

Odessa
Ankara
GEORGIA
ARM. AZER.
Baku
TURKMEN.

Madeira
(Port.)

Algiers
Annaba
Constantine
Rabat
Tétouan
Casablanca
Fès
MOROCCO
Marrakesh

Mediterranean Sea
Tunis
TUNISIA
MALTA
Sfax
Tripoli
Misrātah
Benghazi

Sicily
GREECE
Athens
Crete
CYPRUS
Aleppo
SYRIA
Mosul
TURKEY
Tigris
Baghdād
Eşfahān
TEHRĀN

Canary Is.
(Sp.)

El Aaiún
WESTERN SAHARA
Dakhla

Tropic of Cancer
Fdérik

ALGERIA
In Salah
S a h a r a

LIBYA
Marzūq
Al Jawf

EGYPT
CAIRO
El Faiyûm
Asyût
Aswân

Alexandria
Port Said
Suez
ISRAEL
JORDAN
Tel Aviv-
Jaffa
Jerusalem
LEB.
Damascus
Syrian Desert
I R A Q
Basra
KUWAIT
The Gulf
BAHRAIN
QATAR

IRAN

SAUDI
ARABIA
Medina
Jedda
Mecca
Riyadh

Ras
Nouâdhibou
MAURITANIA
Nouakchott
Tombouctou

Senegal
Niger
NIGER
Agadès
Niamey

CHAD
L. Chad
Abéché
Ndjamena

SUDAN
El Fâsher
El Obeid
Khartoum
Omdurmân
Wâd Medani
Atbara
Atbara

Red Sea
ERITREA
Mesewa
Asmera
Wâdi Halfa
Port Sudan

YEMEN
G. of Aden
Socotra
(Yemen)
Ras Asir

C. VERDE IS.
Praia
St-Louis
C. Vert
Dakar
SENEGAL
GAMBIA
Banjul
GUINEA-
BISSAU
Bissau
Conakry
GUINEA
Freetown
SIERRA
LEONE

MALI
Bamako
BURKINA
FASO
Ouagadougou
Bobo-
Dioulasso
Kano
Maiduguri
Chari

NIGERIA
Abuja
Benue

L. Tana
Blue Nile
White Nile
Malakâl
Bahr el Jebel
Wau

DJIBOUTI
Djibouti
Berbera
Addis Ababa
Harer
ETHIOPIA
Shabelle

IVORY
COAST
Yamoussoukro
Bouaké
LIBERIA
Monrovia
Abidjan
GHANA
Kumasi
Sekondi-
Takoradi
TOGO
Lomé
Accra
BENIN
Porto
Novo
Ibadan
Lagos
Enugu
Port
Harcourt
CAMEROON
Douala
Malabo
Yaoundé
EQUATORIAL
GUINEA
SÃO TOMÉ & PRINCIPE
C. Lopez
Annobón

Bight of Benin
Gulf of Guinea
Equator

CENTRAL
AFRICAN REP.
Bangui
Oubangui
Mbandaka
Congo
Kisangani
L. Albert
L. Edward
UGANDA
Kampala
RWANDA
Kigali
L. Kivu
BURUNDI
Bujumbura
L. Victoria
Kisumu
Nairobi
KENYA
Mombasa
L. Turkana
Tana
SOMALI REP.
Mogadishu
Kismayu

Juba

GABON
Libreville
CONGO
Brazzaville
Pointe Noire
CABINDA
(Angola)
Kinshasa
Matadi
CONGO
(DEM. REP. OF THE)
Kasai
Kananga

TANZANIA
Dodoma
Dar es Salaam
Zanzibar
L. Tanganyika
L. Mweru
SEYCHELLES

INDIAN
OCEAN

SOUTH
ATLANTIC
OCEAN

Ascension I.
(U.K.)
St. Helena
(U.K.)

Luanda
Lobito
Huambo
ANGOLA
Namibe
C. Fria
Cunene
Cubango
Cuango

Likasi
Lubumbashi
Ndola
ZAMBIA
Lusaka
Livingstone
Lilongwe
MALAWI
L. Malawi
Blantyre
COMOROS
Aldabra
Is.
C. Delgado
Moçambique
Mayotte
(Fr.)
Antsiranana
Mahajanga

NAMIBIA
Windhoek
BOTSWANA
Gaborone
Limpopo
ZIMBABWE
Harare
Bulawayo
Zambezi
MOZAMBIQUE
Beira
Maputo
Mbabane
SWAZ.
Mozambique Channel
Toamasina
Antananarivo
MADAGASCAR
Fianarantsoa
Réunion
(Fr.)
MAURITIUS

Tropic of Capricorn

Orange
Vaal
Kimberley
Johannesburg
Pretoria
LESOTHO
Maseru
Durban
SOUTH AFRICA
Cape Town
C. of Good Hope
C. Agulhas
Port
Elizabeth
East
London

Tristan da Cunha
(U.K.)

Projection: Azimuthal Equidistant
West from Greenwich
East from Greenwich
CARTOGRAPHY BY PHILIP'S.
● Dakar Capital Cities
1 : 42 000 000
200 0 200 400 600 800 1000 1200 miles
200 0 200 400 600 800 1000 1200 1400 1600 1800 km

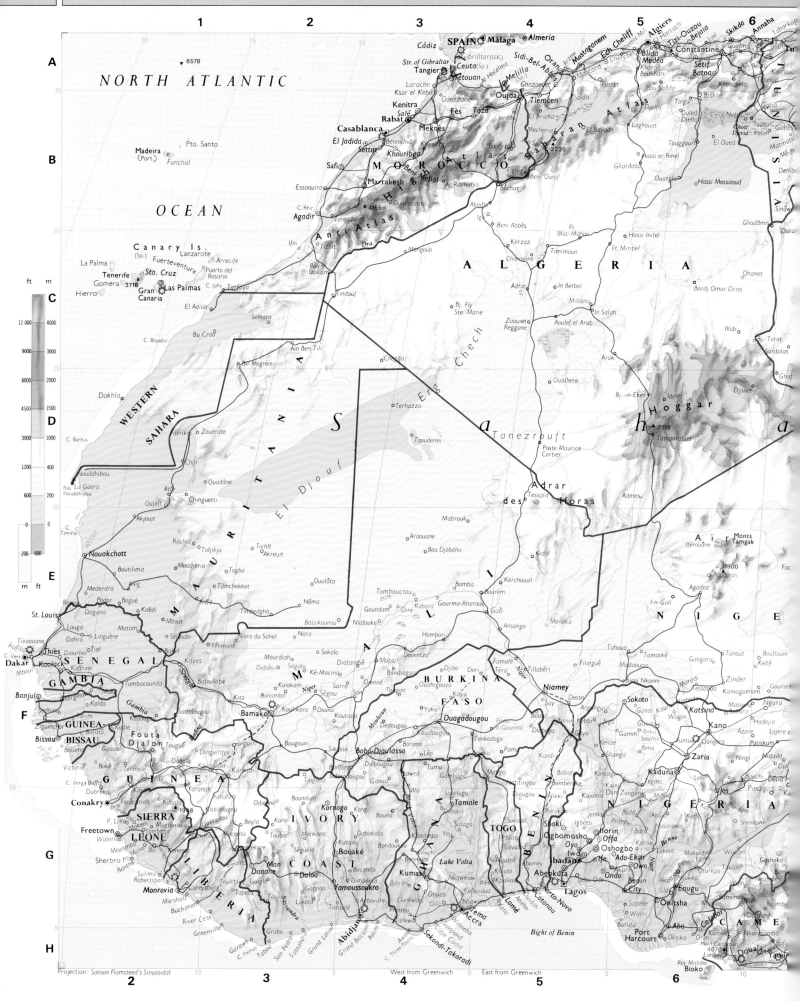

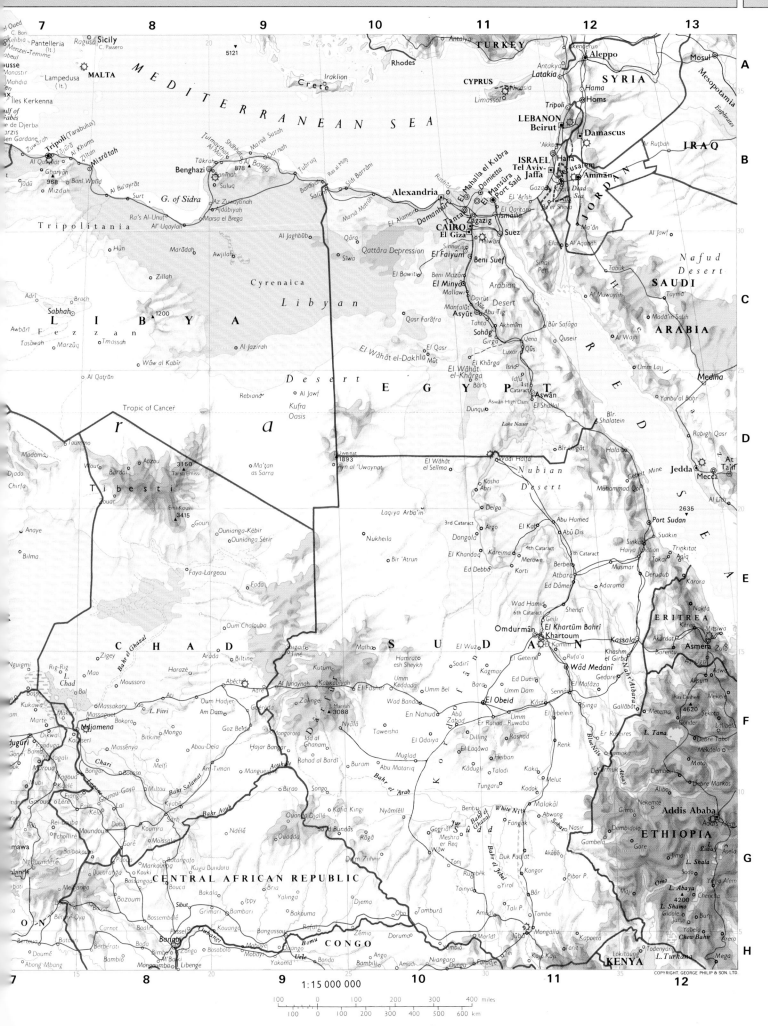

MEDITERRANEAN SEA

TURKEY

SYRIA

IRAQ

LIBYA

EGYPT

SUDAN

CHAD

CENTRAL AFRICAN REPUBLIC

ETHIOPIA

ERITREA

SAUDI ARABIA

ENYA

CONGO

1:15 000 000

100   0   100   200   300   400 miles
100   0   100 200 300 400 500 600 km

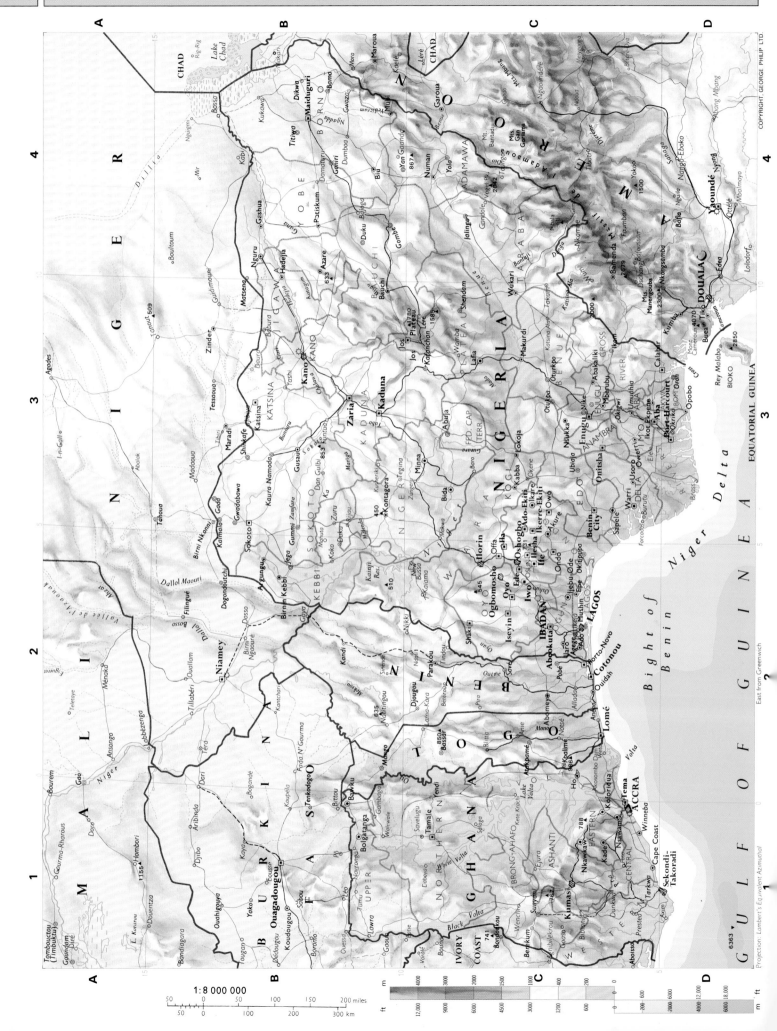

1:8 000 000

Projection: Lambert's Equivalent Azimuthal

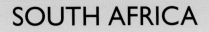

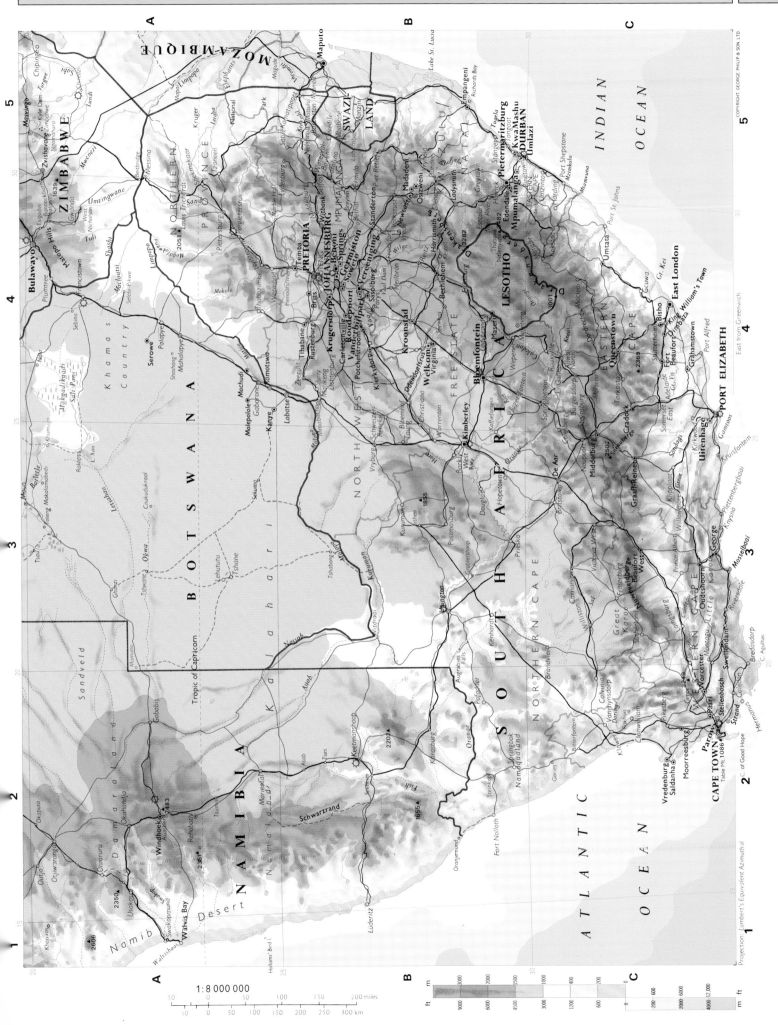

1:8 000 000

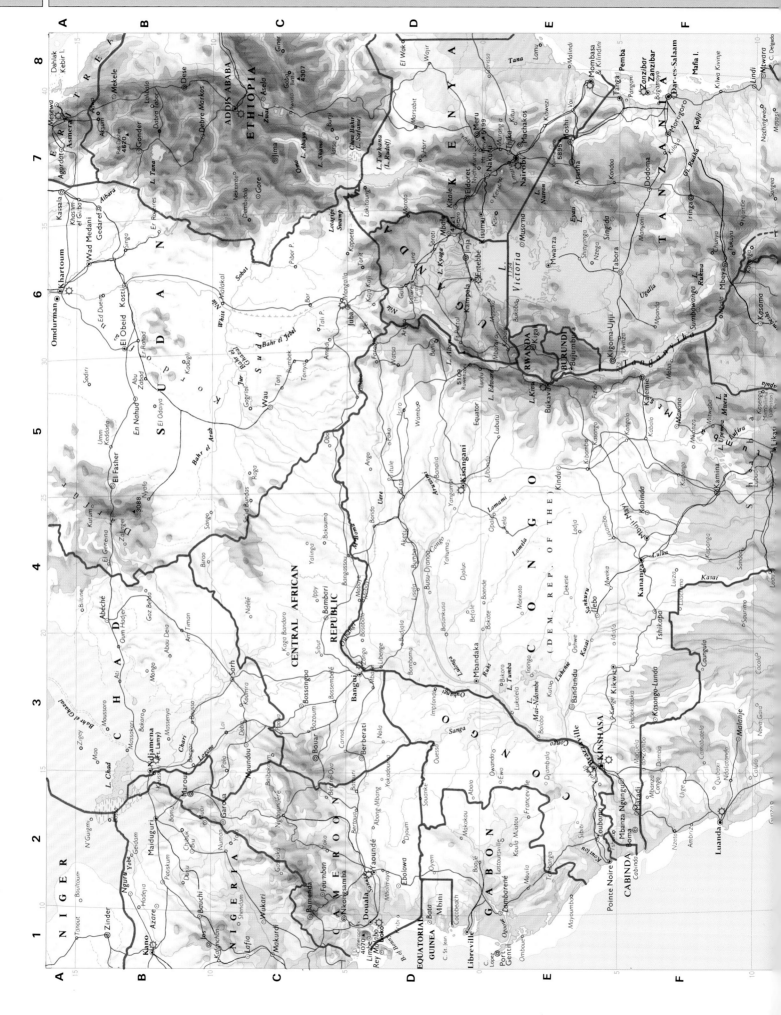

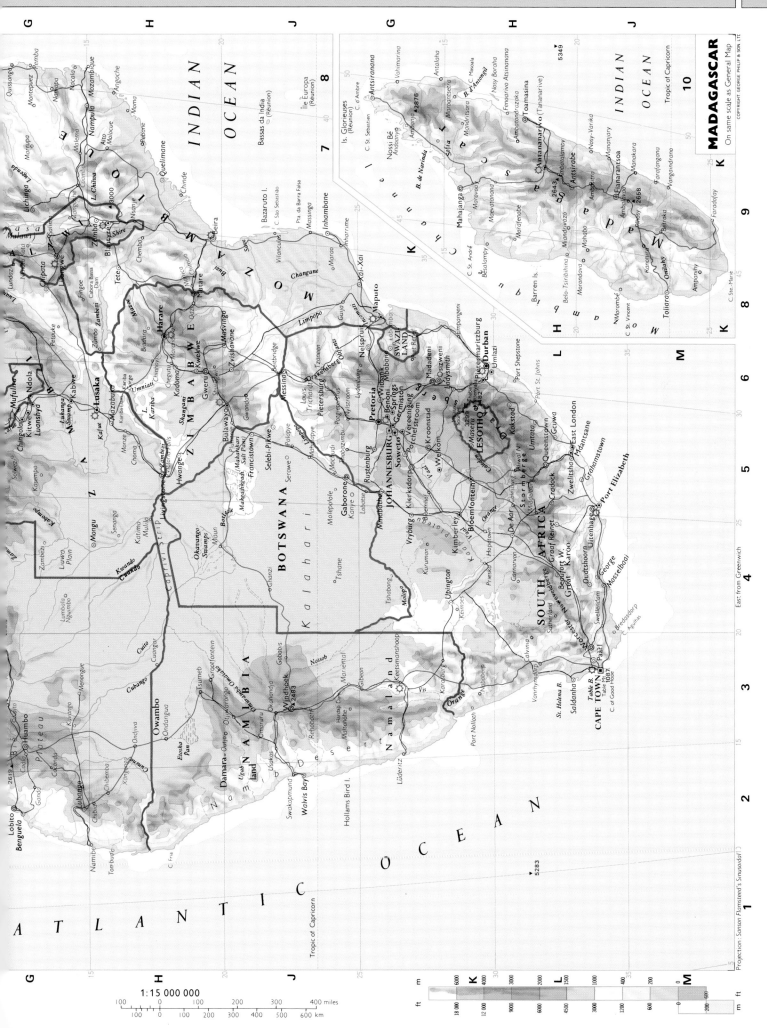

MADAGASCAR
On same scale as General Map

COPYRIGHT GEORGE PHILIP & SON LTD

INDIAN OCEAN

ATLANTIC OCEAN

1:15 000 000

Projection: Sanson Flamsteed's Sinusoidal

NAURU

Tamana

K I R I B A T I

Baker

Equator

▾6195

Abariringa

▲3 Bougainville

ibi

Choiseul

Santa Isabel

SOLOMON

ISLANDS

Namumea

Phoenix Is.

New
Georgia

Malaita

Honiara ○ ▲2331

Carondelet

Guadalcanal

San
Cristóbal

TUVALU

(Ellice Is.) Funafuti ○ Funafuti

A

Rennell

▾7223

Santa Cruz Is.

Nukulaelae

Tokelau
Is.
(N.Z.)

B

Fataka

Rotuma.

Banks Is.

Espíritu Santo ▲1880

VANUATU
(New Hebrides)

Mata-Utu ✿
Wallis & Futuna ○ Uvea
Horn   (Fr.)

SAMOA

Savai'i

Apia
○ ✿

American
Samoa

C

Malakula

Port-Vila ○✿ Efate

Vanua Levu

Niuafo'ou

Upolu

Tutuila

Chesterfield Is.

Viti Levu

FIJI

▲1324
○ Suva

Lau Is.

Vavau Is.

▲1628

Loyalty Is.

▾7569

New
Caledonia
(Fr.)

Nouméa ○

Ha'apai Is.

TONGA

Niue
✿ (N.Z.)

D

Matthew

Ceve-i-Ra

Nuku'Alofa ✿
Tongatapu Is. ○

P   A   C   I   F   I   C

▾5303

Cook Is.
(N.Z.)

O   C   E   A   N

10 882 ▾

Tropic of Capricorn

E

Norfolk
(Austr.)

Raoul

Kermadec Is.
(N.Z.)

Lord Howe
(Austr.)

▾734

F

10 047 ▾

Tasman   Sea

North C.

Kaitaia

Whangarei

▾5267

Auckland

North Island

G

Hamilton

Bay of
Plenty

New Plymouth

Rotorua

Gisborne

NEW
ZEALAND

Ruapehu
2797

Napier

Wanganui

Palmerston
North

Nelson

Cook's Strait

Wellington

Greymouth

Blenheim

South Island

H

Southern Alps

Aoraki-Mt. Cook
3753

Christchurch

Wakatipu

Timaru

Invercargill

Dunedin

Chatham
(N.Z.)

Stewart

J

West from Greenwich

1 : 20 000 000

100   0   100   200   300   400   500 miles

100   0   200   400   600   800 km

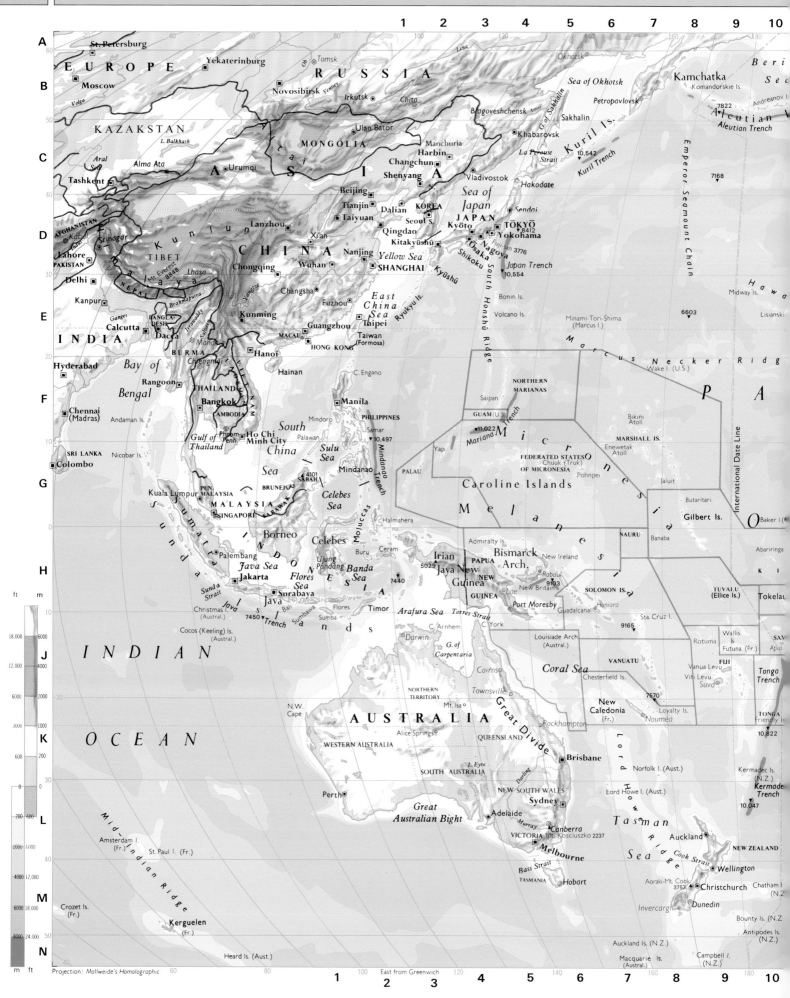

11 12 13 14 15 16 17 18 19 20

ALASKA

GREENLAND
C. Farewell
Bristol Bay
6969
Gulf of Alaska
Juneau
Prince of Wales I.
Prince Rupert
Queen Charlotte Is.
Kitimat
Edmonton

Hudson Bay

Labrador

NORTH AMERICA

NORTH

Newfoundland

Vancouver
Vancouver I.
Victoria
Seattle
Calgary
Regina
Winnipeg
L. Winnipeg
Montréal
Québec
Pr. Edward I.
Saint John

Portland
Boise
Minneapolis
L. Superior
Ottawa
Toronto
L. Huron
L. Michigan
Detroit
Buffalo
Boston
C. Sable

CHICAGO
Pittsburgh
L. Ontario
L. Erie
NEW YORK
Philadelphia

C. Mendocino
Salt Lake City
Denver
Kansas
St. Louis
Cincinnati
Baltimore
Washington

San Francisco
4418
UNITED STATES
Oklahoma
Memphis
Atlanta
C. Hatteras

ATLANTIC

6741
Los Angeles
San Diego
Ciudad Juárez
Dallas
Mississippi
Appalachian Mts.
Jacksonville
Bermuda (U.K.)

OCEAN

6225
San Antonio
Houston
New Orleans

Hawaiian Is.
(U.S.)
Tropic of Cancer
Sierra Madre
Gulf of California
Monterrey
Gulf of Mexico
Miami
Florida Strait
BAHAMAS
Oahu
Honolulu
Hawaii
Revilla Gigedo Is.
(Mexico)
Guadalajara
México
Mérida
Havana
CUBA
West Indies
Hispaniola
DOM. REP.
9200

PACIFIC
Puebla
5700
Acapulco
7680
JAMAICA
HAITI
Kingston
PUERTO RICO
Leeward Is.

BELIZE
Yucatan Channel
Caribbean Sea
BARBADOS

Palmyra Is. (U.S.)
GUATEMALA
HONDURAS
Windward Is.
TRINIDAD & TOBAGO
Teraina
Tabuaeran
Clipperton I. (Fr.)
Guatemala
Salvador
NICARAGUA
Managua
Barranquilla
Maracaibo

Kiritimati
EL SALVADOR
CENTRAL AMERICA
San José
Colón
Panamá
Caracas
Orinoco
VENEZUELA

Jarvis I. (U.S.)
Cocos I.
COSTA RICA
PANAMA
Canal

EAN
Medellín
Bogotá

Malden I.
Starbuck I.
Equator
Galápagos
(Ecuador)
C. Pariñas
Cali
COLOMBIA

Tongareva
Penrhyn Is.
Guayaquil
Quito
ECUADOR
Iquitos
Manaus
Amazon

Manihiki
Suwarrow Is.
Vostok I.
Flint I.
Caroline I.
BRAZIL

Marquesas Is.
Trujillo
SOUTH

Cook Islands
(N.Z.)
Society Is.
Leeward Is.
Tuamotu Archipelago
PERU
Lima
6369
AMERICA

Manuae
Windward Is.
Tahiti
FRENCH POLYNESIA
Cuzco
L. Titicaca
Illampu & Ancohuma
6550

Rarotonga
Mururoa
Arequipa
La Paz
BOLIVIA

Austral
Tropic of Capricorn
Peru-
6866

Tubuai Is.
(Austral Is.)
Pitcairn I. (U.K.)
Ducie I. (U.K.)
Iquique
Chile
8050
Antofagasta
Trench
PARAGUAY

Rapa Iti
Easter Is.
(Chile)
Sala-y-Gomez
(Chile)
San Félix (Chile)
San Ambrosio (Chile)
Asunción

Tucumán
Pto. Alegre

Arch. de Juan Fernández
(Chile)
6960
Córdoba
URUGUAY

East Pacific Ridge
Valparaíso
Rosario
Montevideo

Santiago
Buenos Aires

Pacific-Antarctic Ridge
Concepción
ARGENTINA
Río de la Plata

SOUTH

Chile Rise
ATLANTIC

Chonos Arch.
OCEAN

G. of Penas
6212
Falkland Is. (U.K.)

Punta Arenas
Str. of Magellan
Tierra del Fuego
South Georgia
C. Horn

11 12 13 14 15 16 17 18 19 20

West from Greenwich

COPYRIGHT. GEORGE PHILIP & SON. LTD.

1:54 000 000

1:15 000 000

100   0   100   200   300   400 miles
100   0   100   200   300   400   500   600 km

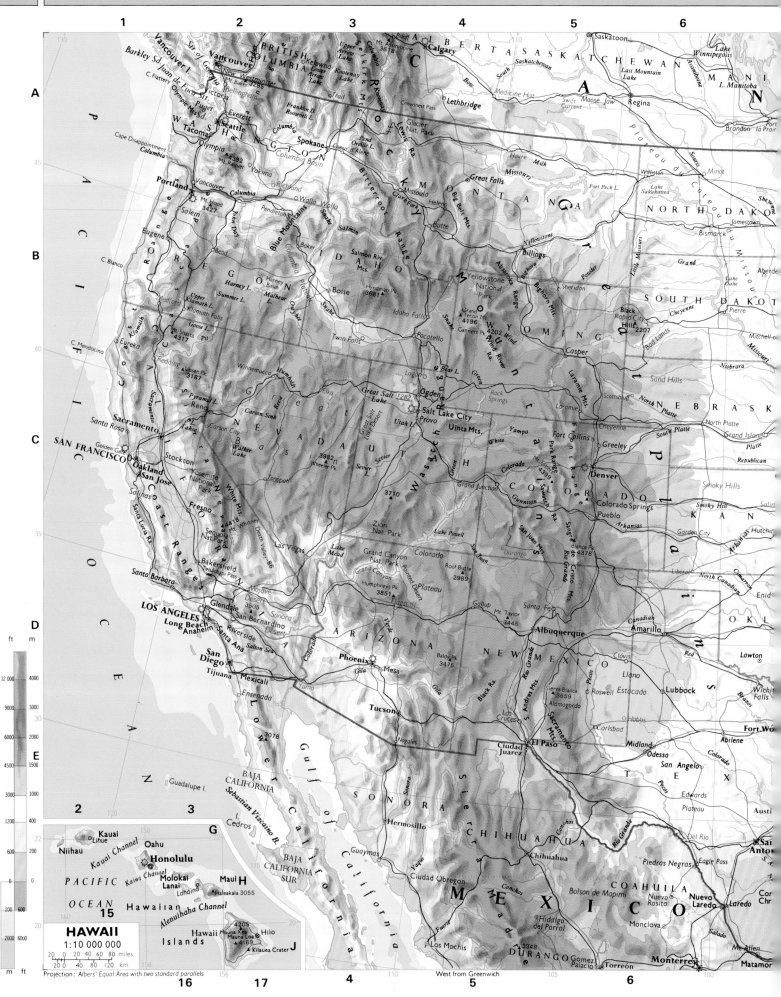

40

UNITED STATES

1   2   3   4   5   6

A

B

C

D

E

PACIFIC

OCEAN

BRITISH COLUMBIA
Vancouver I.
Str. of Georgia
Vancouver
New Westminster
Victoria
C. Flattery
Olympic Mts.
Puget Sd.
W. Tacoma
Everett
Seattle
Bellingham
Olympia
Cape Disappointment
Columbia
WASHINGTON
Mt. Baker, 3285
Mt. Rainier 4392
Yakima
Richland
Portland
Mt. Hood 3427
Vancouver
Salem
Columbia
Eugene
Bend
C. Blanco
OREGON
Blue Mountains
John Day
Pendleton
Walla Walla
Columbia Basin
Spokane
Coeur d'Alene
Pend Oreille L.
Lewis Ra.
Franklin D. Roosevelt L.
Kootenay Lake
Lower Arrow Lake
Upper Arrow Lake
Kelowna
Trail
Crowsnest Pass
Calgary
Banff
Mt. Assiniboine
3618
ALBERTA
Lethbridge
Medicine Hat
Swift Current
Moose Jaw
Regina
SASKATCHEWAN
Last Mountain Lake
Saskatoon
Saskatchewan
Lake Winnipegosis
MANI
L. Manitoba
Brandon
Port la Prair.
Assiniboine
N

Harney L.
Malheur L.
Summer L.
Upper Klamath L.
Klamath Falls
Medford
Roseburg
Klamath
C. Mendocino
Eureka
Redding
Lassen Pk. 3187
Mt. Shasta 4317
Goose L.
Pit
Winnemucca
Humboldt
Reno
Pyramid L.
Carson Sink
Carson City
Tahoe
Walker Lake
Sacramento
Santa Rosa
SAN FRANCISCO
Golden Gate
Oakland
San Jose
Stockton
Yosemite National Park
Fresno
NEVADA
Wheeler Pk. 3982
Tonopah
Boise
Salmon Riv. Mts.
Twin Falls
Idaho Falls
Pocatello
Snake
Owyhee
Harney Basin
IDAHO
Bitterroot Range
Butte
Helena
Missoula
Clark Fork
Salmon
Baker
Bend
Great Falls
Havre
Milk
Missouri
Fort Peck L.
MONTANA
Yellowstone
Billings
Big Belt Mts.
Bighorn Mts.
Sheridan
Powder
Little Missouri
Williston
Lake Sakakawea
Minot
NORTH DAKOTA
Jamestown
Bismarck
Grand
Aberd.
Lake Oahe
SOUTH DAKOTA
Pierre
Bad Lands
Black Hills 2207
Rapid City
Cheyenne
Missouri
Mitchell
Niobrara
Sand Hills
Scottsbluff
North Platte
NEBRASKA
Grand Island
Platte
Republican
Smoky Hills
Smoky Hill
Saln
KAN
Garden City
Liberal
North Canadian
Enid
OKL
Lawton
Wichita Falls
Fort Wo
Abilene
TEX
San Angelo
Colorado
Midland
Odessa
Pecos
Edwards Plateau
Austi
Del Rio
San Anto
Eagle Pass
Piedras Negras
Nuevo Laredo
Laredo
COAHUILA
Monclova
Monterrey
Matamor
McAllen
Salado
DURANGO
Gomez Palacio
Torreón
Bolson de Mapimi
Hidalgo del Parral 3348
MEXICO
CHIHUAHUA
Chihuahua
Conchos
Los Mochis
Ciudad Obregon
Guaymas
Yaqui
Fuerte
Hermosillo
SONORA
Nogales
Ciudad Juarez
El Paso
Las Cruces
Sierra Blanca 3659
Alamogordo
Carlsbad
Hobbs
Roswell
Llano Estacado
Lubbock
Brazos
Red
Clovis
Amarillo
Canadian
Santa Fe
Albuquerque
Mt. Taylor 3445
Gallup
Roof Butte 2989
Grand Canyon
Painted Desert
NEW MEXICO
Rio Grande
Andres Mts.
Black Ra.
Gila
ARIZONA
Humphreys Pk. 3851
Flagstaff
Colorado Plateau
Lake Powell
Grand Canyon Nat. Park
Grand Canyon Nat. Park
Zion Nat. Park
Baldy Pk. 3476
Phoenix
Mesa
Gila
Tucson
Yuma
Gila
Salton Sea
Colorado
Mexicali
Tijuana
Ensenada
San Diego
Santa Ana
Riverside
San Bernardino
Anaheim
Long Beach
LOS ANGELES
Glendale
Mojave Desert
3505
Sonora Desert
Death Valley -86
Mt. Whitney 4418
Sequoia Nat. Park
Bakersfield
Tehachapi Pass
Santa Barbara
Santa Lucia Ra.
Coast Ranges
Salinas
3078
BAJA CALIFORNIA
Sebastian Vizcaino B.
I. Cedros
Guadalupe I.
BAJA CALIFORNIA SUR
SONORA
Gulf of California
Sierra Madre
CHIHUAHUA
MEXICO
3348

Great Salt Lake 1282
Great Salt Lake Desert
Salt Lake City
Ogden
Provo
Utah L.
3710
Sevier
Sevier L.
UTAH
Wasatch Ra.
Rocky Mountains
Bear L.
Logan
Green
Wind River Ra.
Gannett Pk. 4202
Grand Teton Mt. 4196
Yellowstone National Park
Absaroka Range
WYOMING
Casper
Laramie Mts.
Laramie
Cheyenne
Rock Springs
White
Yampa
Colorado
Grand Junction
Gunnison
Uinta Mts.
COLORADO
Mt. Elbert 4399
Park Range
Front Range
Fort Collins
Greeley
Denver
Colorado Springs
Pueblo
Arkansas
Sawatch Ra.
San Juan Mts.
Durango
Blanca Pk. 4378
Sangre de Cristo Mts.
Rio Grande
PLA
P l a i n
North Platte
South Platte
Arkansas
Cimarron
Pecos
Las Vegas
Lake Mead

Walker Lake
White Mts.

PACIFIC OCEAN

ft   m

12 000   4000

9000   3000

6000   2000

4500   1500

3000   1000

1500   400

600   200

0   0

200   600

2000   6000

m   ft

Lower California

G
Kauai
Lihue
Niihau
Kauai Channel
Oahu
Honolulu
Molokai
Lanai
Lahaina
Kaiwi Channel
Maui **H**
Haleakala 3055
Hawaiian Channel
Alenuihaha Channel
Mauna Kea 4205
Hilo
Mauna Loa 4169
Kilauea Crater
Hawaii **J**
Islands
PACIFIC OCEAN
HAWAII
1:10 000 000

15

2   3

120
158
156
160
22
20

16   17

0   20   40   60   80 miles
0   20   40   60   80   120 km

Projection: Albers' Equal Area with two standard parallels

West from Greenwich

110   105   100

130
45
40
35
30
25

16   17   4   5   6

8 9 10 11 12 13

Lake Winnipeg

Albany

O

L A N T

A

A

D

Moosonee

Nottaway

Chibougamau L.

St. Lawrence

Rimouski

Matane

L. Seul

Missinaibi

L. Matagami

Gull L.

L. St. John

Chicoutima

Edmundston

Simli

Sioux Lookout

Lake Nipigon

Kenogami

Abitibi

Moose

Cabonga Res.

Baskatong Res.

Gouin Res.

La Tuque

NEW BRUNSWICK

A

Winnipeg

Kenora

Longlac

Hearst

Abitibi Lake Rouyn

Ottawa

Quebec

Presque Isle

Lake of the Woods

Thunder Bay

I. Royale

Sault Ste. Marie

Timmins

Trois-Rivières

Sherbrooke

MAINE

Bangor

183 above S.L.

Lake Superior

Wawa

Chapleau

Sudbury

North Bay

Ottawa

MONTREAL

L. Champlain

Bemidji

Moorhead

MINNESOTA Duluth

Marquette

Escanaba

L. Nipissing

Algonquin Park

Hull

Ottawa

VERMONT

Burlington

White Mts.

NEW HAMPSHIRE

Portland

Augusta

B

Fargo

Brainerd

St. Cloud

Menominee

Manitoulin

Georgian Bay

Owen Sound

Barrie Simcoe

Peterborough

Kingston

Watertown

Adirondack Mts.

Glens Falls

Concord

Manchester

Martha's

Minneapolis **St. Paul**

Eau Claire

Appleton

Green Bay

Lake Huron 177 above

Oshawa

TORONTO

Lake Ontario

Rochester

Syracuse

Utica

Troy

Albany

Worcester

Springfield

Providence

Boston

C. Cod

Fall River

Brookings

Rochester

WISCONSIN

Madison

Cadillac

Bay City

Kitchener Hamilton

Niagara Falls

Buffalo

NEW YORK

Binghamton

Catskill Mts.

Hartford

CONN.

New Haven

Martha's Vineyard

Mankato

La Crosse Fond du Lac

Sheboygan

177

Saginaw

Flint

London

Sarnia

Lake Erie

Jamestown

Scranton

Wilkes Barre

Bridgeport

Long I.

NEW YORK

Mason City

Waterloo

Madison

Milwaukee Grand Rapids

Lansing

Kalamazoo

Ann Arbor

DETROIT

Windsor

Euclid

Cleveland

Youngstown

Williamsport

PENNSYLVANIA

Allentown

Reading

Jersey City

Fort Dodge

Dubuque

Rockford

Racine

Kenosha

Evanston

South Bend

Gary Ft. Wayne

Lima

Loruin

Akron

Canton

Altoona

Harrisburg

Trenton

PHILADELPHIA

Ames

Des Moines

Davenport

CHICAGO

Hammond

Muncie

Mansfield

Pittsburgh

Wheeling

JERSEY

Camden

Atlantic City

Council Bluffs

Burlington

Peoria

Lafayette

Dayton

Columbus

Ohio

Parkersburg

Baltimore

Dover

C. May

Delaware Bay

C

Champaign

Springfield

Decatur

Indianapolis

INDIANA

Terre Haute

Bloomington

Cincinnati

WEST VIRGINIA

Charleston

Cumberland

Washington

D.C.

Annapolis

Chesapeake Bay

St. Joseph

Quincy

ILLINOIS

Covington

Charlottesville

Potomac

DEL.

Manhattan

Columbia Missouri

St. Louis

E. St. Louis

Evansville

Louisville

Lexington

Huntington

Kanawha

Richmond

Newport News

C. Charles

Topeka

Kansas City

Jefferson

MISSOURI

Owensboro

KENTUCKY

Kentucky

Charleston

Lynchburg

Roanoke

Portsmouth

Norfolk

Osage

L. of the Ozarks

Carbondale

Ohio

Green Bowling Green

Danville

Rocky Mount

Albemarle Sd.

Tulsa

Springfield

Cape Girardeau

Paducah

Clarksville

Cumberland

Kingsport

Winston Salem

Greensboro

Durham

Pamlico

C. Hatteras

Joplin

Fayetteville

Boston Mts.

White

Jonesboro

Nashville

TENNESSEE

Oak Ridge

Knoxville 2037

NORTH CAROLINA

Raleigh

Neuse

OKLAHOMA CITY

Fort Smith

ARKANSAS

Jackson

Florence

Asheville

Charlotte

Fayetteville

C. Fear

D

Fort Smith

Little Rock

Ouachita Mts.

Memphis

Huntsville

Chattanooga

Greenville

Anderson

Columbia

Florence

Wilmington

C. Fear

Sherman

Texarkana

Pine Bluff

Florence

Rome

SOUTH CAROLINA

Texarkana

Red River

MISSISSIPPI

ALABAMA

Birmingham

GEORGIA

Columbus

Augusta

Savannah

Charleston

Dallas

Tyler

Longview

Shreveport

Monroe

Vicksburg

Jackson

Meridian

Tuscaloosa

Atlanta

Macon

Savannah

Beaumont

Alexandria

LOUISIANA

Hattiesburg

Montgomery

Chattahoochee

Albany

Dothan

Valdosta

Jacksonville

E

Houston Pasadena

Port Arthur

Lake Charles

Lafayette

Baton Rouge

Biloxi

Mobile

Pensacola

Panama City

Tallahassee

Gainesville

Daytona Beach

C. Canaveral

Galveston

Brazos

New Orleans

Houma

C. S. Blas

FLORIDA

Orlando

Indian River

BAHAMAS

Delta of the Mississippi

Tampa

Lakeland

West Palm Beach

Grand Bahama I.

Gt. Abaco

Freeport

St. Petersburg

Tampa B.

Sarasota

L. Okeechobee

Ft. Myers

Fort Lauderdale

Miami

Eleuthera I.

Nassau

New Providence

Exuma Sound

Cat I.

F

Brownsville Rio Grande

GULF OF MEXICO

C. Sable

Everglades

Florida Bay

Key West

Florida Keys

Andros I.

Long I.

8 9 10 11 12

1:12 000 000

50 0 50 100 150 200 250 300 miles

50 0 50 100 150 200 250 300 350 400 450 500 km

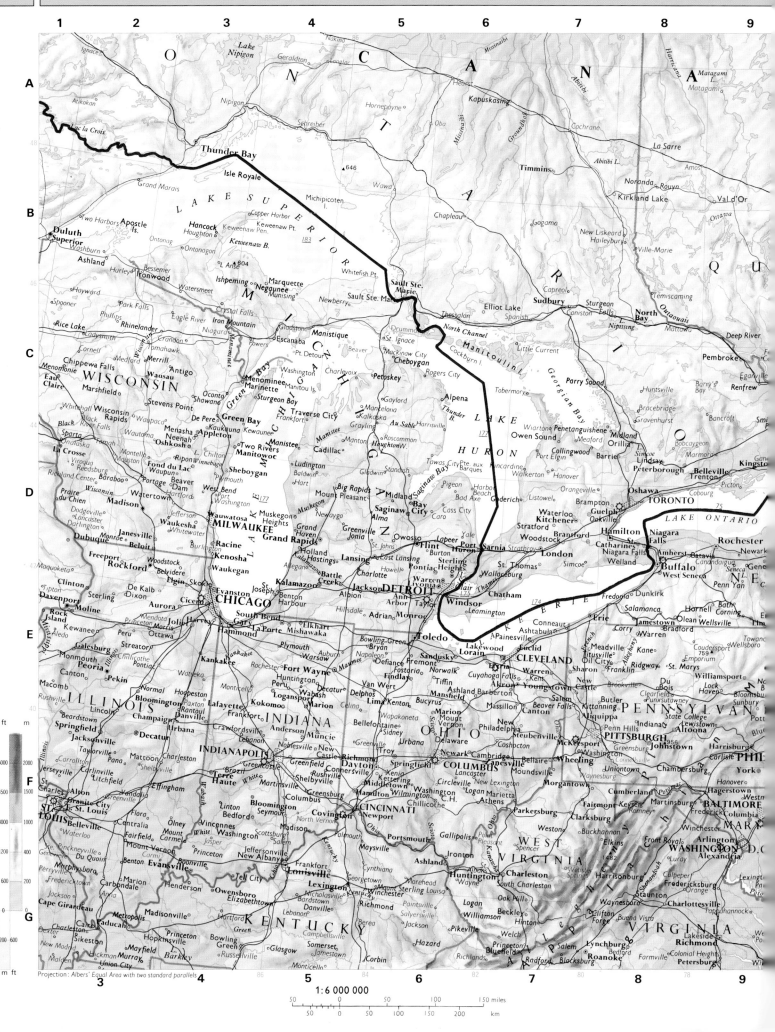

NORTH AMERICA
Political 1 : 70 000 000

A
B
C
D
E
F
G

Columbus
C. Fear
Atlanta
Augusta
Macon
Charleston
umbus
Savannah
any
ahassee
Jacksonville
Daytona Beach
Orlando
C. Canaveral
Tampa
ersburg
West Palm Beach
L. Okeechobee
Grand Bahama I.
Freeport
Gt. Abaco I.
Miami
Fort Lauderdale
New Providence I.
C. Sable
Eleuthera I.
Key West
Nassau
Cat I.
Florida
Andros I.
BAHAMAS
S. Salvador
Havana
Matanzas
Cárdenas
Sagua la Grande
Long I.
Tropic of Cancer
Sta. Clara
Morón
Mayaguana
I. de Juventud
Cienfuegos
Sancti Spiritus
Camagüey
Acklins
Turks & Caicos Is. (U.K.)
GREATER
Ciego de Avila
Holguin
Gt. Inagua I.
Manzanillo
2000
Guantánamo
PUERTO RICO (U.S.A.)
Grand Cayman (U.K.)
Bayamo
Santiago de Cuba
Santiago
San Francisco de Macorís
San Juan
St. Thomas (U.S.A.)
Charlotte Amalie
Virgin Is. (U.K.)
Anguilla (Fr. & Neth.)
St. Martin
Montego Bay
Cap Haitien
Gonaives
1175
DOMINICAN REP.
La Romana
1338
Caguas
St. Croix (U.S.A.)
ST. KITTS–NEVIS
ANTIGUA & BARBUDA
JAMAICA
Kingston
Les Cayes
Port au Prince
2280
Hispaniola
Santo Domingo
Ponce
Mayagüez
St. John's
Montserrat (U.K.)
Guadeloupe (Fr.)
Pointe à Pitre
Barahona
Bani
ANTILLES
Leeward Islands
LESSER
DOMINICA
Caratasca Lagoon
Fort de France
Martinique (Fr.)
C. Gracias á Dios
CARIBBEAN SEA
ANTILLES
Windward
ST. LUCIA
Providencia (Col.)
Pta. Gallinas
Gulf of Venezuela
Aruba (Neth.)
Curaçao
Willemstad
Bonaire
ST. VINCENT
BARBADOS
Bridgetown
San Andrés (Col.)
Pen. de la Guajira
Pen de NETH. Paraguaná ANTILLES
La Blanquilla (Ven.)
& THE GRENADINES Islands
GRENADA
Bluefields
Santa Marta
Tobago
Margarita
Barranquilla
Port of Spain
Punto Fijo
Coro
La Tortuga (Ven.)
Carúpano
TRINIDAD & TOBAGO
Limón
Cartagena
5800
Sierra Nevada de Santa Marta
Maracaibo
Cabimas
Caracas
Barcelona
Cumana
2596
G. of Paria
San Fernando
Delta of the Orinoco
Vol. Barú
3374
Colón
Panama
G. of Darién
Sincelejo
L. de Maracaibo
Maracay
Valencia
Barquisimeto
Maturin
David
Azuero Pen.
G. of Panama
Valera
El Tigre
Ciudad Guayana
Georgetown
Coiba
Atrato
Cauca
Mérida
5007
Cord. de Mérida
Barinas
San Fernando de Apure
Ciudad Bolívar
Orinoco
New Amsterdam
Barrancabermeja
3960
Cúcuta
4100
San Cristóbal
Arauca
Arauca
Apure
VENEZUELA
2285
Pto. Ayacucho
Angel Falls
2560
Roraima
2810
Quibdó
Medellín
Bucaramanga
Meta
GUYANA
SURINAM
Manizales
Pereira
Tunja
COLOMBIA
Caura
Caroni
Sierra Pacaraima
Sa. Parima
280
Buenaventura
Armenia
Olima 5215
Girardot
Bogotá
Guaviare
Cali
4750
Guaviare
Casiquiare
Popayán
4646
BRAZIL

ATLANTIC OCEAN

Bermuda (U.K.)
Hamilton

1:15 000 000

100 0 100 200 300 400 miles
100 0 100 200 300 400 500 600 km

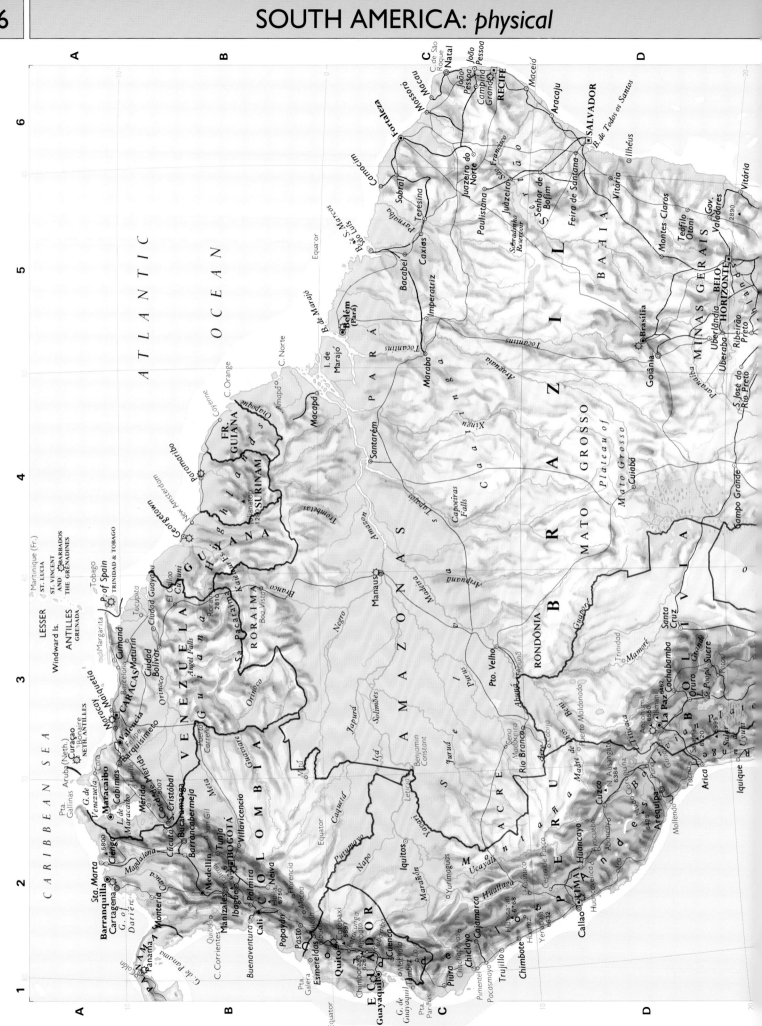

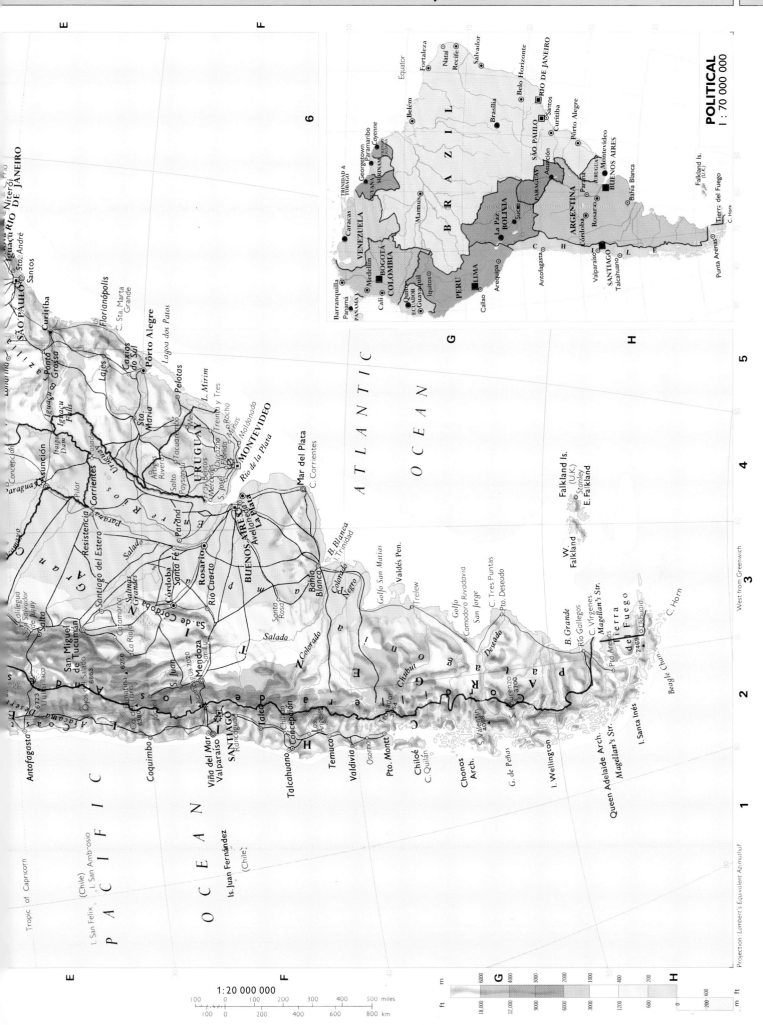

POLITICAL
1 : 70 000 000

1 : 20 000 000

Projection: Lambert's Equivalent Azimuthal

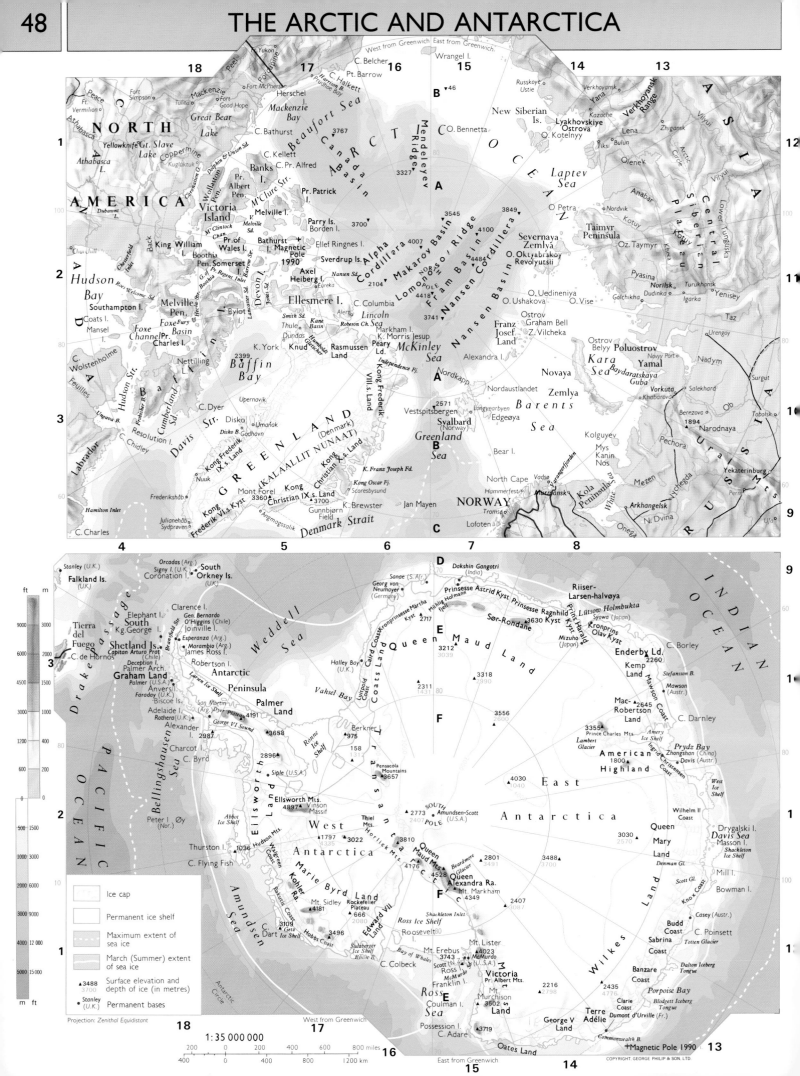

WORLD
THEMATIC MAPS

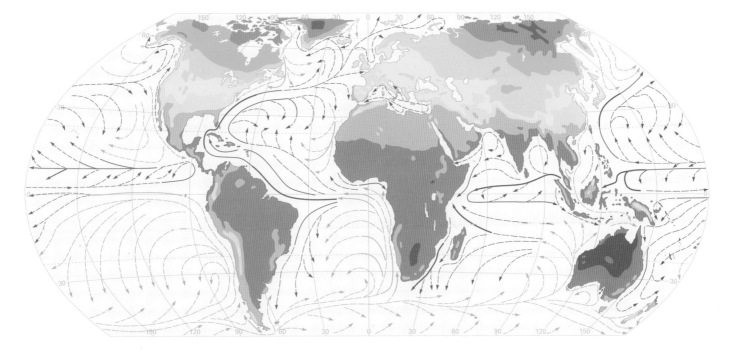

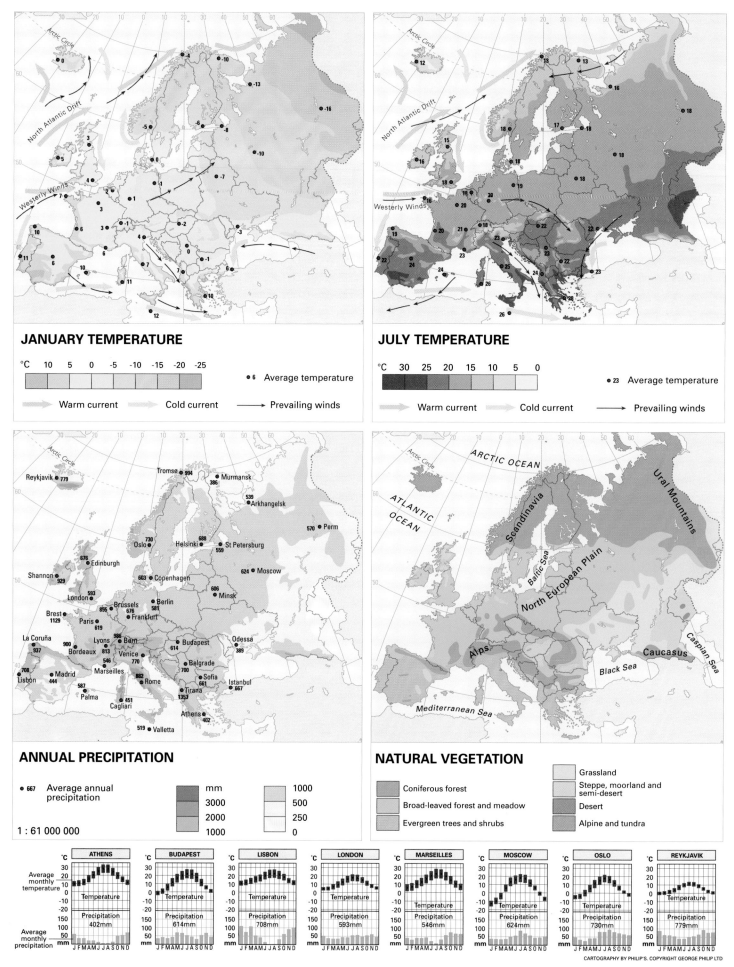

JANUARY TEMPERATURE

°C 10 5 0 -5 -10 -15 -20 -25

• 6 Average temperature

Warm current   Cold current   Prevailing winds

JULY TEMPERATURE

°C 30 25 20 15 10 5 0

• 23 Average temperature

Warm current   Cold current   Prevailing winds

ANNUAL PRECIPITATION

• 667 Average annual precipitation

mm   1000
3000   500
2000   250
1000   0

1 : 61 000 000

NATURAL VEGETATION

Coniferous forest

Broad-leaved forest and meadow

Evergreen trees and shrubs

Grassland

Steppe, moorland and semi-desert

Desert

Alpine and tundra

CARTOGRAPHY BY PHILIP'S. COPYRIGHT GEORGE PHILIP LTD

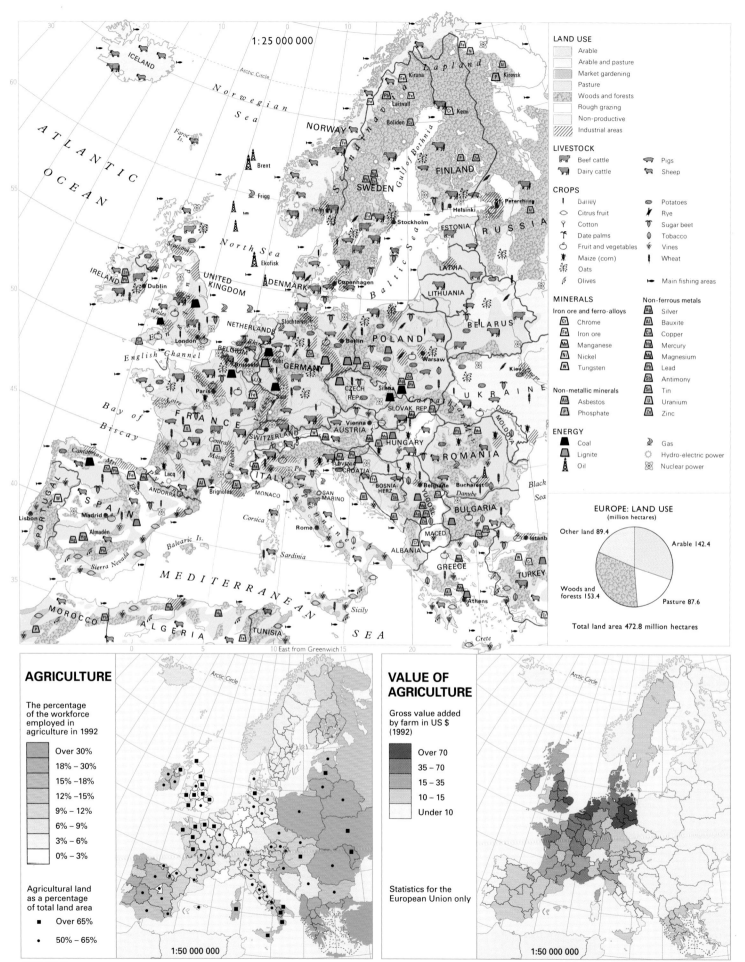

1:25 000 000

LAND USE
- Arable
- Arable and pasture
- Market gardening
- Pasture
- Woods and forests
- Rough grazing
- Non-productive
- Industrial areas

LIVESTOCK
- Beef cattle
- Dairy cattle
- Pigs
- Sheep

CROPS
- Barley
- Citrus fruit
- Cotton
- Date palms
- Fruit and vegetables
- Maize (corn)
- Oats
- Olives
- Potatoes
- Rye
- Sugar beet
- Tobacco
- Vines
- Wheat
- Main fishing areas

MINERALS

Iron ore and ferro-alloys
- Cr Chrome
- Fe Iron ore
- Mn Manganese
- Ni Nickel
- W Tungsten

Non-metallic minerals
- As Asbestos
- P Phosphate

Non-ferrous metals
- Ag Silver
- Al Bauxite
- Cu Copper
- Hg Mercury
- Mg Magnesium
- Pb Lead
- Sb Antimony
- Sn Tin
- U Uranium
- Zn Zinc

ENERGY
- Coal
- Lignite
- Oil
- Gas
- Hydro-electric power
- Nuclear power

EUROPE: LAND USE
(million hectares)

Other land 89.4
Arable 142.4
Woods and forests 153.4
Pasture 87.6

Total land area 472.8 million hectares

AGRICULTURE

The percentage of the workforce employed in agriculture in 1992
- Over 30%
- 18% – 30%
- 15% – 18%
- 12% – 15%
- 9% – 12%
- 6% – 9%
- 3% – 6%
- 0% – 3%

Agricultural land as a percentage of total land area
- ■ Over 65%
- ● 50% – 65%

1:50 000 000

Projection: *Bonne*

VALUE OF AGRICULTURE

Gross value added by farm in US $ (1992)
- Over 70
- 35 – 70
- 15 – 35
- 10 – 15
- Under 10

Statistics for the European Union only

1:50 000 000

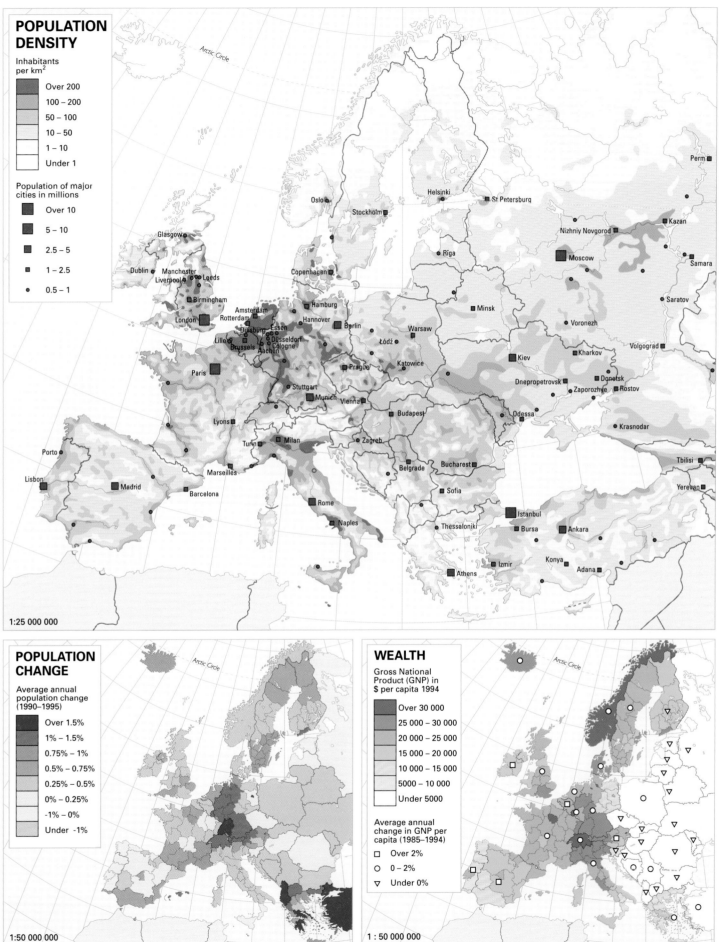

POPULATION DENSITY

Inhabitants per km²

- Over 200
- 100 – 200
- 50 – 100
- 10 – 50
- 1 – 10
- Under 1

Population of major cities in millions

- Over 10
- 5 – 10
- 2.5 – 5
- 1 – 2.5
- 0.5 – 1

1:25 000 000

POPULATION CHANGE

Average annual population change (1990–1995)

- Over 1.5%
- 1% – 1.5%
- 0.75% – 1%
- 0.5% – 0.75%
- 0.25% – 0.5%
- 0% – 0.25%
- -1% – 0%
- Under -1%

1:50 000 000

WEALTH

Gross National Product (GNP) in $ per capita 1994

- Over 30 000
- 25 000 – 30 000
- 20 000 – 25 000
- 15 000 – 20 000
- 10 000 – 15 000
- 5000 – 10 000
- Under 5000

Average annual change in GNP per capita (1985–1994)

- □ Over 2%
- ○ 0 – 2%
- ▽ Under 0%

1 : 50 000 000

Projection: *Bonne*

CARTOGRAPHY BY PHILIP'S. COPYRIGHT GEORGE PHILIP LTD

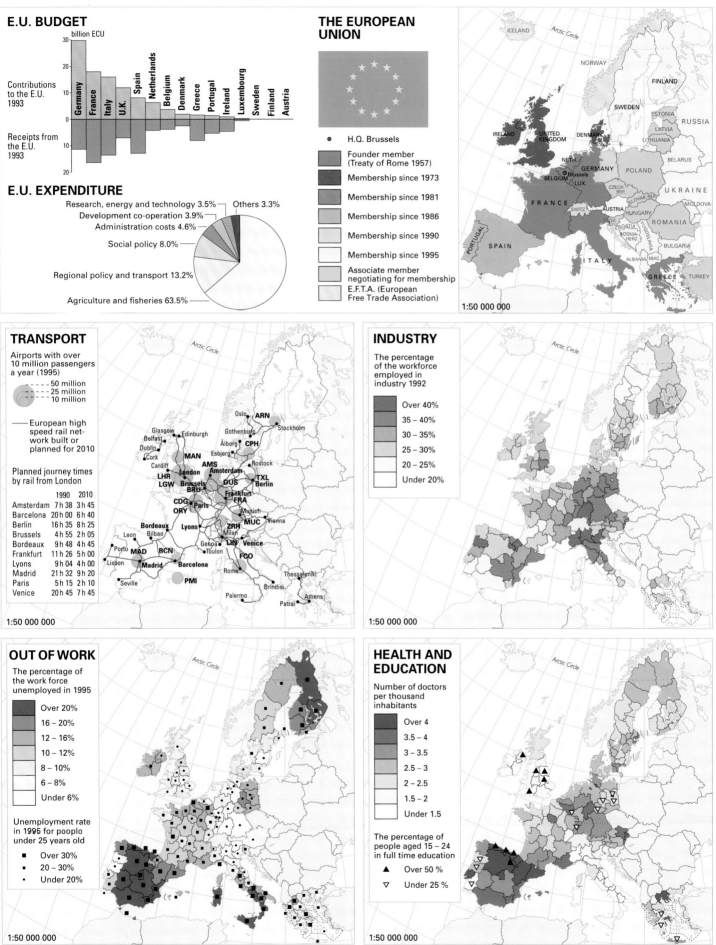

E.U. BUDGET

billion ECU

Contributions to the E.U. 1993

Receipts from the E.U. 1993

Germany
France
Italy
U.K.
Spain
Netherlands
Belgium
Denmark
Greece
Portugal
Ireland
Luxembourg
Sweden
Finland
Austria

E.U. EXPENDITURE

Research, energy and technology 3.5%
Development co-operation 3.9%
Administration costs 4.6%
Social policy 8.0%
Regional policy and transport 13.2%
Agriculture and fisheries 63.5%
Others 3.3%

THE EUROPEAN UNION

● H.Q. Brussels

Founder member (Treaty of Rome 1957)
Membership since 1973
Membership since 1981
Membership since 1986
Membership since 1990
Membership since 1995
Associate member negotiating for membership
E.F.T.A. (European Free Trade Association)

1:50 000 000

TRANSPORT

Airports with over 10 million passengers a year (1995)
50 million
25 million
10 million

— European high speed rail network built or planned for 2010

Planned journey times by rail from London

	1990	2010
Amsterdam	7 h 38	3 h 45
Barcelona	20 h 00	6 h 40
Berlin	16 h 35	8 h 25
Brussels	4 h 55	2 h 05
Bordeaux	9 h 48	4 h 45
Frankfurt	11 h 26	5 h 00
Lyons	9 h 04	4 h 00
Madrid	21 h 32	9 h 20
Paris	5 h 15	2 h 10
Venice	20 h 45	7 h 45

1:50 000 000

INDUSTRY

The percentage of the workforce employed in industry 1992

Over 40%
35 – 40%
30 – 35%
25 – 30%
20 – 25%
Under 20%

1:50 000 000

OUT OF WORK

The percentage of the work force unemployed in 1995

Over 20%
16 – 20%
12 – 16%
10 – 12%
8 – 10%
6 – 8%
Under 6%

Unemployment rate in 1995 for people under 25 years old

■ Over 30%
■ 20 – 30%
● Under 20%

1:50 000 000

HEALTH AND EDUCATION

Number of doctors per thousand inhabitants

Over 4
3.5 – 4
3 – 3.5
2.5 – 3
2 – 2.5
1.5 – 2
Under 1.5

The percentage of people aged 15 – 24 in full time education

▲ Over 50 %
▽ Under 25 %

1:50 000 000

Projection: *Bonne*

CARTOGRAPHY BY PHILIP'S. COPYRIGHT GEORGE PHILIP LTD

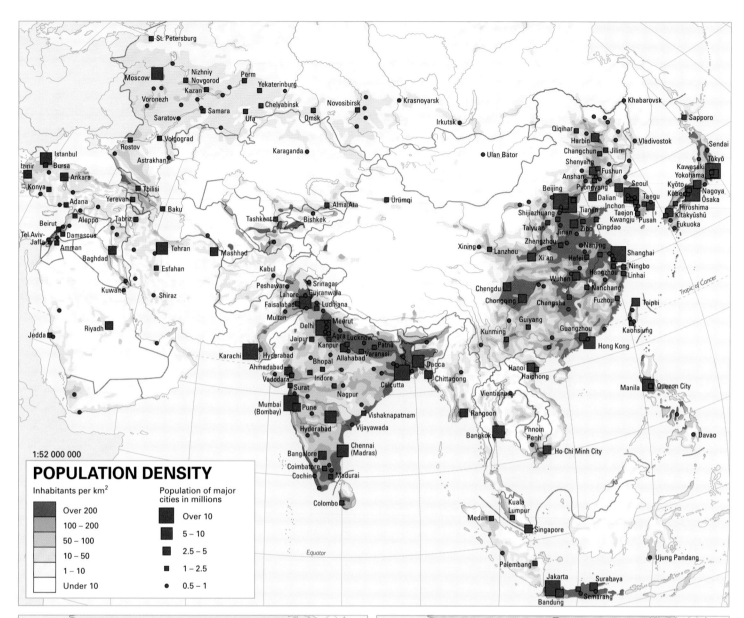

1:52 000 000

POPULATION DENSITY

Inhabitants per km²

	Over 200
	100 – 200
	50 – 100
	10 – 50
	1 – 10
	Under 10

Population of major cities in millions

■	Over 10
■	5 – 10
■	2.5 – 5
▪	1 – 2.5
•	0.5 – 1

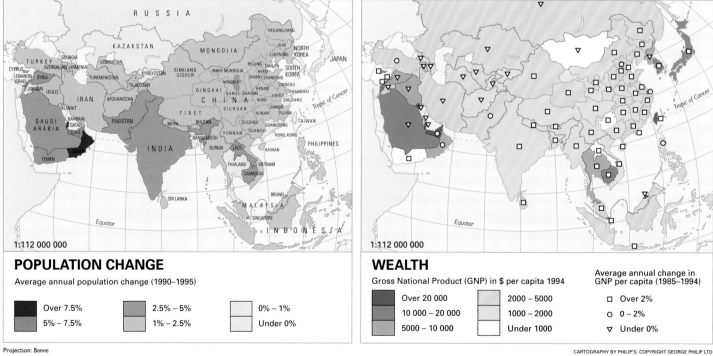

1:112 000 000

POPULATION CHANGE

Average annual population change (1990–1995)

	Over 7.5%		2.5% – 5%		0% – 1%
	5% – 7.5%		1% – 2.5%		Under 0%

1:112 000 000

WEALTH

Gross National Product (GNP) in $ per capita 1994

	Over 20 000		2000 – 5000
	10 000 – 20 000		1000 – 2000
	5000 – 10 000		Under 1000

Average annual change in GNP per capita (1985–1994)

□	Over 2%
○	0 – 2%
▽	Under 0%

Projection: *Bonne*

CARTOGRAPHY BY PHILIP'S. COPYRIGHT GEORGE PHILIP LTD

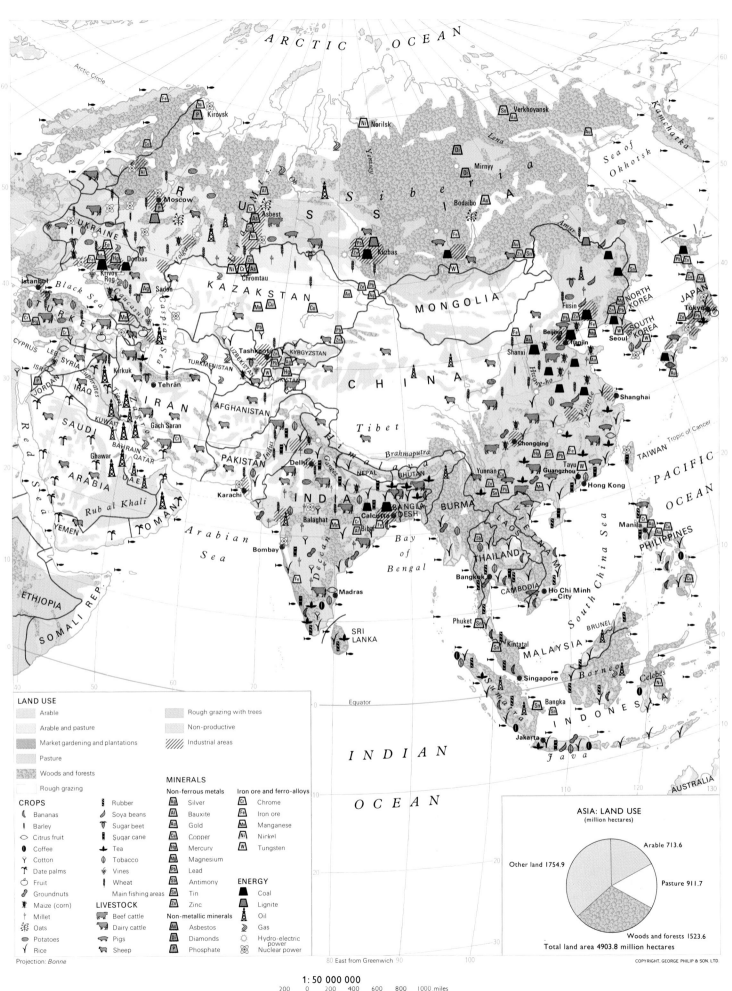

ARCTIC OCEAN

Arctic Circle

Kirovsk

Verkhoyansk

Norilsk

Lena

Mirnyy

Bodaibo

R U S S I A N S i b e r i a

Sea of Okhotsk

Kamchatka

Moscow

U r a l M t s.

Ob

Yenisey

Asbest

UKRAINE

Volga

Kuzbas

Amur

Istanbul

Black Sea

Krivoy Rog

Donbas

Saden

Caucasus

Caspian Sea

KAZAKSTAN

Chromtau

MONGOLIA

NORTH KOREA

JAPAN

Tokyo

TURKEY

CYPRUS

LEB.

SYRIA

Euphrates

Tigris

Kirkuk

Tashkent

TURKMENISTAN

UZBEKISTAN

KYRGYZSTAN

TAJIKISTAN

Fusin

Beijing

Tianjin

SOUTH KOREA

Seoul

ISR.

JORDAN

IRAQ

KUWAIT

Tehrān

AFGHANISTAN

C H I N A

Shanxi

Huang-ho

Shanghai

SAUDI ARABIA

BAHRAIN QATAR

Gach Saran

I R A N

Zagros Mts.

Tibet

Chongqing

Yangtze

TAIWAN

Tropic of Cancer

Ghawar

U.A.E.

OMAN

PAKISTAN

Indus

Himalaya

Brahmaputra

NEPAL

BHUTAN

Yunnan

Guangzhou

Hong Kong

PACIFIC OCEAN

YEMEN

Rub al Khali

Delhi

Karachi

Ganges

I N D I A

Deccan

Bombay

BANGLA DESH

Calcutta

Bihar

Balaghat

BURMA

Bay of Bengal

LAOS

VIETNAM

Manila

PHILIPPINES

Red Sea

ETHIOPIA

SOMALI REP.

Arabian Sea

Madras

SRI LANKA

THAILAND

Bangkok

CAMBODIA

Ho Chi Minh City

South China Sea

Phuket

Kintatal

MALAYSIA

BRUNEI

Singapore

Borneo

Celebes

Bangka

S u m a t r a

I N D O N E S I A

Equator

Jakarta

J a v a

I N D I A N

O C E A N

AUSTRALIA

LAND USE

Arable	Rough grazing with trees
Arable and pasture	Non-productive
Market gardening and plantations	//// Industrial areas
Pasture	
Woods and forests	
Rough grazing	

CROPS

Bananas		Rubber	
Barley		Soya beans	
Citrus fruit		Sugar beet	
Coffee		Sugar cane	
Cotton		Tea	
Date palms		Tobacco	
Fruit		Vines	
Groundnuts		Wheat	
Maize (corn)		Main fishing areas	
Millet			
Oats		**LIVESTOCK**	
Potatoes		Beef cattle	
Rice		Dairy cattle	
		Pigs	
		Sheep	

MINERALS

Non-ferrous metals

		Iron ore and ferro-alloys	
Ag Silver		Cr Chrome
Al Bauxite		Fe Iron ore
Au Gold		Mn Manganese
Cu Copper		Ni Nickel
Hg Mercury		W Tungsten
Mg Magnesium		
Pb Lead		**ENERGY**
Sb Antimony		Coal
Sn Tin		Lignite
Zn Zinc		Oil

Non-metallic minerals

As Asbestos	Gas
Di Diamonds	Hydro-electric power
P Phosphate	Nuclear power

ASIA: LAND USE
(million hectares)

Other land 1754.9

Arable 713.6

Pasture 911.7

Woods and forests 1523.6

Total land area 4903.8 million hectares

Projection: *Bonne*

80 East from Greenwich 90   100

COPYRIGHT. GEORGE PHILIP & SON. LTD.

1 : 50 000 000

200	0	200	400	600	800	1000 miles
200	0	400	800	1200	1600 km	

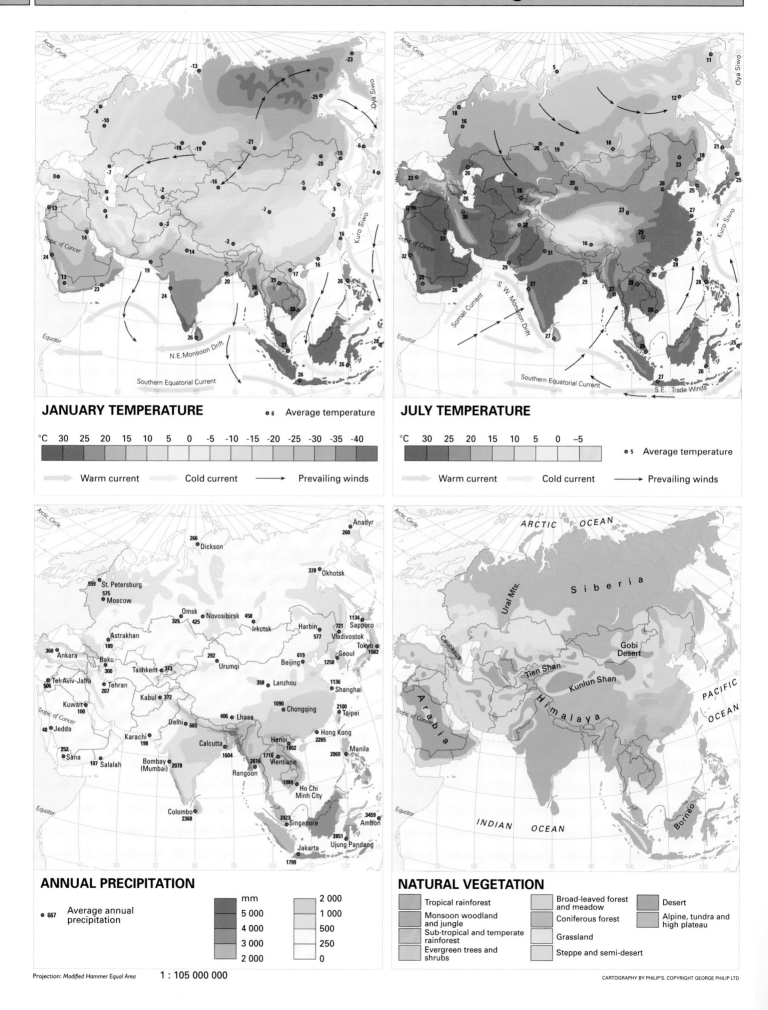

JANUARY TEMPERATURE

● 6　Average temperature

°C　30　25　20　15　10　5　0　-5　-10　-15　-20　-25　-30　-35　-40

⟶ Warm current　⟶ Cold current　⟶ Prevailing winds

JULY TEMPERATURE

°C　30　25　20　15　10　5　0　–5

● 5　Average temperature

⟶ Warm current　⟶ Cold current　⟶ Prevailing winds

ANNUAL PRECIPITATION

● 667　Average annual precipitation

mm	
5 000	2 000
4 000	1 000
3 000	500
2 000	250
	0

NATURAL VEGETATION

- Tropical rainforest
- Monsoon woodland and jungle
- Sub-tropical and temperate rainforest
- Evergreen trees and shrubs
- Broad-leaved forest and meadow
- Coniferous forest
- Grassland
- Steppe and semi-desert
- Desert
- Alpine, tundra and high plateau

Projection: Modified Hammer Equal Area　　1 : 105 000 000

CARTOGRAPHY BY PHILIP'S. COPYRIGHT GEORGE PHILIP LTD

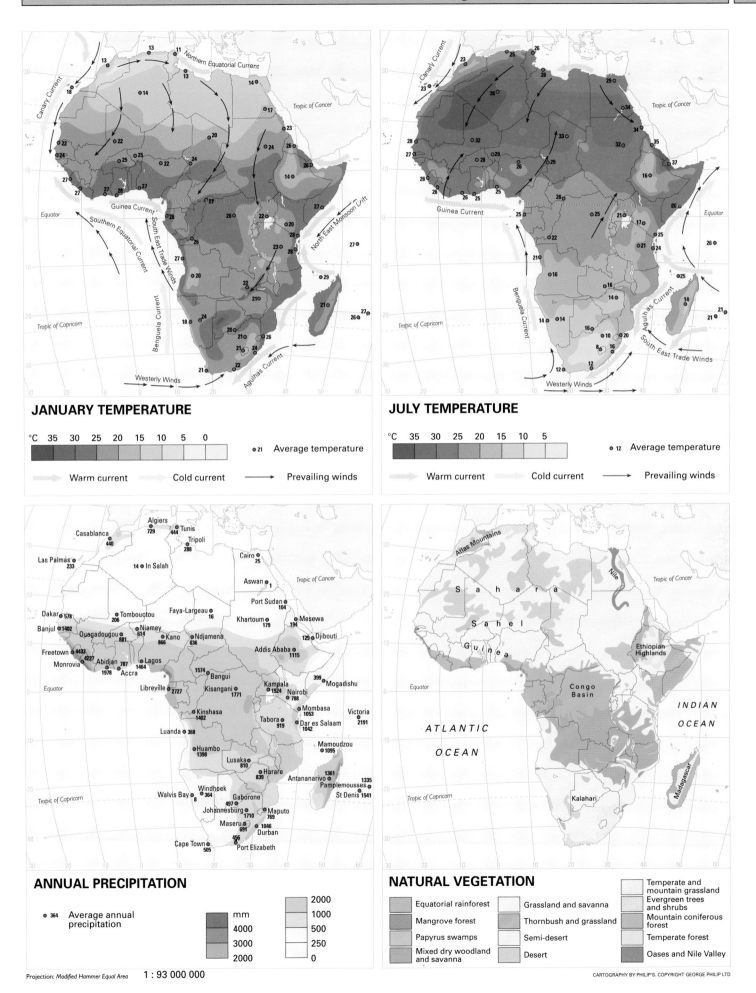

JANUARY TEMPERATURE

°C 35 30 25 20 15 10 5 0

• 21 Average temperature

Warm current   Cold current   → Prevailing winds

JULY TEMPERATURE

°C 35 30 25 20 15 10 5

• 12 Average temperature

Warm current   Cold current   → Prevailing winds

ANNUAL PRECIPITATION

• 364 Average annual precipitation

mm	
4000	2000
3000	1000
2000	500
	250
	0

Projection: *Modified Hammer Equal Area*   1 : 93 000 000

NATURAL VEGETATION

- Equatorial rainforest
- Mangrove forest
- Papyrus swamps
- Mixed dry woodland and savanna
- Grassland and savanna
- Thornbush and grassland
- Semi-desert
- Desert
- Temperate and mountain grassland
- Evergreen trees and shrubs
- Mountain coniferous forest
- Temperate forest
- Oases and Nile Valley

CARTOGRAPHY BY PHILIP'S. COPYRIGHT GEORGE PHILIP LTD

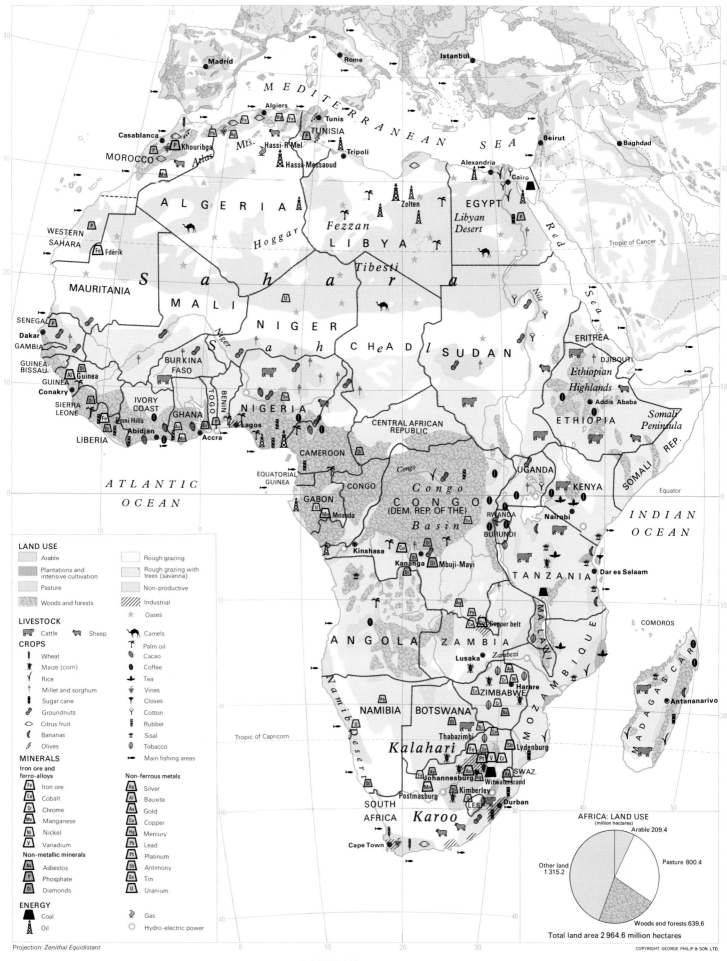

LAND USE

Arable	Rough grazing
Plantations and intensive cultivation	Rough grazing with trees (savanna)
Pasture	Non-productive
Woods and forests	Industrial

LIVESTOCK

Cattle   Sheep   Camels

CROPS

Wheat   Palm oil
Maize (corn)   Cacao
Rice   Coffee
Millet and sorghum   Tea
Sugar cane   Vines
Groundnuts   Cloves
Citrus fruit   Cotton
Bananas   Rubber
Olives   Sisal
               Tobacco
               Main fishing areas

MINERALS

Iron ore and ferro-alloys

Fe Iron ore
Co Cobalt
Cr Chrome
Mn Manganese
Ni Nickel
V   Vanadium

Non-metallic minerals

As Asbestos
P   Phosphate
Di Diamonds

Non-ferrous metals

Ag Silver
Al Bauxite
Au Gold
Cu Copper
Hg Mercury
Pb Lead
Pt Platinum
Sb Antimony
Sn Tin
U   Uranium

ENERGY

Coal   Gas
Oil   Hydro-electric power

AFRICA: LAND USE
(million hectares)

Arable 209.4

Pasture 800.4

Woods and forests 639.6

Other land 1 315.2

Total land area 2 964.6 million hectares

Projection: *Zenithal Equidistant*

1:40 000 000

COPYRIGHT. GEORGE PHILIP & SON. LTD.

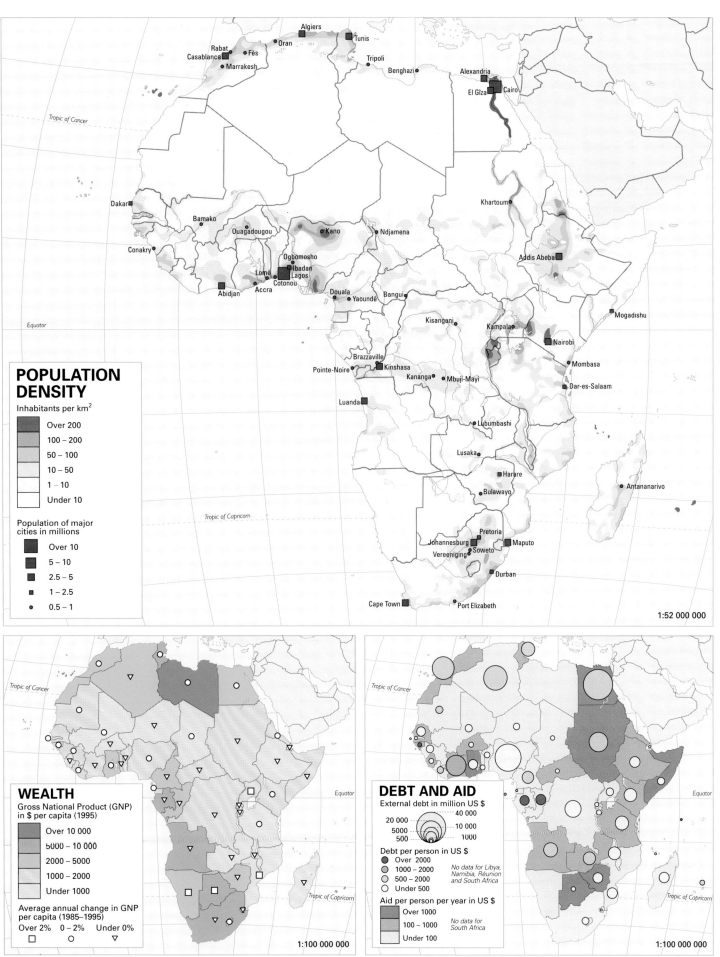

POPULATION DENSITY

Inhabitants per km²

- Over 200
- 100 – 200
- 50 – 100
- 10 – 50
- 1 – 10
- Under 10

Population of major cities in millions

- Over 10
- 5 – 10
- 2.5 – 5
- 1 – 2.5
- 0.5 – 1

1:52 000 000

WEALTH

Gross National Product (GNP) in $ per capita (1995)

- Over 10 000
- 5000 – 10 000
- 2000 – 5000
- 1000 – 2000
- Under 1000

Average annual change in GNP per capita (1985–1995)

Over 2%   0 – 2%   Under 0%
□   ○   ▽

1:100 000 000

DEBT AND AID

External debt in million US $

20 000
5000
500
40 000
10 000
1000

Debt per person in US $

- Over 2000
- 1000 – 2000
- 500 – 2000
- Under 500

No data for Libya, Namibia, Réunion and South Africa

Aid per person per year in US $

- Over 1000
- 100 – 1000
- Under 100

No data for South Africa

1:100 000 000

Projection: *Zenithal Equidistant*

CARTOGRAPHY BY PHILIP'S. COPYRIGHT GEORGE PHILIP LTD

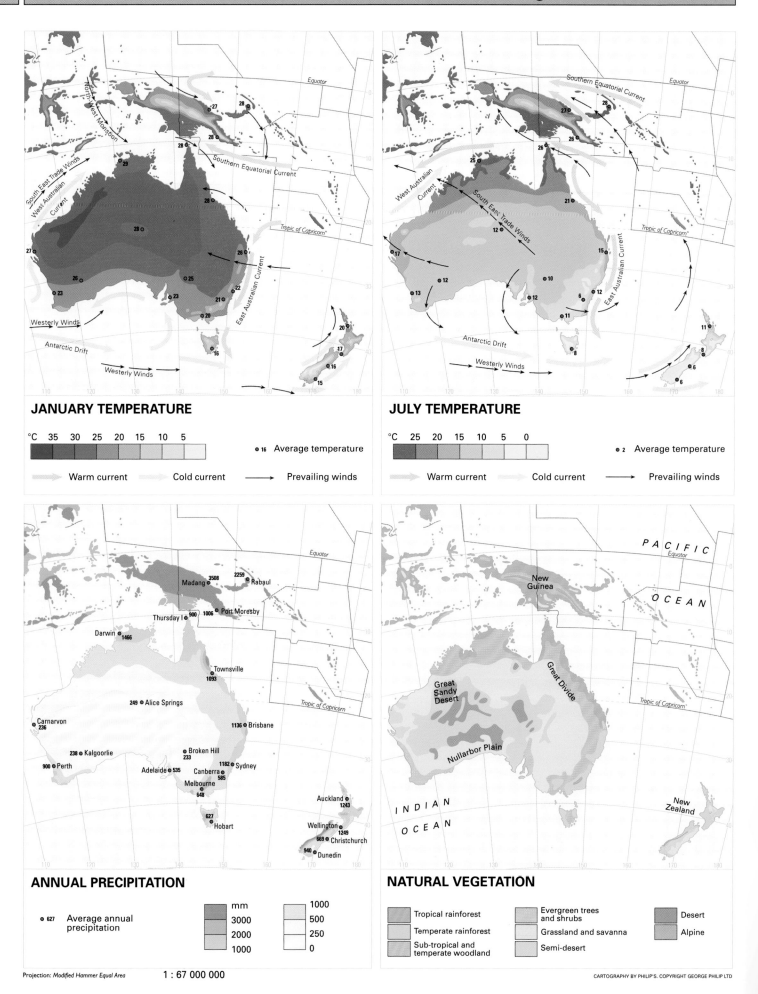

JANUARY TEMPERATURE

°C 35 30 25 20 15 10 5

● 16 Average temperature

⟹ Warm current   ⟹ Cold current   → Prevailing winds

JULY TEMPERATURE

°C 25 20 15 10 5 0

● 2 Average temperature

⟹ Warm current   ⟹ Cold current   → Prevailing winds

ANNUAL PRECIPITATION

● 627 Average annual precipitation

mm	
3000	1000
2000	500
1000	250
	0

NATURAL VEGETATION

- Tropical rainforest
- Temperate rainforest
- Sub-tropical and temperate woodland
- Evergreen trees and shrubs
- Grassland and savanna
- Semi-desert
- Desert
- Alpine

Projection: *Modified Hammer Equal Area*   1 : 67 000 000

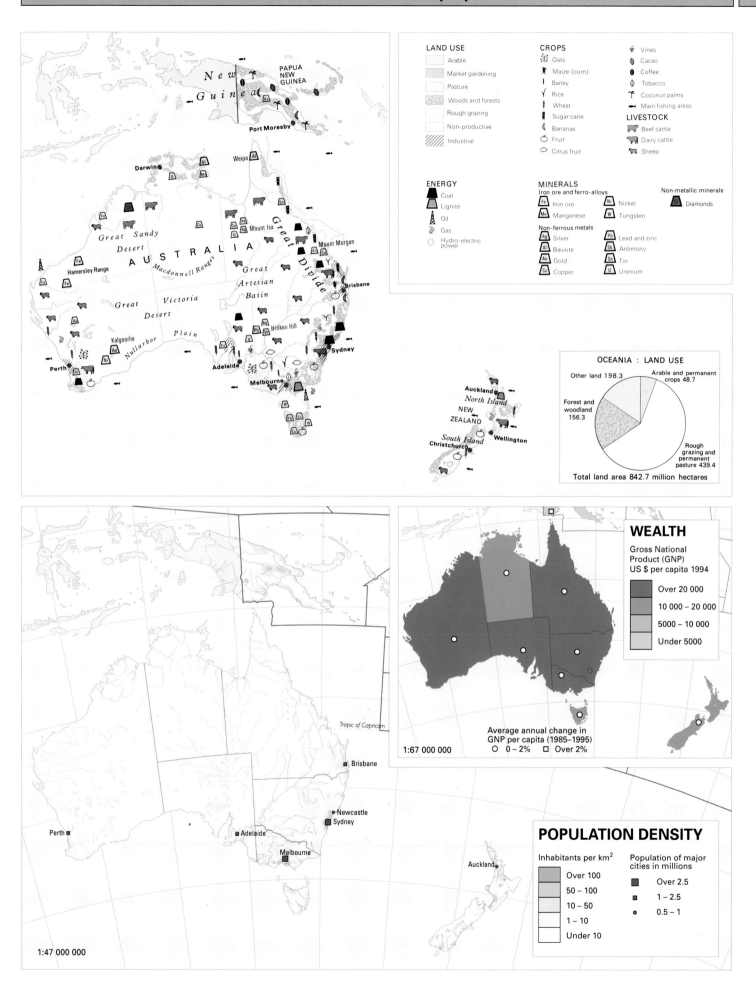

LAND USE
- Arable
- Market gardening
- Pasture
- Woods and forests
- Rough grazing
- Non-productive
- Industrial

CROPS
- Oats
- Maize (corn)
- Barley
- Rice
- Wheat
- Sugar cane
- Bananas
- Fruit
- Citrus fruit
- Vines
- Cacao
- Coffee
- Tobacco
- Coconut palms
- Main fishing areas

LIVESTOCK
- Beef cattle
- Dairy cattle
- Sheep

ENERGY
- Coal
- Lignite
- Oil
- Gas
- Hydro-electric power

MINERALS
Iron ore and ferro-alloys
- Fe Iron ore
- Mn Manganese
- Ni Nickel
- W Tungsten

Non-ferrous metals
- Ag Silver
- Al Bauxite
- Au Gold
- Cu Copper
- Pb Lead and zinc
- Sb Antimony
- Sn Tin
- U Uranium

Non-metallic minerals
- Di Diamonds

OCEANIA : LAND USE

Other land 198.3

Arable and permanent crops 48.7

Forest and woodland 156.3

Rough grazing and permanent pasture 439.4

Total land area 842.7 million hectares

WEALTH

Gross National Product (GNP) US $ per capita 1994
- Over 20 000
- 10 000 – 20 000
- 5000 – 10 000
- Under 5000

1:67 000 000

Average annual change in GNP per capita (1985–1995)
- ○ 0 – 2%
- □ Over 2%

POPULATION DENSITY

Inhabitants per km²
- Over 100
- 50 – 100
- 10 – 50
- 1 – 10
- Under 10

Population of major cities in millions
- Over 2.5
- 1 – 2.5
- 0.5 – 1

1:47 000 000

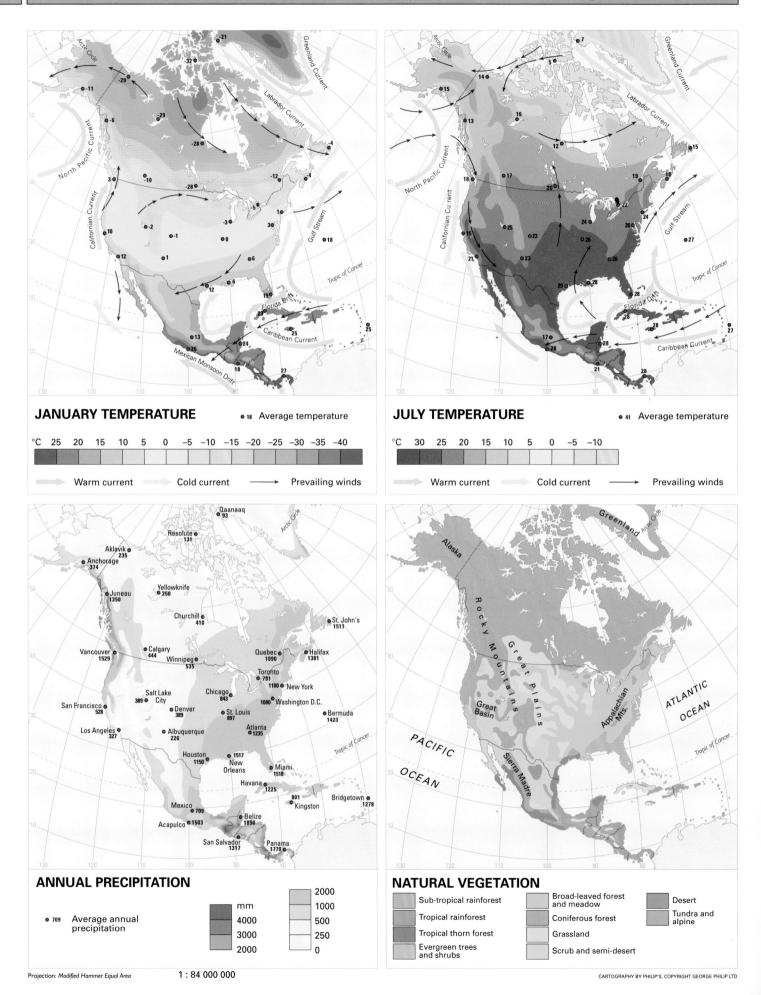

JANUARY TEMPERATURE
● 18 Average temperature

°C 25 20 15 10 5 0 –5 –10 –15 –20 –25 –30 –35 –40

▸ Warm current   ▸ Cold current   → Prevailing winds

JULY TEMPERATURE
● 41 Average temperature

°C 30 25 20 15 10 5 0 –5 –10

▸ Warm current   ▸ Cold current   → Prevailing winds

ANNUAL PRECIPITATION

● 709 Average annual precipitation

mm
2000
1000
500
250
0

4000
3000
2000

Qaanaaq 93
Resolute 131
Aklavik 235
Anchorage 374
Yellowknife 250
Juneau 1350
Churchill 410
St. John's 1511
Vancouver 1529
Calgary 444
Winnipeg 535
Quebec 1090
Halifax 1381
Toronto 791
New York 1100
Salt Lake City 389
Chicago 843
Washington D.C. 1080
San Francisco 528
Denver 389
St. Louis 897
Bermuda 1423
Los Angeles 327
Albuquerque 226
Atlanta 1235
Houston 1150
New Orleans 1517
Miami 1518
Havana 1225
Kingston 801
Bridgetown 1278
Mexico 709
Belize 1890
Acapulco 1503
San Salvador 1317
Panama 1770

NATURAL VEGETATION

Sub-tropical rainforest
Tropical rainforest
Tropical thorn forest
Evergreen trees and shrubs
Broad-leaved forest and meadow
Coniferous forest
Grassland
Scrub and semi-desert
Desert
Tundra and alpine

Alaska
Greenland
Rocky Mountains
Great Plains
Great Basin
Sierra Madre
Appalachian Mts.
PACIFIC OCEAN
ATLANTIC OCEAN

Projection: *Modified Hammer Equal Area*   1 : 84 000 000

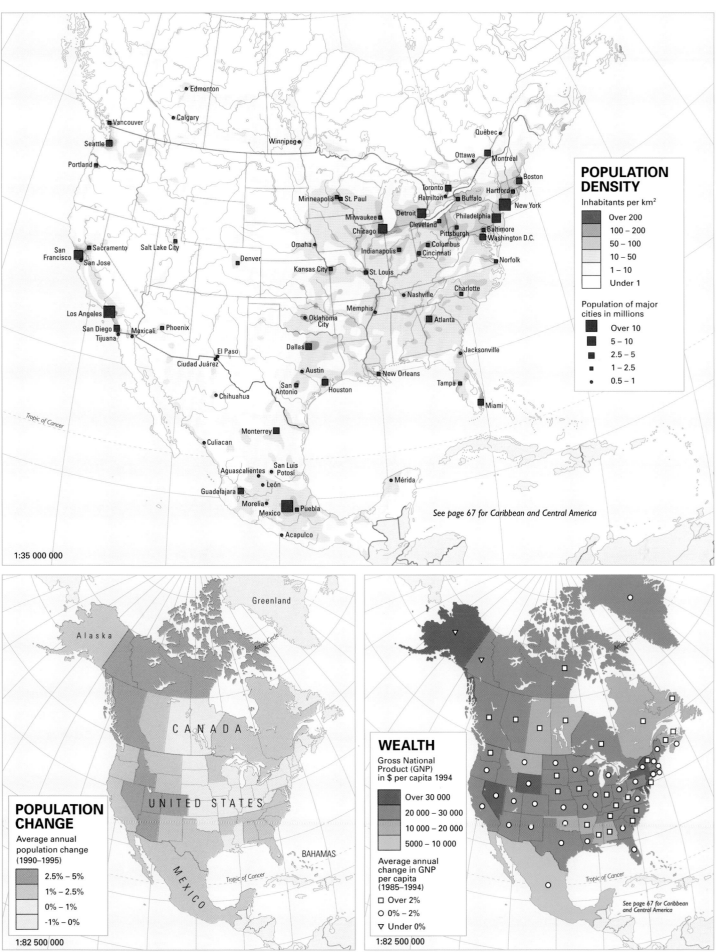

POPULATION DENSITY

Inhabitants per km²

- Over 200
- 100 – 200
- 50 – 100
- 10 – 50
- 1 – 10
- Under 1

Population of major cities in millions

- Over 10
- 5 – 10
- 2.5 – 5
- 1 – 2.5
- 0.5 – 1

See page 67 for Caribbean and Central America

1:35 000 000

POPULATION CHANGE

Average annual population change (1990–1995)

- 2.5% – 5%
- 1% – 2.5%
- 0% – 1%
- -1% – 0%

1:82 500 000

WEALTH

Gross National Product (GNP) in $ per capita 1994

- Over 30 000
- 20 000 – 30 000
- 10 000 – 20 000
- 5000 – 10 000

Average annual change in GNP per capita (1985–1994)

- □ Over 2%
- ○ 0% – 2%
- ▽ Under 0%

See page 67 for Caribbean and Central America

1:82 500 000

Projection: Polyconic

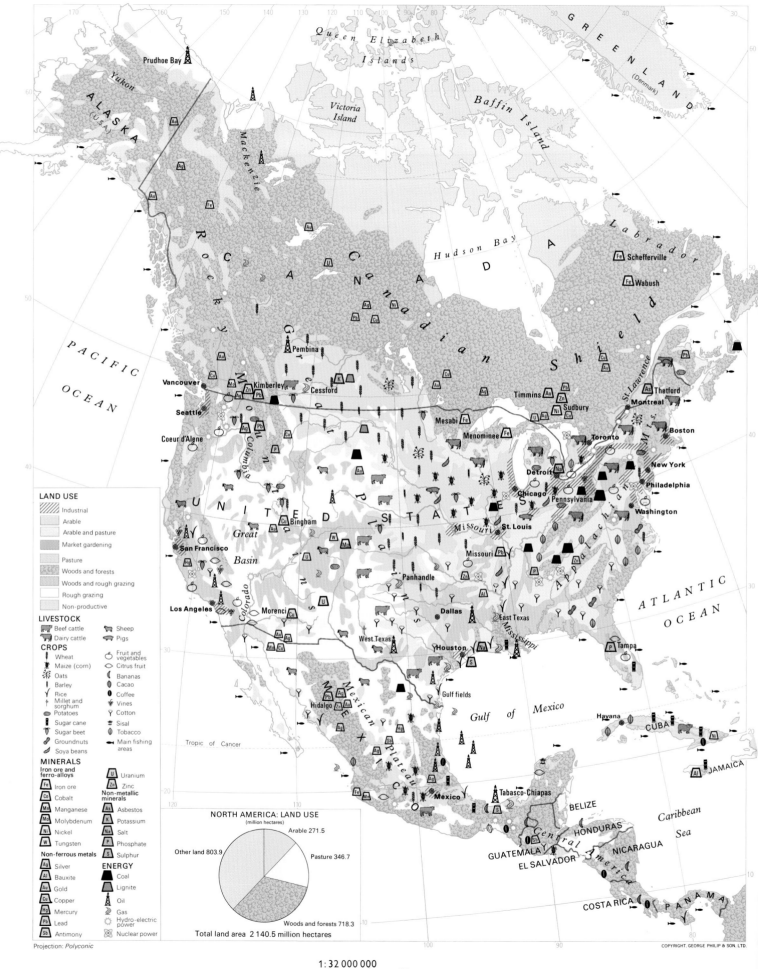

GREENLAND (Denmark)

Queen Elizabeth Islands

Victoria Island

Baffin Island

Hudson Bay

PACIFIC OCEAN

ALASKA (U.S.A.)

Yukon

Prudhoe Bay

Mackenzie

CANADA

Canadian Shield

Labrador

Scheffervile

Wabush

Vancouver

Seattle

Coeur d'Alene

Kimberley

Cessford

Pembina

Timmins

Sudbury

Mesabi

Menominee

Toronto

Detroit

Chicago

St. Louis

Montreal

Boston

New York

Philadelphia

Washington

Thetford

St. Lawrence

UNITED STATES

Great Basin

San Francisco

Los Angeles

Bingham

Morenci

Panhandle

Dallas

West Texas

Houston

Missouri

Missouri

Mississippi

Appalachian

East Texas

Gulf fields

Tampa

ATLANTIC OCEAN

Gulf of Mexico

Havana

CUBA

JAMAICA

Hidalgo

MEXICO

Mexican Plateau

Mexico

Tabasco-Chiapas

BELIZE

GUATEMALA

EL SALVADOR

HONDURAS

NICARAGUA

Central America

Caribbean Sea

COSTA RICA

PANAMA

Tropic of Cancer

Great Plains

Columbia

Colorado

Rocky Mountains

LAND USE

- Industrial
- Arable
- Arable and pasture
- Market gardening
- Pasture
- Woods and forests
- Woods and rough grazing
- Rough grazing
- Non-productive

LIVESTOCK

- Beef cattle
- Dairy cattle
- Sheep
- Pigs

CROPS

- Wheat
- Maize (corn)
- Oats
- Barley
- Rice
- Millet and sorghum
- Potatoes
- Sugar cane
- Sugar beet
- Groundnuts
- Soya beans
- Fruit and vegetables
- Citrus fruit
- Bananas
- Cacao
- Coffee
- Vines
- Cotton
- Sisal
- Tobacco
- Main fishing areas

MINERALS

Iron ore and ferro-alloys
- Fe Iron ore
- Co Cobalt
- Mn Manganese
- Mo Molybdenum
- Ni Nickel
- W Tungsten

Non-metallic minerals
- As Asbestos
- K Potassium
- Na Salt
- P Phosphate
- S Sulphur

Non-ferrous metals
- Ag Silver
- Al Bauxite
- Au Gold
- Cu Copper
- Hg Mercury
- Pb Lead
- Sb Antimony

- U Uranium
- Zn Zinc

ENERGY

- Coal
- Lignite
- Oil
- Gas
- Hydro-electric power
- Nuclear power

NORTH AMERICA: LAND USE
(million hectares)

Arable 271.5

Other land 803.9

Pasture 346.7

Woods and forests 718.3

Total land area 2 140.5 million hectares

Projection: *Polyconic*

COPYRIGHT. GEORGE PHILIP & SON, LTD.

1 : 32 000 000

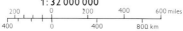

200   0   200   400   600 miles

400   0   400   800 km

SOUTH AMERICA: LAND USE
(million hectares)

Other land 283.5

Arable 104.1

Pasture 441.8

Woods and forests 924.3

Total land area 1 753.7 million hectares

PACIFIC

OCEAN

ATLANTIC

OCEAN

Tropic of Capricorn

Projection: Lambert's Equivalent Azimuthal

COPYRIGHT GEORGE PHILIP & SON LTD

LAND USE

- Industrial
- Arable
- Market gardening and plantations
- Pasture
- Woods and forests
- Rough grazing
- Non-productive

LIVESTOCK

- Beef cattle
- Sheep
- Dairy cattle
- Pigs

CROPS

- Wheat
- Coconut palms
- Maize (corn)
- Cacao
- Rice
- Coffee
- Millet and sorghum
- Tea
- Potatoes
- Vines
- Sugar cane
- Cotton
- Groundnuts
- Rubber
- Fruit and vegetables
- Tobacco
- Citrus fruit
- Main fishing areas
- Bananas

MINERALS

Iron ore and ferro-alloys

- Fe Iron ore
- Cr Chrome
- Mn Manganese
- Mo Molybdenum
- W Tungsten

Non-metallic minerals

- N Saltpetre

ENERGY

- Coal
- Oil

Non-ferrous metals

- Ag Silver
- Al Bauxite
- Au Gold
- Cu Copper
- Pb Lead
- Sb Antimony
- Sn Tin
- Zn Zinc
- Nuclear power
- Gas
- Hydro-electric power

1:30 000 000

200   0   200   400   600 miles

200   0   200   400   600   800 km

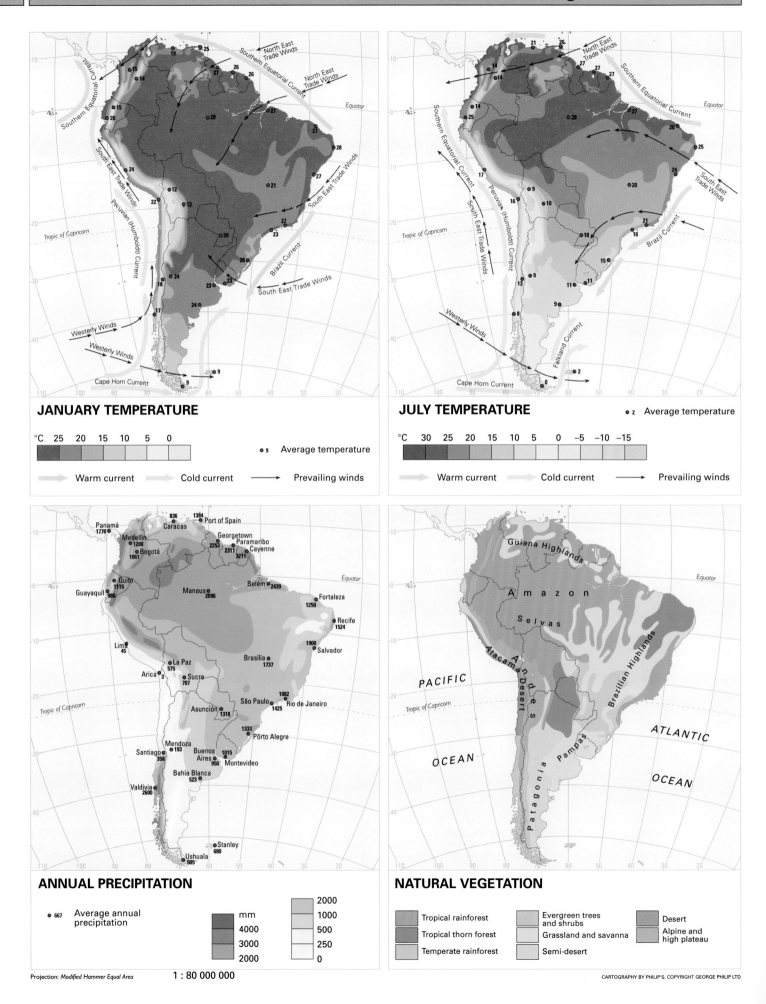

JANUARY TEMPERATURE

°C 25 20 15 10 5 0

• 9 Average temperature

Warm current   Cold current   Prevailing winds

JULY TEMPERATURE

• 2 Average temperature

°C 30 25 20 15 10 5 0 –5 –10 –15

Warm current   Cold current   Prevailing winds

ANNUAL PRECIPITATION

• 667 Average annual precipitation

mm | 2000
4000 | 1000
3000 | 500
2000 | 250
 | 0

Projection: *Modified Hammer Equal Area*   1 : 80 000 000

NATURAL VEGETATION

Tropical rainforest

Tropical thorn forest

Temperate rainforest

Evergreen trees and shrubs

Grassland and savanna

Semi-desert

Desert

Alpine and high plateau

CARTOGRAPHY BY PHILIP'S. COPYRIGHT GEORGE PHILIP LTD

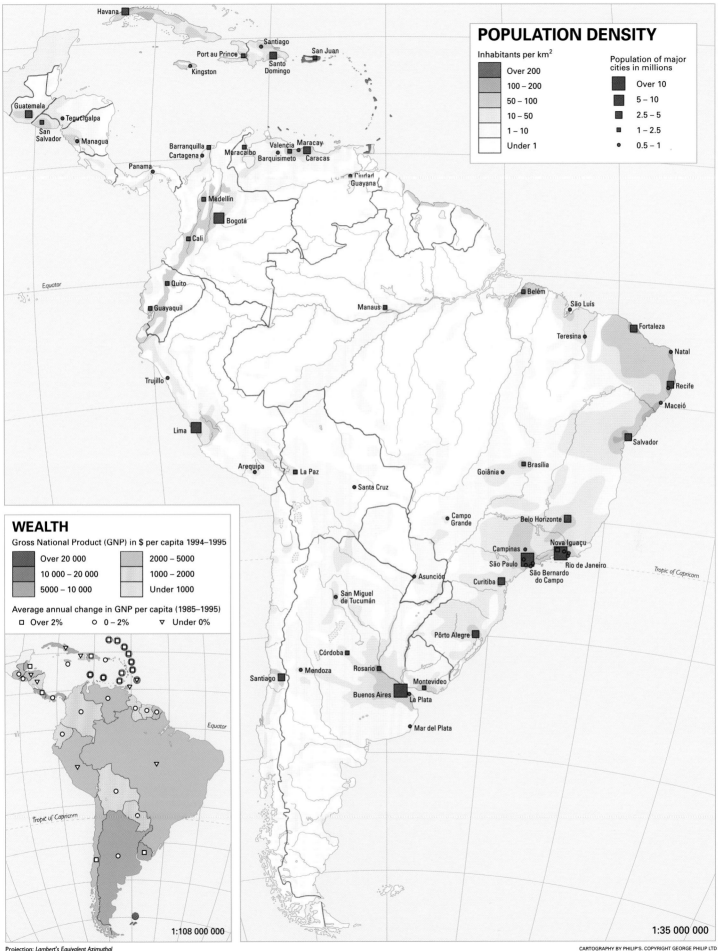

POPULATION DENSITY

Inhabitants per km²

Over 200
100 – 200
50 – 100
10 – 50
1 – 10
Under 1

Population of major cities in millions

Over 10
5 – 10
2.5 – 5
1 – 2.5
0.5 – 1

Havana
Santiago
Port au Prince
Kingston
Santo Domingo
San Juan
Guatemala
Tegucigalpa
San Salvador
Managua
Panama
Barranquilla
Cartagena
Maracaibo
Valencia
Barquisimeto
Maracay
Caracas
Ciudad Guayana
Medellín
Bogotá
Cali
Quito
Guayaquil
Manaus
Belém
São Luís
Fortaleza
Teresina
Natal
Recife
Maceió
Salvador
Trujillo
Lima
Arequipa
La Paz
Santa Cruz
Goiânia
Brasília
Campo Grande
Belo Horizonte
Campinas
São Paulo
Nova Iguaçu
Rio de Janeiro
São Bernardo do Campo
Curitiba
Asunción
San Miguel de Tucumán
Pôrto Alegre
Córdoba
Mendoza
Rosario
Santiago
Montevideo
Buenos Aires
La Plata
Mar del Plata

Equator

Tropic of Capricorn

WEALTH

Gross National Product (GNP) in $ per capita 1994–1995

Over 20 000
10 000 – 20 000
5000 – 10 000
2000 – 5000
1000 – 2000
Under 1000

Average annual change in GNP per capita (1985–1995)

□ Over 2%   ○ 0 – 2%   ▽ Under 0%

Equator

Tropic of Capricorn

1:108 000 000

1:35 000 000

Projection: *Lambert's Equivalent Azimuthal*

CARTOGRAPHY BY PHILIP'S. COPYRIGHT GEORGE PHILIP LTD

180
80 160 140 120 100 80 60 40 20

Queen Elizabeth Is. Ellesmere I. Greenland
Bering Str. Victoria I. +North Magnetic Pole Baffin
60 Yukon Mt. McKinley Island Arctic Circ
Bering 6194 Gt. Bear L. Davis Str.
Sea Mackenzie Gt. Slave L. Hudson Str. Iceland
Aleutian Is. Hudson Labrador C. Farewell British
Vancouver I. Bay Isles
L. Winnipeg Newfoundland
40 Great St. Lawrence C. Race
Lakes
Mt. Whitney Arkansas Missouri Ohio Appalachian Mts. Iberi
4418 Pen
C. Hatteras Azores Atlas M
Lower Colorado Bermuda
California Rio Grande Canary Is. Tropic of Canc
20 Gulf of Bahama S
Mauna Kea Sierra Madre Mexico Florida Str. Islands A T L A N T I C
Hawaiian Is. 4202 Popocatepetl Cuba C. Verde C. Verde
5452 Yucatan Greater Hispaniola Is.
Citlaltepetl Jamaica Antilles
5700 Caribbean Sea Lesser O C E A N
Palmyra Is. Antilles G
Llanos Orinoco Guiana Highlands
Tabuaeran Isthmus Roraima C. Palmas
0 Kiritimati P A C I F I C of Panama 2772
Galapagos Chimborazo Negro Equator
Is. 6267 Amazon C. de São Roque Ascension
Phoenix Is. Madeira S e l v a s
Tokelau Is. Marquesas Is. Tocantins St. Helena
Samoa Is. O C E A N Mato Grosso Brazilian Highlands
Society Is. Tuamotu L. Titicaca C. Frio
Cook Is. Tahiti Archipelago Gran Chaco Paraguay Tropic of Capric
20 Tonga Tubuai Is. Atacama Paraná Pampas
Is. Pitcairn I. Desert R. de la Plata Tristan da Cu
Easter I. Ojos del Salado
6863 Negro
Kermadec Is. Aconcagua Patagonia
6960
40 Falkland Is.
Chatham Is. Tierra del Fuego S. Georgia
Magellan's Str. C. Horn
Drake Passage
Graham Antarctic Antarctic C
Land Peninsula
60 Palmer Weddell Sea
Land Caird Coast
Ellsworth Land 40 20 Coats Land
Ross Sea Byrd Land 80 60 West from Green
80 180 160 140 120 100

Projection: Hammer Equal Area

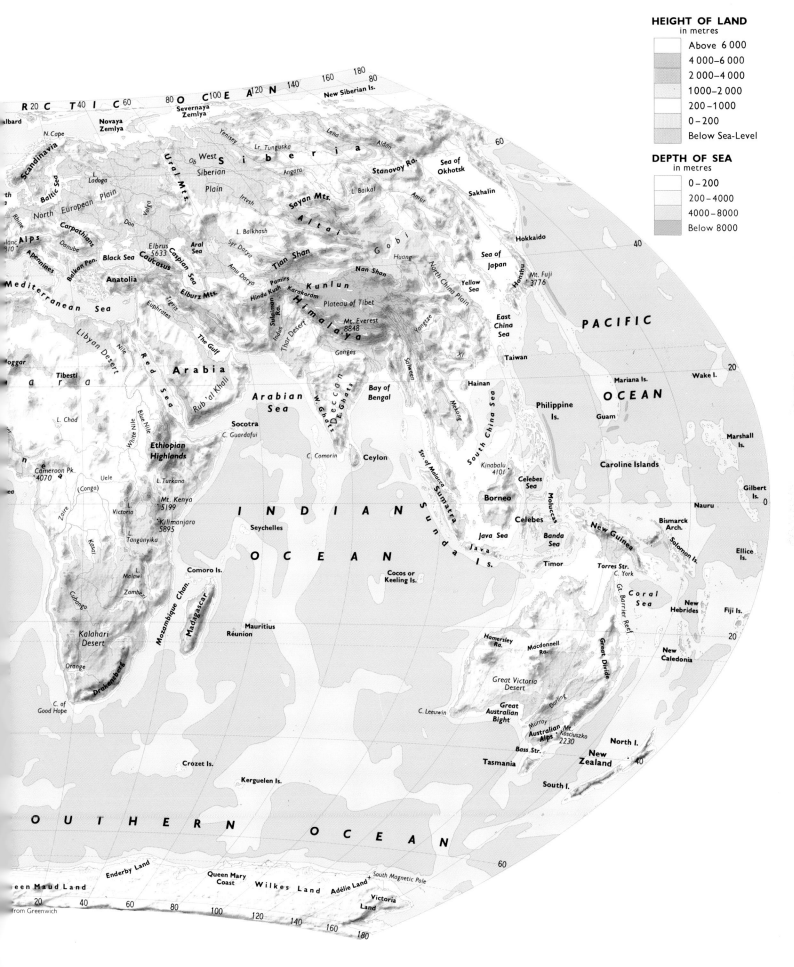

HEIGHT OF LAND
in metres

- Above 6 000
- 4 000 – 6 000
- 2 000 – 4 000
- 1000 – 2 000
- 200 – 1000
- 0 – 200
- Below Sea-Level

DEPTH OF SEA
in metres

- 0 – 200
- 200 – 4000
- 4000 – 8000
- Below 8000

ARCTIC OCEAN

Svalbard · N. Cape · Novaya Zemlya · Severnaya Zemlya · New Siberian Is.

Scandinavia · Baltic Sea · L. Ladoga · Ob · West Siberian Plain · S i b e r i a · Yenisey · Lr. Tunguska · Lena · Aldan · Stanovoy Ra. · Sea of Okhotsk

North European Plain · Ural Mts. · Volga · Irtysh · Angara · Sayan Mts. · L. Baikal · Amur · Sakhalin

Rhine · Carpathians · Danube · Don · L. Balkhash · A l t a i · Gobi · Hokkaido

Mt. Blanc 4810 · Alps · Apennines · Balkan Pen. · Black Sea · Caucasus · Elbrus 5633 · Aral Sea · Caspian Sea · Syr Darya · Tian Shan · Huang · North China Plain · Sea of Japan · Honshu · Mt. Fuji 3776

Mediterranean Sea · Anatolia · Elburz Mts. · Amu Darya · Pamirs · Hindu Kush · Karakoram · Kunlun · Nan Shan · Yellow Sea · East China Sea · Taiwan

Libyan Desert · Tigris · Euphrates · The Gulf · Sulaiman Ra. · Indus · H i m a l a y a · Plateau of Tibet · Mt. Everest 8848 · Yangtze · Xi

Hoggar · Tibesti · Arabia · Red Sea · Rub 'al Khali · Thar Desert · Ganges · Saltween · PACIFIC OCEAN

Sahara · L. Chad · White Nile · Blue Nile · Socotra · Arabian Sea · W. Ghats · Deccan · E. Ghats · Bay of Bengal · Hainan · Mariana Is. · Wake I.

Cameroon Pk. 4070 · Ethiopian Highlands · C. Guardafui · C. Comorin · Ceylon · Philippine Is. · Guam · Caroline Islands · Marshall Is.

Uele · (Congo) · L. Turkana · Mt. Kenya 5199 · Mekong · Str. of Malacca · Kinabalu 4101 · South China Sea · Nauru · Gilbert Is.

Zaire · L. Victoria · Kilimanjaro 5895 · Seychelles · I N D I A N · Sumatra · Borneo · Celebes Sea · Moluccas · New Guinea · Bismarck Arch. · Solomon Is. · Ellice Is.

Kasai · L. Tanganyika · O C E A N · Celebes · Banda Sea · Java Sea · Java · Timor · Torres Str. · C. York · Ellice Is.

Cubango · Zambezi · Comoro Is. · Mozambique Chan. · Madagascar · Mauritius · Réunion · Cocos or Keeling Is. · Coral Sea · New Hebrides · Fiji Is.

Kalahari Desert · Orange · Hamersley Ra. · Macdonnell Ra. · Great Dividing Range · New Caledonia

Drakensberg · C. of Good Hope · Crozet Is. · Kerguelen Is. · Great Victoria Desert · C. Leeuwin · Great Australian Bight · Murray · Australian Alps · Mt. Kosciuszko 2230 · Darling · North I. · Bass Str. · Tasmania · New Zealand · South I.

S O U T H E R N   O C E A N

Queen Maud Land · Enderby Land · Queen Mary Coast · Wilkes Land · Adélie Land · + South Magnetic Pole · Victoria Land

from Greenwich

1 : 80 000 000

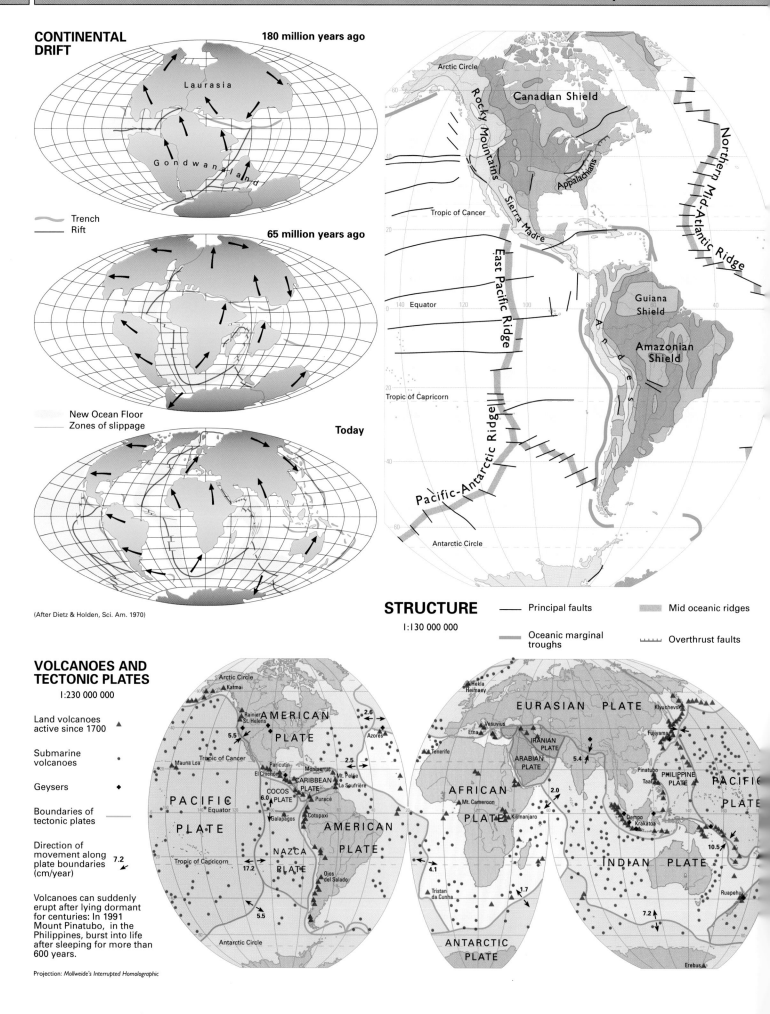

CONTINENTAL DRIFT

180 million years ago

Laurasia

Gondwanaland

~~~ Trench
— Rift

65 million years ago

New Ocean Floor
— Zones of slippage

Today

(After Dietz & Holden, Sci. Am. 1970)

Arctic Circle

Canadian Shield

Rocky Mountains

Appalachians

Tropic of Cancer

Sierra Madre

East Pacific Ridge

Equator

Andes

Guiana Shield

Amazonian Shield

Tropic of Capricorn

Pacific-Antarctic Ridge

Antarctic Circle

Northern Mid-Atlantic Ridge

STRUCTURE

1:130 000 000

— Principal faults

▬ Oceanic marginal troughs

▨ Mid oceanic ridges

ᚒᚒᚒ Overthrust faults

VOLCANOES AND TECTONIC PLATES

1:230 000 000

Land volcanoes active since 1700 ▲

Submarine volcanoes ·

Geysers ✚

Boundaries of tectonic plates —

Direction of movement along plate boundaries (cm/year) 7.2

Volcanoes can suddenly erupt after lying dormant for centuries: In 1991 Mount Pinatubo, in the Philippines, burst into life after sleeping for more than 600 years.

Projection: Mollweide's Interrupted Homolographic

Arctic Circle
Katmai
Rainier
St. Helens
AMERICAN PLATE
2.6
5.5
Azores
Mauna Loa
Tropic of Cancer
2.5
Paricutin
El Chichón
Montserrat
COCOS PLATE
6.0
CARIBBEAN PLATE
Mt. Pelée
La Soufrière
Puracé
PACIFIC
Equator
Galapagos
Cotopaxi
PLATE
AMERICAN PLATE
NAZCA PLATE
Tropic of Capricorn
17.2
Ojos del Salado
5.5
Antarctic Circle

Hekla
Heimaey
EURASIAN PLATE
Klyuchevsk
Vesuvius
Etna
IRANIAN PLATE
ARABIAN PLATE
5.4
Fujiyama
Tenerife
Pinatubo
Taal
PHILIPPINE PLATE
PACIFIC PLATE
AFRICAN PLATE
2.0
Mt. Cameroon
Kilimanjaro
Dempo
Krakatoa
10.5
INDIAN PLATE
4.1
Tristan da Cunha
1.7
Ruapehu
7.2
ANTARCTIC PLATE
Erebus

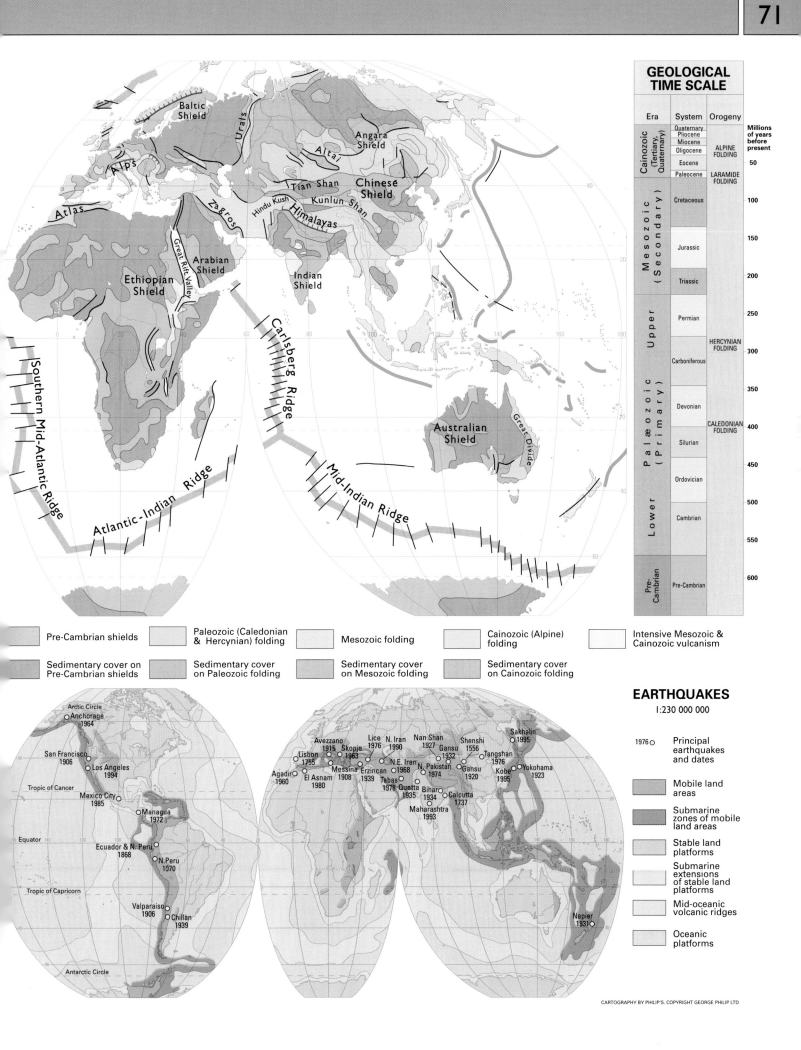

GEOLOGICAL TIME SCALE

Era	System	Orogeny	Millions of years before present
Cainozoic (Tertiary, Quaternary)	Quaternary		
	Pliocene		
	Miocene	ALPINE FOLDING	50
	Oligocene		
	Eocene		
	Paleocene	LARAMIDE FOLDING	
Mesozoic (Secondary)	Cretaceous		100
	Jurassic		150
	Triassic		200
Palæozoic (Primary) — Upper	Permian		250
	Carboniferous	HERCYNIAN FOLDING	300
	Devonian		350
Palæozoic (Primary) — Lower	Silurian	CALEDONIAN FOLDING	400
	Ordovician		450
	Cambrian		500
			550
Pre-Cambrian	Pre-Cambrian		600

Legend (geological map):
- Pre-Cambrian shields
- Paleozoic (Caledonian & Hercynian) folding
- Mesozoic folding
- Cainozoic (Alpine) folding
- Intensive Mesozoic & Cainozoic vulcanism
- Sedimentary cover on Pre-Cambrian shields
- Sedimentary cover on Paleozoic folding
- Sedimentary cover on Mesozoic folding
- Sedimentary cover on Cainozoic folding

Map labels: Baltic Shield, Urals, Angara Shield, Altai, Alps, Tian Shan, Chinese Shield, Atlas, Zagros, Hindu Kush, Kunlun Shan, Himalayas, Great Rift Valley, Arabian Shield, Ethiopian Shield, Indian Shield, Carlsberg Ridge, Southern Mid-Atlantic Ridge, Atlantic-Indian Ridge, Mid-Indian Ridge, Australian Shield, Great Divide.

EARTHQUAKES

1:230 000 000

- 1976 ○ Principal earthquakes and dates
- Mobile land areas
- Submarine zones of mobile land areas
- Stable land platforms
- Submarine extensions of stable land platforms
- Mid-oceanic volcanic ridges
- Oceanic platforms

Earthquake labels: Arctic Circle, Anchorage 1964, San Francisco 1906, Los Angeles 1994, Tropic of Cancer, Mexico City 1985, Managua 1972, Equator, Ecuador & N. Peru 1868, N. Peru 1970, Tropic of Capricorn, Valparaiso 1906, Chillan 1939, Antarctic Circle; Avezzano 1915, Lisbon 1755, Skopje 1963, Lice 1976, N. Iran 1990, Nan Shan 1927, Shenshi 1556, Gansu 1932, Sakhalin 1995, Agadir 1960, Messina 1908, Erzincan 1939, N.E. Iran 1968, N. Pakistan 1974, Gansu 1920, Tangshan 1976, Yokohama 1923, El Asnam 1980, Tabas 1978, Quetta 1935, Bihar 1934, Calcutta 1737, Kobe 1995, Maharashtra 1993, Napier 1931.

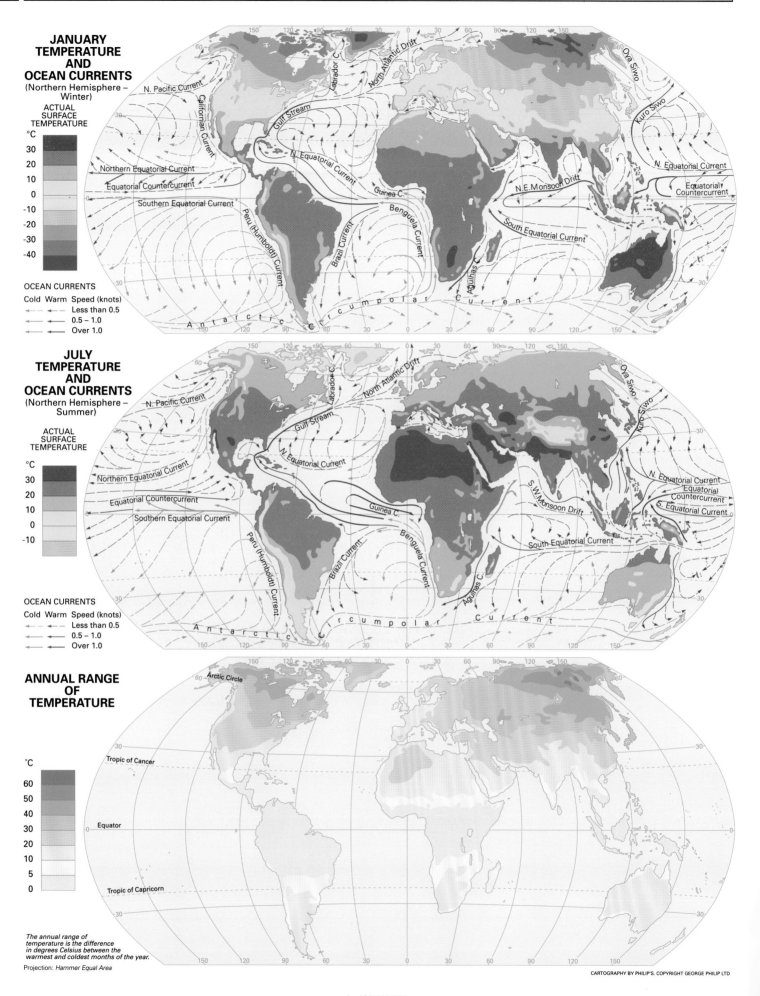

JANUARY TEMPERATURE AND OCEAN CURRENTS
(Northern Hemisphere – Winter)

ACTUAL SURFACE TEMPERATURE
°C
30
20
10
0
-10
-20
-30
-40

OCEAN CURRENTS
Cold Warm Speed (knots)
Less than 0.5
0.5 – 1.0
Over 1.0

JULY TEMPERATURE AND OCEAN CURRENTS
(Northern Hemisphere – Summer)

ACTUAL SURFACE TEMPERATURE
°C
30
20
10
0
-10

OCEAN CURRENTS
Cold Warm Speed (knots)
Less than 0.5
0.5 – 1.0
Over 1.0

ANNUAL RANGE OF TEMPERATURE

°C
60
50
40
30
20
10
5
0

The annual range of temperature is the difference in degrees Celsius between the warmest and coldest months of the year.

Projection: Hammer Equal Area

CARTOGRAPHY BY PHILIP'S. COPYRIGHT GEORGE PHILIP LTD

I : 190 000 000

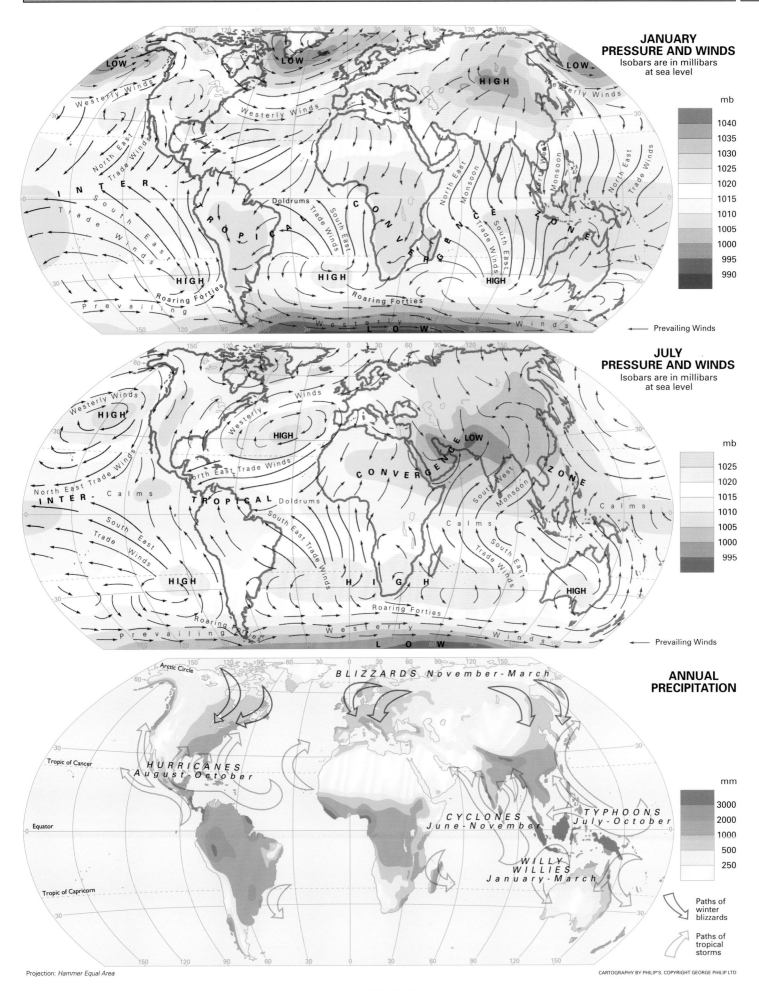

JANUARY PRESSURE AND WINDS
Isobars are in millibars at sea level

mb
1040
1035
1030
1025
1020
1015
1010
1005
1000
995
990

⟵ Prevailing Winds

JULY PRESSURE AND WINDS
Isobars are in millibars at sea level

mb
1025
1020
1015
1010
1005
1000
995

⟵ Prevailing Winds

ANNUAL PRECIPITATION

mm
3000
2000
1000
500
250

Paths of winter blizzards

Paths of tropical storms

Projection: *Hammer Equal Area*

1 : 190 000 000

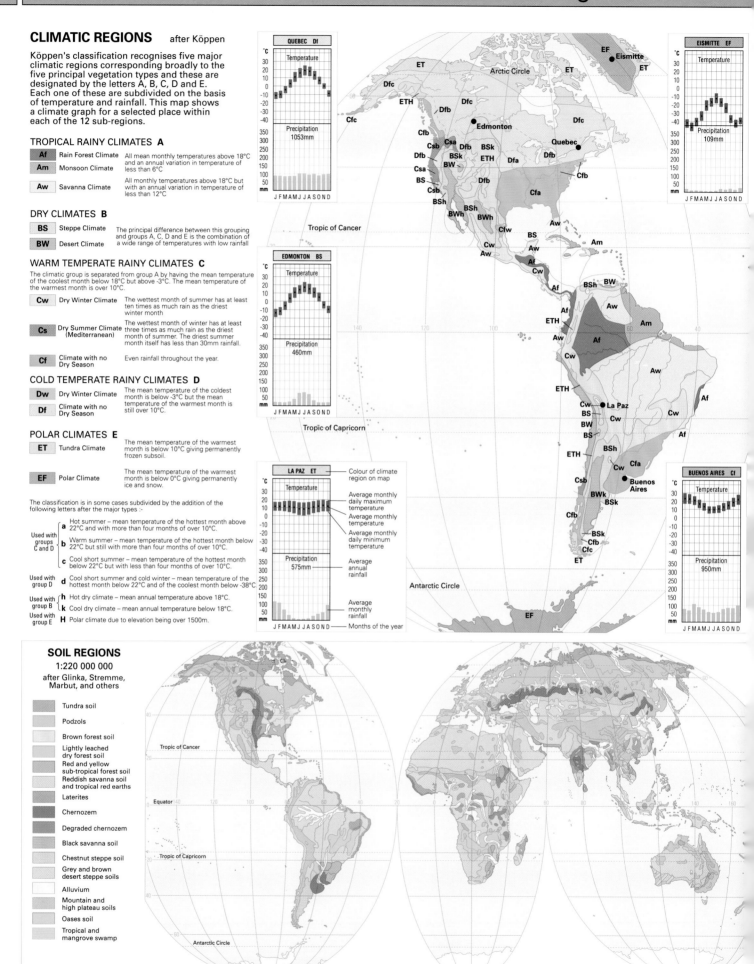

CLIMATIC REGIONS after Köppen

Köppen's classification recognises five major climatic regions corresponding broadly to the five principal vegetation types and these are designated by the letters A, B, C, D and E. Each one of these are subdivided on the basis of temperature and rainfall. This map shows a climate graph for a selected place within each of the 12 sub-regions.

TROPICAL RAINY CLIMATES A

Af	Rain Forest Climate	All mean monthly temperatures above 18°C and an annual variation in temperature of less than 6°C
Am	Monsoon Climate	
Aw	Savanna Climate	All monthly temperatures above 18°C but with an annual variation in temperature of less than 12°C

DRY CLIMATES B

BS	Steppe Climate	The principal difference between this grouping and groups A, C, D and E is the combination of a wide range of temperatures with low rainfall
BW	Desert Climate	

WARM TEMPERATE RAINY CLIMATES C

The climatic group is separated from group A by having the mean temperature of the coolest month below 18°C but above -3°C. The mean temperature of the warmest month is over 10°C.

Cw	Dry Winter Climate	The wettest month of summer has at least ten times as much rain as the driest winter month
Cs	Dry Summer Climate (Mediterranean)	The wettest month of winter has at least three times as much rain as the driest month of summer. The driest summer month itself has less than 30mm rainfall.
Cf	Climate with no Dry Season	Even rainfall throughout the year.

COLD TEMPERATE RAINY CLIMATES D

Dw	Dry Winter Climate	The mean temperature of the coldest month is below -3°C but the mean temperature of the warmest month is still over 10°C
Df	Climate with no Dry Season	

POLAR CLIMATES E

ET	Tundra Climate	The mean temperature of the warmest month is below 10°C giving permanently frozen subsoil.
EF	Polar Climate	The mean temperature of the warmest month is below 0°C giving permanently ice and snow.

The classification is in some cases subdivided by the addition of the following letters after the major types :-

Used with groups C and D
- **a** Hot summer – mean temperature of the hottest month above 22°C and with more than four months of over 10°C.
- **b** Warm summer – mean temperature of the hottest month below 22°C but still with more than four months of over 10°C.
- **c** Cool short summer – mean temperature of the hottest month below 22°C but with less than four months of over 10°C.

Used with group D
- **d** Cool short summer and cold winter – mean temperature of the hottest month below 22°C and of the coolest month below -38°C.

Used with group B
- **h** Hot dry climate – mean annual temperature above 18°C.
- **k** Cool dry climate – mean annual temperature below 18°C.

Used with group E
- **H** Polar climate due to elevation being over 1500m.

QUEBEC Df
Temperature
Precipitation 1053mm

EISMITTE EF
Temperature
Precipitation 109mm

EDMONTON BS
Temperature
Precipitation 460mm

LA PAZ ET
Temperature
Precipitation 575mm

- Colour of climate region on map
- Average monthly daily maximum temperature
- Average monthly temperature
- Average monthly daily minimum temperature
- Average annual rainfall
- Average monthly rainfall
- Months of the year

BUENOS AIRES Cf
Temperature
Precipitation 950mm

SOIL REGIONS
1:220 000 000
after Glinka, Stremme, Marbut, and others

- Tundra soil
- Podzols
- Brown forest soil
- Lightly leached dry forest soil
- Red and yellow sub-tropical forest soil
- Reddish savanna soil and tropical red earths
- Laterites
- Chernozem
- Degraded chernozem
- Black savanna soil
- Chestnut steppe soil
- Grey and brown desert steppe soils
- Alluvium
- Mountain and high plateau soils
- Oases soil
- Tropical and mangrove swamp

Projection: *Interrupted Mollweide's Homolographic*

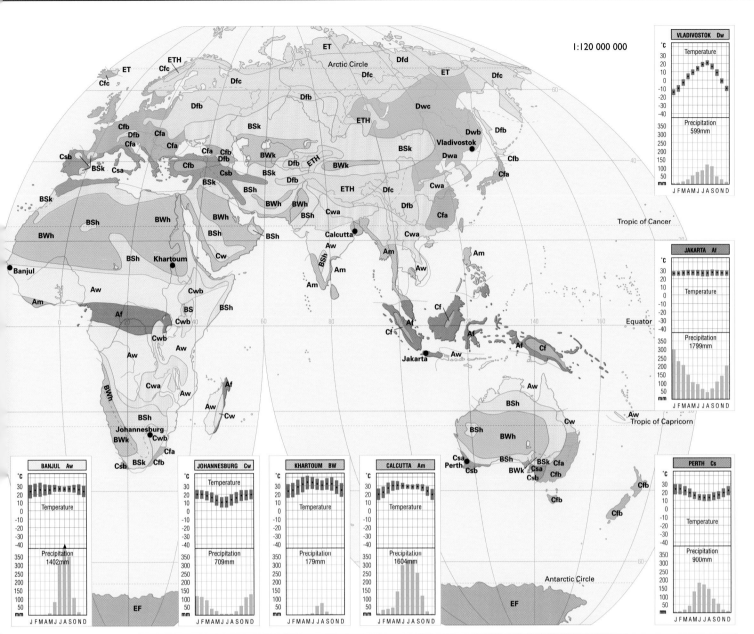

1:120 000 000

VLADIVOSTOK Dw
Temperature
Precipitation 599mm

JAKARTA Af
Temperature
Precipitation 1799mm

BANJUL Aw
Temperature
Precipitation 1402mm

JOHANNESBURG Cw
Temperature
Precipitation 709mm

KHARTOUM BW
Temperature
Precipitation 179mm

CALCUTTA Am
Temperature
Precipitation 1604mm

PERTH Cs
Temperature
Precipitation 900mm

NATURAL VEGETATION

1:220 000 000
after Austin Miller

- Tropical rainforest
- Subtropical and temperate rainforest
- Monsoon woodland and open jungle
- Subtropical and temperate woodland, scrub and bush
- Tropical savanna, with low trees and bush
- Tropical savanna and grasslands
- Dry semi-desert, with shrub and grass
- Desert shrub
- Desert
- Dry steppe and shrub
- Temperate grasslands, prairie and steppe
- Mediterranean hardwood forest and scrub
- Temperate deciduous forest and meadow
- Temperate deciduous and coniferous forest
- Northern coniferous forest (taiga)
- Mountainous forest, mainly coniferous
- High plateau steppe and tundra
- Arctic tundra
- Polar and mountainous ice desert

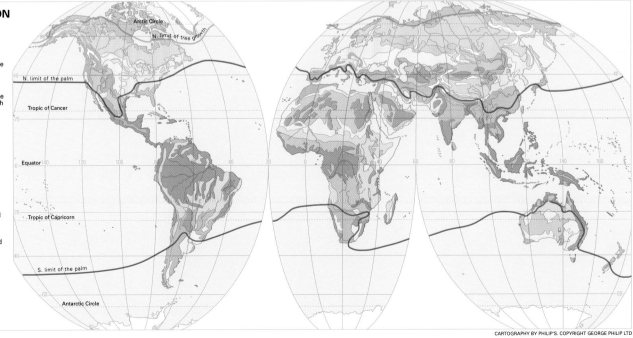

CARTOGRAPHY BY PHILIP'S. COPYRIGHT GEORGE PHILIP LTD

	Jan	Feb	
Addis Ababa Ethiopia 2410m			Height of meteorological station above sea level in metres
Temperature Daily Max.°C	23	24	Average monthly maximum temperature in degrees Celsius
Daily Min.°C	6	7	Average monthly minimum temperature in degrees Celsius
Average Monthly °C	14	15	Average monthly temperature in degrees Celsius
Rainfall Monthly Total mm	13	35	Average monthly precipitation in millimetres
Sunshine Hours per Day	8.7	8.2	Average daily duration of bright sunshine per month in hours

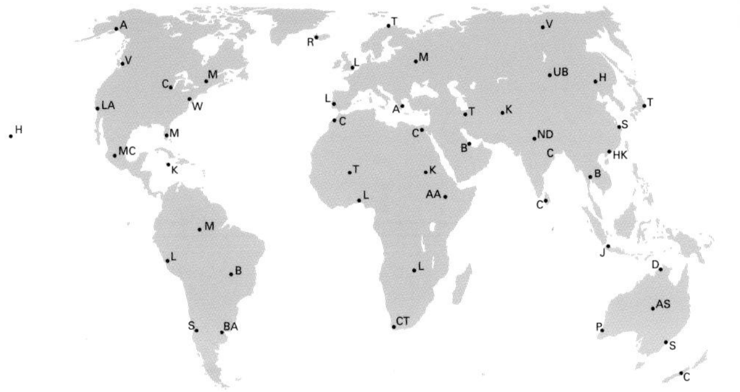

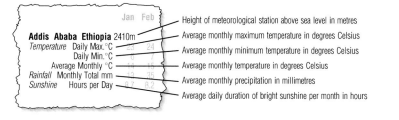

Addis Ababa Ethiopia 2410m

	Jan	Feb	Mar	Apr	May	June	July	Aug	Sep	Oct	Nov	Dec	Year
Temperature Daily Max.°C	23	24	25	24	25	23	20	20	21	22	23	22	23
Daily Min.°C	6	7	9	10	9	10	11	11	10	7	5	5	8
Average Monthly °C	14	15	17	17	17	16	16	15	15	15	14	14	15
Rainfall Monthly Total mm	13	35	67	91	81	117	247	255	167	29	8	5	1115
Sunshine Hours per Day	8.7	8.2	7.6	8.1	6.5	4.8	2.8	3.2	5.2	7.6	6.7	7	6.4

Alice Springs Australia 580m

	Jan	Feb	Mar	Apr	May	June	July	Aug	Sep	Oct	Nov	Dec	Year
Temperature Daily Max.°C	35	35	32	27	23	19	19	23	27	31	33	35	28
Daily Min.°C	21	20	17	12	8	5	4	6	10	15	18	20	13
Average Monthly °C	28	27	25	20	15	12	12	14	18	23	25	27	21
Rainfall Monthly Total mm	44	33	27	10	15	13	7	8	7	18	29	38	249
Sunshine Hours per Day	10.3	10.4	9.3	9.2	8	8	8.9	9.8	10	9.7	10.1	10	9.5

Anchorage USA 183m

	Jan	Feb	Mar	Apr	May	June	July	Aug	Sep	Oct	Nov	Dec	Year
Temperature Daily Max.°C	-7	-3	0	7	13	18	19	17	13	6	-2	-6	-6
Daily Min.°C	-15	-12	-9	-2	4	8	10	9	5	-2	-9	-14	-2
Average Monthly °C	-11	-7	-4	3	9	13	15	13	9	2	-5	-10	-4
Rainfall Monthly Total mm	20	18	13	11	13	25	47	64	64	47	28	24	374
Sunshine Hours per Day	2.4	4.1	6.6	8.3	8.3	9.2	8.5	6	4.4	3.1	2.6	1.6	5.4

Athens Greece 107m

	Jan	Feb	Mar	Apr	May	June	July	Aug	Sep	Oct	Nov	Dec	Year
Temperature Daily Max.°C	13	14	16	20	25	30	33	33	29	24	19	15	23
Daily Min.°C	6	7	8	11	16	20	23	23	19	15	12	8	14
Average Monthly °C	10	10	12	16	20	25	28	28	24	20	15	11	18
Rainfall Monthly Total mm	62	37	37	23	23	14	6	7	15	51	56	71	402
Sunshine Hours per Day	3.9	5.2	5.8	7.7	8.9	10.7	11.9	11.5	9.4	6.8	4.8	3.8	7.3

Bahrain City Bahrain 2m

	Jan	Feb	Mar	Apr	May	June	July	Aug	Sep	Oct	Nov	Dec	Year
Temperature Daily Max.°C	20	21	25	29	33	36	37	38	36	32	27	22	30
Daily Min.°C	14	15	18	22	25	29	31	32	29	25	22	16	23
Average Monthly °C	17	18	21	25	29	32	34	35	32	29	25	19	26
Rainfall Monthly Total mm	18	12	10	9	2	0	0	0	0	0.4	3	16	70
Sunshine Hours per Day	5.9	6.9	7.9	8.8	10.6	13.2	12.1	12	12	10.3	7.7	6.4	9.5

Bangkok Thailand 10m

	Jan	Feb	Mar	Apr	May	June	July	Aug	Sep	Oct	Nov	Dec	Year
Temperature Daily Max.°C	32	33	34	35	34	33	32	32	32	31	31	31	33
Daily Min.°C	20	23	24	26	25	25	25	24	24	24	23	20	24
Average Monthly °C	26	28	29	30	30	29	28	28	28	28	27	26	28
Rainfall Monthly Total mm	9	30	36	82	165	153	168	183	310	239	55	8	1438
Sunshine Hours per Day	8.2	8	8	10	7.5	6.1	4.7	5.2	5.2	6.1	7.3	7.8	7

Brasilia Brazil 910m

	Jan	Feb	Mar	Apr	May	June	July	Aug	Sep	Oct	Nov	Dec	Year
Temperature Daily Max.°C	28	28	28	28	27	27	27	29	30	29	28	27	28
Daily Min.°C	18	18	18	17	15	13	13	14	16	18	18	18	16
Average Monthly °C	23	23	23	22	21	20	20	21	23	24	23	22	22
Rainfall Monthly Total mm	252	204	227	93	17	3	6	3	30	127	255	343	1560
Sunshine Av. Monthly Dur.	5.8	5.7	6	7.4	8.7	9.3	9.6	9.8	7.9	6.5	4.8	4.4	7.2

Buenos Aires Argentina 25m

	Jan	Feb	Mar	Apr	May	June	July	Aug	Sep	Oct	Nov	Dec	Year
Temperature Daily Max.°C	30	29	26	22	18	14	14	16	18	21	25	28	22
Daily Min.°C	17	17	16	12	9	5	6	6	8	10	14	16	11
Average Monthly °C	23	23	21	17	13	10	10	11	13	15	19	22	16
Rainfall Monthly Total mm	79	71	109	89	76	61	56	61	79	86	84	99	950
Sunshine Hours per Day	9.2	8.5	7.5	6.8	4.9	3.5	3.8	5.2	6	6.8	8.1	8.5	6.6

Cairo Egypt 75m

	Jan	Feb	Mar	Apr	May	June	July	Aug	Sep	Oct	Nov	Dec	Year
Temperature Daily Max.°C	19	21	24	28	32	35	35	35	33	30	26	21	28
Daily Min.°C	9	9	12	14	18	20	22	22	20	18	14	10	16
Average Monthly °C	14	15	18	21	25	28	29	28	26	24	20	16	22
Rainfall Monthly Total mm	4	4	3	1	2	1	0	0	1	1	3	7	27
Sunshine Hours per Day	6.9	8.4	8.7	9.7	10.5	11.9	11.7	11.3	10.4	9.4	8.3	6.4	9.5

Calcutta India 5m

	Jan	Feb	Mar	Apr	May	June	July	Aug	Sep	Oct	Nov	Dec	Year
Temperature Daily Max.°C	27	29	34	36	35	34	32	32	32	32	29	26	31
Daily Min.°C	13	15	21	24	25	26	26	26	26	23	18	13	21
Average Monthly °C	20	22	27	30	30	30	29	29	29	28	23	20	26
Rainfall Monthly Total mm	10	30	34	44	140	297	325	332	253	114	20	5	1604
Sunshine Hours per Day	8.6	8.7	8.9	9	8.7	5.4	4.1	4.1	5.1	6.5	8.3	8.4	7.1

Cape Town South Africa 44m

	Jan	Feb	Mar	Apr	May	June	July	Aug	Sep	Oct	Nov	Dec	Year
Temperature Daily Max.°C	26	26	25	23	20	18	17	18	19	21	24	25	22
Daily Min.°C	15	15	14	11	9	7	7	7	8	10	13	15	11
Average Monthly °C	21	20	20	17	14	13	12	12	14	16	18	20	16
Rainfall Monthly Total mm	12	19	17	42	67	98	68	76	36	45	12	13	505
Sunshine Hours per Day	11.4	10.2	9.4	7.7	6.1	5.7	6.4	6.6	7.6	8.6	10.2	10.9	8.4

Casablanca Morocco 59m

	Jan	Feb	Mar	Apr	May	June	July	Aug	Sep	Oct	Nov	Dec	Ye
Temperature Daily Max.°C	17	18	20	21	22	24	26	26	26	24	21	18	
Daily Min.°C	8	9	11	12	15	18	19	20	18	15	12	10	
Average Monthly °C	13	13	15	16	18	21	23	23	22	20	17	14	
Rainfall Monthly Total mm	78	61	54	37	20	3	0	1	6	28	58	94	
Sunshine Hours per Day	5.2	6.3	7.3	9	9.4	9.7	10.2	9.7	9.1	7.4	5.9	5.3	

Chicago USA 186m

	Jan	Feb	Mar	Apr	May	June	July	Aug	Sep	Oct	Nov	Dec	Ye
Temperature Daily Max.°C	0.6	1.5	6.4	14.1	20.6	26.4	28.9	28	23.8	17.4	8.4	2.1	
Daily Min.°C	-7	-6	-2	5	11	16	20	19	14	8	0	-5	
Average Monthly °C	-3	-2	2	9	16	21	24	23	19	13	4	-2	
Rainfall Monthly Total mm	47	41	70	77	96	103	86	80	69	71	56	48	
Sunshine Hours per Day	4	5	6.6	6.9	8.9	10.2	10	9.2	8.2	6.9	4.5	3.7	

Christchurch New Zealand 5m

	Jan	Feb	Mar	Apr	May	June	July	Aug	Sep	Oct	Nov	Dec	Ye
Temperature Daily Max.°C	21	21	19	17	13	11	10	11	14	17	19	21	
Daily Min.°C	12	12	10	7	4	2	1	3	5	7	8	11	
Average Monthly °C	16	16	15	12	9	6	6	7	9	12	13	16	
Rainfall Monthly Total mm	56	46	43	46	76	69	61	58	51	51	51	61	
Sunshine Hours per Day	7	6.5	5.6	4.7	4.3	3.9	4.1	4.7	5.6	6.1	6.9	6.3	

Colombo Sri Lanka 10m

	Jan	Feb	Mar	Apr	May	June	July	Aug	Sep	Oct	Nov	Dec	Ye
Temperature Daily Max.°C	30	31	31	31	30	30	29	29	30	29	29	30	
Daily Min.°C	22	22	23	24	25	25	25	25	25	24	23	22	
Average Monthly °C	26	26	27	28	28	27	27	27	27	27	26	26	
Rainfall Monthly Total mm	101	66	118	230	394	220	140	102	174	348	333	142	
Sunshine Hours per Day	7.9	9	8.1	7.2	6.4	5.4	6.1	6.3	6.2	6.5	6.4	7.8	

Darwin Australia 30m

	Jan	Feb	Mar	Apr	May	June	July	Aug	Sep	Oct	Nov	Dec	Ye
Temperature Daily Max.°C	32	32	33	33	33	31	31	32	33	34	34	33	
Daily Min.°C	25	25	25	24	23	21	19	21	23	25	26	26	
Average Monthly °C	29	29	29	29	28	26	25	26	28	29	30	29	
Rainfall Monthly Total mm	405	309	279	77	8	2	0	1	15	48	108	214	
Sunshine Hours per Day	5.8	5.8	6.6	9.8	9.3	10	9.9	10.4	10.1	9.4	9.6	6.8	

Harbin China 175m

	Jan	Feb	Mar	Apr	May	June	July	Aug	Sep	Oct	Nov	Dec	Ye
Temperature Daily Max.°C	-14	-9	0	12	21	26	29	27	20	12	-1	-11	
Daily Min.°C	-26	-23	-12	-1	7	14	18	16	8	0	-12	-22	
Average Monthly °C	-20	-16	-6	6	14	20	23	22	14	6	-7	-17	
Rainfall Monthly Total mm	4	6	17	23	44	92	167	119	52	36	12	5	
Sunshine Hours per Day	6.4	7.8	8	7.8	8.3	8.6	8.6	8.2	7.2	6.9	6.1	5.7	

Hong Kong China 35m

	Jan	Feb	Mar	Apr	May	June	July	Aug	Sep	Oct	Nov	Dec	Ye
Temperature Daily Max.°C	18	18	20	24	28	30	31	31	30	27	24	20	
Daily Min.°C	13	13	16	19	23	26	26	26	25	23	19	15	
Average Monthly °C	16	15	18	22	25	28	28	28	27	25	21	17	
Rainfall Monthly Total mm	30	60	70	133	332	479	286	415	364	33	46	17	
Sunshine Hours per Day	4.7	3.5	3.1	3.8	5	5.4	6.8	6.5	6.6	7	6.2	5.5	

Honolulu Hawaii 5m

	Jan	Feb	Mar	Apr	May	June	July	Aug	Sep	Oct	Nov	Dec	Ye
Temperature Daily Max.°C	26	26	26	27	28	29	29	29	30	29	28	26	
Daily Min.°C	19	19	19	20	21	22	23	23	23	22	21	20	
Average Monthly °C	23	22	23	23	24	26	26	26	26	26	24	23	
Rainfall Monthly Total mm	96	84	73	33	25	8	11	23	25	47	55	76	
Sunshine Hours per Day	7.3	7.7	8.3	8.6	8.8	9.1	9.4	9.3	9.2	8.3	7.5	6.2	

Jakarta Indonesia 10m

	Jan	Feb	Mar	Apr	May	June	July	Aug	Sep	Oct	Nov	Dec	Ye
Temperature Daily Max.°C	29	29	30	31	31	31	31	31	31	31	30	29	
Daily Min.°C	23	23	23	24	24	23	23	23	23	23	23	23	
Average Monthly °C	26	26	27	27	27	27	27	27	27	27	27	26	
Rainfall Monthly Total mm	300	300	211	147	114	97	64	43	66	112	142	203	
Sunshine Av. Monthly Dur.	6.1	6.5	7.7	8.5	8.4	8.5	9.1	9.5	9.6	9	7.7	7.1	

Kabul Afghanistan 1791 m

	Jan	Feb	Mar	Apr	May	June	July	Aug	Sep	Oct	Nov	Dec	Ye
Temperature Daily Max.°C	2	4	12	19	26	31	33	33	30	22	17	8	
Daily Min.°C	-8	-6	1	6	11	13	16	15	11	6	1	-3	
Average Monthly °C	-3	-1	6	13	18	22	25	24	20	14	9	3	
Rainfall Monthly Total mm	28	61	72	117	33	1	7	1	0	1	37	14	
Sunshine Av. Monthly Dur.	5.9	6	5.7	6.8	10.1	11.5	11.4	11.2	9.8	9.4	7.8	6.1	

Khartoum Sudan 380m

	Jan	Feb	Mar	Apr	May	June	July	Aug	Sep	Oct	Nov	Dec	Ye
Temperature Daily Max.°C	32	33	37	40	42	41	38	36	38	39	35	32	
Daily Min.°C	16	17	20	23	26	27	26	25	25	25	21	17	
Average Monthly °C	24	25	28	32	34	34	32	30	32	32	28	25	
Rainfall Monthly Total mm	0	0	0	1	7	5	56	80	28	2	0	0	
Sunshine Av. Monthly Dur.	10.6	11.2	10.4	10.8	10.4	10.1	8.6	8.6	9.6	10.3	10.8	10.6	

		Jan	Feb	Mar	Apr	May	June	July	Aug	Sep	Oct	Nov	Dec	Year
gston Jamaica 35m														
perature	Daily Max.°C	30	30	30	31	31	32	32	32	32	31	31	31	31
	Daily Min.°C	20	20	20	21	22	24	23	23	23	23	22	21	22
	Average Monthly °C	25	25	25	26	26	28	28	28	27	27	26	26	26
fall	Monthly Total mm	23	15	23	31	102	89	38	91	99	180	74	36	801
hine	Av. Monthly Dur.	8.3	8.8	8.7	8.7	8.3	7.8	8.5	8.5	7.6	7.3	8.3	7.7	8.2
os Nigeria 40m														
perature	Daily Max.°C	32	33	33	32	31	29	28	28	29	30	31	32	31
	Daily Min.°C	22	23	23	23	23	22	22	21	22	22	23	22	22
	Average Monthly °C	27	28	28	28	27	26	25	24	25	26	27	27	26
fall	Monthly Total mm	28	41	99	99	203	300	180	56	180	190	63	25	1464
hine	Av. Monthly Dur.	5.9	6.8	6.3	6.1	5.6	3.8	2.8	3.3	3	5.1	6.6	6.5	5.2
a Peru 120m														
perature	Daily Max.°C	28	29	29	27	24	20	20	19	20	22	24	26	24
	Daily Min.°C	19	20	19	17	16	15	14	14	14	15	16	17	16
	Average Monthly °C	24	24	24	22	20	17	17	16	17	18	20	21	20
all	Monthly Total mm	1	1	1	1	5	5	8	8	8	3	3	1	45
hine	Av. Monthly Dur.	6.3	6.8	6.9	6.7	4	1.4	1.1	1	1.1	2.5	4.1	5	3.9
on Portugal 77m														
erature	Daily Max.°C	14	15	17	20	21	25	27	28	26	22	17	15	21
	Daily Min.°C	8	8	10	12	13	15	17	17	17	14	11	9	13
	Average Monthly °C	11	12	14	16	17	20	22	23	21	18	14	12	17
all	Monthly Total mm	111	76	109	54	44	16	3	4	33	62	93	103	708
hine	Av. Monthly Dur.	4.7	5.9	6	8.3	9.1	10.6	11.4	10.7	8.4	6.7	5.2	4.6	7.7
lon (Kew) United Kingdom 5m														
erature	Daily Max.°C	6	7	10	13	17	20	22	21	19	14	10	7	14
	Daily Min.°C	2	2	3	6	8	12	14	13	11	8	5	4	7
	Average Monthly °C	4	5	7	9	12	16	18	17	15	11	8	5	11
all	Monthly Total mm	54	40	37	37	46	45	57	59	49	57	64	48	593
hine	Av. Monthly Dur.	1.7	2.3	3.5	5.7	6.7	7	6.6	6	5	3.3	1.9	1.4	4.3
Angeles USA 30m														
erature	Daily Max.°C	18	18	18	19	20	22	24	24	24	23	22	19	21
	Daily Min.°C	7	8	9	11	13	15	17	17	16	14	11	9	12
	Average Monthly °C	12	13	14	15	17	18	21	21	20	18	16	14	17
all	Monthly Total mm	69	74	46	28	3	3	0	0	5	10	28	61	327
hine	Av. Monthly Dur.	6.9	8.2	8.9	8.8	9.5	10.3	11.7	11	10.1	8.6	8.2	7.6	9.2
ka Zambia 1154m														
erature	Daily Max.°C	26	26	26	27	25	23	23	26	29	31	29	27	27
	Daily Min.°C	17	17	16	15	12	10	9	11	15	18	18	17	15
	Average Monthly °C	22	22	21	21	18	17	16	19	22	25	23	22	21
ll	Monthly Total mm	224	173	90	19	3	1	0	1	1	17	85	196	810
ine	Av. Monthly Dur.	5.1	5.4	6.9	8.9	9	9	9.1	9.6	9.5	9	7	5.5	7.8
aus Brazil 45m														
erature	Daily Max.°C	31	31	31	31	31	31	32	33	34	34	33	32	32
	Daily Min.°C	24	24	24	24	24	24	24	24	24	25	25	24	24
	Average Monthly °C	28	28	28	27	28	28	28	29	29	29	29	28	28
ll	Monthly Total mm	278	278	300	287	193	99	61	41	62	112	165	220	2096
ine	Av. Monthly Dur.	3.9	4	3.6	3.9	5.4	6.9	7.9	8.2	7.5	6.6	5.9	4.9	5.7
co City Mexico 2309m														
erature	Daily Max.°C	21	23	26	27	26	25	23	24	23	22	21	21	24
	Daily Min.°C	5	6	7	9	10	11	11	11	11	9	6	5	8
	Average Monthly °C	13	15	16	18	18	18	17	17	17	16	14	13	16
ll	Monthly Total mm	8	4	9	23	57	111	160	149	119	46	16	7	709
ine	Av. Monthly Dur.	7.3	8.1	8.5	8.1	7.8	7	6.2	6.4	5.6	6.3	7	7.3	7.1
i USA 2m														
rature	Daily Max.°C	24	25	27	28	30	31	32	32	31	29	27	25	28
	Daily Min.°C	14	15	16	19	21	23	24	24	24	22	18	15	20
	Average Monthly °C	19	20	21	23	25	27	28	28	27	25	22	20	24
l	Monthly Total mm	51	48	58	99	163	188	170	178	241	208	71	43	1518
ine	Av. Monthly Dur.	7.7	8.3	8.7	9.4	8.9	8.5	8.7	8.4	7.1	6.5	7.5	7.1	8.1
real Canada 57m														
rature	Daily Max.°C	-6	-4	2	11	18	23	26	25	20	14	5	-3	11
	Daily Min.°C	-13	-11	-5	2	9	14	17	16	11	6	0	-9	3
	Average Monthly °C	-9	-8	-2	6	13	19	22	20	16	10	3	-6	7
l	Monthly Total mm	87	76	86	83	81	91	98	87	96	84	89	89	1047
ne	Av. Monthly Dur.	2.8	3.4	4.5	5.2	6.7	7.7	8.2	7.7	5.6	4.3	2.4	2.2	5.1
ow Russia 156m														
rature	Daily Max.°C	-6	-4	1	9	18	22	24	22	17	10	1	-5	9
	Daily Min.°C	-14	-16	-11	-1	5	9	12	9	4	-2	-6	-12	-2
	Average Monthly °C	-10	-10	-5	4	12	15	18	16	10	4	-2	-8	4
l	Monthly Total mm	31	28	33	35	52	67	74	74	58	51	36	36	575
ne	Av. Monthly Dur.	1	1.9	3.7	5.2	7.8	8.3	8.4	7.1	4.4	2.4	1	0.6	4.4
Delhi India 220m														
rature	Daily Max.°C	21	24	29	36	41	39	35	34	34	34	28	23	32
	Daily Min.°C	6	10	14	20	26	28	27	26	24	17	11	7	18
	Average Monthly °C	14	17	22	28	33	34	31	30	29	26	20	15	25
	Monthly Total mm	25	21	13	8	13	77	178	184	123	10	2	11	665
ne	Av. Monthly Dur.	7.7	8.2	8.2	8.7	9.2	7.9	6	6.3	6.9	9.4	8.7	8.3	8

		Jan	Feb	Mar	Apr	May	June	July	Aug	Sep	Oct	Nov	Dec	Year
Perth Australia 60m														
Temperature	Daily Max.°C	29	30	27	25	21	18	17	18	19	21	25	27	23
	Daily Min.°C	17	18	16	14	12	10	9	9	10	11	14	16	13
	Average Monthly °C	23	24	22	19	16	14	13	13	15	16	19	22	18
Rainfall	Monthly Total mm	8	13	22	44	128	189	177	145	84	58	19	13	900
Sunshine	Av. Monthly Dur.	10.4	9.8	8.8	7.5	5.7	4.8	5.4	6	7.2	8.1	9.6	10.4	7.8
Reykjavik Iceland 18m														
Temperature	Daily Max.°C	2	3	5	6	10	13	15	14	12	8	5	4	8
	Daily Min.°C	-3	-3	-1	1	4	7	9	8	6	3	0	-2	3
	Average Monthly °C	0	0	2	4	7	10	12	11	9	5	3	1	5
Rainfall	Monthly Total mm	89	64	62	56	42	42	50	56	67	94	78	79	779
Sunshine	Av. Monthly Dur.	0.8	2	3.6	4.5	5.9	6.1	5.8	5.4	3.5	2.3	1.1	0.3	3.7
Santiago Chile 520m														
Temperature	Daily Max.°C	30	29	27	24	19	15	15	17	19	22	26	29	23
	Daily Min.°C	12	11	10	7	5	3	3	4	6	7	9	11	7
	Average Monthly °C	21	20	18	15	12	9	9	10	12	15	17	20	15
Rainfall	Monthly Total mm	3	3	5	13	64	84	76	56	31	15	8	5	363
Sunshine	Av. Monthly Dur.	10.8	8.9	8.5	5.5	3.6	3.3	3.3	3.6	4.8	6.1	8.7	10.1	6.4
Shanghai China 5m														
Temperature	Daily Max.°C	8	8	13	19	24	28	32	32	27	23	17	10	20
	Daily Min.°C	-1	0	4	9	14	19	23	23	19	13	7	2	11
	Average Monthly °C	3	4	8	14	19	23	27	27	23	18	12	6	15
Rainfall	Monthly Total mm	48	59	84	94	94	180	147	142	130	71	51	36	1136
Sunshine	Av. Monthly Dur.	4	3.7	4.4	4.8	5.4	4.7	6.9	7.5	5.3	5.6	4.7	4.5	5.1
Sydney Australia 40m														
Temperature	Daily Max.°C	26	26	25	22	19	17	17	18	20	22	24	25	22
	Daily Min.°C	18	19	17	14	11	9	8	9	11	13	16	17	14
	Average Monthly °C	22	22	21	18	15	13	12	13	16	18	20	21	18
Rainfall	Monthly Total mm	89	101	127	135	127	117	117	76	74	71	74	74	1182
Sunshine	Av. Monthly Dur.	7.5	7	6.4	6.1	5.7	5.3	6.1	7	7.3	7.5	7.5	7.5	6.8
Tehran Iran 1191m														
Temperature	Daily Max.°C	9	11	16	21	29	30	37	36	29	24	16	11	22
	Daily Min.°C	-1	1	4	10	16	20	23	23	18	12	6	1	11
	Average Monthly °C	4	6	10	15	22	25	30	29	23	18	11	6	17
Rainfall	Monthly Total mm	37	23	36	31	14	2	1	1	1	5	29	27	207
Sunshine	Av. Monthly Dur.	5.9	6.7	7.5	7.4	8.6	11.6	11.2	11	10.1	7.6	6.9	6.3	8.4
Timbuktu Mali 269m														
Temperature	Daily Max.°C	31	35	38	41	43	42	38	35	38	40	37	31	37
	Daily Min.°C	13	16	18	22	26	27	25	24	24	23	18	14	21
	Average Monthly °C	22	25	28	31	34	34	32	30	31	31	28	23	29
Rainfall	Monthly Total mm	0	0	0	1	4	20	54	93	31	3	0	0	206
Sunshine	Av. Monthly Dur.	9.1	9.6	9.6	9.7	9.8	9.4	9.6	9	9.3	9.5	9.5	8.9	9.4
Tokyo Japan 5m														
Temperature	Daily Max.°C	9	9	12	18	22	25	29	30	27	20	16	11	19
	Daily Min.°C	-1	-1	3	4	13	17	22	23	19	13	7	1	10
	Average Monthly °C	4	4	8	11	18	21	25	26	23	17	11	6	14
Rainfall	Monthly Total mm	48	73	101	135	131	182	146	147	217	220	101	61	1562
Sunshine	Av. Monthly Dur.	6	5.9	5.7	6	6.2	5	5.8	6.6	4.5	4.4	4.8	5.4	5.5
Tromsø Norway 100m														
Temperature	Daily Max.°C	-2	-2	0	3	7	12	16	14	10	5	2	0	5
	Daily Min.°C	-6	-6	-5	-2	1	6	9	8	5	1	-2	-4	0
	Average Monthly °C	-4	-4	-3	0	4	9	13	11	7	3	0	-2	3
Rainfall	Monthly Total mm	96	79	91	65	61	59	56	80	109	115	88	95	994
Sunshine	Av. Monthly Dur.	0.1	1.6	2.9	6.1	5.7	6.9	7.9	4.8	3.5	1.7	0.3	0	3.52
Ulan Bator Mongolia 1305m														
Temperature	Daily Max.°C	-19	-13	-4	7	13	21	22	21	14	6	-6	-16	4
	Daily Min.°C	-32	-29	-22	-8	-2	7	11	8	2	-8	-20	-28	-11
	Average Monthly °C	-26	-21	-13	-1	6	14	16	14	8	-1	-13	-22	-4
Rainfall	Monthly Total mm	1	1	2	5	10	28	76	51	23	5	5	2	209
Sunshine	Av. Monthly Dur.	6.4	7.8	8	7.8	8.3	8.6	8.6	8.2	7.2	6.9	6.1	5.7	7.5
Vancouver Canada 5m														
Temperature	Daily Max.°C	6	7	10	14	17	20	23	22	19	14	9	7	14
	Daily Min.°C	0	1	3	5	8	11	13	12	10	7	3	2	6
	Average Monthly °C	3	4	6	9	13	16	18	17	14	10	6	4	10
Rainfall	Monthly Total mm	214	161	151	90	69	65	39	44	83	172	198	243	1529
Sunshine	Av. Monthly Dur.	1.6	3	3.8	5.9	7.5	7.4	9.5	8.2	6	3.7	2	1.4	5
Vorkhoyanck Russia 137m														
Temperature	Daily Max.°C	-47	-40	-20	-1	11	21	24	21	12	-8	-33	-42	-8
	Daily Min.°C	-51	-48	-40	-25	-7	4	6	1	-6	-20	-39	-50	-23
	Average Monthly °C	-49	-44	-30	-13	2	12	15	11	3	-14	-36	-46	-16
Rainfall	Monthly Total mm	7	5	5	4	5	25	33	30	13	11	10	7	155
Sunshine	Av. Monthly Dur.	0	2.6	6.9	9.6	9.7	10	9.7	7.5	4.1	2.4	0.6	0	5.4
Washington USA 22m														
Temperature	Daily Max.°C	7	8	12	19	25	29	31	30	26	20	14	8	19
	Daily Min.°C	-1	-1	2	8	13	18	21	20	16	10	4	-1	9
	Average Monthly °C	3	3	7	13	19	24	26	25	21	15	9	4	14
Rainfall	Monthly Total mm	84	68	96	85	103	88	108	120	100	78	75	75	1080
Sunshine	Av. Monthly Dur.	4.4	5.7	6.7	7.4	8.2	8.8	8.6	8.2	7.5	6.5	5.3	4.5	6.8

AGRICULTURAL PRODUCTION

Staple Crops

Wheat

China 18.9% India 12.2% U.S.A. 11.0% France 5.7% Russia 4.6% Canada 4.6%

World total (1996): 584,874,000 tonnes

Rice

China 34.0% India 21.7% Indonesia 9.0% Bangladesh 4.8% Vietnam 4.5% Thailand 4.3% Burma 3.6%

World total (1996): 562,259,000 tonnes

Millet

India 33.2% Nigeria 18.3% China 16.1% Niger 6.4%

World total (1996): 29,563,000 tonnes

Rye

Poland 27.7% Germany 20.0% Russia 18.1% Belarus 9.5% Ukraine 5.3%

World total (1996): 23,156,000 tonnes

Maize

U.S.A. 36.4% China 21.8% Brazil 7.0%

World total (1996): 576,821,000 tonnes

Potatoes

China 16.0% Russia 14.0% Poland 8.7% U.S.A. 7.1% India 6.5% Ukraine 5.2% Germany 3.6%

World total (1996): 294,834,000 tonnes

Soya

U.S.A. 47.1% Brazil 20.4% China 10.7% Argentina 9.6%

World total (1996): 130,302,000 tonnes

Cassava

Nigeria 19.2% Brazil 15.6% Thailand 11.1% Congo (Zaire) 10.7% Indonesia 9.4% Ghana 4.2% India 3.7% Tanzania 3.6%

World total (1996): 162,942,000 tonnes

Animal Products

Milk

U.S.A. 15.2% Russia 8.4% India 6.9% Germany 6.0% France 5.5% Brazil 3.8% Ukraine 3.7%

World total (1996): 466,317,000 tonnes

Butter

India 19.0% U.S.A. 8.9% Germany 7.2% France 6.1% Russia 6.2% Pakistan 5.5% New Zealand 4.6%

World total (1996): 6,565,000 tonnes

Lamb and Mutton

China 15.1% Australia 8.5% N. Zealand 7.9% U.K. 5.2% Turkey 3.8% Iran 3.6% Russia 3.6% Pakistan 3.6%

World total (1996): 7,289,000 tonnes

Beef and Veal

U.S.A. 21.7% Brazil 8.6% China 6.5% Russia 5.3% Argentina 4.6% France 3.6%

World total (1996): 53,956,000 tonnes

Pork

China 45.1% U.S.A. 9.7% Germany 4.3%

World total (1996): 85,761,000 tonnes

Sugars

Sugarcane

Brazil 26.0% India 22.2% China 6.0% Thailand 5.0% Pakistan 4.0% Mexico 3.6%

World total (1996): 1,192,555,000 tonnes

Sugar beet

France 11.5% Ukraine 11.2% Germany 9.8% U.S.A. 9.6% Russia 7.2% China 5.2% Poland 5.0% Italy 5.0% Turkey 4.2%

World total (1996): 255,500,000 tonnes

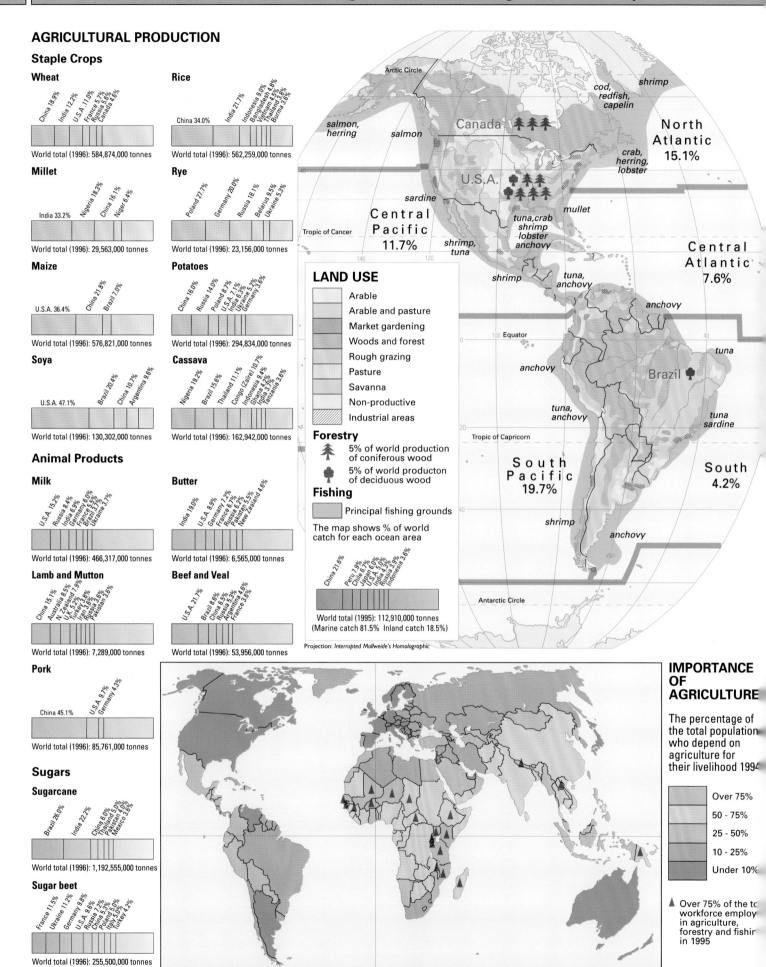

LAND USE

- Arable
- Arable and pasture
- Market gardening
- Woods and forest
- Rough grazing
- Pasture
- Savanna
- Non-productive
- Industrial areas

Forestry

🌲 5% of world production of coniferous wood

🌳 5% of world producton of deciduous wood

Fishing

■ Principal fishing grounds

The map shows % of world catch for each ocean area

China 21.6% Peru 7.9% Chile 6.7% Japan 6.0% U.S.A. 5.0% India 4.3% Russia 3.9% Indonesia 3.6%

World total (1995): 112,910,000 tonnes
(Marine catch 81.5% Inland catch 18.5%)

Projection: *Interrupted Mollweide's Homolographic*

North Atlantic 15.1%
Central Pacific 11.7%
Central Atlantic 7.6%
South Pacific 19.7%
South 4.2%

Projection: *Modified Hammer Equal Area*

IMPORTANCE OF AGRICULTURE

The percentage of the total population who depend on agriculture for their livelihood 1994

- Over 75%
- 50 - 75%
- 25 - 50%
- 10 - 25%
- Under 10%

▲ Over 75% of the total workforce employed in agriculture, forestry and fishing in 1995

1:110 000 000

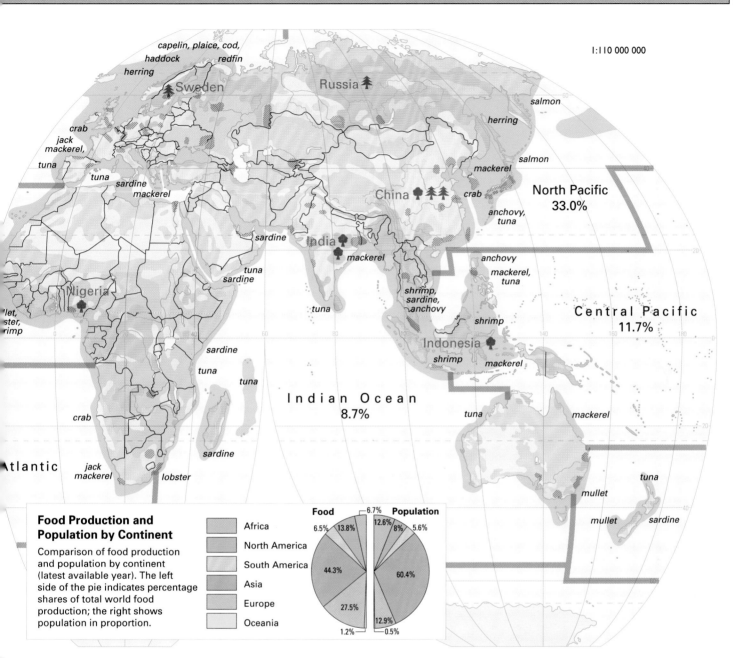

capelin, plaice, cod, haddock, redfin

herring

Sweden

Russia

salmon

crab
jack mackerel,
tuna

herring

tuna

sardine
mackerel

mackerel

salmon

China

crab

anchovy,
tuna

North Pacific
33.0%

sardine

India

mackerel

anchovy
mackerel,
tuna

Nigeria

tuna
sardine

tuna

shrimp,
sardine,
anchovy

shrimp

Central Pacific
11.7%

let,
ster,
rimp

tuna

Indonesia

shrimp

mackerel

sardine

tuna

tuna

Indian Ocean
8.7%

tuna

mackerel

crab

jack
mackerel

lobster

sardine

mullet

tuna

Atlantic

sardine

mullet

sardine

Food Production and Population by Continent

Comparison of food production and population by continent (latest available year). The left side of the pie indicates percentage shares of total world food production; the right shows population in proportion.

Africa
North America
South America
Asia
Europe
Oceania

Food   6.7%   **Population**

6.5%   13.8%   12.6%   8%   5.6%

44.3%   60.4%

27.5%   12.9%

1.2%   0.5%

TRADE IN AGRICULTURAL PRODUCTS

Balance of trade in agricultural products (food and live animals) by value (latest available year)

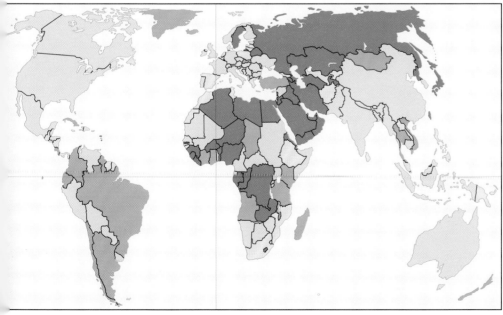

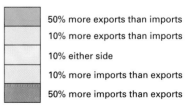

50% more exports than imports
10% more exports than imports
10% either side
10% more imports than exports
50% more imports than exports

CARTOGRAPHY BY PHILIP'S. COPYRIGHT GEORGE PHILIP LTD

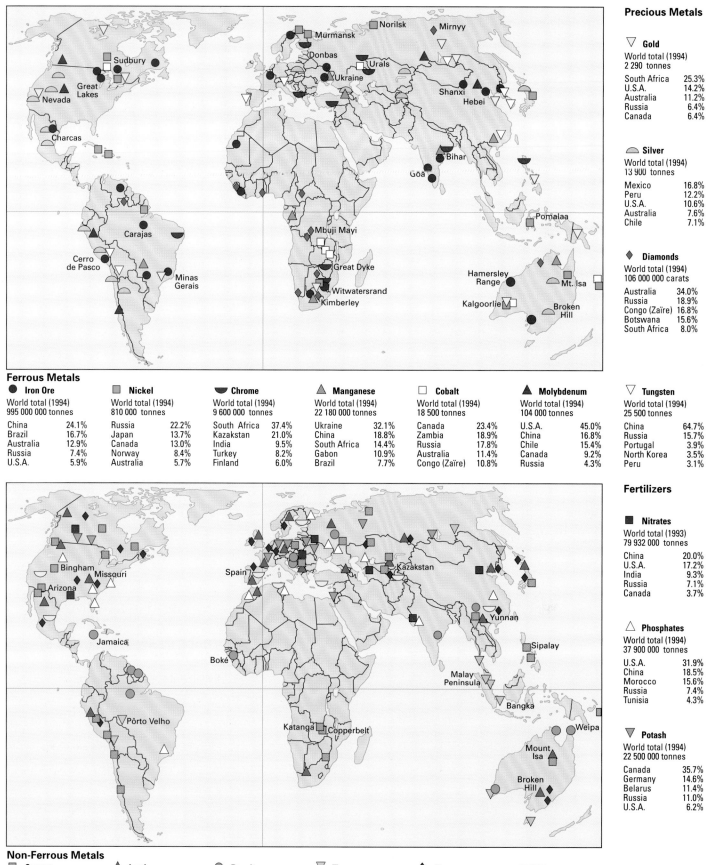

Precious Metals

▽ **Gold**
World total (1994)
2 290 tonnes

South Africa	25.3%
U.S.A.	14.2%
Australia	11.2%
Russia	6.4%
Canada	6.4%

◖ **Silver**
World total (1994)
13 900 tonnes

Mexico	16.8%
Peru	12.2%
U.S.A.	10.6%
Australia	7.6%
Chile	7.1%

◆ **Diamonds**
World total (1994)
106 000 000 carats

Australia	34.0%
Russia	18.9%
Congo (Zaïre)	16.8%
Botswana	15.6%
South Africa	8.0%

Ferrous Metals

● **Iron Ore**	■ **Nickel**	◗ **Chrome**	▲ **Manganese**	☐ **Cobalt**	▲ **Molybdenum**	▽ **Tungsten**
World total (1994)	World total (1994)	World total (1994)	World total (1994)	World total (1994)	World total (1994)	World total (1994)
995 000 000 tonnes	810 000 tonnes	9 600 000 tonnes	22 180 000 tonnes	18 500 tonnes	104 000 tonnes	25 500 tonnes
China 24.1%	Russia 22.2%	South Africa 37.4%	Ukraine 32.1%	Canada 23.4%	U.S.A. 45.0%	China 64.7%
Brazil 16.7%	Japan 13.7%	Kazakstan 21.0%	China 18.8%	Zambia 18.9%	China 16.8%	Russia 15.7%
Australia 12.9%	Canada 13.0%	India 9.5%	South Africa 14.4%	Russia 17.8%	Chile 15.4%	Portugal 3.9%
Russia 7.4%	Norway 8.4%	Turkey 8.2%	Gabon 10.9%	Australia 11.4%	Canada 9.2%	North Korea 3.5%
U.S.A. 5.9%	Australia 5.7%	Finland 6.0%	Brazil 7.7%	Congo (Zaïre) 10.8%	Russia 4.3%	Peru 3.1%

Fertilizers

■ **Nitrates**
World total (1993)
79 932 000 tonnes

China	20.0%
U.S.A.	17.2%
India	9.3%
Russia	7.1%
Canada	3.7%

△ **Phosphates**
World total (1994)
37 900 000 tonnes

U.S.A.	31.9%
China	18.5%
Morocco	15.6%
Russia	7.4%
Tunisia	4.3%

▽ **Potash**
World total (1994)
22 500 000 tonnes

Canada	35.7%
Germany	14.6%
Belarus	11.4%
Russia	11.0%
U.S.A.	6.2%

Non-Ferrous Metals

■ **Copper**	▲ **Lead**	● **Bauxite**	▽ **Tin**	◆ **Zinc**	◗ **Mercury**
World total (1994)	World total (1994)	World total (1994)	World total (1994)	World total (1994)	World total (1994)
9 750 000 tonnes	5 380 000 tonnes	107 000 000 tonnes	199 000 tonnes	7 360 000 tonnes	1 760 tonnes
U.S.A. 17.5%	U.S.A. 23.4%	Australia 39.0%	China 26.6%	China 13.2%	China 28.4%
Chile 13.1%	France 8.3%	Guinea 13.5%	Malaysia 21.1%	Japan 9.7%	Algeria 27.0%
Japan 11.5%	China 7.6%	Brazil 7.6%	Indonesia 15.6%	Canada 9.4%	Spain 17.0%
Russia 6.0%	U.K. 6.4%	India 5.0%	Brazil 15.2%	Germany 4.9%	Kyrgyzstan 11.4%
Canada 5.7%	Germany 6.2%	China 3.5%	Bolivia 7.7%	U.S.A. 4.8%	Finland 5.7%

Projection: *Modified Hammer Equal Area*

CARTOGRAPHY BY PHILIP'S. COPYRIGHT GEORGE PH

ENERGY PRODUCTION

Primary energy production expressed in kilograms of coal equivalent per person 1994

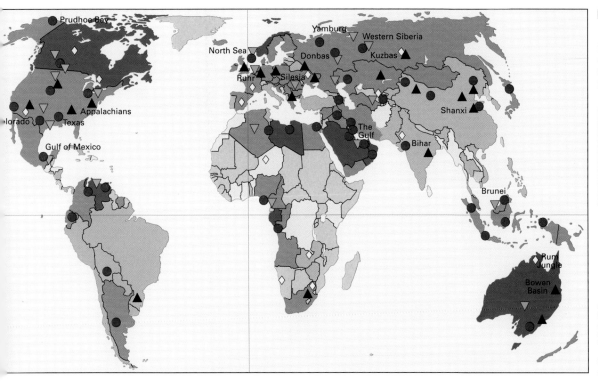

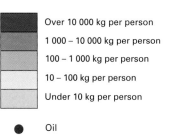

- Over 10 000 kg per person
- 1 000 – 10 000 kg per person
- 100 – 1 000 kg per person
- 10 – 100 kg per person
- Under 10 kg per person

- ● Oil
- ▽ Natural gas
- ▲ Coal and lignite
- ◇ Uranium (the fuel used to generate nuclear power)

In developing countries traditional fuels are still very important. Sometimes called biomass fuels, they include wood, charcoal and dried dung. The pie graph for Nigeria at the foot of the page shows their importance.

Oil		Natural Gas		Coal (bituminous)		Coal (lignite)		Uranium		Nuclear Power		Hydro-Electric Power	
World total (1994) 183 500 000 tonnes		World total (1993) 2 658 000 000 tonnes of coal equivalent		World total (1993) 3 160 000 000 tonnes		World total (1993) 1 265 000 000 tonnes		World total (1993) 32 532 tonnes (metal content)		World total (1994) 820 000 000 tonnes of coal equivalent		World total (1994) 922 000 000 tonnes of coal equivalent	
di Arabia	13.2%	Canada	28.2%	China	36.0%	U.S.A.	23.7%	Canada	28.2%	U.S.A.	31.0%	Canada	12.8%
A.	12.6%	Nigeria	9.0%	U.S.A.	17.6%	Germany	17.5%	Niger	9.0%	France	16.3%	U.S.A.	12.2%
sia	9.9%	Kazakstan	8.3%	India	7.9%	Russia	9.1%	Kazakstan	8.3%	Japan	11.8%	Former U.S.S.R.	10.4%
	5.7%	Uzbekistan	8.0%	Russia	6.3%	China	7.4%	Uzbekistan	8.0%	Former U.S.S.R.	7.9%	Brazil	10.3%
co	4.9%	Russia	7.4%	Australia South Africa}	5.8%	Poland	5.4%	Russia	7.4%	Germany	6.9%	China	6.9%

ENERGY CONSUMPTION

Primary energy consumption expressed in kilograms of coal equivalent per person 1994

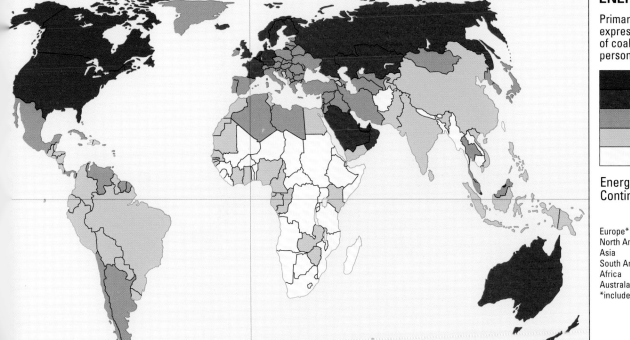

- Over 10 000 kg per person
- 5 000 – 10 000 kg per person
- 1 000 – 5 000 kg per person
- 100 – 1 000 kg per person
- Under 100 kg per person

Energy consumption by Continent 1991

		Change 1990-91
Europe*	38.3%	(-0.2%)
North America	30.0%	(+2.4%)
Asia	25.0%	(+1.9%)
South America	3.0%	(-2.9%)
Africa	2.4%	(-0.4%)
Australasia	1.3%	(no change)

*includes former U.S.S.R.

ion: Modified Hammer Equal Area

- Coal & Lignite
- Oil
- Natural gas
- Hydro-electricity
- Nuclear electricity
- Traditional Fuels

TYPE OF ENERGY CONSUMED BY SELECTED COUNTRIES 1993

NIGERIA   CHINA   JAPAN   FRANCE   USA   NORWAY

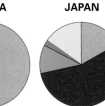
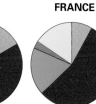

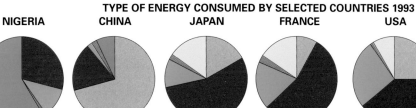

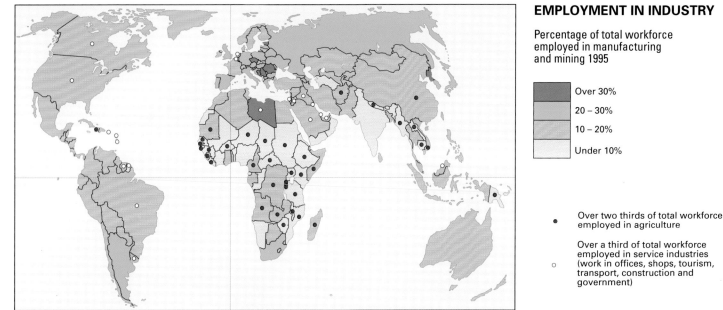

EMPLOYMENT IN INDUSTRY

Percentage of total workforce employed in manufacturing and mining 1995

- Over 30%
- 20 – 30%
- 10 – 20%
- Under 10%

● Over two thirds of total workforce employed in agriculture

○ Over a third of total workforce employed in service industries (work in offices, shops, tourism, transport, construction and government)

INDUSTRIAL PRODUCTION

Industrial output (mining, manufacturing, construction, energy and water production), top 40 nations, US $ billion (1991)

1.	U.S.A.	1,627	21. Saudi Arabia	56
2.	Japan	1,412	22. Indonesia	48
3.	Germany	614	23. Spain	47
4.	Italy	380	24. Argentina	46
5.	France	348	25. Poland	39
6.	U.K.	324	26. Norway	38
7.	Former U.S.S.R.	250	27. Finland	37
8.	Brazil	161	28. Thailand	36
9.	China	155	29. Turkey	33
10.	South Korea	127	30. Denmark	31
11.	Canada	117	31. Israel	23
12.	Australia	93	32. Iran	20
	Netherlands	93	33. Ex- Czechoslovakia	19
14.	Taiwan	86	34. Hong Kong	17
15.	Mexico	85	Portugal (1989)	17
16.	Sweden	70	36. Algeria	16
17.	Switzerland (1989)	61	Greece	16
18.	India	60	38. Iraq	15
19.	Austria	59	Philippines	15
	Belgium	59	Singapore	15

Graphs show the top ten producing countries for selected industrial goods.

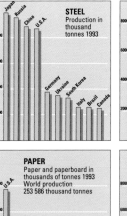

RUBBER Natural and synthetic rubber in thousands of tonnes 1993 World production 13 081 thousand tonnes

Synthetic rubber

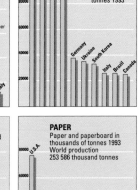

STEEL Production in thousand tonnes 1993

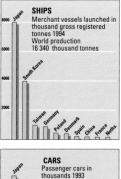

SHIPS Merchant vessels launched in thousand gross registered tonnes 1994 World production 16 340 thousand tonnes

TELEVISION SETS Production in thousands 1992

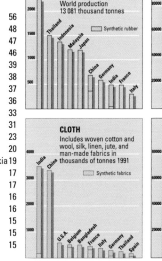

CLOTH Includes woven cotton and wool, silk, linen, jute, and man-made fabrics in thousands of tonnes 1991

Synthetic fabrics

PAPER Paper and paperboard in thousands of tonnes 1993 World production 253 586 thousand tonnes

CARS Passenger cars in thousands 1993

RADIO RECEIVERS Production in thousands 1991

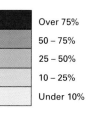

INDUSTRY AND TRADE

Manufactured goods (inc. machinery & transport) as a percentage of total exports (latest available year)

- Over 75%
- 50 – 75%
- 25 – 50%
- 10 – 25%
- Under 10%

The Far East and South-East Asia (Japan 98.3%, Macau 97.8%, Taiwan 92.7%, Hong Kong 93.0%, South Korea 93.4%) are most dominant, but many countries in Europe (e.g. Slovenia 92.4%) are also heavily dependent on manufactured goods.

Projection: *Modified Hammer Equal Area*

CARTOGRAPHY BY PHILIP'S. COPYRIGHT GEORGE PHILIP LTD

DEPENDENCE ON TRADE

Value of exports as a percentage
of G.N.P. (Gross National Product)
1995

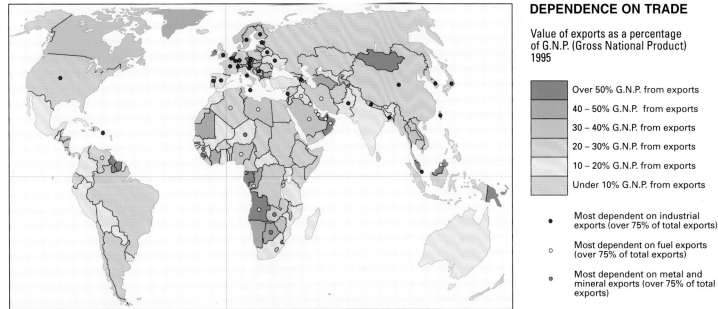

Over 50% G.N.P. from exports

40 – 50% G.N.P. from exports

30 – 40% G.N.P. from exports

20 – 30% G.N.P. from exports

10 – 20% G.N.P. from exports

Under 10% G.N.P. from exports

● Most dependent on industrial
exports (over 75% of total exports)

○ Most dependent on fuel exports
(over 75% of total exports)

◉ Most dependent on metal and
mineral exports (over 75% of total
exports)

BALANCE OF TRADE

Value of exports in proportion to
the value of imports 1995

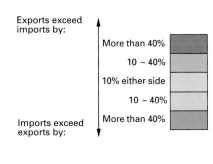

Exports exceed
imports by:

More than 40%

10 – 40%

10% either side

10 – 40%

Imports exceed
exports by:

More than 40%

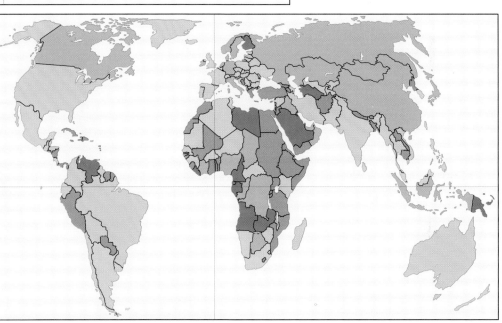

SHARE OF WORLD TRADE

Percentage share of total world
exports by value 1995

Over 10% of world trade

5 – 10% of world trade

1 – 5% of world trade

0.5 – 1% of world trade

0.1 – 0.5% of world trade

Under 0.1% of world trade

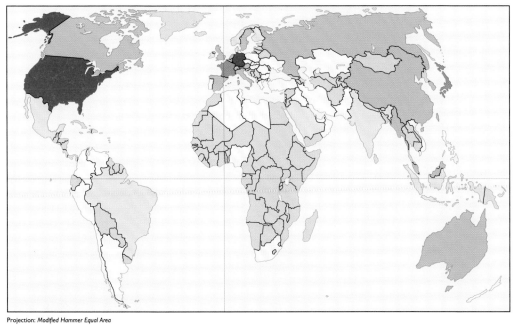

Projection: *Modified Hammer Equal Area*

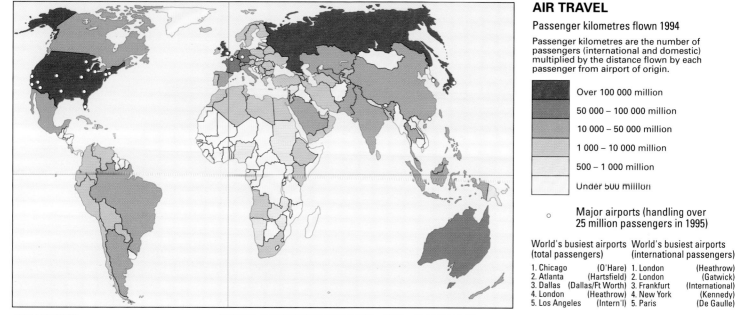

AIR TRAVEL

Passenger kilometres flown 1994

Passenger kilometres are the number of passengers (international and domestic) multiplied by the distance flown by each passenger from airport of origin.

- Over 100 000 million
- 50 000 – 100 000 million
- 10 000 – 50 000 million
- 1 000 – 10 000 million
- 500 – 1 000 million
- Under 500 million

○   Major airports (handling over 25 million passengers in 1995)

World's busiest airports (total passengers)		World's busiest airports (international passengers)	
1. Chicago	(O'Hare)	1. London	(Heathrow)
2. Atlanta	(Hartsfield)	2. London	(Gatwick)
3. Dallas	(Dallas/Ft Worth)	3. Frankfurt	(International)
4. London	(Heathrow)	4. New York	(Kennedy)
5. Los Angeles	(Intern'l)	5. Paris	(De Gaulle)

TOURISM

Tourism receipts as a percentage of G.N.P. (Gross National Product) 1994

- Over 10% of G.N.P from tourism
- 5 – 10% of G.N.P. from tourism
- 2.5 – 5% of G.N.P. from tourism
- 1 – 2.5% of G.N.P. from tourism
- 0.5 – 1% of G.N.P. from tourism
- Under 0.5% of G.N.P. from tourism

Countries spending the most on promoting tourism, millions of US $ (1996)		Fastest growing tourist destinations, % change in receipts (1994–5)	
Australia	88	South Korea	49%
Spain	79	Czech Republic	27%
U.K.	79	India	21%
France	73	Russia	19%
Singapore	54	Philippines	18%

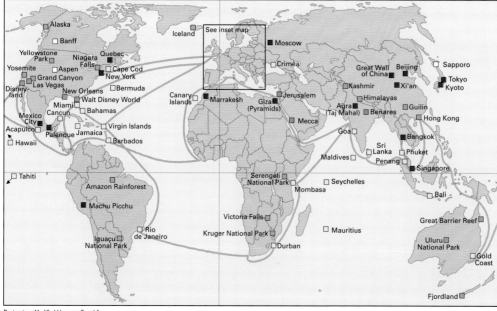

TOURIST DESTINATIONS

- ■ Cultural & historical centres
- □ Coastal resorts
- □ Ski resorts
- ■ Centres of entertainment
- ■ Places of pilgrimage
- ■ Places of great natural beauty
- —— Popular holiday cruise routes

TIME ZONES

Note: Certain of the time zones are affected by the incidence of "Summer Time" in countries where it is adopted.

- Zones using Greenwich Mean Time
- Zones slow of Greenwich Mean Time
- Half hour zones
- Zones fast of Greenwich Mean Time
- International boundaries
- Time zone boundaries
- International date line
- Selected air routes
- 10PM Actual Solar Time when noon at Greenwich is shown along the top of the map.
- 10 Hours slow or fast of Greenwich Mean Time

Equatorial scale: 1:220 000 000

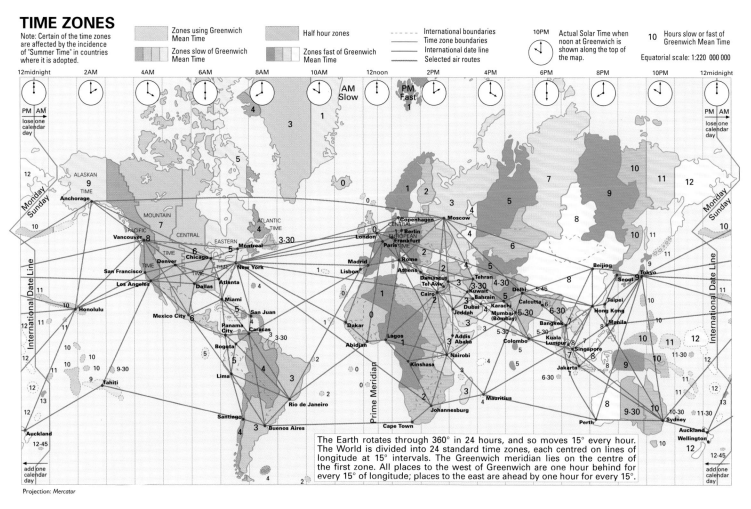

The Earth rotates through 360° in 24 hours, and so moves 15° every hour. The World is divided into 24 standard time zones, each centred on lines of longitude at 15° intervals. The Greenwich meridian lies on the centre of the first zone. All places to the west of Greenwich are one hour behind for every 15° of longitude; places to the east are ahead by one hour for every 15°.

Projection: *Mercator*

DISTANCE TABLE

The table shows air distances in miles and kilometres between twenty-four major cities. Known as 'Great Circle' distances, these measure the shortest routes between cities, which aircraft use where possible.

Kms (lower-left) / Miles (upper-right)

	Beijing	Bogota	Buenos Aires	Cairo	Calcutta	Caracas	Chicago	Hong Kong	Honolulu	Johannesburg	Lagos	London	Los Angeles	Mexico City	Moscow	Nairobi	New York	Paris	Rio de Janeiro	Rome	Singapore	Sydney	Tokyo	Wellington
Beijing	Beijing	9263	11972	4688	2031	8947	6588	1220	5070	7276	7119	5057	6251	7742	3600	5727	6828	5106	10773	5049	2783	5561	1304	6700
Bogota	14908	Bogota	2911	6971	10223	637	2710	10480	5697	7125	5319	5262	3478	1961	6758	7672	2481	5358	2820	5831	11990	8903	8851	7527
Buenos Aires	19268	4685	Buenos Aires	7341	10268	3167	5599	11481	7558	5025	4919	6917	6122	4591	8374	6463	5298	6867	1214	6929	9867	7332	11410	6202
Cairo	7544	11218	11814	Cairo	3541	6340	6127	5064	8838	3894	2432	2180	7580	7687	1803	2197	5605	1994	6149	1325	5137	8959	5947	10268
Calcutta	3269	16453	16524	5699	Calcutta	9609	7978	1653	7048	5256	5727	4946	8152	9494	3438	3839	7921	4883	9366	4486	1800	5678	3195	7055
Caracas	14399	1026	5096	10203	15464	Caracas	2502	10166	6009	6847	4810	4664	3612	2228	6175	7173	2131	4738	2825	5196	11407	9534	8801	8154
Chicago	10603	4361	9011	9860	12839	4027	Chicago	7783	4247	8689	5973	3949	1742	1694	4971	8005	711	4132	5311	4809	9369	9243	6299	8358
Hong Kong	1963	16865	18478	8150	2659	16360	12526	Hong Kong	5543	6669	7360	5980	7232	8775	4439	5453	8047	5984	11001	5769	1615	4582	1786	5857
Honolulu	8160	9169	12164	14223	11343	9670	6836	8921	Honolulu	11934	10133	7228	2558	3781	7036	10739	4958	7437	8290	8026	6721	5075	3854	4669
Johannesburg	11710	11467	8088	6267	8459	11019	13984	10732	19206	Johannesburg	2799	5637	10362	9063	5692	1818	7979	5426	4420	4811	5381	6860	8418	7308
Lagos	11457	8561	7916	3915	9216	7741	9612	11845	16308	4505	Lagos	3118	7713	6879	3886	2366	5268	2929	3750	2510	6925	9643	8376	9973
London	8138	8468	11131	3508	7961	7507	6356	9623	11632	9071	5017	London	5442	5552	1552	4237	3463	212	5778	889	6743	10558	5942	11691
Los Angeles	10060	5596	9852	12200	13120	5812	2804	11639	4117	16676	12414	8758	Los Angeles	1549	6070	9659	2446	5645	6310	6331	8776	7502	5475	6719
Mexico City	12460	3156	7389	12372	15280	3586	2726	14122	6085	14585	11071	8936	2493	Mexico City	6664	9207	2090	5717	4780	6365	10321	8058	7024	6897
Moscow	5794	10877	13477	2902	5534	9938	8000	7144	11323	9161	6254	2498	9769	10724	Moscow	3942	4666	1545	7184	1477	5237	9008	4651	10283
Nairobi	9216	12347	10402	3536	6179	11544	12883	8776	17282	2927	3807	6819	15544	14818	6344	Nairobi	7358	4029	5548	3350	4635	7552	6996	8490
New York	10988	3000	0520	9020	12747	3430	1145	12950	7980	12841	8477	5572	3936	3264	7510	11842	New York	3626	4832	4280	9531	9935	6741	8951
Paris	8217	8622	11051	3210	7858	7625	6650	9630	11968	8732	4714	342	9085	9200	2486	6485	5836	Paris	5708	687	6671	10539	6038	11798
Rio de Janeiro	17338	4539	1953	9896	15073	4546	8547	17704	13342	7113	6035	9299	10155	7693	11562	8928	7777	9187	Rio de Janeiro	5725	9763	8389	11551	7367
Rome	8126	9383	11151	2133	7219	8363	7739	9284	12916	7743	4039	1431	10188	10243	2376	5391	6888	1105	9214	Rome	6229	10143	6127	11523
Singapore	4478	19296	15879	8267	2897	18359	15078	2599	10816	8660	11145	10852	14123	16610	8428	7460	15339	10737	15712	10025	Singapore	3915	3306	5298
Sydney	8949	14327	11800	14418	9138	15343	14875	7374	8168	11040	15519	16992	12073	12969	14497	12153	15989	16962	13501	16324	6300	Sydney	4861	1383
Tokyo	2099	14245	18362	9571	5141	14164	10137	2874	6202	13547	13480	9562	8811	11304	7485	11260	10849	9718	18589	9861	5321	7823	Tokyo	5762
Wellington	10782	12113	9981	16524	11354	13122	13451	9427	7513	11761	16050	18814	10814	11100	16549	13664	14405	18987	11855	18545	8526	2226	9273	Wellington

CARTOGRAPHY BY PHILIP'S.

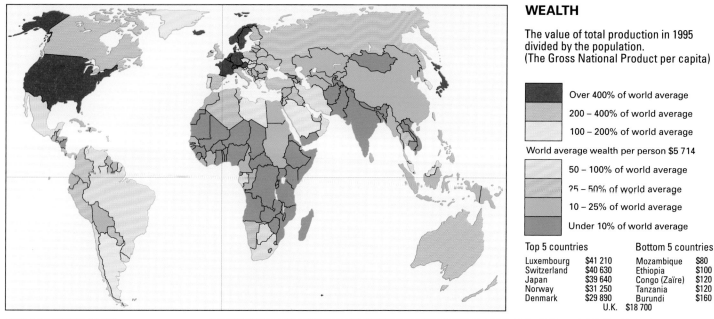

WEALTH

The value of total production in 1995 divided by the population. (The Gross National Product per capita)

Over 400% of world average

200 – 400% of world average

100 – 200% of world average

World average wealth per person $5 714

50 – 100% of world average

25 – 50% of world average

10 – 25% of world average

Under 10% of world average

Top 5 countries		Bottom 5 countries	
Luxembourg	$41 210	Mozambique	$80
Switzerland	$40 630	Ethiopia	$100
Japan	$39 640	Congo (Zaïre)	$120
Norway	$31 250	Tanzania	$120
Denmark	$29 890	Burundi	$160
		U.K.	$18 700

CAR OWNERSHIP

Number of people per car (latest available year)

Over 1000 people per car

500 – 1000 people per car

100 – 500 people per car

25 – 100 people per car

5 – 25 people per car

Under 5 people per car

Most people per car		Most cars (millions)	
Nepal	4247	U.S.A.	143.8
Bangladesh	2618	Germany	39.1
Cambodia	2328	Japan	39.0
Somalia	1790	Italy	29.6
Ethiopia	1423	France	24.0

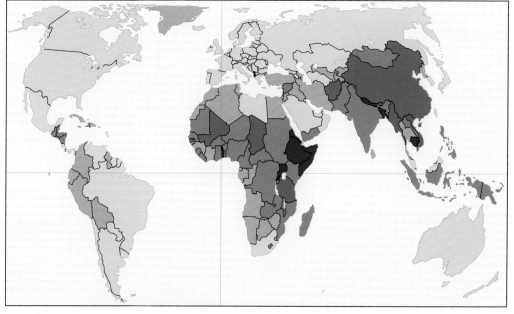

HUMAN DEVELOPMENT INDEX

The Human Development Index (H.D.I.) 1994 includes social and economic indicators and is calculated by the U.N. Development Programme as a measure of national human progress. Wealthy developed countries measure highest on the index.

H.D.I. over 0.900

H.D.I. 0.700 – 0.899

H.D.I. 0.500 – 0.699

H.D.I. 0.300 – 0.499

H.D.I. under 0.299

H.D.I. not available

Top 5 countries		Bottom 5 countries	
Canada	0.960	Mali	0.229
France	0.946	Burkina Faso	0.221
Norway	0.943	Niger	0.206
U.S.A.	0.942	Rwanda	0.187
Iceland	0.942	Sierra Leone	0.176
		U.K.	0.931

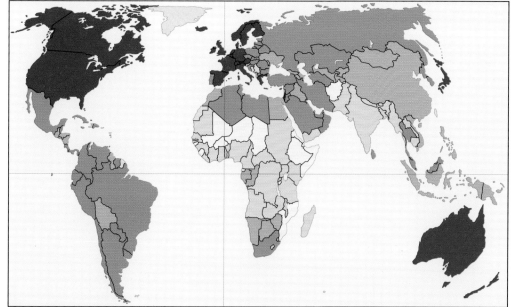

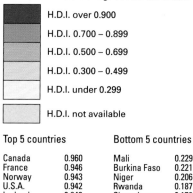

Projection: *Modified Hammer Equal Area*

HEALTH CARE

Number of people per doctor 1993

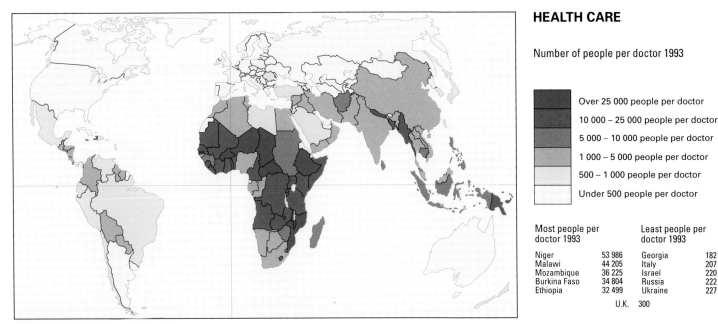

- Over 25 000 people per doctor
- 10 000 – 25 000 people per doctor
- 5 000 – 10 000 people per doctor
- 1 000 – 5 000 people per doctor
- 500 – 1 000 people per doctor
- Under 500 people per doctor

Most people per doctor 1993		Least people per doctor 1993	
Niger	53 986	Georgia	182
Malawi	44 205	Italy	207
Mozambique	36 225	Israel	220
Burkina Faso	34 804	Russia	222
Ethiopia	32 499	Ukraine	227
		U.K.	300

ILLITERACY & EDUCATION

Percentage of total population unable to read or write 1995

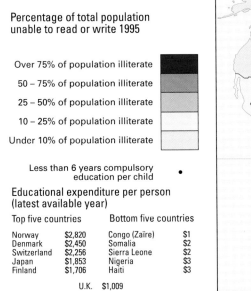

- Over 75% of population illiterate
- 50 – 75% of population illiterate
- 25 – 50% of population illiterate
- 10 – 25% of population illiterate
- Under 10% of population illiterate

• Less than 6 years compulsory education per child

Educational expenditure per person (latest available year)

Top five countries		Bottom five countries	
Norway	$2,820	Congo (Zaïre)	$1
Denmark	$2,450	Somalia	$2
Switzerland	$2,256	Sierra Leone	$2
Japan	$1,853	Nigeria	$3
Finland	$1,706	Haiti	$3
U.K.	$1,009		

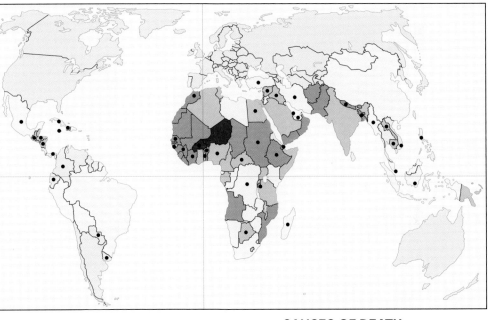

FERTILITY & EDUCATION
Fertility rates compared with female education, selected countries (1992–1995)

Fertility rate: average number of children borne per woman

Percentage of females aged 12 – 17 in secondary education

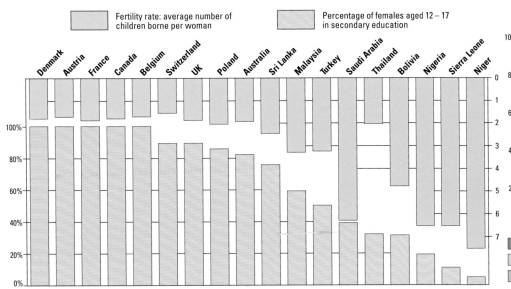

Denmark, Austria, France, Canada, Belgium, Switzerland, UK, Poland, Australia, Sri Lanka, Malaysia, Turkey, Saudi Arabia, Thailand, Bolivia, Nigeria, Sierra Leone, Niger

CAUSES OF DEATH

Causes of death for selected countries by percentage (1992–1994)

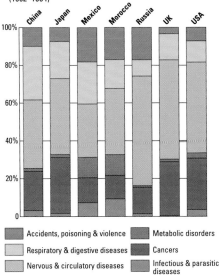

China, Japan, Mexico, Morocco, Russia, UK, USA

- Accidents, poisoning & violence
- Metabolic disorders
- Respiratory & digestive diseases
- Cancers
- Nervous & circulatory diseases
- Infectious & parasitic diseases

AGE DISTRIBUTION PYRAMIDS

The bars represent the percentage of the total population (males plus females) in the age group shown.

Developed countries such as the U.K. have populations evenly spread across age groups and usually a growing percentage of elderly people. Developing countries such as Kenya have the great majority of their people in the younger age groups, about to enter their most fertile years.

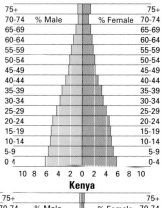
World

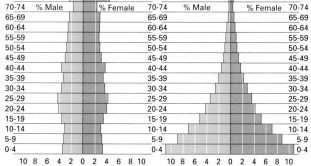
U.K. — **Kenya**

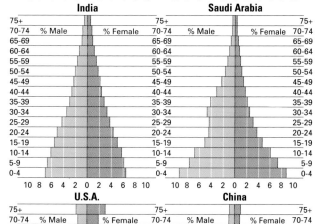
India — **Saudi Arabia**

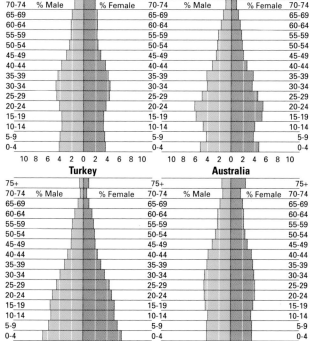
U.S.A. — **China**

Turkey — **Australia**

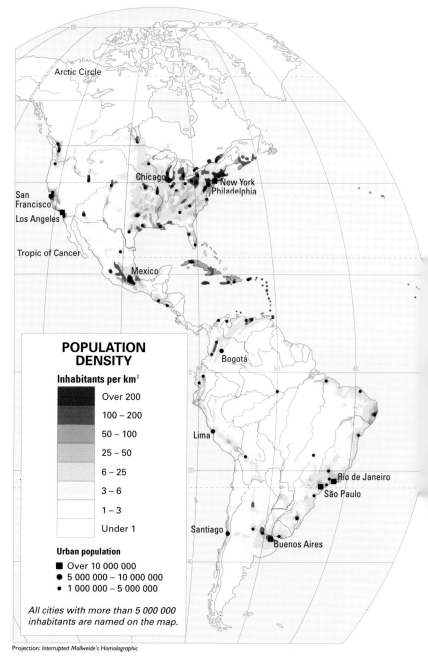

POPULATION DENSITY

Inhabitants per km²

- Over 200
- 100 – 200
- 50 – 100
- 25 – 50
- 6 – 25
- 3 – 6
- 1 – 3
- Under 1

Urban population

- ■ Over 10 000 000
- ● 5 000 000 – 10 000 000
- • 1 000 000 – 5 000 000

All cities with more than 5 000 000 inhabitants are named on the map.

Projection: *Interrupted Mollweide's Homolographic*

POPULATION CHANGE 1930-2020

Population totals are in millions

Figures in italics represent the percentage average annual increase for the period show

	1930	1930-1960	1960	1960-1990	1990	1990-2020	2020
World	2013	*1.4%*	3019	*1.9%*	5292	*1.4%*	8062
Africa	155	*2.0%*	281	*2.85*	648	*2.7%*	1441
North America	135	*1.3%*	199	*1.1%*	276	*0.6%*	327
Latin America*	129	*1.8%*	218	*2.4%*	448	*1.6%*	719
Asia	1073	*1.5%*	1669	*2.1%*	3108	*1.4%*	4680
Europe	355	*0.6%*	425	*0.55*	498	*0.1%*	514
Oceania	10	*1.4%*	16	*1.75*	27	*1.1%*	37
C.I.S.†	176	*0.7%*	214	*1.0%*	288	*0.6%*	343

* *South America plus Central America, Mexico, and the West Indies*
† *Commonwealth of Independent States, formerly the U.S.S.R.*

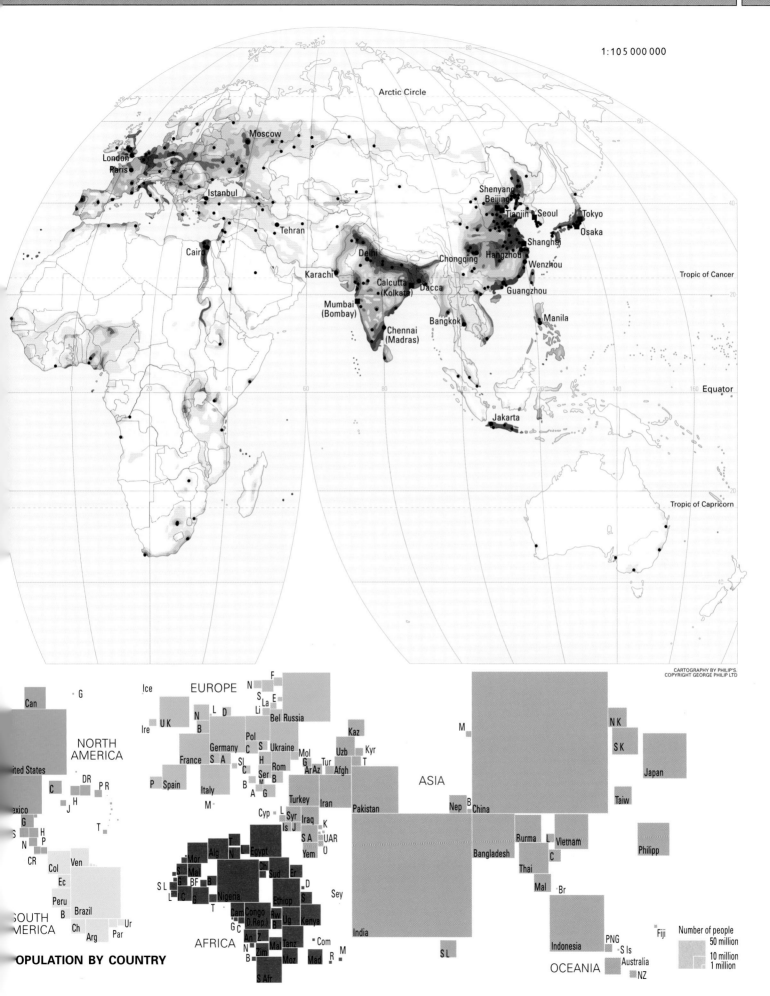

1:105 000 000

Arctic Circle

Moscow

London
Paris

Istanbul

Tehran

Cair

Karachi

Delhi

Calcutta
(Kolkata)

Dacca

Chongqing

Hangzhou

Shenyang
Beijing

Tianjin

Seoul

Tokyo

Osaka

Shanghai

Wenzhou

Guangzhou

Mumbai
(Bombay)

Chennai
(Madras)

Bangkok

Manila

Tropic of Cancer

Equator

Jakarta

Tropic of Capricorn

CARTOGRAPHY BY PHILIP'S.
COPYRIGHT GEORGE PHILIP LTD

EUROPE

Ice

G

Can

NORTH
AMERICA

N

Ire

UK

B

F

S
La

E

Li

L
N

D

Bel

Russia

Kaz

M

N K

S K

Japan

United States

C

DR

P R

Pol

S

Ukraine

Uzb

Kyr

H

J

Germany

France

S A

C

H

Ser

Mol

Ar

Az

Tur

Afgh

ASIA

China

Taiw

P

Spain

Italy

Sl

B

M

C

G

B

Turkey

Iran

Pakistan

Nep

B

Mexico

S

G

H

N

P

Cyp

L

Syr

Iraq

Is

J

S A

UAR

K

U

Philipp

CR

Col

Ven

Yem

Burma

L

Vietnam

Ec

Mor

Alg

F

N

Egypt

Ch

Sud

Er

Thai

C

Peru

S L

L

Mal

BF

C

B

Nigeria

G

B

D

Ethiop

S

Sey

Bangladesh

Mal

Br

SOUTH
AMERICA

B

Brazil

Ch

Arg

Par

Ur

T

Cam

Congo
(D.Rep.)

G C

An

Z

Rw

B

Ug

Kenya

Com

M

India

Indonesia

PNG

S Is

Fiji

AFRICA

Mal

Tanz

B

Zim

Moz

Mad

R

S L

OCEANIA

Australia

NZ

POPULATION BY COUNTRY

Number of people
50 million
10 million
1 million

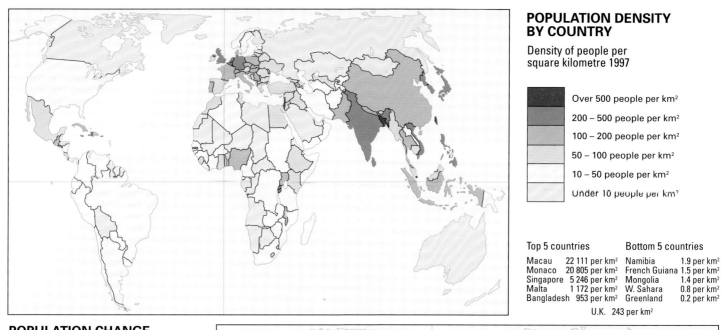

POPULATION DENSITY BY COUNTRY

Density of people per square kilometre 1997

- Over 500 people per km²
- 200 – 500 people per km²
- 100 – 200 people per km²
- 50 – 100 people per km²
- 10 – 50 people per km²
- Under 10 people per km²

Top 5 countries		Bottom 5 countries	
Macau	22 111 per km²	Namibia	1.9 per km²
Monaco	20 805 per km²	French Guiana	1.5 per km²
Singapore	5 246 per km²	Mongolia	1.4 per km²
Malta	1 172 per km²	W. Sahara	0.8 per km²
Bangladesh	953 per km²	Greenland	0.2 per km²
		U.K.	243 per km²

POPULATION CHANGE 1990-2000

The predicted population change for the years 1990-2000

- Over 40% population gain
- 30 – 40% population gain
- 20 – 30% population gain
- 10 – 20% population gain
- 0 – 10% population gain
- No change or population loss

Top 5 countries		Bottom 5 countries	
Kuwait	+75.9%	Belgium	-0.1%
Namibia	+62.5%	Hungary	-0.2%
Afghanistan	+60.1%	Grenada	-2.4%
Mali	+55.5%	Germany	-3.2%
Tanzania	+54.6%	Tonga	-3.2%
		U.K.	+2.0%

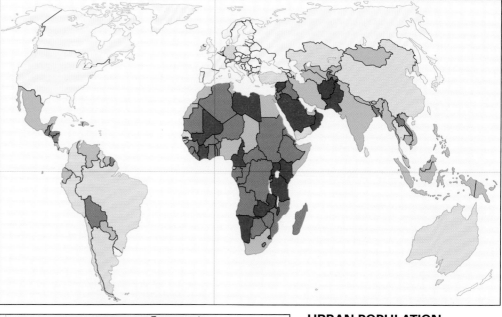

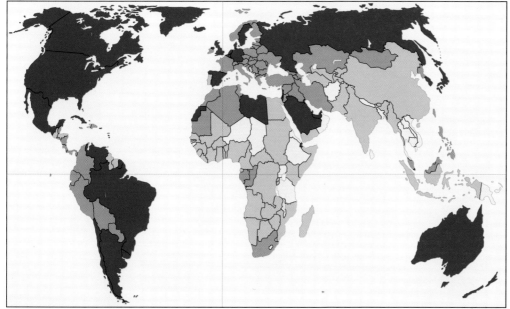

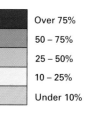

URBAN POPULATION

Percentage of total population living in towns and cities 1995

- Over 75%
- 50 – 75%
- 25 – 50%
- 10 – 25%
- Under 10%

Most urbanized		Least urbanized	
Singapore	100%	Bhutan	6%
Belgium	97%	Rwanda	6%
Kuwait	97%	Burundi	7%
Iceland	92%	Uganda	12%
Venezuela	92%	Malawi	13%
		U.K.	89%

Projection: *Modified Hammer Equal Area*

CHILD MORTALITY

The number of babies who died
under the age of one
(average 1990–95)

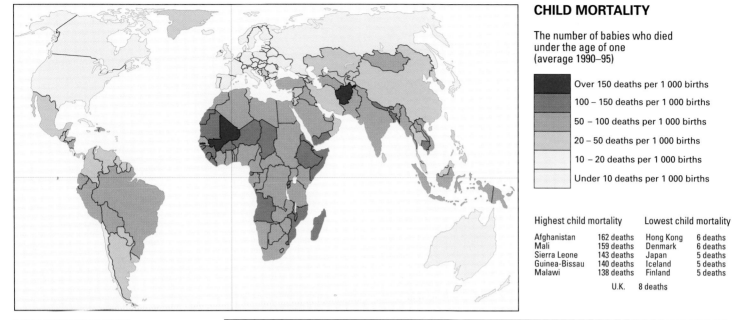

Over 150 deaths per 1 000 births

100 – 150 deaths per 1 000 births

50 – 100 deaths per 1 000 births

20 – 50 deaths per 1 000 births

10 – 20 deaths per 1 000 births

Under 10 deaths per 1 000 births

Highest child mortality		Lowest child mortality	
Afghanistan	162 deaths	Hong Kong	6 deaths
Mali	159 deaths	Denmark	6 deaths
Sierra Leone	143 deaths	Japan	5 deaths
Guinea-Bissau	140 deaths	Iceland	5 deaths
Malawi	138 deaths	Finland	5 deaths
	U.K.	8 deaths	

LIFE EXPECTANCY

Average expected lifespan
of babies born in 1997

Over 75 years

70 – 75 years

65 – 70 years

60 – 65 years

55 – 60 years

50 – 55 years

Under 50 years

Highest life expectancy		Lowest life expectancy	
Iceland	81 years	Tanzania	42 years
Japan	80 years	Niger	41 years
Australia	80 years	Uganda	40 years
Canada	79 years	Rwanda	39 years
Luxembourg	79 years	Malawi	35 years
	U.K.	77 years	

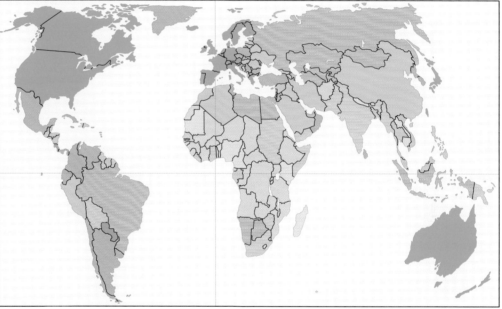

FAMILY SIZE

The average number of children a woman
can expect to bear during her lifetime 1995

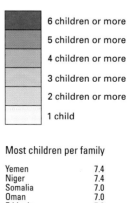

6 children or more

5 children or more

4 children or more

3 children or more

2 children or more

1 child

Most children per family

Yemen	7.4
Niger	7.4
Somalia	7.0
Oman	7.0
Ethiopia	7.0
U.K.	1.7

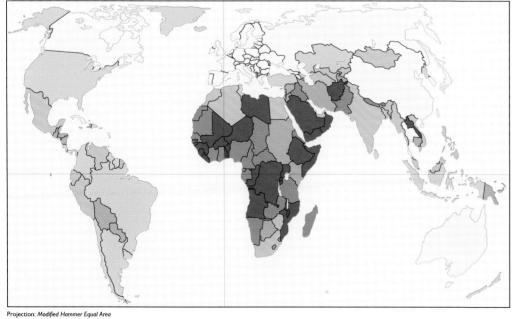

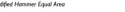

Projection: *Modified Hammer Equal Area*

CARTOGRAPHY BY PHILIP'S. COPYRIGHT GEORGE PHILIP LTD

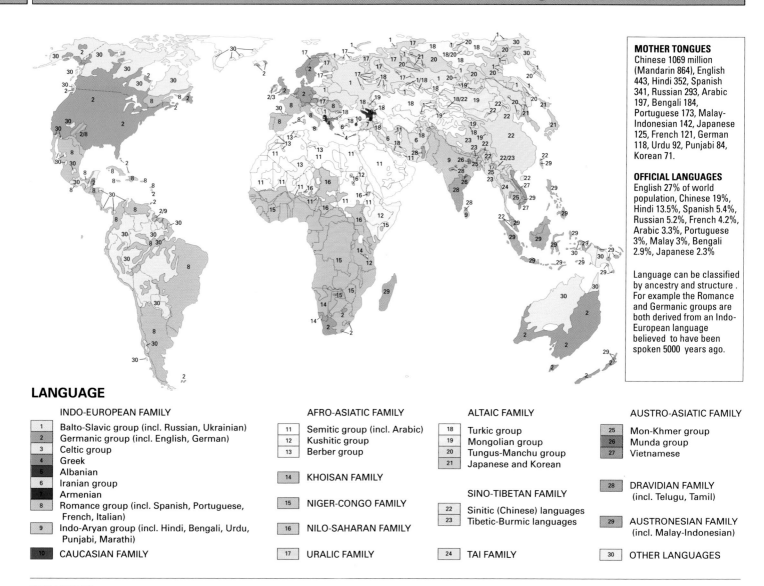

MOTHER TONGUES
Chinese 1069 million (Mandarin 864), English 443, Hindi 352, Spanish 341, Russian 293, Arabic 197, Bengali 184, Portuguese 173, Malay-Indonesian 142, Japanese 125, French 121, German 118, Urdu 92, Punjabi 84, Korean 71.

OFFICIAL LANGUAGES
English 27% of world population, Chinese 19%, Hindi 13.5%, Spanish 5.4%, Russian 5.2%, French 4.2%, Arabic 3.3%, Portuguese 3%, Malay 3%, Bengali 2.9%, Japanese 2.3%

Language can be classified by ancestry and structure. For example the Romance and Germanic groups are both derived from an Indo-European language believed to have been spoken 5000 years ago.

LANGUAGE

INDO-EUROPEAN FAMILY
1	Balto-Slavic group (incl. Russian, Ukrainian)
2	Germanic group (incl. English, German)
3	Celtic group
4	Greek
5	Albanian
6	Iranian group
7	Armenian
8	Romance group (incl. Spanish, Portuguese, French, Italian)
9	Indo-Aryan group (incl. Hindi, Bengali, Urdu, Punjabi, Marathi)
10	CAUCASIAN FAMILY

AFRO-ASIATIC FAMILY
11	Semitic group (incl. Arabic)
12	Kushitic group
13	Berber group
14	KHOISAN FAMILY
15	NIGER-CONGO FAMILY
16	NILO-SAHARAN FAMILY
17	URALIC FAMILY

ALTAIC FAMILY
18	Turkic group
19	Mongolian group
20	Tungus-Manchu group
21	Japanese and Korean

SINO-TIBETAN FAMILY
22	Sinitic (Chinese) languages
23	Tibetic-Burmic languages
24	TAI FAMILY

AUSTRO-ASIATIC FAMILY
25	Mon-Khmer group
26	Munda group
27	Vietnamese
28	DRAVIDIAN FAMILY (incl. Telugu, Tamil)
29	AUSTRONESIAN FAMILY (incl. Malay-Indonesian)
30	OTHER LANGUAGES

RELIGION

- ▲ Roman Catholicism
- Orthodox and other Eastern Churches
- • Protestantism
- Sunni Islam
- Shia Islam
- Buddhism
- Hinduism
- Confucianism
- ✶ Judaism
- Shintoism
- Primitive Religions

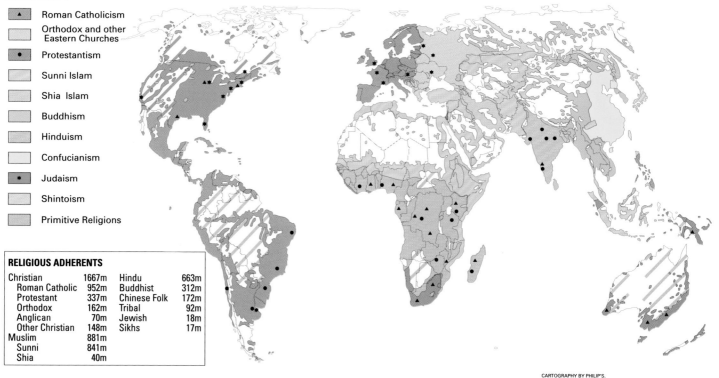

RELIGIOUS ADHERENTS

Christian	1667m	Hindu	663m
Roman Catholic	952m	Buddhist	312m
Protestant	337m	Chinese Folk	172m
Orthodox	162m	Tribal	92m
Anglican	70m	Jewish	18m
Other Christian	148m	Sikhs	17m
Muslim	881m		
Sunni	841m		
Shia	40m		

CARTOGRAPHY BY PHILIP'S.

UNITED NATIONS

Created in 1945 to promote peace and co-operation and based in New York, the United Nations is the world's largest international organization, with 185 members and an annual budget of US $2.6 billion (1996–97). Each member of the General Assembly has one vote, while the permanent members of the 15-nation Security Council – USA, Russia, China, UK and France – hold a veto. The Secretariat is the UN's principal administrative arm. The 54 members of the Economic and Social Council are responsible for economic, social, cultural, educational, health and related matters. The UN has 16 specialized agencies – based in Canada, France, Switzerland and Italy, as well as the USA – which help members in fields such as education (UNESCO), agriculture (FAO), medicine (WHO) and finance (IFC). By the end of 1994, all the original 11 trust territories of The Trusteeship Council had become independent.

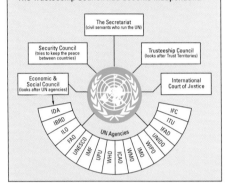

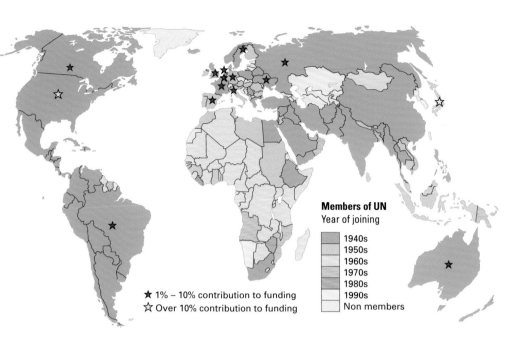

Members of UN
Year of joining

- 1940s
- 1950s
- 1960s
- 1970s
- 1980s
- 1990s
- Non members

★ 1% – 10% contribution to funding
☆ Over 10% contribution to funding

MEMBERSHIP OF THE UN In 1945 there were 51 members; by December 1994 membership had increased to 185 following the admission of Palau. There are 7 independent states which are not members of the UN – Kiribati, Nauru, Switzerland, Taiwan, Tonga, Tuvalu and the Vatican City. All the successor states of the former USSR had joined by the end of 1992. The official languages of the UN are Chinese, English, French, Russian, Spanish and Arabic.
FUNDING The UN budget for 1996–97 was US $2.6 billion. Contributions are assessed by the members' ability to pay, with the maximum 25% of the total, the minimum 0.01%. Contributions for 1996 were: USA 25.0%, Japan 15.4%, Germany 9.0%, France 6.4%, UK 5.3%, Italy 5.2%, Russia 4.5%, Canada 3.1%, Spain 2.4%, Brazil 1.6%, Netherlands 1.6%, Australia 1.5%, Sweden 1.2%, Ukraine 1.1%, Belgium 1.0%.

INTERNATIONAL ORGANIZATIONS

EU European Union (evolved from the European Community in 1993). The 15 members - Austria, Belgium, Denmark, Finland, France, Germany, Greece, Ireland, Italy, Luxembourg, Netherlands, Portugal, Spain, Sweden and the UK - aim to integrate economies, co-ordinate social developments and bring about political union. These members of what is now the world's biggest market share agricultural and industrial policies and tariffs on trade. The original body, the European Coal and Steel Community (ECSC), was created in 1951 following the signing of the Treaty of Paris.
EFTA European Free Trade Association (formed in 1960). Portugal left the original 'Seven' in 1989 to join what was then the EC, followed by Austria, Finland and Sweden in 1995. Only 4 members remain: Norway, Iceland, Switzerland and Liechtenstein.
ACP African-Caribbean-Pacific (formed in 1963). Members have economic ties with the EU.
NATO North Atlantic Treaty Organization (formed in 1949). It continues after 1991 despite the winding up of the Warsaw Pact. There are 19 member nations.
OAS Organization of American States (formed in 1948). It aims to promote social and economic co-operation between developed countries of North America and developing nations of Latin America.
ASEAN Association of South-east Asian Nations (formed in l967). Burma and Laos joined inJuly l997.
OAU Organization of African Unity (formed in 1963). Its 53 members represent over 94% of Africa's population. Arabic, French, Portuguese and English are recognized as working languages.
LAIA Latin American Integration Association (1980). Its aim is to promote freer regional trade.
OECD Organization for Economic Co-operation and Development (formed in 1961). It comprises the 29 major Western free-market economies. 'G7' is its' inner group' comprising the USA, Canada, Japan, UK, Germany, Italy and France. Russia attended the G7 summit in June 1997 ('Summit of the Eight').
COMMONWEALTH The Commonwealth of Nations evolved from the British Empire; it comprises 16 Queen's realms, 32 republics and 5 indigenous monarchies, giving a total of 53.
OPEC Organization of Petroleum Exporting Countries (formed in 1960). It controls about three-quarters of the world's oil supply. Gabon left the organization in 1996.

OAS | EFTA | EU | OAU | COLOMBO PLAN

ARAB LEAGUE (formed in 1945). The League's aim is to promote economic, social, political and military co-operation. There are 21 member nations.
COLOMBO PLAN (formed in 1951). Its 26 members aim to promote economic and social development in Asia and the Pacific.

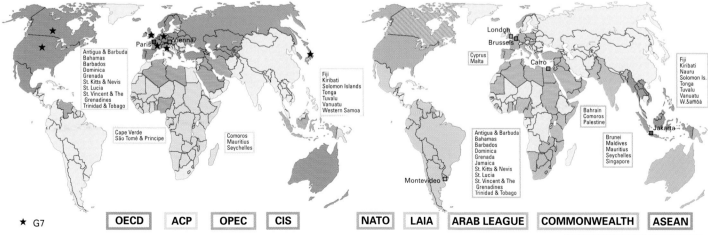

★ G7

OECD | ACP | OPEC | CIS

NATO | LAIA | ARAB LEAGUE | COMMONWEALTH | ASEAN

CARTOGRAPHY BY PHILIP'S. COPYRIGHT GEORGE PHILIP LTD

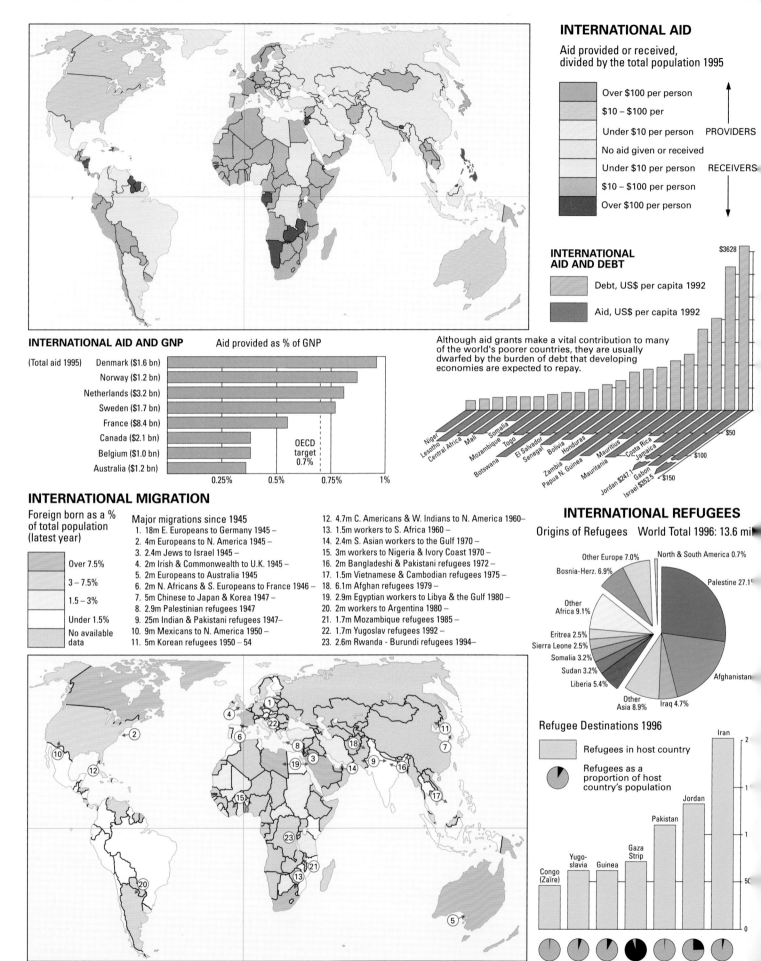

INTERNATIONAL AID

Aid provided or received,
divided by the total population 1995

- Over $100 per person
- $10 – $100 per — PROVIDERS
- Under $10 per person
- No aid given or received
- Under $10 per person — RECEIVERS
- $10 – $100 per person
- Over $100 per person

INTERNATIONAL AID AND DEBT

- Debt, US$ per capita 1992
- Aid, US$ per capita 1992

Although aid grants make a vital contribution to many of the world's poorer countries, they are usually dwarfed by the burden of debt that developing economies are expected to repay.

$3628

Niger, Lesotho, Central Africa, Mali, Somalia, Mozambique, Togo, Botswana, El Salvador, Senegal, Bolivia, Honduras, Zambia, Papua N. Guinea, Mauritius, Mauritania, Costa Rica, Jamaica, Jordan $247.1, Gabon, Israel $352.5

$50, $100, $150

INTERNATIONAL AID AND GNP

Aid provided as % of GNP

(Total aid 1995)

- Denmark ($1.6 bn)
- Norway ($1.2 bn)
- Netherlands ($3.2 bn)
- Sweden ($1.7 bn)
- France ($8.4 bn)
- Canada ($2.1 bn)
- Belgium ($1.0 bn)
- Australia ($1.2 bn)

OECD target 0.7%

0.25%   0.5%   0.75%   1%

INTERNATIONAL MIGRATION

Foreign born as a %
of total population
(latest year)

- Over 7.5%
- 3 – 7.5%
- 1.5 – 3%
- Under 1.5%
- No available data

Major migrations since 1945
1. 18m E. Europeans to Germany 1945 –
2. 4m Europeans to N. America 1945 –
3. 2.4m Jews to Israel 1945 –
4. 2m Irish & Commonwealth to U.K. 1945 –
5. 2m Europeans to Australia 1945
6. 2m N. Africans & S. Europeans to France 1946 –
7. 5m Chinese to Japan & Korea 1947 –
8. 2.9m Palestinian refugees 1947
9. 25m Indian & Pakistani refugees 1947–
10. 9m Mexicans to N. America 1950 –
11. 5m Korean refugees 1950 – 54

12. 4.7m C. Americans & W. Indians to N. America 1960–
13. 1.5m workers to S. Africa 1960 –
14. 2.4m S. Asian workers to the Gulf 1970 –
15. 3m workers to Nigeria & Ivory Coast 1970 –
16. 2m Bangladeshi & Pakistani refugees 1972 –
17. 1.5m Vietnamese & Cambodian refugees 1975 –
18. 6.1m Afghan refugees 1979 –
19. 2.9m Egyptian workers to Libya & the Gulf 1980 –
20. 2m workers to Argentina 1980 –
21. 1.7m Mozambique refugees 1985 –
22. 1.7m Yugoslav refugees 1992 –
23. 2.6m Rwanda - Burundi refugees 1994–

INTERNATIONAL REFUGEES

Origins of Refugees   World Total 1996: 13.6 mi

- Other Europe 7.0%
- Bosnia-Herz. 6.9%
- Other Africa 9.1%
- Eritrea 2.5%
- Sierra Leone 2.5%
- Somalia 3.2%
- Sudan 3.2%
- Liberia 5.4%
- Other Asia 8.9%
- North & South America 0.7%
- Palestine 27.1%
- Afghanistan
- Iraq 4.7%

Refugee Destinations 1996

- Refugees in host country
- Refugees as a proportion of host country's population

Iran, Jordan, Pakistan, Gaza Strip, Guinea, Yugoslavia, Congo (Zaïre)

Projection: *Modified Hammer Equal Area*

HOUSING

Number of people per household
(latest available year)

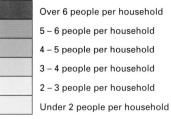

- Over 6 people per household
- 5 – 6 people per household
- 4 – 5 people per household
- 3 – 4 people per household
- 2 – 3 people per household
- Under 2 people per household

Expenditure on housing and energy as a percentage of total consumer spending

▲ Over 20% spent

△ Under 5% spent

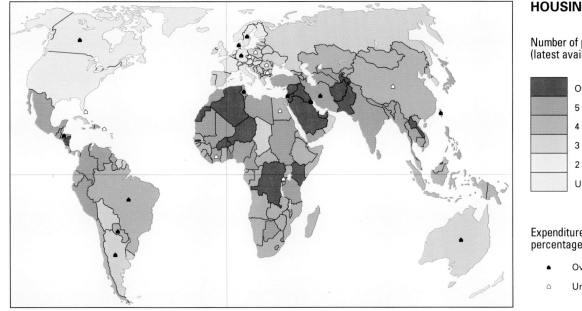

WATER SUPPLY

Percentage of total population with access to safe drinking water (average 1990 – 1996)

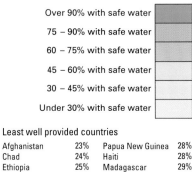

- Over 90% with safe water
- 75 – 90% with safe water
- 60 – 75% with safe water
- 45 – 60% with safe water
- 30 – 45% with safe water
- Under 30% with safe water

Least well provided countries

Afghanistan	23%	Papua New Guinea	28%
Chad	24%	Haiti	28%
Ethiopia	25%	Madagascar	29%

Average daily domestic water consumption per person

△ Under 80 litres   ▲ Over 320 litres

80 litres of water a day is considered necessary for a reasonable quality of life

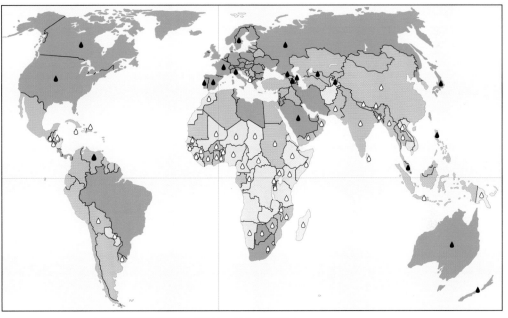

DAILY FOOD CONSUMPTION

Average daily food intake in calories per person 1992

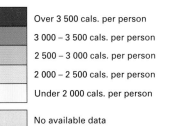

- Over 3 500 cals. per person
- 3 000 – 3 500 cals. per person
- 2 500 – 3 000 cals. per person
- 2 000 – 2 500 cals. per person
- Under 2 000 cals. per person
- No available data

Top 5 countries		Bottom 5 countries	
Ireland	3 847	Mozambique	1 680
Greece	3 815	Liberia	1 640
Cyprus	3 779	Ethiopia	1 610
U.S.A.	3 732	Afghanistan	1 523
Spain	3 708	Somalia	1 499

U.K.   3 317

Malnutrition in children under 5 years

■ Over 50% of children

▪ 25 – 50% of children

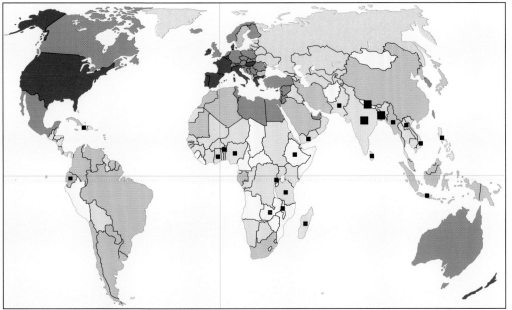

Projection: *Modified Hammer Equal Area*

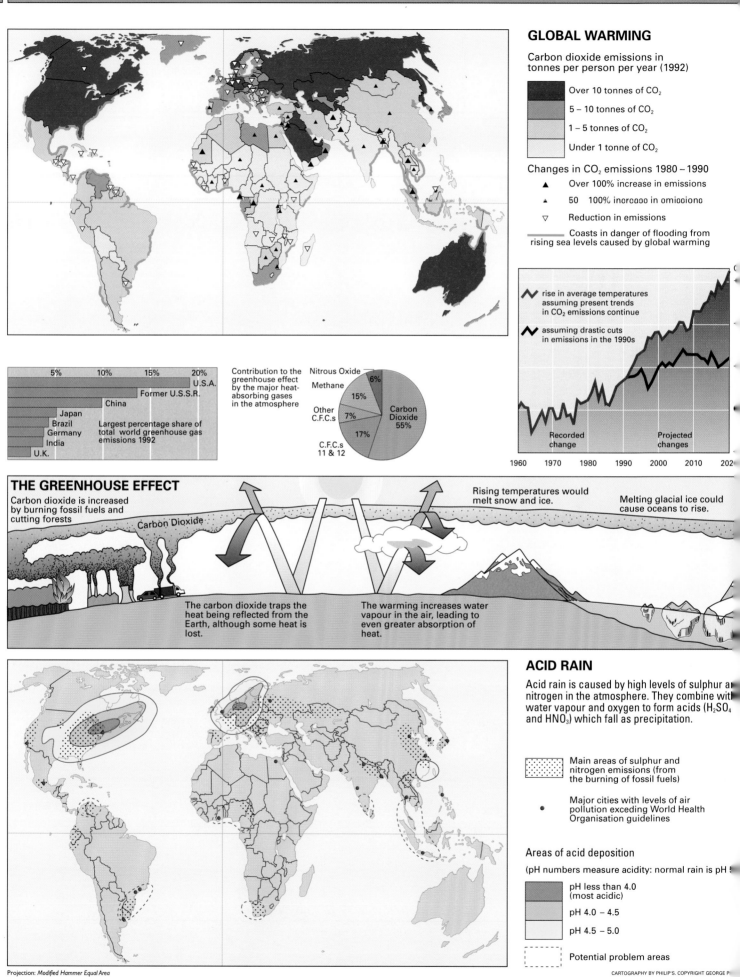

GLOBAL WARMING

Carbon dioxide emissions in tonnes per person per year (1992)

Over 10 tonnes of CO_2

5 – 10 tonnes of CO_2

1 – 5 tonnes of CO_2

Under 1 tonne of CO_2

Changes in CO_2 emissions 1980 – 1990

▲   Over 100% increase in emissions

▴   50 – 100% increase in emissions

▽   Reduction in emissions

——   Coasts in danger of flooding from rising sea levels caused by global warming

rise in average temperatures assuming present trends in CO_2 emissions continue

assuming drastic cuts in emissions in the 1990s

Recorded change   Projected changes

1960   1970   1980   1990   2000   2010   202

5%   10%   15%   20%

U.S.A.

Former U.S.S.R.

China

Japan

Brazil

Germany   Largest percentage share of total world greenhouse gas emissions 1992

India

U.K.

Contribution to the greenhouse effect by the major heat-absorbing gases in the atmosphere

Nitrous Oxide 6%

Methane 15%

Other C.F.C.s 7%

Carbon Dioxide 55%

C.F.C.s 11 & 12 17%

THE GREENHOUSE EFFECT

Carbon dioxide is increased by burning fossil fuels and cutting forests

Carbon Dioxide

Rising temperatures would melt snow and ice.

Melting glacial ice could cause oceans to rise.

The carbon dioxide traps the heat being reflected from the Earth, although some heat is lost.

The warming increases water vapour in the air, leading to even greater absorption of heat.

ACID RAIN

Acid rain is caused by high levels of sulphur an nitrogen in the atmosphere. They combine wit water vapour and oxygen to form acids (H_2SO_4 and HNO_3) which fall as precipitation.

Main areas of sulphur and nitrogen emissions (from the burning of fossil fuels)

•   Major cities with levels of air pollution exceeding World Health Organisation guidelines

Areas of acid deposition

(pH numbers measure acidity: normal rain is pH 5

pH less than 4.0 (most acidic)

pH 4.0 – 4.5

pH 4.5 – 5.0

Potential problem areas

Projection: *Modified Hammer Equal Area*

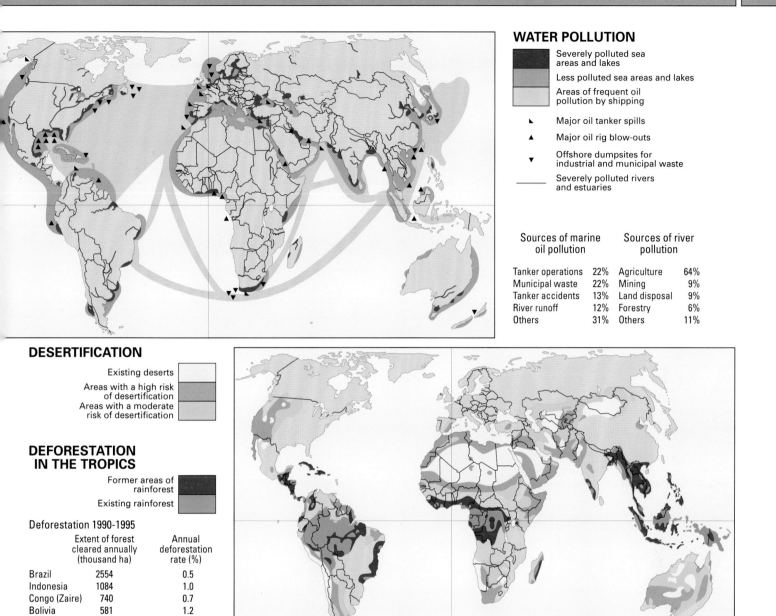

WATER POLLUTION

- Severely polluted sea areas and lakes
- Less polluted sea areas and lakes
- Areas of frequent oil pollution by shipping

- ◤ Major oil tanker spills
- ▲ Major oil rig blow-outs
- ▼ Offshore dumpsites for industrial and municipal waste
- ─── Severely polluted rivers and estuaries

Sources of marine oil pollution		Sources of river pollution	
Tanker operations	22%	Agriculture	64%
Municipal waste	22%	Mining	9%
Tanker accidents	13%	Land disposal	9%
River runoff	12%	Forestry	6%
Others	31%	Others	11%

DESERTIFICATION

- Existing deserts
- Areas with a high risk of desertification
- Areas with a moderate risk of desertification

DEFORESTATION IN THE TROPICS

- Former areas of rainforest
- Existing rainforest

Deforestation 1990-1995

	Extent of forest cleared annually (thousand ha)	Annual deforestation rate (%)
Brazil	2554	0.5
Indonesia	1084	1.0
Congo (Zaire)	740	0.7
Bolivia	581	1.2
Mexico	508	0.9
Venezuela	503	1.1
Malaysia	400	2.4

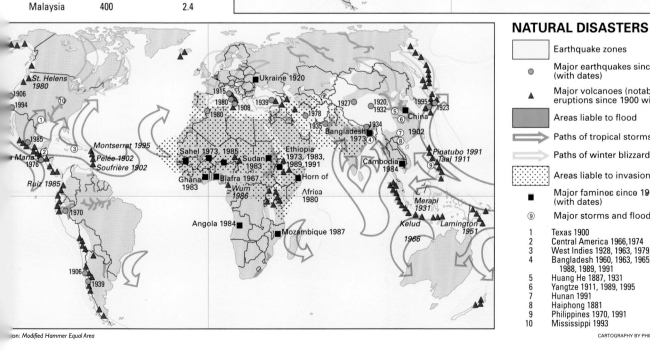

NATURAL DISASTERS

- Earthquake zones
- ● Major earthquakes since 1900 (with dates)
- ▲ Major volcanoes (notable eruptions since 1900 with dates)
- Areas liable to flood
- ⇒ Paths of tropical storms
- ⇒ Paths of winter blizzards
- Areas liable to invasion by locusts
- ■ Major famines since 1900 (with dates)
- ⑨ Major storms and floods

1 Texas 1900
2 Central America 1966, 1974
3 West Indies 1928, 1963, 1979, 1988
4 Bangladesh 1960, 1963, 1965, 1970, 1985, 1988, 1989, 1991
5 Huang He 1887, 1931
6 Yangtze 1911, 1989, 1995
7 Hunan 1991
8 Haiphong 1881
9 Philippines 1970, 1991
10 Mississippi 1993

Projection: Modified Hammer Equal Area

CARTOGRAPHY BY PHILIP'S. COPYRIGHT GEORGE PHILIP LTD

	Population									Land and Agriculture					Energy	Trade	
	Population Total 1997	Population Density 1997	Average Annual Change 1970-80	Average Annual Change 1990-97	Birth Rate 1997	Death Rate 1997	Fertility Rate 1995	Life Expectancy Average 1997	Urban Population 1995	Land Area	Arable and Permanent Crops	Permanent grassland	Forest	Agriculture Population 1995	Consumption per capita 1994	Imports per capita 1995	Exports per capita 1995
	millions	persons per km²	%	%	births per thousand population	deaths per thousand population	children	years	%	thousand km²	% of land area	% of land area	% of land area	% of economically active pop.	tonnes of coal	US $	US $
Afghanistan	23	35	1.7	4.8	43	18	6.9	46	20	652	12	46	3	69	0.04	19	6
Albania	3.6	131	2.3	1.5	22	8	2.6	68	37	27.4	26	15	38	54	0.3	178	42
Algeria	29.3	12	3.1	2.3	28	6	3.5	69	56	2382	3	13	2	24	1.58	375	375
Angola	11.2	9	3.3	1.6	44	17	6.9	47	32	1247	3	43	18	74	0.08	198	309
Argentina	35.4	13	1.7	1.3	20	8	2.7	74	88	2737	10	52	19	11	2.15	579	603
Armenia	3.8	134	2	1.9	17	8	1.8	69	69	28.4	20	54	15	15	0.61	105	603
Australia	18.4	2	1.6	1.2	14	7	1.9	80	86	7644	6	54	19	5	7.61	3342	2942
Austria	8.2	99	0.1	1.1	11	10	1.5	77	65	82.7	18	24	39	7	4.16	8253	7166
Azerbaijan	7.7	89	1.8	1	22	9	2.3	65	56	86.1	23	52	11	30	2.6	105	86
Bahamas	0.3	28	2.1	1.5	18	6	2	73	85	10	1	0	32	5	2.97	4439	5418
Bangladesh	124	953	2.8	1	30	11	3.5	56	18	130	74	5	15	62	0.09	55	27
Barbados	0.3	616	0.4	0.6	15	8	1.8	75	46	0.43	37	5	12	6	1.58	2946	915
Belarus	10.5	51	0.7	0.3	11	13	1.4	69	69	208	31	14	34	18	3.38	297	243
Belgium	10.2	335	0.2	0.5	12	10	1.6	77	97	30.5	24	21	21	3	6.86	14702	16078
Benin	5.8	52	2.5	2.9	46	13	6	53	36	111	17	4	31	60	0.05	125	34
Bolivia	7.7	7	2.6	2.4	32	10	4.5	60	62	1084	2	24	53	45	0.49	192	149
Bosnia-Herzegovina	3.6	70	1	-2.7	6	7	1	60	41	51.2	16	24	39	10	0.36	204	12
Botswana	1.5	3	3.8	2.2	33	7	4.4	62	31	567	1	45	47	39	...	1153	1302
Brazil	159.5	19	2.4	1.4	20	9	2.4	62	78	8457	6	22	58	19	3.26	345	298
Bulgaria	8.6	77	0.4	-0.7	8	14	1.2	71	71	111	38	16	35	11	3.26	598	606
Burkina Faso	10.9	40	2.3	2.8	46	20	6.7	42	27	274	13	22	50	92	0.05	54	53
Burma	47.5	72	2.4	1.9	30	11	3.4	57	27	658	15	1	49	72	0.08	30	19
Burundi	6.3	243	1.6	0.5	42	15	6.5	49	7	25.7	46	39	13	91	0.02	39	18
Cambodia	10.5	59	-0.8	3.5	43	15	4.7	50	21	177	22	8	69	73	0.02	43	24
Cameroon	13.8	30	2.7	2.6	42	14	5.7	52	45	465	15	4	77	68	0.14	94	154
Canada	30.2	3	1.2	1.9	13	7	1.7	79	77	9221	5	3	54	3	11.21	5676	6491
Central African Rep.	3.4	5	2.3	1.8	40	18	5.1	45	39	623	3	5	75	79	0.04	54	52
Chad	6.8	5	2.1	2.5	44	17	5.9	48	22	1259	3	36	26	81	0.01	67	77
Chile	14.7	20	1.6	1.6	18	6	2.3	75	85	749	6	18	22	17	1.45	1121	1130
China	1210	130	1.8	1.2	17	7	1.9	70	29	9326	10	43	14	71	0.92	106	122
Colombia	35.9	35	2.3	1.2	21	5	2.8	73	73	1039	5	39	48	24	1	395	288
Congo	2.7	8	2.8	2.9	39	17	6	46	59	342	0	29	58	45	0.34	259	325
Congo (Zaïre)	47.2	21	2.9	4.1	48	17	6	47	29	2267	3	7	77	66	0.06	8	9
Costa Rica	3.5	69	2.8	2.2	23	4	2.8	76	50	51.1	10	46	31	22	0.87	977	811
Croatia	4.9	86	0.4	0.2	10	11	1.5	73	55	56.4	22	20	38	15	1.59	1586	969
Cuba	11.3	102	1.3	0.8	13	7	1.7	75	75	110	31	27	24	16	1.14	258	146
Cyprus	0.8	83	0.2	1.4	15	8	2.2	77	68	9.24	15	0	13	10	3.03	4986	1661
Czech Rep.	10.5	136	0.5	0.3	11	11	1.3	74	65	77	44	12	34	11	4.97	2450	2099
Denmark	5.4	126	0.4	0.3	12	10	1.8	78	86	42.4	56	7	10	4	5.15	8266	9378
Dominican Rep.	8.2	168	2.6	1.8	23	6	2.9	69	62	48.4	31	43	12	21	0.65	376	97
Ecuador	11.8	43	3	1.6	25	5	3.2	72	59	277	11	18	56	29	0.77	366	376
Egypt	63	63	2.1	2.6	28	9	3.4	62	45	995	4	0	0	33	0.66	199	58
El Salvador	6	287	2.3	1.8	27	6	3.7	69	52	20.7	35	29	5	32	0.5	504	176
Estonia	1.5	34	0.8	-1.1	12	14	1.3	68	73	43.2	27	7	48	14	4.9	1714	1240
Ethiopia	58.5	53	2.4	3.5	46	18	7	47	13	1101	11	20	13	86	0.03	19	7
Finland	5.2	17	0.4	0.6	11	11	1.8	76	63	305	9	0	76	7	7.4	5502	7744
France	58.8	107	0.6	0.7	13	9	1.7	79	74	550	35	19	27	4	5.15	4763	4941
Gabon	1.2	5	4.8	1.5	28	13	5.2	56	73	258	2	18	77	45	0.87	667	2055
Gambia, The	1.2	120	3.3	4.9	44	19	5.3	53	26	10	17	19	10	80	0.1	192	32
Georgia	5.5	78	0.8	0	14	9	1.9	68	58	69.7	16	24	33	25	0.85	39	22
Germany	82.3	236	0.1	0.5	9	11	1.2	76	87	349	34	15	31	3	5.48	5445	6227
Ghana	18.1	80	2.2	2.7	34	11	5.1	57	36	228	19	37	42	56	0.14	129	74
Greece	10.6	82	0.9	0.8	10	10	1.4	78	65	129	27	41	20	20	3.22	2056	899
Guatemala	11.3	104	2.8	2.9	33	7	4.7	66	42	108	18	24	54	51	0.29	310	203
Guinea	7.5	30	1.4	3.8	42	18	6.5	46	30	246	3	44	27	85	0.08	116	97
Guinea-Bissau	1.2	41	4.2	2.6	39	16	6	49	22	28.1	12	38	38	84	0.1	66	22
Guyana	0.8	4	0.7	-0.8	19	10	2.4	59	35	197	3	6	84	20	0.6	594	558
Haiti	7.4	269	1.7	1.8	33	15	4.4	50	32	27.6	33	18	5	66	0.04	91	16
Honduras	6.3	56	3.4	3	33	6	4.6	69	48	112	18	14	54	33	0.31	205	178
Hungary	10.2	110	0.4	-0.6	11	15	1.6	69	64	92.3	54	12	19	14	3.27	1472	1217
Iceland	0.3	3	1.1	1.2	17	6	2.1	81	92	100	0	23	1	10	6.7	6500	6678
India	980	330	2.2	2.5	25	9	3.2	60	27	2973	57	4	23	62	0.37	37	33
Indonesia	203.5	112	2.3	1.8	23	8	2.7	62	33	1812	17	7	62	53	0.47	211	234
Iran	69.5	42	3.2	3.5	33	6	4.5	68	58	1636	11	27	7	36	1.88	537	348
Iraq	22.5	51	3.6	2.5	43	6	5.4	67	73	437	12	9	4	12	1.76	278	383

Wealth							Social Indicators								Aid	
GNP 1995	GNP per capita 1995	Real GDP per capita 1995	Average Annual growth of Real GNP per capita 1985-95	GDP share Agriculture 1995	GDP share Industry 1995	GDP share services 1995	HDI Human Development Index 1994	Food Intake	Population per doctor 1993	% of GNP spent on health 1990-95	% of GNP spent on education 1993-94	%o GNP spent on military 1995	Adult Illiteracy		given (*) and received per capita 1994	
million US $	US $	US $	%	%	%	%		calories per day	persons	%	%	%	Female %	Male %	US $	
5000	300	800	-6	52	32	16	...	1523	7000	...	...	9.1	85	53	10	Afghanistan
2199	670	2750	-7	56	21	23	0.655	2605	735	2.7	3	2.8	0	0	21	Albania
44609	1600	5300	-2.6	13	47	40	0.737	2897	1062	4.6	5.6	2.5	51	26	11	Algeria
4422	410	1310	-6.1	12	59	29	0.335	1839	23725	4	...	4.8	71	44	40	Angola
278431	8030	8310	1.9	6	31	63	0.884	2880	330	10.6	3.8	1.7	4	4	7	Argentina
2752	730	2260	-15.1	44	35	21	0.651	...	261	7.8	7.3	4.4	2	1	27	Armenia
337909	18720	18940	1.4	3	28	69	0.931	3179	500	8.4	6	2.5	...	...	*62	Australia
216547	26890	21250	1.9	2	34	64	0.932	3497	231	9.7	5.5	1	0	0	*82	Austria
3601	480	1460	-16.3	27	32	41	0.636	...	257	7.5	5.5	5	4	1	3	Azerbaijan
3297	11940	14710	-1	3	9	88	0.894	2624	700	...	3.9	0.6	2	1	15	Bahamas
28599	240	1380	2.1	31	18	51	0.368	2019	12884	2.4	2.3	1.8	74	51	11	Bangladesh
1745	6560	10620	-0.2	5	17	78	0.907	3207	1000	5	7.5	0.7	3	2	...	Barbados
21356	2070	4220	-5.2	13	35	52	0.806	...	236	6.4	6.1	3.3	3	1	11	Belarus
250710	24710	21660	2.2	2	31	67	0.932	3681	274	8.2	5.6	1.7	0	0	*81	Belgium
2034	370	1760	-0.4	34	12	54	0.368	2532	14216	1.7	...	1.3	74	51	53	Benin
5905	800	2540	1.7	17	30	53	0.589	2094	2348	5	5.4	2.6	24	10	96	Bolivia
11650	2600	...	1.8	...	...	...	...	...	600	...	...	...	23	3	...	Bosnia-Herzegovina
4381	3020	5580	6	5	46	49	0.673	2266	5151	1.9	8.5	7.1	40	20	64	Botswana
579787	3640	5400	-0.7	14	37	49	0.783	2824	844	7.4	1.6	1.5	17	17	2	Brazil
11225	1330	4480	-2.2	13	34	53	0.78	2831	306	4	4.5	3.3	3	1	6	Bulgaria
2417	230	780	-0.1	34	27	39	0.221	2387	34804	5.5	3.6	2.4	91	71	48	Burkina Faso
45100	1000	1050	0.4	63	9	28	0.475	2598	12528	0.9	2.4	6.2	22	11	3	Burma
984	160	630	-1.3	56	18	26	0.247	1941	17153	0.9	3.8	5.3	78	51	46	Burundi
2718	270	1084	2	51	14	35	0.348	2021	9374	7.2	...	4.7	47	20	57	Cambodia
8615	650	2110	-7	39	23	38	0.468	1981	11996	1.4	3.1	1.8	48	25	35	Cameroon
573695	19380	21130	0.4	3	30	67	0.96	3094	464	9.8	7.6	1.6	2	2	*73	Canada
1123	340	1070	-2	44	13	43	0.355	1690	25920	1.7	2.8	1.8	48	32	50	Central African Rep.
1144	180	700	0.5	44	22	34	0.288	1989	30030	1.8	2.2	2.6	65	38	38	Chad
59151	4160	9520	6.1	8	34	58	0.891	2582	942	6.5	2.9	3.8	5	5	11	Chile
744890	620	2920	8	21	48	31	0.626	2727	1063	3.8	2.6	5.7	27	10	3	China
70263	1910	6130	2.8	14	32	54	0.848	2677	1105	7.4	3.7	2	9	9	6	Colombia
1784	680	2050	-3.2	10	38	52	0.5	2296	3713	6.8	8.3	1.7	33	17	50	Congo
5313	120	490	-8.5	51	16	33	0.381	2060	15150	2.4	1	2	32	13	4	Congo (Zaïre)
8884	2610	5850	2.9	17	24	59	0.889	2883	1133	8.5	4.7	0.3	5	5	8	Costa Rica
5508	3250	3960	-20	12	25	63	0.76	...	500	10.1	...	12.6	5	1	...	Croatia
3700	1250	3000	-10	...	...	...	0.723	2833	275	7.9	6.6	2.8	5	4	6	Cuba
8510	11500	13000	4.6	6	43	51	0.907	3779	450	3.9	4.3	4.5	7	2	30	Cyprus
39990	3870	9770	-1.8	6	39	55	0.882	...	273	9.9	5.9	2.8	0	0	5	Czech Rep.
146027	29890	21230	1.5	4	29	67	0.927	3664	360	6.6	8.5	1.8	0	0	*273	Denmark
11390	1460	3870	2.1	15	22	63	0.718	2286	949	5.3	1.9	1.3	18	18	16	Dominican Rep.
5997	1390	4220	0.8	12	36	52	0.775	2583	652	5.3	3	3.4	12	8	21	Ecuador
45507	790	3820	1.1	20	21	59	0.614	3335	1316	4.9	5	4.3	61	36	35	Egypt
9057	1610	2610	2.9	14	22	64	0.592	2663	1515	5	1.6	1.8	30	27	54	El Salvador
4252	2860	4220	-4.3	8	28	64	0.776	...	253	5.9	5.8	5.3	0	0	22	Estonia
5722	100	450	-0.5	57	10	33	0.244	1610	32499	1.1	6.4	2.1	75	55	16	Ethiopia
5174	20580	17760	-0.2	6	37	57	0.94	3018	406	8.3	8.4	2	0	0	*59	Finland
1051	24990	21030	1.5	2	27	71	0.946	3633	334	9.7	5.8	3.1	1	1	*137	France
3759	3490	3650	-1.6	9	59	32	0.562	2500	1987	0.5	3.2	1.7	47	26	138	Gabon
354	320	930	0.3	28	15	57	0.281	2360	14000	1.8	2.7	3.8	75	47	43	Gambia, The
2358	440	1470	-17	67	22	11	0.637	...	182	0.3	1.9	3.4	1	0	106	Georgia
2343	27510	20070	1.9	1	30	69	0.924	3344	367	9.5	4.8	2	0	0	*81	Germany
6719	390	1990	1.5	46	16	38	0.468	2199	22970	3.5	3.1	1.2	47	24	38	Ghana
85885	8210	11710	1.2	21	36	43	0.923	3815	312	6.4	3	4.6	7	2	...	Greece
14255	1340	3340	0.3	25	19	56	0.572	2255	3999	2.7	1.6	1.4	51	38	21	Guatemala
3593	550	1100	1.4	24	31	45	0.271	2389	7445	0.9	2.2	1.4	78	50	62	Guinea
265	250	790	1.8	46	24	30	0.291	2556	3500	1.1	2.8	3	58	32	113	Guinea-Bissau
493	590	2420	0.8	50	35	15	0.649	2384	3000	10.4	5	1.1	2	1	...	Guyana
1777	250	910	-5.2	44	12	44	0.338	1706	10855	3.6	1.4	2.1	58	52	104	Haiti
3566	600	1900	0.2	21	33	46	0.575	2305	1266	5.6	4	1.3	27	27	75	Honduras
42129	4120	6410	-1	8	33	59	0.857	3503	306	7.3	6.7	1.4	1	1	7	Hungary
6686	24950	20460	0.3	13	29	58	0.942	3058	360	6.9	5.4	...	0	0	...	Iceland
319660	340	1400	3.1	29	29	42	0.446	2395	2459	3.5	3.8	2.5	62	35	2	India
190105	980	3800	6	17	42	41	0.668	2752	7028	1.5	1.3	1.6	22	10	7	Indonesia
63000	4800	5470	0.5	25	34	41	0.78	2860	3142	4.5	5.9	3.9	24	22	3	Iran
16200	1800	3150	...	28	20	52	0.531	2121	1659	...	5.1	14.8	55	29	16	Iraq

	Population									Land and Agriculture					Energy	Trade	
	Population Total 1997	Population Density 1997	Average Annual Change 1970-80	Average Annual Change 1990-97	Birth Rate 1997	Death Rate 1997	Fertility Rate 1995	Life Expectancy Average 1997	Urban Population 1995	Land Area	Arable and Permanent Crops	Permanent grassland	Forest	Agriculture Population 1995	Consumption per capita 1994	Imports per capita 1995	Exports per capita 1995
	millions	persons per km²	%	%	births per thousand population	deaths per thousand population	children	years	%	thousand km²	% of land area	% of land area	% of land area	% of economically active pop.	tonnes of coal	US $	US $
Ireland	3.6	53	1.4	0.5	13	9	1.9	76	58	68.9	19	45	5	13	4.31	9237	12469
Israel	5.9	286	2.7	3.6	20	6	2.4	78	91	20.6	21	7	6	3	3.26	5337	3436
Italy	57.8	196	0.5	0.2	10	10	1.2	78	67	294	38	15	23	7	3.95	3562	4038
Ivory Coast	15.1	47	4	3.4	42	17	5.3	45	46	318	12	41	34	57	0.26	231	301
Jamaica	2.6	240	1.3	0.8	22	6	2.4	75	53	10.8	20	24	17	24	1.66	1089	545
Japan	125.9	334	1.1	0.3	10	8	1.5	80	78	377	12	2	66	6	4.98	2684	3540
Jordan	5.6	63	2.4	4.9	36	4	4.8	73	72	88.9	5	9	1	15	1.01	680	325
Kazakstan	17	6	1.3	0.2	19	10	2.3	64	58	2670	13	70	4	21	5.93	40	70
Kenya	31.9	56	3.8	4.1	32	11	4.7	54	25	570	8	37	30	78	0.12	98	62
Korea, North	24.5	203	2.2	1.7	22	5	2.2	71	61	120	17	0	61	34	4.21	75	41
Korea, South	46.1	466	1.8	1.1	16	6	1.8	74	75	98.7	21	1	65	14	3.77	3013	2788
Kyrgyzstan	4.7	24	2	0.8	26	9	3.3	64	40	191	7	44	4	31	0.76	71	76
Laos	5.2	23	1.7	3.3	41	13	6.5	53	22	231	4	3	54	77	0.04	40	20
Latvia	2.5	38	0.7	-1.3	12	15	1.3	67	72	64.1	28	13	46	14	2.3	697	520
Lebanon	3.2	313	0.8	2.5	28	6	2.8	70	87	10.2	30	1	8	4	1.83	2058	197
Lesotho	2.1	69	2.3	2.7	32	14	4.6	52	23	30.4	11	66	0	39	...	520	58
Liberia	3	30	3.1	2.9	42	12	6.5	59	45	96.8	4	21	48	70	0.06	116	197
Libya	5.5	3	4.4	2.8	44	7	6.1	65	86	1760	1	8	0	6	3.34	1240	2596
Lithuania	3.7	57	0.9	-0.1	14	13	1.5	68	71	65.2	47	7	31	18	3.04	696	545
Luxembourg	0.4	163.5	0.7	1.9	13	8	1.7	79	88	2.6	...	...	...	...	12.82	20295	16090
Macedonia	2.2	86	1.6	0.9	13	9	2.2	72	60	24.9	26	25	39	17	1.9	600	500
Madagascar	15.5	27	2.7	4.8	42	14	5.8	53	27	582	5	41	40	76	0.04	36	25
Malawi	10.3	109	3.2	3.1	41	25	6.6	35	13	94.1	18	20	39	86	0.04	49	41
Malaysia	20.9	64	2.4	2.2	26	5	3.4	70	52	329	23	1	68	23	2.29	3751	3563
Mali	11	9	2.3	4.4	51	19	6.8	47	27	1220	2	25	10	84	0.02	70	42
Malta	0.4	1172	1.1	0.9	15	7	1.9	79	88	0.32	41	0	0	2	1.97	7951	5170
Mauritania	2.4	2	2.4	2.5	47	15	5.2	50	54	1025	0	38	4	49	0.61	284	223
Mauritius	1.2	569	1.6	1.1	19	7	2.2	71	44	2.03	52	3	22	12	0.7	1797	1410
Mexico	97.4	51	2.9	1.8	26	5	3	74	75	1909	13	39	26	24	2.03	508	520
Moldova	4.5	132	1.1	0.3	17	12	2	65	50	33.7	66	13	13	31	1.55	185	162
Mongolia	2.5	2	2.8	1.9	25	8	3.4	61	60	1567	1	75	9	29	1.55	158	208
Morocco	28.1	63	2.4	1.6	27	6	3.4	70	52	446	21	47	20	41	0.47	315	172
Mozambique	19.1	24	2.6	4.3	44	18	6.2	45	32	784	4	56	22	81	0.03	45	10
Namibia	1.7	2	2.5	2	37	8	5	65	34	823	1	46	15	45	...	916	881
Nepal	22.1	162	2.6	2.1	37	12	5.3	54	13	137	17	15	42	93	0.03	64	16
Netherlands	15.9	469	0.8	0.9	12	9	1.6	78	89	33.9	28	31	10	4	7.22	11419	12680
New Zealand	3.7	14	1	1.1	15	8	2.1	77	86	268	14	50	28	10	5.47	3951	3882
Nicaragua	4.6	39	3	2.5	33	6	4.1	66	63	119	10	45	26	23	0.36	212	115
Niger	9.7	8	3	3.3	54	24	7.4	41	16	1267	3	8	2	89	0.06	37	27
Nigeria	118	130	2.2	3.1	43	12	5.5	55	38	911	36	44	12	38	0.21	71	94
Norway	4.4	14	0.5	0.8	11	11	1.9	78	73	307	3	0	27	5	7.44	7563	9632
Oman	2.4	11	4.2	6.9	38	4	7	71	13	212	0	5	0	42	5.41	1994	2682
Pakistan	136	176	2.6	2.8	35	11	5.2	59	34	771	28	6	5	48	0.33	88	62
Panama	2.7	37	2.5	1.7	22	5	2.7	74	55	74.4	9	20	44	22	1.2	955	238
Papua New Guinea	4.4	10	2.5	1.8	33	10	4.8	58	16	453	1	0	93	78	0.29	357	651
Paraguay	5.2	13	3	2.8	30	4	4	74	52	397	6	55	32	35	0.38	669	196
Peru	24.5	19	2.7	1.3	24	6	3.1	70	72	1280	3	21	66	33	0.46	392	237
Philippines	73.5	247	2.6	2.4	29	7	3.7	66	52	298	31	4	46	42	0.43	403	249
Poland	38.8	127	0.9	0.1	12	10	1.6	72	64	304	48	13	29	26	3.51	753	593
Portugal	10.1	110	0.8	-0.3	11	10	1.4	76	36	92	32	11	36	14	2.13	3261	2280
Puerto Rico	3.8	432	1.7	1.4	18	8	2.1	75	77	8.86	9	26	16	3	3.07	4300	5900
Romania	22.6	98	0.9	-0.3	10	12	1.4	70	55	230	43	21	29	19	2.54	453	349
Russia	147.8	9	0.6	0	11	16	1.4	64	75	16996	8	5	45	12	6	261	427
Rwanda	7	284	3.3	-0.4	39	21	6.2	39	6	24.7	47	28	10	91	0.03	46	10
Saudi Arabia	19.1	9	5	4.4	38	5	6.2	70	79	2150	2	56	1	14	5.77	1539	2335
Senegal	8.9	46	2.9	2.8	45	11	5.7	57	42	193	12	30	39	74	0.16	156	103
Sierra Leone	4.6	64	2.1	1.5	47	18	6.5	48	35	71.6	8	31	28	67	0.05	30	6
Singapore	3.2	5246	1	2.5	16	5	1.7	79	100	0.61	2	0	5	1	9.67	41639	39553
Slovak Rep.	5.4	112	1.7	0.3	13	9	1.5	73	58	48.1	34	17	41	12	4.07	1250	1025
Slovenia	2	99	0.9	0.2	8	10	1.3	75	50	20.3	14	25	54	5	3.11	4793	4199
Somalia	9.9	16	3.8	1.9	44	13	7	56	27	627	2	69	26	74	0.05	26	5
South Africa	42.3	35	2.3	1.6	27	12	3.9	56	57	1221	11	67	7	11	2.73	718	653
Spain	39.3	79	1.1	0	10	9	1.2	79	77	499	40	21	32	9	3.01	2890	2334
Sri Lanka	18.7	289	1.7	1.2	18	6	2.3	73	22	64.6	29	7	32	47	0.16	290	212
Sudan	31	13	3	3	41	11	4.8	56	35	2376	5	46	18	68	0.06	44	21

Wealth							Social Indicators								Aid	
GNP 1995	GNP per capita 1995	Real GDP per capita 1995	Average Annual growth of Real GNP per capita 1985-95	GDP share Agriculture 1995	GDP share Industry 1995	GDP share services 1995	HDI Human Development Index 1994	Food Intake	Population per doctor 1993	% of GNP spent on health 1990-95	% of GNP spent on education 1993-94	%o GNP spent on military 1995	Adult Illiteracy Female	Adult Illiteracy Male	given (*) and received per capita 1994	
million US $	US $	US $	%	%	%	%	1994	calories per day	persons	%	%	%	%	%	US $	
52765	14710	15680	5.2	9	37	54	0.929	3847	632	7.9	6.4	1.2	0	0	*35	Ireland
87875	15920	16490	2.5	3	32	65	0.913	3050	220	4.1	6	9.2	7	3	226	Israel
88085	19020	19870	1.7	3	31	66	0.921	3561	207	8.3	5.2	1.8	4	2	*37	Italy
9548	660	1580	-4.3	31	20	49	0.368	2491	11739	3.4	...	1	70	50	87	Ivory Coast
3803	1510	3540	3.7	9	38	53	0.736	2607	6420	5.4	4.7	0.6	11	19	43	Jamaica
3587	39640	22110	2.9	2	38	60	0.94	2903	608	7	4.7	1.1	0	0	*106	Japan
6354	1510	4060	-2.8	8	27	65	0.73	3022	554	7.9	3.8	6.7	21	7	127	Jordan
22143	1330	3010	-8.6	12	30	58	0.709	...	254	2.2	5.4	3	4	1	2	Kazakstan
7583	280	1380	0.1	29	17	54	0.463	2075	21970	1.9	6.8	2.3	30	14	42	Kenya
24000	1000	4000	-8	...	...	...	0.765	2833	370	...	...	25.2	5	5	1	Korea, North
435137	9700	11450	7.6	7	43	50	0.89	3285	951	5.4	4.5	3.4	2	2	1	Korea, South
3158	700	1800	-6.9	44	24	32	0.635	...	303	3.5	6.8	3.5	4	1	19	Kyrgyzstan
1694	350	2500	2.7	52	18	30	0.459	2259	4446	2.6	2.3	4.2	56	31	66	Laos
5708	2270	3370	-6.6	9	31	60	0.711	...	278	3.7	6.5	3.2	0	0	14	Latvia
10673	2660	4800	2.7	7	24	69	0.794	3317	537	5.3	2	5.3	10	5	48	Lebanon
1519	770	1780	1.5	10	56	34	0.457	2201	24095	3.5	4.8	5.5	38	19	57	Lesotho
2300	850	1000	1.5	...	...	...	...	1640	25000	8.2	...	4.8	78	46	23	Liberia
8000	7000	6000	1	8	48	44	0.801	3308	957	...	9.6	5.5	37	12	1	Libya
7070	1900	4120	-11.7	11	36	53	0.762	...	235	4.8	4.5	2.4	2	1	14	Lithuania
16876	41210	37930	1	1	33	66	0.899	...	460	6.3	3.1	0.9	0	0	*148	Luxembourg
1813	860	4000	-15	19	44	37	0.748	...	427	7.7	5.6	...	16	6	...	Macedonia
3178	230	640	-2	34	13	53	0.35	2135	8385	1	1.9	1.1	27	12	23	Madagascar
1623	170	750	-0.7	42	27	31	0.32	1825	44205	2.3	3.4	1.2	58	28	40	Malawi
78321	3890	9020	5.7	13	43	44	0.832	2888	2441	1.4	5.3	4.5	22	11	6	Malaysia
2410	250	550	0.6	46	17	37	0.229	2278	18376	1.3	2.1	2.4	77	61	57	Mali
4070	11000	13000	5.1	3	28	69	0.887	3486	410	12.1	5.1	1.1	4	4	...	Malta
1049	460	1540	0.5	27	30	43	0.355	2685	15772	1.5	...	1.9	74	50	99	Mauritania
3815	3380	13210	5.7	9	33	58	0.831	...	1165	2.2	3.7	0.5	21	13	21	Mauritius
4596	3320	6400	0.1	8	26	66	0.853	3146	615	5.3	5.8	0.9	13	8	4	Mexico
3996	920	1600	-8.2	50	28	22	0.612	...	250	5.1	5.5	3.7	6	1	5	Moldova
767	310	1950	-3.8	21	46	33	0.661	1899	371	4.7	5.2	2.4	23	11	88	Mongolia
9545	1110	3340	0.8	14	33	53	0.566	2984	4665	3.4	5.4	4.3	69	43	19	Morocco
1353	80	810	3.6	33	21	46	0.281	1680	36225	4.6	6.2	3.7	77	42	66	Mozambique
3098	2000	4150	2.8	14	29	57	0.57	2134	4328	7.6	8.7	2.7	26	22	125	Namibia
4391	200	1170	2.4	42	22	36	0.347	1957	13634	5	2.9	1	86	59	21	Nepal
1039	24000	19950	1.8	3	27	70	0.94	3222	399	8.8	5.5	2.2	0	0	*172	Netherlands
1655	14340	16360	0.6	7	25	68	0.937	3669	518	7.5	7.3	1.7	1	1	*31	New Zealand
1659	380	2000	-5.8	33	20	47	0.53	2293	2039	7.8	3.8	1.8	33	35	155	Nicaragua
1961	220	750	-2.1	39	18	43	0.206	2257	53986	2.2	3.1	0.9	93	79	30	Niger
28411	260	1220	1.2	43	27	30	0.393	2124	5208	2.7	1.3	2.9	53	33	2	Nigeria
6077	31250	21940	1.6	3	36	61	0.943	3244	308	7.3	9.2	2.6	0	0	*255	Norway
10578	4820	8140	0.3	3	48	49	0.718	...	1131	2.5	4.5	15.1	76	42	29	Oman
59991	460	2230	1.2	26	24	50	0.445	2315	1923	0.8	2.7	6.5	76	50	6	Pakistan
7235	2750	5980	-0.4	11	18	71	0.864	2242	562	7.5	5.2	1.3	10	9	19	Panama
4976	1160	2420	2.1	26	38	36	0.525	2613	12754	2.8	...	1.3	37	19	88	Papua New Guinea
8158	1690	3650	1.1	24	22	54	0.706	2670	1231	4.3	2.9	1.4	9	7	30	Paraguay
5019	2310	3770	-1.6	7	38	55	0.717	1882	939	4.9	1.5	1.6	17	6	18	Peru
865	1050	2850	1.5	22	32	46	0.672	2257	8273	2.4	2.4	1.6	6	5	109	Philippines
7829	2790	5400	-0.4	6	39	55	0.834	3301	451	4.6	5.5	2.5	2	1	40	Poland
6689	9740	12670	3.7	6	40	54	0.89	3634	353	7.6	5.4	2.9	13	13	*27	Portugal
7750	7500	7000	2.1	1	42	57	...	...	350	...	...	...	10	10	...	Puerto Rico
3488	1480	4360	-4	21	49	30	0.748	3051	538	3.3	3.1	3.1	5	1	3	Romania
948	2240	4480	-5.1	7	38	55	0.792	...	222	4.8	4.4	7.4	3	0	12	Russia
128	180	540	-5	37	17	46	0.187	1821	24967	1.9	3.8	4.4	48	30	92	Rwanda
3540	7040	9500	-1.9	6	51	43	0.774	2735	749	2.2	6.4	10.6	50	29	1	Saudi Arabia
5070	600	1780	-1.2	20	18	62	0.326	2262	18192	1.6	4.2	1.9	77	57	82	Senegal
762	180	580	-3.4	42	27	31	0.176	1694	11000	1.6	1.4	5.7	82	55	45	Sierra Leone
831	26730	22770	6.2	0	36	64	0.9	...	714	3.5	3.3	5.9	14	4	6	Singapore
848	2950	3610	-2.6	6	33	61	0.873	...	287	6.3	4.9	2.8	0	0	6	Slovak Rep.
328	8200	10400	-1	5	39	56	0.886	...	500	7.9	6.2	1.5	0	0	...	Slovenia
625	500	1000	-2.3	65	9	26	...	1499	13300	1.5	0.4	0.9	52	39	61	Somalia
918	3160	5030	-1	5	31	64	0.716	2695	1500	7.9	7.1	2.9	18	18	10	South Africa
347	13580	14520	2.6	3	31	66	0.934	3708	261	7.4	4.7	1.5	6	2	*31	Spain
616	700	3250	2.7	23	25	52	0.711	2273	6843	1.9	3.2	4.9	13	7	31	Sri Lanka
000	750	1050	0.6	36	18	46	0.333	2202	10000	0.3	...	4.3	65	42	8	Sudan

	Population									Land and Agriculture					Energy	Trade	
	Population Total 1997	Population Density 1997	Average Annual Change 1970-80	Average Annual Change 1990-97	Birth Rate 1997	Death Rate 1997	Fertility Rate 1995	Life Expectancy Average 1997	Urban Population 1995	Land Area	Arable and Permanent Crops	Permanent grassland	Forest	Agriculture Population 1995	Consumption per capita 1994	Imports per capita 1995	Exports per capita 1995
	millions	persons per km²	%	%	births per thousand population	deaths per thousand population	children	years	%	thousand km²	% of land area	% of land area	% of land area	% of economically active pop.	tonnes of coal	US $	US $
Surinam	0.5	3	-0.6	1.5	24	6	2.6	70	52	156	0	0	96	20	2.01	1565	873
Swaziland	1	55	3	3.1	43	10	4.6	58	29	17.2	11	62	7	34	...	1090	855
Sweden	8.9	22	0.3	0.7	11	11	1.7	78	84	412	7	1	68	4	6.79	7299	9051
Switzerland	7.1	180	0.2	1	11	10	1.5	78	61	39.6	11	29	32	5	4.5	10938	11088
Syria	15.3	83	3.5	2.9	39	6	4.8	67	52	184	30	45	3	33	1.28	325	280
Taiwan	21.7	603	2	0.9	15	6	1.8	76	76	36	26	11	52	19	2.5	4868	5238
Tajikistan	6	42	3	1.8	34	8	4.2	65	32	143	6	25	4	38	0.58	93	84
Tanzania	31.2	35	3.4	2.8	41	20	5.8	42	24	884	4	40	38	83	0.04	55	23
Thailand	60.8	119	2.7	0.9	17	7	1.8	69	19	511	41	2	26	60	1.07	1236	946
Togo	4.5	82	2.6	3.4	46	10	6.4	58	31	54.4	45	4	17	62	0.08	94	51
Trinidad & Tobago	1.3	253	1.1	0.2	16	7	2.1	70	70	5.13	24	2	46	9	7.53	1329	1904
Tunisia	9.2	59	2.2	1.9	24	5	2.9	73	57	155	32	20	4	24	0.75	886	614
Turkey	63.5	83	2.3	1.1	22	5	2.7	72	65	770	36	16	26	51	1.16	579	350
Turkmenistan	4.8	10	2.7	3.9	29	9	3.8	62	47	488	3	64	9	36	3.68	250	533
Uganda	20.8	104	3	2.4	45	21	6.7	40	12	200	34	9	32	83	0.03	50	22
Ukraine	51.5	85	0.6	-0.1	12	15	1.5	67	69	604	59	13	18	18	4.39	192	187
United Kingdom	58.6	243	0.1	0.3	13	11	1.7	77	90	242	25	46	10	2	5.33	4527	4130
United States	268	28	1.1	1	15	9	2.1	76	77	9573	20	25	30	3	11.39	2929	2222
Uruguay	3.3	19	0.4	0.7	17	9	2.2	75	90	175	7	77	5	14	0.78	899	660
Uzbekistan	23.8	56	2.9	2.1	29	8	3.7	65	42	425	11	50	3	34	2.94	111	138
Venezuela	22.5	26	3.5	1.9	24	5	3.1	72	92	882	4	20	34	11	3.75	553	854
Vietnam	77.1	237	2.3	2.1	22	7	3.1	67	20	325	21	1	30	69	0.16	30	30
Yemen	16.5	31	1.9	5.6	45	9	7.4	60	34	528	3	30	4	57	0.33	165	74
Yugoslavia	10.5	103	1	0.3	14	10	1.9	72	54	102	40	21	26	20	1.22	533	452
Zambia	9.5	13	3.2	2.4	44	24	5.7	45	45	743	7	40	43	74	0.19	12	94
Zimbabwe	12.1	31	3.1	3.7	32	19	3.8	60	32	387	7	44	23	67	0.7	231	183

	Land area thousand sq km	Population 1997 thousands
American Samoa	0.2	62
Andorra	0.45	75
Anguilla	0.1	10
Antigua & Barbuda	0.44	66
Aruba	0.19	70
Ascension I.	0.09	1.1
Bahrain	0.68	605
Belize	22.8	228
Bermuda	0.05	65
Bhutan	47	1790
British Virgin Is.	0.15	13
Brunei	5.27	300
Cape Verde Is.	4.03	410
Cayman Is.	0.26	35
Cocos Is.	0.01	1
Comoros	2.23	630
Cook Is.	0.23	20
Djibouti	23.2	650
Dominica	0.75	78
Equatorial Guinea	28.1	420
Eritrea	101	3500
Falkland Is.	12.2	2
Faroe Is.	1.4	45
Fiji	18.3	800
French Guiana	88.2	155

	Land area thousand sq km	Population 1997 thousands
French Polynesia	3.66	226
Gaza Strip	0.36	900
Gibraltar	0.01	28
Greenland	342	57
Grenada	0.34	99
Guadeloupe	1.69	440
Guam	0.55	161
Kiribati	0.73	85
Kuwait	17.8	2050
Liechtenstein	0.16	32
Macau	0.02	450
Maldives	0.3	275
Marshall Is.	0.18	60
Martinique	1.06	405
Mayotte	0.37	105
Micronesia	0.7	127
Monaco	0.002	33
Montserrat	0.1	12
Nauru	0.02	53
Netherlands Antilles	0.8	12
New Caledonia	18.3	210
Niue	0.26	192
Norfolk I.	0.04	2
Northern Marianas	0.48	2
Palau	0.49	17

	Land area thousand sq km	Population thousands
Pitcairn I.	0.05	0.
Qatar	11	
Réunion	2.5	
St Kitts-Nevis	0.36	
St Helena	0.3	
St Lucia	0.61	
St Pierre & Miquelon	0.23	
St Vincent & the Grenadines	0.39	
San Marino	0.06	
Sâo Tomé & Principe	0.96	
Seychelles	0.45	
Solomon Is.	28	
Svalbard	63	
Tokelau	0.01	
Tonga	0.72	
Turks & Caicos Is.	0.43	
Tuvalu	0.03	
United Arab Emirates	83.6	
US Virgin Is.	0.34	
Vanuatu	12.2	
Vatican City	0.0004	
Wallis & Futuna Is.	0.2	
West Bank	5.9	
Western Sahara	267	
Western Samoa	2.83	

Wealth							Social Indicators								Aid	
GNP 1995	GNP per capita 1995	Real GDP per capita 1995	Average Annual growth of Real GNP per capita 1985-95	GDP share Agriculture 1995	GDP share Industry 1995	GDP share services 1995	HDI Human Development Index 1994	Food Intake	Population per doctor 1993	% of GNP spent on health 1990-95	% of GNP spent on education 1993-94	%o GNP spent on military 1995	Adult Illiteracy		given (*) and received per capita 1994	
million US $	US $	US $	%	%	%	%		calories per day	persons	%	%	%	Female %	Male %	US $	
360	880	2250	0.7	22	23	55	0.792	2547	1200	2.9	3.6	3.9	9	5	183	Surinam
1051	1170	2880	0.6	10	25	65	0.582	2706	9250	7.2	6.8	...	24	22	59	Swaziland
9720	23750	18540	-0.1	2	32	66	0.936	2972	394	7.7	8.4	2.9	0	0	*189	Sweden
36014	40630	25860	0.2	3	32	65	0.93	3379	580	9.6	5.6	1.9	0	0	*135	Switzerland
15780	1120	5320	1	18	43	39	0.755	3175	1159	2.1	4.2	6.8	44	14	25	Syria
52000	12000	13000	7	3	42	55	...	3048	800	4.3		4.8	10	3	...	Taiwan
1976	340	920	-13	27	45	28	0.58	...	424	6.4	9.5	6.9	3	1	5	Tajikistan
3703	120	640	0.9	58	17	25	0.357	2018	22000	2.8	5	2.7	43	21	30	Tanzania
59630	2740	7540	8.4	11	40	49	0.833	2432	4416	5.3	3.8	2.5	8	4	15	Thailand
1266	310	1130	-2.8	38	21	41	0.365	2242	11385	1.7	6.1	2.5	63	33	47	Togo
4851	3770	8610	-1.6	3	42	55	0.88	2585	1520	3.9	4.5	1.3	3	1	20	Trinidad & Tobago
16369	1820	5000	1.8	12	29	59	0.748	3330	1549	5.9	6.3	2	45	21	8	Tunisia
69452	2780	5580	2.2	16	31	53	0.772	3429	976	4.2	3.3	3.6	28	8	5	Turkey
4125	920	3500	-9.6	31	31	38	0.723	...	306	2.8	7.9	1.9	3	1	3	Turkmenistan
4668	240	1470	2.8	50	14	36	0.328	2159	22399	3.9	1.9	2.6	50	26	43	Uganda
84084	1630	2400	-9.2	18	42	40	0.689	...	227	5.4	8.2	3	3	0	5	Ukraine
94734	18700	19260	1.4	2	32	66	0.931	3317	300	6.9	5.4	3.1	0	0	*53	United Kingdom
00007	26980	26980	1.4	2	26	72	0.942	3732	421	14.3	5.5	3.8	5	4	*33	United States
6458	5170	6630	3.3	9	26	65	0.883	2750	500	8.5	2.5	2.6	2	3	26	Uruguay
21979	970	2370	-3.9	33	34	33	0.662	...	282	3.5	11	3.6	4	1	1	Uzbekistan
75382	3020	7900	0.5	5	38	57	0.861	2618	633	7.1	5.1	1.1	10	8	4	Venezuela
17634	240	1200	4.2	28	30	42	0.557	2250	2279	5.2	...	4.3	9	4	8	Vietnam
4044	260	850	3.1	22	27	51	0.361	2203	4498	2.6	4.6	3.9	74	47	13	Yemen
4750	1400	4000	1.8	26	36	38	...	...	232	5.1	...	...	11	2	...	Yugoslavia
3605	400	930	-1	22	40	38	0.369	1931	10917	3.3	2.6	1.9	29	14	221	Zambia
5933	540	2030	-0.6	15	36	49	0.513	1985	7384	2.1	8.3	4.2	20	10	45	Zimbabwe

y figures for Luxembourg are included in those Belgium.

energy, the figures for South Africa include those otswana, Lesotho, Swaziland and Namibia.

sign ... means that figures are not available.

ulation Total. This is an estimate for the mid- 1997.

ulation Density. This is the total population ed by the land area, both quoted in the table.

ulation Change. This shows the average al percentage change for the two periods, -80 and 1990-97.

h and Death Rates and Life Expectancy. e are estimates from the US Census Bureau. Birth and Death rates are the number of those rrences per year, per thousand population. Life ctancy is the number of years that a child born can expect to live if the levels of mortality of last throughout its life. The figure is the age ot that for men and women.

lity Rate. This is the average number of ren born to a woman in her lifetime.

an Population. This is the percentage of the population living in urban areas. The definition an is that of the individual nations and often des quite small towns.

Land Area. This is the total area of the country less the area covered by major lakes and rivers.

Arable Land and Permanent Crops. This excludes fallow land but includes temporary pasture.

Forest and Woodland. This includes natural and planted woodland and land recently cleared of timber which will be replanted.

Agricultural Population. This is the percentage of the economically active population working in agriculture. It includes those working in forestry, hunting and fishing.

Energy. All forms of energy have been expressed in an approximate equivalent of tonnes of coal per person.

Trade. The trade figures are for 1994 or 1995. In a few cases the figure is older than this but is the latest available. The total Import and Export figures have been divided by the population to give a figure in US $ per capita.

Gross National Product (GNP). This figure is an estimate of the value of a country's production and the average production per person for 1995, in US $. The GNP measures the value of goods and services produced in a country, plus the balance, positive or negative, of income from abroad, for example, from investments, interest on capital, money returned from workers abroad, etc. The Gross Domestic Product (GDP), is the GNP less the foreign balances. The adjoining three columns show the percentage contribution to the GDP made by the

agricultural, mining and manufacturing and service sectors of the economy. The average annual rate of change is for the GNP per capita in PPP $ during the period 1985-95

Real GDP per capita. Using official exchange rates to convert national currencies into US $ makes no attempt to reflect the varying domestic purchasing powers of the local currency. The UN has made these estimates of Real GDP taking into account these local purchasing values and they are called Purchasing Power Parity $.

Human Development Index. This is a calculation made by the UN Development Programme, using 1994 data and takes into account not only national income, but also life expectancy, adult literacy and the years in education. It is a measure of national human progress. The wealthy developed countries have an index approaching 1, and the figures range down to some of the poorer with an index of less than 0.1.

Food Intake. The figures are the average intake per person in calories per day. They are for 1992 and are the latest estimates that are available.

Adult Illiteracy. This is the percentage of the male and female population aged 15 and over who cannot read or write a simple sentence.

Aid. The bulk of the table is concerned with aid received but aid given is shown by an asterisk.

To convert square kilometres to square miles multiply by 0.39.

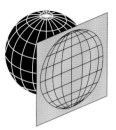

AZIMUTHAL OR ZENITHAL PROJECTIONS

These are constructed by the projection of part of the graticule from the globe onto a plane tangential to any single point on it. This plane may be tangential to the equator (equatorial case), the poles (polar case) or any other point (oblique case). Any straight line drawn from the point at which the plane touches the globe is the shortest distance from that point and is known as a great circle. In its Gnomonic construction any straight line on the map is a great circle, but there is great exaggeration towards the edges and this reduces its general uses. There are five different ways of transferring the graticule onto the plane and these are shown below. The diagrams below also show how the graticules vary, using the polar case as the example.

MAP PROJECTIONS

A map projection is the systematic depiction of the imaginary grid of lines of latitude and longitude from a globe onto a flat surface. The grid of lines is called the graticule and it can be constructed either by graphical means or by mathematical formulae to form the basis of a map. As a globe is three dimensional it is not possible to depict its surface on a flat map without some form of distortion. Preservation of one of the basic properties listed below can only be secured at the expense of the others and the choice of projection is often a compromise solution.

Correct Area
In these projections the areas from the globe are to scale on the map. This is particularly useful in the mapping of densities and distributions. Projections with this property are termed Equal Area, Equivalent or Homolographic.

Correct Distance
In these projections the scale is correct along the meridians, or in the case of the Azimuthal Equidistant scale is true along any line drawn from the centre of the projection. They are called Equidistant.

Correct Shape
This property can only be true within small areas as it is achieved only by having a uniform scale distortion along both x and y axes of the projection. The projections are called Conformal or Orthomorphic.

Map projections can be divided into three broad categories - azimuthal, conic and cylindrical. Cartographers use different projections from these categories depending on the map scale, the size of the area to be mapped, and what they want the map to show.

| Equidistant | Equal-Area | Orthographic | Gnomonic | Stereographic (conformal) |

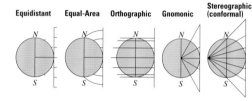

Polar Case
The polar case is the simplest to construct and the diagram on the right shows the differing effects of all five methods of construction comparing their coverage, distortion etc., using North America as the example.

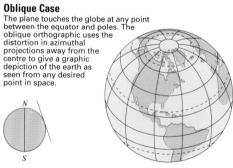

Oblique Case
The plane touches the globe at any point between the equator and poles. The oblique orthographic uses the distortion in azimuthal projections away from the centre to give a graphic depiction of the earth as seen from any desired point in space.

Equatorial Case
The example shown here is Lambert's Equivalent Azimuthal. It is the only projection which is both equal area and where bearing is true from the centre.

CONICAL PROJECTIONS

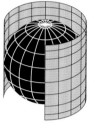

These use the projection of the graticule from the globe onto a cone which is tangential to a line of latitude (termed the standard parallel). This line is always an arc and scale is always true along it. Because of its method of construction it is used mainly for depicting the temperate latitudes around the standard parallel i.e. where there is least distortion. To reduce the distortion and include a larger range of latitudes, the projection may be constructed with the cone bisecting the surface of the globe so that there are two standard parallels each of which is true to scale. The distortion is thus spread more evenly between the two chosen parallels.

Simple Conical with one standard parallel

Bonne
This is a modification of the simple conic whereby the true scale along the meridians is sacrificed to enable the accurate representation of areas. However scale is true along each parallel but shapes are distorted at the edges.

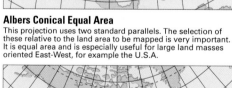

Albers Conical Equal Area
This projection uses two standard parallels. The selection of these relative to the land area to be mapped is very important. It is equal area and is especially useful for large land masses oriented East-West, for example the U.S.A.

CYLINDRICAL AND OTHER WORLD PROJECTIONS

This group of projections are those which permit the whole of the Earth's surface to be depicted on one map. They are a very large group of projections and the following are only a few of them. Cylindrical projections are constructed by the projection of the graticule from the globe onto a cylinder tangential to the globe. Although cylindrical projections can depict all the main land masses, there is considerable distortion of shape and area towards the poles. One cylindrical projection, Mercator overcomes this shortcoming by possesing the unique navigational property that any straight line drawn on it is a line of constant bearing (loxodrome). It is used for maps and charts between 15° either side of the equator. Beyond this enlargement of area is a serious drawback, although it is used for navigational charts at all latitudes.

Simple Cylindrical   **Cylindrical with two standard parallels**

Mercator

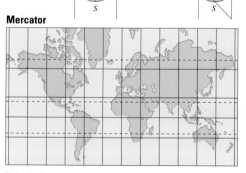

Eckert IV (pseudocylindrical equal area)

Hammer (polyconic equal area)

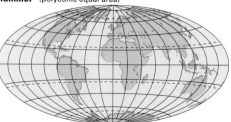

SATELLITE IMAGERY AND REMOTE SENSING

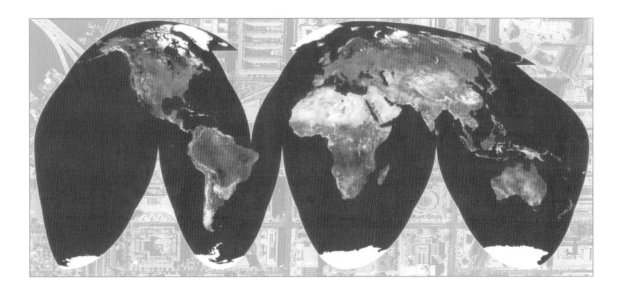

All satellite images in this section courtesy of NPA Group Limited, Edenbridge, Kent (www.satmaps.com)
Philip's would like to acknowledge the valuable assistance of Richard Chiles and the staff at NPA in the preparation of this section.

The first satellite to monitor our environment systematically was launched as long ago as April 1961. It was called TIROS-1 and was designed specifically to record atmospheric change. The first of the generation of Earth resources satellites was Landsat-1, launched in July 1972.

The succeeding two or three decades have seen a revolution in our ability to survey and map our global environment. Digital sensors mounted on satellites now scan vast areas of the Earth's surface day and night. They collect and relay back to Earth huge volumes of geographical data which is processed and stored by computers.

Satellite Imagery and Remote Sensing

Continuous development and refinement, and freedom from national access restrictions, have meant that sensors on these satellite platforms are increasingly replacing surface and airborne data-gathering techniques. Twenty-four hours a day, satellites are scanning and measuring the Earth's surface and atmosphere, adding to an ever-expanding range of geographic and geophysical data available to help us identify and manage the problems of our human and physical environments. Remote sensing is the science of extracting information from such images.

Satellite Orbits

Most Earth-observation satellites (such as the Landsat, SPOT and IRS series) are in a near-polar, Sun-synchronous orbit (*see diagram opposite*). At altitudes of around 700–900 km the satellites revolve around the Earth approximately every 100 minutes and on each orbit cross a particular line of latitude at the same local (solar) time. This ensures that the satellite can obtain coverage of most of the globe, replicating the coverage typically within 2–3 weeks. In more recent satellites, sensors can be pointed sideways from the orbital path, and 'revisit' times with high-resolution frames can thus be reduced to a few days.

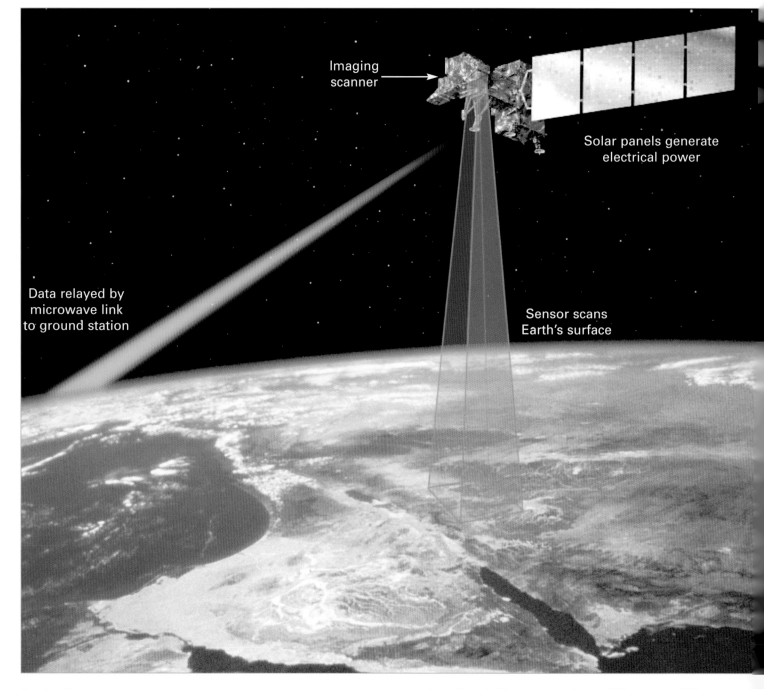

Imaging scanner

Solar panels generate electrical power

Data relayed by microwave link to ground station

Sensor scans Earth's surface

Landsat-7

This is the latest addition to the Landsat Earth-observation satellite programme, orbiting at 705 km above the Earth. With onboard recorders, the satellite can store data until it passes within range of a ground station. Basic geometric and radiometric corrections are then applied before distribution of the imagery to users.

Exceptions to these Sun-synchronous orbits include the geostationary meteorological satellites, such as Meteosat. These have a 36,000 km high orbit and rotate around the Earth every 24 hours, thus remaining above the same point on the equator. These satellites acquire frequent images showing cloud and atmospheric moisture movements for almost a full hemisphere.

In addition, there is the Global Positioning System (GPS) satellite 'constellation', which orbits at a height of 20,200 km, consisting of 24 satellites. These circle the Earth in six different orbital planes, enabling us to fix our position on the Earth's surface to an accuracy of a few centimetres. Although developed for military use, this system is now available to individuals through hand-held receivers and in-car navigation systems. The other principal commercial uses are for surveying and air and sea navigation.

Digital Sensors

Early satellite designs involved images being exposed to photographic film and returned to Earth by capsule for processing, a technique still sometimes used today. However, even the first commercial satellite imagery, from Landsat-1, used digital imaging sensors and transmitted the data back to ground stations (*see diagram opposite*).

Passive, or optical, sensors record the radiation reflected from the Earth for specific wavebands. Active sensors transmit their own microwave radiation, which is reflected from the Earth's surface back to the satellite and recorded. The SAR (synthetic aperture radar) Radarsat images on page 118 are examples of the latter.

Whichever scanning method is used, each satellite records image data of constant width but potentially several thousand kilometres in length. Once the data has been received on Earth, it is usually split into approximately square sections or 'scenes' for distribution.

Spectral Resolution, Wavebands and False-Colour Composites

Satellites can record data from many sections of the electromagnetic spectrum (wavebands) simultaneously. Since we can only see images made from the three primary colours (red, green and blue), a selection of any three wavebands needs to be made in order to form a picture that will enable visual interpretation of the scene to be made. When any combination other than the visible bands are used, such as near or middle infrared, the resulting image is termed a 'false-colour composite'. An example of this is shown on page 109.

The selection of these wavebands depends on the purpose of the final image – geology, hydrology, agronomy and environmental

---

GEOGRAPHIC INFORMATION SYSTEMS

A Geographic Information System (GIS) enables any available geospatial data to be compiled, presented and analysed using specialized computer software.

Many aspects of our lives now benefit from the use of GIS – from the management and maintenance of the networks of pipelines and cables that supply our homes, to the exploitation or protection of the natural resources that we use. Much of this is at a regional or national scale and the data collected from satellites form an important part of our interpretation and understanding of the world around us.

GIS systems are used for many aspects of central planning and modern life, such as defence, land use, reclamation, telecommunications and the deployment of emergency services. Commercial companies can use demographic and infrastructure data within a GIS to plan marketing strategies, identifying where their services would be most needed, and thus decide where best to locate their businesses. Insurance companies use GIS to determine premiums based on population distribution, crime figures and the likelihood of natural disasters, such as flooding or subsidence.

Whatever the application, all the geographically related information that is available can be input and prepared in a GIS, so that a user can display the specific information of interest, or combine data to produce further information which might answer or help resolve a specific problem. From analysis of the data that has been acquired, it is often possible to use a GIS to generate a 'model' of possible future situations and to see what impact might result from decisions and actions taken. A GIS can also monitor change over time, to aid the observation and interpretation of long-term change.

A GIS can utilize a satellite image to extract useful information and map large areas, which would otherwise take many man-years of labour to achieve on the ground. For industrial applications, including hydrocarbon and mineral exploration, forestry, agriculture, environmental monitoring and urban development, such dramatic and beneficial increases in efficiency have made it possible to evaluate and undertake projects and studies in parts of the world that were previously considered inaccessible, and on a scale that would not have been possible before.

---

requirements each have their own optimum waveband combinations. The following pages give an indication of the variety and detail provided by satellite imagery.

SELECTED REMOTE SENSING SATELLITES

Year Launched	Satellite	Country	Repeat Cycle
Passive Sensors (Optical)			
1972	Landsat-1 MSS	USA	18 days
1975	Landsat-2 MSS	USA	18 days
1978	Landsat-3 MSS	USA	18 days
1978	NOAA AVHRR	USA	12 hours
1981	Cosmos TK-350	Russia	varied
1982	Landsat-4 TM	USA	16 days
1984	Landsat-5 TM	USA	16 days
1986	SPOT-1	France	26 days
1988	IRS-1A	India	22 days
1988	SPOT-2	France	26 days
1989	Cosmos KVR-1000	Russia	varied
1991	IRS-1B	India	22 days
1992	SPOT-3	France	26 days
1995	IRS-1C	India	24 days
1997	IRS-1D	India	24 days
1998	SPOT-4	France	26 days
1999	Landsat-7 ETM	USA	16 days
1999	UoSAT-12	UK	n/a
1999	IKONOS-2	USA	n/a
Active Sensors (Synthetic Aperture Radar)			
1991	ERS-1	Europe	up to 168 days
1992	JERS-1	Japan	44 days
1995	ERS-2	Europe	35 days
1995	Radarsat	Canada	16 days

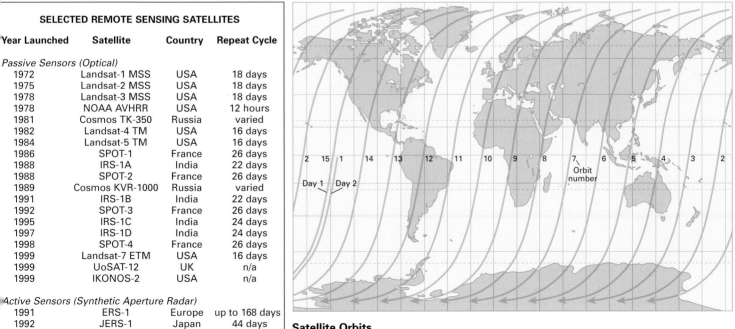

Satellite Orbits
Landsat-7 makes over 14 orbits per day in its Sun-synchronous orbit. During the full 16 days of a repeat cycle, coverage of the areas between those shown is achieved.

Natural-colour and false-colour composites

These images show the salt ponds at the southern end of San Francisco Bay, which now form the San Francisco Bay National Wildlife Refuge. They demonstrate the difference between 'natural colour' (*left*) and 'false colour' (*right*) composites.

The image on the left is made from visible red, green and blue wavelengths. The colours correspond closely to those one would observe from an aircraft. The salt ponds appear green or orange-red due to the colour of the sediments they contain. The urban areas appear grey and vegetation is either dark green (trees) or light brown (dry grass).

The right-hand image is made up of near-infrared, visible red and

visible green wavelengths. These wavebands are represented here in red, green and blue, respectively. Since chlorophyll in healthy vegetation strongly reflects near-infrared light, this is clearly visible as red in the image.

False-colour composite imagery is therefore very sensitive to the presence of healthy vegetation. The image above thus shows better discrimination between the 'leafy' residential urban areas, such as Palo Alto (south-west of the Bay) from other urban areas by the 'redness' of the trees. The high chlorophyll content of watered urban grass areas shows as bright red, contrasting with the dark red of trees and the brown of natural, dry grass. *(EROS)*

Europe at Night

This image was derived as part of the Defense Meteorological Satellite Program. The sensor recorded all the emissions of near-infrared radiation at night, mainly the lights from cities, towns and villages. Note also the 'lights' in the North Sea from the flares of the oil production platforms. This project was the first systematic attempt to record human settlement on a global scale using remote sensing. *(NOAA)*

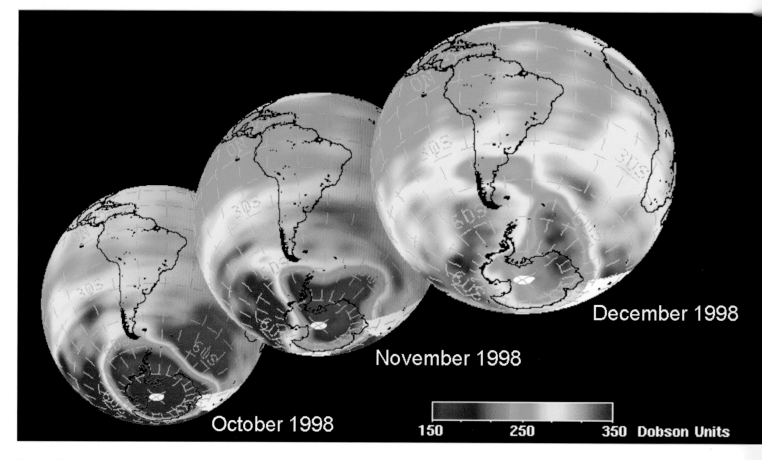

December 1998

November 1998

October 1998

150   250   350 **Dobson Units**

Ozone Distribution

The Global Ozone Monitoring Experiment (GOME) sensor was launched in April 1995. This instrument can measure a range of atmospheric trace constituents, in particular global ozone distributions. Environmental and public health authorities need this up-to-date information to alert people to health risks. Low ozone levels result in increased UV-B radiation, which is harmful and can cause cancers, cataracts and impact the human immune system. 'Dobson Units' indicate the level of ozone depletion (norma levels are around 280DU). *(DLR)*

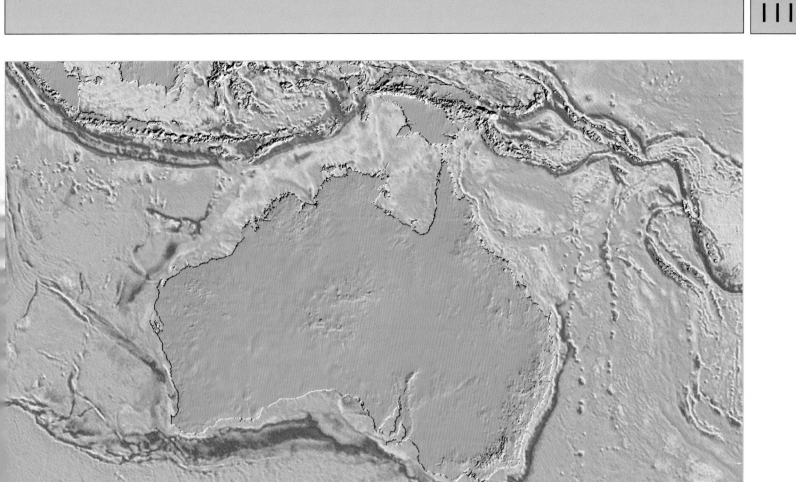

Gravitational Fields

The strength of the Earth's gravitational field at its surface varies according to the ocean depth and the density of local rocks. This causes local variations in the sea level. Satellites orbiting in precisely determined orbits are able to measure the sea level to an accuracy of a few centimetres. These variations give us a better understanding of the geological structure of the sea floor. Information from these sensors can also be used to determine ocean wave heights, which relate to surface wind speed, and are therefore useful in meteorological forecasting. *(NPA)*

Weather Monitoring

Geostationary and polar orbiting satellites monitor the Earth's cloud and atmospheric moisture movements, giving us an insight into the global workings of the atmosphere and permitting us to predict weather change. *(J-2)*

Hurricane Andrew

Although Hurricane Andrew, which hit Florida on 23 August 1992, was the most expensive natural disaster ever to strike the USA, its effects would have been far more disastrous had its path not been precisely tracked by large scale satellite images such as this from the AVHRR sensor. *(NOAA)*

Western Grand Canyon, Arizona, USA
This false-colour image shows in red the sparse vegetation on the limestone plateau, including sage, mesquite and grasses. Imagery such as this is used to monitor this and similar fragile environments. The sediment-laden river, shown as blue-green, can be seen dispersing into Lake Mead to the north-west. Side canyons cross the main canyon in straight lines, showing where erosion along weakened fault lines has occurred. *(EROS)*

Niger Delta, West Africa
The River Niger is the third longest river in Africa after the Nile and Congo. Deltas are by nature constantly evolving sedimentary features and often contain many ecosystems within them. In the case of the Niger Delta, there are also vast hydrocarbon reserves beneath it with associated wells and pipelines. Satellite imagery helps to plan activity and monitor this fragile and changing environment. *(EROS)*

Ayers Rock and Mt Olga, Northern Territory, Australia
These two huge outliers are the remnants of Precambrian mountain ranges created some 500 million years ago and then eroded away. Ayers Rock (*right*) rises 345 m above the surrounding land and has been a part of Aboriginal life for over 10,000 years. Their dramatic coloration, caused by oxidized iron in the sandstone, attracts visitors from around the world. The Yulara tourist resort (shown in blue) and the airport can be made out to the north of Ayers Rock. *(EROS)*

Mount St Helens, Washington, USA
A massive volcanic eruption on 18 May 1980 killed 60 people and devastated around 400 sq km of forest within minutes. The blast reduced the mountain peak by 400 m to its current height of 2550 m, and volcanic ash rose some 25 km into the atmosphere. The image shows Mount St Helens eight years after the eruption in 1988. The characteristic volcanic cone has collapsed in the north, resulting in the devastating 'liquid' flow of mud and rock. *(EROS)*

Kuwait City, Kuwait

This image shows Kuwait after the war with Iraq, which took place in 1991. During this conflict, more than 600 oil wells were set on fire and over 300 oil lakes were formed (visible as dark areas to the south). Satellite imagery helped reduce the costs of mapping these oil spills and enabled the level of damage to be determined prior to clean-up operations. *(Space Imaging)*

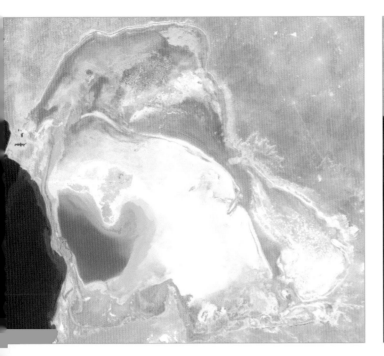

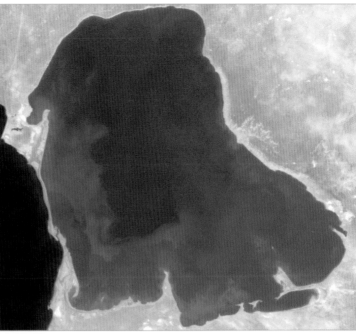

Kara-Bogaz-Gol, Turkmenistan

The Kara-Bogaz-Gol is a large, shallow lagoon joined by a narrow, steep-sided strait to the Caspian Sea. Evaporation makes it one of the most saline bodies of water in the world. Believing the Caspian Sea level was falling, the straight was dammed by the USSR in 1980 with the intention of conserving the water to sustain the salt industry. However, by 1983 it had dried up completely (*left*), leading to widespread wind-blown salt, soil poisoning and health problems downwind to the east. In 1992 the Turkmenistan government began to demolish the dam to re-establish the flow of water from the Caspian Sea (*right*). Satellite imagery has helped monitor and map the Kara-Bogaz-Gol as it has fluctuated in size. *(EROS)*

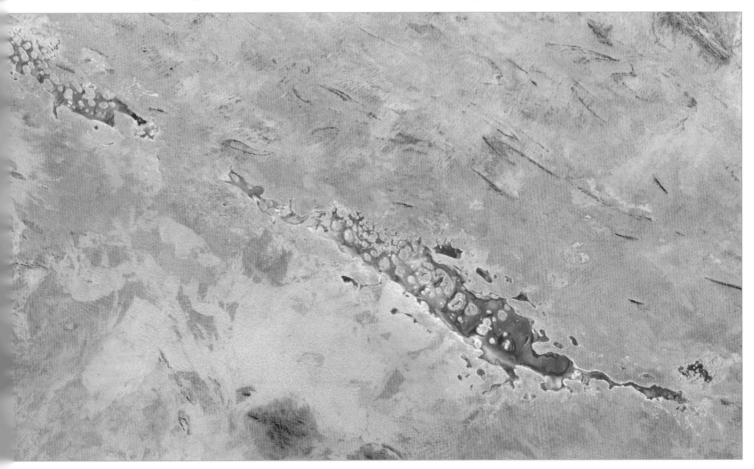

Lake Amadeus, Northern Territory, Australia

This is a saline lake system in the area between the Great Sandy Desert and Ayers Rock. An important wetland environment at the heart of one of the most arid areas in Australia, it supports a wide range of complex habitats and exists due to seepage from the central Australian groundwater system. Changes in its extent in an otherwise remote site can be monitored using satellite imagery such as this Landsat ETM scene. *(EROS)*

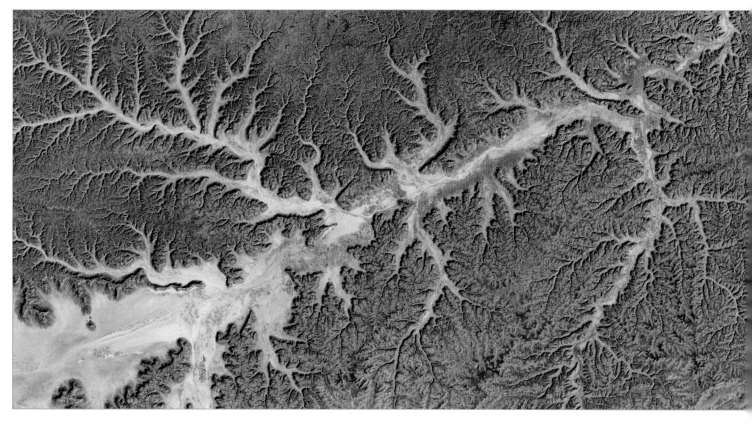

Wadi Hadhramaut, Yemen

Yemen is extremely arid – however, in the past it was more humid and wet, enabling large river systems to carve out the deep and spectacular gorges and dried-out river beds (*wadis*) seen in this image. The erosion has revealed many contrasting rock types. The image has been processed to exaggerate this effect, producing many shades of red, pink and purple, which make geological mapping easier and more cost-effective. *(EROS)*

North Anatolian Fault, Turkey

The east–west trending valley that runs through the centre of the image is formed by the North Anatolian wrench fault. It is the result of Arabia colliding with southern Eurasia, forcing most of Turkey westwards towards Greece. The valley was created by the Kelkit river removing the loosened rock formed by the two tectonic plates grinding together. This active fault has recently caused considerable damage further east in the Gulf of Izmit *(see page 120)*. *(EROS)*

agros Mountains, Iran

hese mountains were formed as Arabia collided with Southern urasia. The centre of this colour-enhanced image shows an nticline that runs east–west. The dark grey features are called *diapirs*, which are bodies of viscous rock salt that are very buoyant and sometimes rise to the surface, spilling and spreading out like a glacier. The presence of salt in the region is important as it stops oil escaping to the surface. *(EROS)*

chuan Basin, China

he north-east/south-west trending ridges in this image are nticlinal folds developed in the Earth's crust as a result of ate collision and compression. Geologists map these folds and the lowlands between them formed by synclinal folds, as they are often the areas where oil or gas are found in commercial quantities. The river shown in this image is the Yangtze, near Chongqing. *(China RSGS)*

Montserrat, Caribbean Sea

Synthetic Aperture Radar (SAR) sensors send out a microwave signal and create an image from the radiation reflected back. The signal penetrates cloud cover and does not need any solar illumina- tion. This image of Montserrat shows how the island can still be seen, despite clouds and the continuing eruption of the Soufrière volcano in the south. The delta visible in the sea to the east is being formed by lava flows pouring down the Tar River Valley. *(Radarsat)*

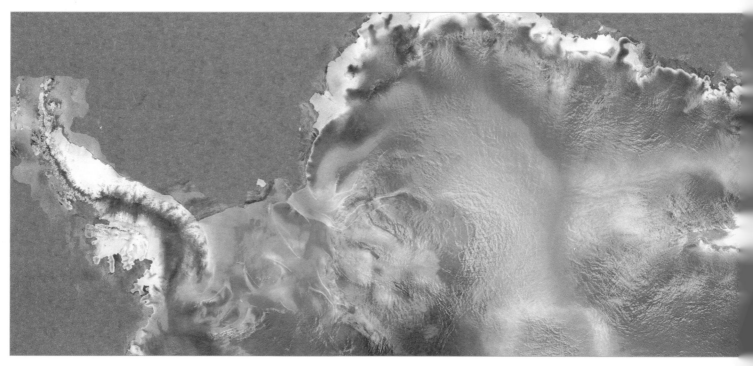

Antarctic Peninsula

SAR image brightness is dependent on surface texture. This image of part of Antarctica clearly shows the Antarctic ice tongues projecting from the Wilkins and George VI Ice Shelves at the south- west end of the peninsula as well as other coastal ice features. Images can be received, even during the winter 'night', and over a period of time form a valuable resource in our ability to monitor the recession of the ice and also the 'calving' of icebergs. *(Radarsat)*

as Vegas, Nevada, USA

vo satellite images viewing the same area of ground from different
rbits can be used to compile a Digital Elevation Model (DEM) of
e Earth's surface. A computer compares the images and calculates
the ground surface elevation to a vertical precision of 8–15 m,
preparing this for thousands of square kilometres in just a few
minutes. Overlaying a colour satellite image on to a DEM produced
the picture of Las Vegas shown here. *(NPA)*

- Urban (tall)
- Urban dense
- Urban
- Industrial
- Paved
- Urban / Tree mix
- Trees (coniferous)
- Trees (deciduous)
- Forest clearing
- Grass or crops
- Open
- Water

attle, Washington, USA

age processing software can use the differing spectral properties
land cover to 'classify' a multispectral satellite image. This
ssification of the area around Seattle was used together with
elevation data to model the transmission of mobile phone signals
before installation of the network. Microwave signals are affected
by the absorption, reflection and scattering of the signal from
vegetation and urban structures as well as the topography. *(NPA)*

Gulf of Izmit, north-west Turkey

On 17 August 1999 an earthquake measuring 7.4 on the Richter scale caused extensive damage and loss of life around Izmit. This image is a composite of two black-and-white images, one recorded on 7 August 1999 and the other on 24 September 1999. The colours in the image indicate change: orange highlights severely damaged buildings and areas where debris has been deposited during the rescue operation; blue indicates areas submerged beneath sea level as a result of the Earth's movement during the earthquake and fire-damaged oil tanks in the north-west. *(NPA)*

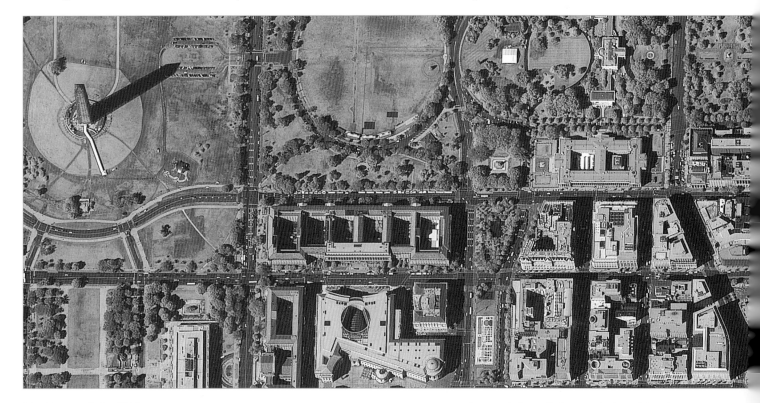

Washington D.C., USA

This image, with the White House seen at top right and the Washington Monument to the left, was recorded on 30 September 1999 by Space Imaging's IKONOS-2 satellite. It was the first satellite image to be commercially available with a ground-sampling interval (pixel size) of 1 m. With a directional sensor, image acquisition attempts can be made in as little as 1–3 days (cloud cover permitting). This level of resolution enables satellite imagery to be used as a data source for many applications that otherwise require expensive aerial surveys to be flown. In addition, data can readily be acquired for projects in remote regions of the world or areas where access is restricted. *(Space Imaging)*

INDEX TO WORLD MAPS

The index contains the names of all the principal places and features shown on the World Maps. Each name is followed by an additional entry in italics giving the country or region within which it is located. The alphabetical order of names composed of two or more words is governed primarily by the first word and then by the second. This is an example of the rule:

New South Wales □, *Australia*.. **34 G8** 33 0S 146 0E
New York □, *U.S.A.* **43 D10** 42 40N 76 0W
New York City, *U.S.A.* **43 E11** 40 45N 74 0W
New Zealand ■, *Oceania*............. **35 J13** 40 0S 176 0E
Newark, *U.S.A.* **43 F10** 39 42N 75 45W

Physical features composed of a proper name (Erie) and a description (Lake) are positioned alphabetically by the proper name. The description is positioned after the proper name and is usually abbreviated:

Erie, L., *N. Amer.* **42 D7** 42 15N 81 0W

Where a description forms part of a settlement or administrative name, however, it is always written in full and put in its true alphabetical position:

Mount Isa, *Australia*...................... **34 E6** 20 42S 139 26E

Names beginning with M' and Mc are indexed as if they were spelt Mac. Names beginning St. are alphabetized under Saint, but Santa and San are all spelt in full and are alphabetized accordingly. If the same placename occurs two or more times in the index and all are in the same country, each is followed by the name of the administrative subdivision in which it is located. The names are placed in the alphabetical order of the subdivision. For example:

Columbus, Ga., *U.S.A.* **41 D10** 32 30N 84 58W
Columbus, Ind., *U.S.A.* **42 F5** 39 14N 85 55W
Columbus, Ohio, *U.S.A.* **42 F6** 39 57N 83 1W

The number in bold type which follows each name in the index refers to the number of the map page where that feature or place will be found. This is usually the largest scale at which the place or feature appears.

The letter and figure which are in bold type immediately after the page number give the grid square on the map page, within which the feature is situated. The letter represents the latitude and the figure the longitude. In some cases the feature itself may fall within the specified square, while the name is outside.

For a more precise location, the geographical co-ordinates which follow the letter-figure references give the latitude and the longitude of each place. The first set of figures represent the latitude, which is the distance north or south of the Equator measured as an angle at the centre of the Earth. The Equator is latitude 0°, the North Pole is 90°N, and the South Pole 90°S.

The second set of figures represent the longitude, which is the distance east or west of the prime meridian, which runs through Greenwich, England. Longitude is also measured as an angle at the centre of the Earth and is given east or west of the prime meridian, from 0° to 180° in either direction.

The unit of measurement for latitude and longitude is the degree, which is subdivided into 60 minutes. Each index entry states the position of a place in degrees and minutes, a space being left between the degrees and the minutes. The latitude is followed by N(orth) or S(outh) and the longitude by E(ast) or W(est).

Rivers are indexed to their mouths or confluences, and carry the symbol ↝ after their names. A solid square ■ follows the name of a country, while an open square □ refers to a first order administrative area.

ABBREVIATIONS USED IN THE INDEX

Afghan. – Afghanistan
Ala. – Alabama
Alta. – Alberta
Amer. – America(n)
Arch. – Archipelago
Ariz. – Arizona
Ark. – Arkansas
Atl. Oc. – Atlantic Ocean
B. – Baie, Bahia, Bay, Bucht, Bugt
B.C. – British Columbia
Bangla. – Bangladesh
C. – Cabo, Cap, Cape, Coast
C.A.R. – Central African Republic
C. Prov. – Cape Province
Calif. – California
Cent. – Central
Chan. – Channel
Colo. – Colorado

Conn. – Connecticut
Cord. – Cordillera
Cr. – Creek
D.C. – District of Columbia
Del. – Delaware
Domin. – Dominica
Dom. Rep. – Dominican Republic
E. – East
El Salv. – El Salvador
Eq. Guin. – Equatorial Guinea
Fla. – Florida
Falk. Is. – Falkland Is.
G. – Golfe, Golfo, Gulf
Ga. – Georgia
Guinea–Biss. – Guinea–Bissau
Hd. – Head
Hts. – Heights
I.(s). – Ile, Ilha, Insel,

Isla, Island, Isle(s)
Ill. – Illinois
Ind. – Indiana
Ind. Oc. – Indian Ocean
Ivory C. – Ivory Coast
Kans. – Kansas
Ky. – Kentucky
L. – Lac, Lacul, Lago, Lagoa, Lake, Limni, Loch, Lough
La. – Louisiana
Lux. – Luxembourg
Madag. – Madagascar
Man. – Manitoba
Mass. – Massachusetts
Md. – Maryland
Me. – Maine
Medit. S. – Mediterranean Sea
Mich. – Michigan
Minn. – Minnesota
Miss. – Mississippi

Mo. – Missouri
Mont. – Montana
Mozam.– Mozambique
Mt.(s).– Mont, Monte, Monti, Montaña, Mountain
N. – Nord, Norte, North, Northern
N.B. – New Brunswick
N.C. – North Carolina
N. Cal. – New Caledonia
N. Dak. – North Dakota
N.H. – New Hampshire
N.J. – New Jersey
N. Mex. – New Mexico
N.S. – Nova Scotia
N.S.W. – New South Wales
N.W.T. – North West Territory
N.Y. – New York
N.Z. – New Zealand

Nebr. – Nebraska
Neths. – Netherlands
Nev. – Nevada
Nfld. – Newfoundland
Nic. – Nicaragua

Okla. – Oklahoma
Ont. – Ontario
Oreg. – Oregon
P.E.I. – Prince Edward Island
Pa. – Pennsylvania
Pac. Oc. – Pacific Ocean
Papua N.G. – Papua New Guinea
Pen. – Peninsula, Peninsule
Phil. – Philippines
Pk. – Park, Peak
Plat. – Plateau
Prov. – Province,

Provincial
Pt. – Point
Pta. – Ponta, Punta
Pte. – Pointe
Qué. – Québec
Queens. – Queensland
R. – Rio, River
R.I. – Rhode Island
Ra.(s). – Range(s)
Reg. – Region
Rep. – Republic
Res. – Reserve, Reservoir
S. – San, South
Si. Arabia – Saudi Arabia
S.C. – South Carolina
S. Dak. – South Dakota
S. Leone – Sierra Leone
Sa. – Serra, Sierra
Sask. – Saskatchewan
Scot. – Scotland
Sd. – Sound

Sib. – Siberia
St. – Saint, Sankt, Sint
Str. – Strait, Stretto
Switz. – Switzerland
Tas. – Tasmania
Tenn. – Tennessee
Tex. – Texas
Trin. & Tob. – Trinidad & Tobago
U.A.E. – United Arab Emirates
U.K. – United Kingdom
U.S.A. – United States of America
Va. – Virginia
Vic. – Victoria
Vol. – Volcano
Vt. – Vermont
W. – West
W. Va. – West Virginia
Wash. – Washington
Wis. – Wisconsin

INDEX TO WORLD MAPS

Aachen — Banda

A

Aachen, Germany 10 C4 50 45N 6 6 E
Aalborg, Denmark 6 G9 57 2N 9 54 E
Aarau, Switz. 10 E5 47 23N 8 4 E
Aare →, Switz. 10 E5 47 33N 8 14 E
Aarhus, Denmark 6 G10 56 8N 10 11 E
Abadan, Iran 24 B3 30 22N 48 20 E
Abbeville, France 8 A4 50 6N 1 49 E
Abéché, Chad 29 F9 13 50N 20 35 E
Abeokuta, Nigeria 30 C2 7 3N 3 19 E
Aberdeen, U.K. 7 C5 57 9N 2 5W
Abidjan, Ivory C. 28 G4 5 26N 3 58W
Abitibi L., Canada 42 A8 48 40N 79 40W
Abkhazia □, Georgia 15 F7 43 12N 41 5 E
Abohar, India 23 D5 30 10N 74 10 E
Abu Dhabi, U.A.E. 24 C4 24 28N 54 22 E
Abuja, Nigeria 30 C3 9 16N 7 2 E
Acapulco, Mexico 44 D5 16 51N 99 56W
Accomac, U.S.A. 43 G10 37 43N 75 40W
Accra, Ghana 30 C1 5 35N 0 6W
Acklins I., Bahamas 45 C10 22 30N 74 0W
Aconcagua, Argentina 47 F3 32 39S 70 0W
Acre □, Brazil 46 C2 9 1S 71 0W
Adamawa Highlands, Cameroon 29 G7 7 20N 12 20 E
Adana, Turkey 15 G6 37 0N 35 16 E
Adapazarı, Turkey 15 F5 40 48N 30 25 E
Addis Ababa, Ethiopia 29 G12 9 2N 38 42 E
Adelaide, Australia 34 G6 34 52S 138 30 E
Adelaide, S. Africa 31 C4 32 42S 26 20 E
Aden, Yemen 24 D3 12 45N 45 0 E
Aden, G. of, Asia 24 D3 12 30N 47 30 E
Adirondack Mts., U.S.A. 43 D10 44 0N 74 0W
Admiralty Is., Papua N. G. 36 H6 2 0S 147 0 E
Ado-Ekiti, Nigeria 30 C3 7 38N 5 12 E
Adoni, India 25 D6 15 33N 77 18 E
Adour →, France 8 E3 43 32N 1 32W
Adrar, Algeria 28 C4 27 51N 0 11W
Adrian, U.S.A. 42 E5 41 54N 84 2W
Adriatic Sea, Medit. S. 12 C6 43 0N 16 0 E
Ægean Sea, Medit. S. 13 E11 38 30N 25 0 E
Afghanistan ■, Asia 24 B5 33 0N 65 0 E
'Afīf, Si. Arabia 24 C3 23 53N 42 56 E
Agadès, Niger 30 A3 16 58N 7 59 E
Agadir, Morocco 28 B3 30 28N 9 55W
Agartala, India 23 H13 23 50N 91 23 E
Agen, France 8 D4 44 12N 0 38 E
Agra, India 23 F6 27 17N 77 58 E
Agrigento, Italy 12 F5 37 19N 13 34 E
Aguascalientes, Mexico 44 C4 21 53N 102 12W
Agulhas, C., S. Africa 31 C3 34 52S 20 0 E
Ahmadabad, India 23 H4 23 0N 72 40 E
Ahmadnagar, India 25 D6 19 7N 74 46 E
Ahmadpur, Pakistan 23 E3 29 12N 71 10 E
Ahvaz, Iran 24 B3 31 20N 48 40 E
Ahvenanmaa Is., Finland 6 F11 60 15N 20 0 E
Aïr, Niger 28 E6 18 30N 8 0 E
Aisne →, France 8 B5 49 26N 2 50 E
Aix-en-Provence, France 8 E6 43 32N 5 27 E
Aix-les-Bains, France 8 D6 45 41N 5 53 E
Ajaccio, France 8 F8 41 55N 8 40 E
Ajanta Ra., India 23 J5 20 28N 75 50 E
Ajaria □, Georgia 15 F7 41 30N 42 0 E
Ajmer, India 23 F5 26 28N 74 37 E
Akashi, Japan 19 B4 34 45N 134 58 E
Akita, Japan 19 A7 39 45N 140 7 E
Akola, India 23 J6 20 42N 77 2 E
Akranes, Iceland 6 B2 64 19N 22 5W
Akron, U.S.A. 42 E7 41 5N 81 31W
Aktyubinsk, Kazakstan 15 D10 50 17N 57 10 E
Akure, Nigeria 30 C3 7 15N 5 5 E
Akureyri, Iceland 6 B4 65 40N 18 6W
Al Ḩudaydah, Yemen 24 D3 14 50N 43 0 E
Al Hufūf, Si. Arabia 24 C3 25 25N 49 45 E
Al Jawf, Si. Arabia 24 C2 29 55N 39 40 E
Al Kut, Iraq 24 B3 32 30N 46 0 E
Al Qatif, Si. Arabia 24 C3 26 35N 50 0 E
Al 'Ula, Si. Arabia 24 C2 26 35N 38 0 E
Alabama □, U.S.A. 41 D9 33 0N 87 0W
Aland Is. = Ahvenanmaa Is., Finland 6 F11 60 15N 20 0 E
Alaska □, U.S.A. 38 B5 64 0N 154 0W
Alaska, G. of, Pac. Oc. 38 C5 58 0N 145 0W
Alaska Peninsula, U.S.A. 38 C4 56 0N 159 0W
Alaska Range, U.S.A. 38 B4 62 50N 151 0W
Alba-Iulia, Romania 11 E12 46 8N 23 39 E
Albacete, Spain 9 C5 39 0N 1 50W
Albania ■, Europe 13 D9 41 0N 20 0 E
Albany, Australia 34 H2 35 1S 117 58 E
Albany, Ga., U.S.A. 41 D10 31 35N 84 10W
Albany, N.Y., U.S.A. 43 D11 42 39N 73 45W
Albany →, Canada 39 C11 52 17N 81 31W
Albert L., Africa 32 D6 1 30N 31 0 E
Alberta □, Canada 38 C8 54 40N 115 0W
Albertville, France 8 D7 45 40N 6 22 E
Albi, France 8 E5 43 56N 2 9 E
Albion, U.S.A. 42 D5 42 15N 84 45W
Albuquerque, U.S.A. 40 C5 35 5N 106 39W
Albury, Australia 34 H8 36 3S 146 56 E
Alcalá de Henares, Spain 9 B4 40 28N 3 22W
Aldabra Is., Seychelles 27 G8 9 22S 46 28 E
Aldan →, Russia 18 C14 63 28N 129 35 E
Aleksandrovsk-Sakhalinskiy, Russia 18 D16 50 50N 142 20 E
Alençon, France 8 B4 48 27N 0 4 E
Alès, France 8 D6 44 9N 4 5 E
Alessándria, Italy 12 B3 44 54N 8 37 E
Ålesund, Norway 6 F9 62 28N 6 12 E
Aleutian Is., Pac. Oc. 36 B10 52 0N 175 0W
Alexander Arch., U.S.A. 38 C6 56 0N 136 0W
Alexandria, Egypt 29 B10 31 13N 29 58 E
Alexandria, La., U.S.A. 41 D8 31 18N 92 27W
Alexandria, Va., U.S.A. 42 F9 38 48N 77 3W
Algarve, Portugal 9 D1 36 58N 8 20W
Algeciras, Spain 9 D3 36 9N 5 28W
Algeria ■, Africa 28 C5 28 30N 2 0 E
Algiers, Algeria 28 A5 36 42N 3 8 E
Alicante, Spain 9 C5 38 23N 0 30W
Alice Springs, Australia 34 E5 23 40S 133 50 E
Aligarh, India 23 F7 27 55N 78 10 E
Alipur Duar, India 23 F12 26 30N 89 35 E
Aliquippa, U.S.A. 42 E7 40 37N 80 15W
Aliwal North, S. Africa 31 C4 30 45S 26 45 E
Alkmaar, Neths. 10 B3 52 37N 4 45 E
Allahabad, India 23 G8 25 25N 81 58 E
Allegan, U.S.A. 42 D5 42 32N 85 51W
Allegheny →, U.S.A. 42 E8 40 27N 80 1W
Allegheny Plateau, U.S.A. 42 G7 38 0N 80 0W
Allentown, U.S.A. 43 E10 40 37N 75 29W
Alleppey, India 25 E6 9 30N 76 28 E
Allier →, France 8 C5 46 57N 3 4 E
Alma, U.S.A. 42 D5 43 23N 84 39W
Almaty, Kazakstan 18 E9 43 15N 76 57 E
Almelo, Neths. 10 B4 52 22N 6 42 E
Almería, Spain 9 D4 36 52N 2 27W
Alor, Indonesia 22 D4 8 15S 124 30 E
Alpena, U.S.A. 42 C6 45 4N 83 27W
Alps, Europe 10 E5 46 30N 9 30 E
Alsace, France 8 B7 48 15N 7 25 E
Altai, Mongolia 20 B4 46 40N 92 45 E
Altay, China 20 B3 47 48N 88 10 E
Altoona, U.S.A. 42 E8 40 31N 78 24W
Altun Shan, China 20 C3 38 30N 88 0 E
Alwar, India 23 F6 27 38N 76 34 E
Amadjuak L., Canada 39 B12 65 0N 71 8W
Amagasaki, Japan 19 B4 34 42N 135 20 E
Amarillo, U.S.A. 40 C6 35 13N 101 50W
Amazon →, S. Amer. 46 C4 0 5S 50 0W
Ambala, India 23 D6 30 23N 76 56 E
Ambikapur, India 23 H9 23 15N 83 15 E
Ambon, Indonesia 22 D4 3 35S 128 20 E
American Samoa □, Pac. Oc. 35 C17 14 20S 170 40W
Amiens, France 8 B5 49 54N 2 16 E
Amman, Jordan 24 B2 31 57N 35 52 E
Amos, Canada 42 A8 48 35N 78 5W
Amravati, India 23 J6 20 55N 77 45 E
Amreli, India 23 J3 21 35N 71 17 E
Amritsar, India 23 D5 31 35N 74 57 E
Amroha, India 23 E7 28 53N 78 30 E
Amsterdam, Neths. 10 B3 52 23N 4 54 E
Amsterdam, U.S.A. 43 D10 42 56N 74 11W
Amudarya →, Uzbekistan 18 E7 43 58N 59 34 E
Amundsen Gulf, Canada 38 A7 71 0N 124 0W
Amundsen Sea, Antarctica 48 E1 72 0S 115 0W
Amur →, Russia 18 D16 52 56N 141 10 E
An Najaf, Iraq 24 B3 32 3N 44 15 E
An Nasiriyah, Iraq 24 B3 31 0N 46 15 E
An Nhon, Vietnam 22 B2 13 55N 109 7 E
Anadyr, Russia 18 C19 64 35N 177 20 E
Anadyr, G. of, Russia 18 C20 64 0N 180 0 E
Anaheim, U.S.A. 40 D3 33 50N 117 55W
Anambas Is., Indonesia 22 C2 3 20N 106 30 E
Anantnag, India 23 C5 33 45N 75 10 E
Anar, Iran 24 B4 30 55N 55 13 E
Anatolia, Turkey 15 G5 39 0N 30 0 E
Anchorage, U.S.A. 38 B5 61 13N 149 54W
Ancona, Italy 12 C5 43 38N 13 30 E
Anda, China 21 B7 46 24N 125 19 E
Andalucía □, Spain 9 D3 37 35N 5 0W
Andaman Is., Ind. Oc. 25 D8 12 30N 92 30 E
Anderson, U.S.A. 42 E5 40 10N 85 41W
Andes, S. Amer. 46 E3 20 0S 68 0W
Andhra Pradesh □, India 25 D6 18 0N 79 0 E
Andorra ■, Europe 9 A6 42 30N 1 30 E
Andreanof Is., U.S.A. 38 C2 52 0N 178 0W
Ándria, Italy 12 D7 41 13N 16 17 E
Andros I., Bahamas 45 C9 24 30N 78 0W
Angara →, Russia 18 D11 58 5N 94 20 E
Ånge, Sweden 6 F11 62 31N 15 35 E
Angel Falls, Venezuela 46 B3 5 57N 62 30W
Angerman →, Sweden 6 F11 62 40N 18 0 E
Angers, France 8 C3 47 30N 0 35W
Anglesey, U.K. 7 E4 53 17N 4 20W
Angola ■, Africa 33 G3 12 0S 18 0 E
Angoulême, France 8 D4 45 39N 0 10 E
Angoumois, France 8 D3 45 50N 0 25 E
Anguilla ■, W. Indies 44 J18 18 14N 63 5W
Anhui □, China 21 C6 32 0N 117 0 E
Anjou, France 8 C3 47 20N 0 15W
Ankara, Turkey 15 G5 39 57N 32 54 E
Ann, C., U.S.A. 43 D12 42 38N 70 35W
Ann Arbor, U.S.A. 42 D6 42 17N 83 45W
Annaba, Algeria 28 A6 36 50N 7 46 E
Annapolis, U.S.A. 42 F9 38 59N 76 30W
Annecy, France 8 D7 45 55N 6 8 E
Annobón, Atl. Oc. 27 G4 1 25S 5 36 E
Anshun, China 20 D5 26 18N 105 57 E
Antalya, Turkey 15 G5 36 52N 30 45 E
Antananarivo, Madag. 33 H9 18 55S 47 31 E
Antarctic Pen., Antarctica 48 D4 67 0S 60 0W
Antibes, France 8 E7 43 34N 7 6 E
Anticosti I., Canada 43 A16 49 30N 63 0W
Antigua & Barbuda ■, W. Indies 44 K20 17 20N 61 48W
Antofagasta, Chile 47 E2 23 50S 70 30W
Antsiranana, Madag. 33 G9 12 25S 49 20 E
Antwerp, Belgium 10 C3 51 13N 4 25 E
Anyang, China 21 C6 36 5N 114 21 E
Aomori, Japan 19 F12 40 45N 140 45 E
Aoraki Mt. Cook, N.Z. 35 J13 43 36S 170 9 E
Aparri, Phil. 22 B4 18 22N 121 38 E
Apeldoorn, Neths. 10 B3 52 13N 5 57 E
Apennines, Italy 12 B4 44 0N 10 0 E
Apia, Samoa 35 C16 13 50S 171 50W
Appalachian Mts., U.S.A. 42 G7 38 0N 80 0W
Appleton, U.S.A. 42 C3 44 16N 88 25W
Aqmola = Astana, Kazakstan 18 D9 51 10N 71 30 E
Ar Ramadi, Iraq 24 B3 33 25N 43 20 E
Arabian Desert, Egypt 29 C11 27 30N 32 30 E
Arabian Gulf = Gulf, The, Asia 24 C4 27 0N 50 0 E
Arabian Sea, Ind. Oc. 24 D5 16 0N 65 0 E
Aracaju, Brazil 46 D6 10 55S 37 4W
Arad, Romania 11 E11 46 10N 21 20 E
Arafura Sea, E. Indies 22 D5 9 0S 135 0 E
Aragón □, Spain 9 B5 41 25N 0 40W
Araguaia →, Brazil 46 C5 5 21S 48 41W
Arak, Iran 24 B3 34 0N 49 40 E
Arakan Yoma, Burma 25 C8 20 0N 94 40 E
Aral, Kazakstan 18 E8 46 41N 61 45 E
Aral Sea, Asia 18 E8 44 30N 60 0 E
Arcachon, France 8 D3 44 40N 1 10W
Arctic Ocean, Arctic 48 B17 78 0N 160 0W
Arctic Red River, Canada 38 B6 67 15N 134 0W
Ardabil, Iran 24 B3 38 15N 48 18 E
Ardennes, Belgium 10 D3 49 50N 5 5 E
Arendal, Norway 6 G9 58 28N 8 46 E
Arequipa, Peru 46 D2 16 20S 71 30W
Argentan, France 8 B3 48 45N 0 1W
Argentina ■, S. Amer. 47 F3 35 0S 66 0W
Arima, Trin. & Tob. 44 S20 10 38N 61 17W
Arizona □, U.S.A. 40 D4 34 0N 112 0W
Arkansas □, U.S.A. 41 D8 35 0N 92 30W
Arkansas →, U.S.A. 41 D8 33 47N 91 4W
Arkhangelsk, Russia 14 B7 64 38N 40 36 E
Arles, France 8 E6 43 41N 4 40 E
Arlington, U.S.A. 42 F9 38 53N 77 7W
Arlon, Belgium 10 D3 49 42N 5 49 E
Armenia ■, Asia 15 F7 40 20N 45 0 E
Arnhem, Neths. 10 C3 51 58N 5 55 E
Arnhem Land, Australia 34 C5 13 10S 134 30 E
Arnprior, Canada 42 C9 45 26N 76 21W
Arrah, India 23 G10 25 35N 84 32 E
Arran, U.K. 7 D4 55 34N 5 12W
Arras, France 8 A5 50 17N 2 46 E
Artois, France 8 A5 50 20N 2 30 E
Aru Is., Indonesia 22 D5 6 0S 134 30 E
Arunachal Pradesh □, India 25 C8 28 0N 95 0 E
Arusha, Tanzania 32 E7 3 20S 36 40 E
Arviat, Canada 38 B10 61 10N 94 15W
Asab, Namibia 31 B2 25 30S 18 0 E
Asahigawa, Japan 19 F12 43 46N 142 22 E
Asansol, India 23 H11 23 40N 87 1 E
Asbestos, Canada 43 C12 45 47N 71 58W
Asbury Park, U.S.A. 43 E10 40 13N 74 1W
Ascension I., Atl. Oc. 27 G2 8 0S 14 15W
Ashkhabad, Turkmenistan 18 F7 38 0N 57 50 E
Ashland, Ky., U.S.A. 42 F6 38 28N 82 38W
Ashland, Ohio, U.S.A. 42 E6 40 52N 82 19W
Ashtabula, U.S.A. 42 E7 41 52N 80 47W
Asifabad, India 23 K7 19 20N 79 24 E
Asir □, Si. Arabia 24 D3 18 40N 42 30 E
Asmara, Eritrea 29 E12 15 19N 38 55 E
Assam □, India 23 F13 26 0N 93 0 E
Assen, Neths. 10 B4 53 0N 6 35 E
Assisi, Italy 12 C5 43 4N 12 37 E
Astana, Kazakstan 18 D9 51 10N 71 30 E
Asti, Italy 12 B3 44 54N 8 12 E
Astrakhan, Russia 15 E8 46 25N 48 5 E
Asturias □, Spain 9 A3 43 15N 6 0W
Asunción, Paraguay 47 E4 25 10S 57 30W
Aswân, Egypt 29 D11 24 4N 32 57 E
Atacama Desert, Chile 47 E3 24 0S 69 20W
Atbara, Sudan 29 E11 17 42N 33 59 E
Atbara →, Sudan 29 E11 17 40N 33 56 E
Athabasca →, Canada 38 C8 58 40N 110 50W
Athabasca, L., Canada 38 C9 59 15N 109 15W
Athens, Greece 13 F10 37 58N 23 46 E
Athens, U.S.A. 42 F6 39 20N 82 6W
Atikokan, Canada 42 A2 48 45N 91 37W
Atlanta, U.S.A. 41 D10 33 45N 84 23W
Atlantic City, U.S.A. 43 F10 39 21N 74 27W
Atlantic Ocean 2 E9 0 0 20 0W
Atyraū, Kazakstan 18 E7 47 5N 52 0 E
Au Sable →, U.S.A. 42 C6 44 25N 83 20W
Aube →, France 8 B5 48 34N 3 43 E
Auburn, Ind., U.S.A. 42 E5 41 22N 85 4W
Auburn, N.Y., U.S.A. 42 D9 42 56N 76 34W
Aubusson, France 8 D5 45 57N 2 11 E
Auch, France 8 E4 43 39N 0 36 E
Auckland, N.Z. 35 H13 36 52S 174 46 E
Aude →, France 8 E5 43 13N 3 14 E
Augrabies Falls, S. Africa 31 B3 28 35S 20 20 E
Augsburg, Germany 10 D6 48 25N 10 52 E
Augusta, Ga., U.S.A. 41 D10 33 28N 81 58W
Augusta, Maine, U.S.A. 43 C13 44 19N 69 47W
Aunis, France 8 C3 46 5N 0 50W
Aurangabad, Bihar, India 23 G10 24 45N 84 18 E
Aurangabad, Maharashtra, India 23 K5 19 50N 75 23 E
Aurillac, France 8 D5 44 55N 2 26 E
Aurora, U.S.A. 42 E3 41 45N 88 19W
Austin, U.S.A. 40 D7 30 17N 97 45W
Australia ■, Oceania 34 E5 23 0S 135 0 E
Australian Capital Territory □, Australia 34 H8 35 30S 149 0 E
Austria ■, Europe 10 E8 47 0N 14 0 E
Autun, France 8 C6 46 58N 4 17 E
Auvergne, France 8 D5 45 20N 3 15 E
Auxerre, France 8 C5 47 48N 3 32 E
Avallon, France 8 C5 47 30N 3 53 E
Avellino, Italy 12 D6 40 54N 14 47 E
Avignon, France 8 E6 43 57N 4 50 E
Ávila, Spain 9 B3 40 39N 4 43W
Avranches, France 8 B3 48 40N 1 20W
Axiós →, Greece 13 D10 40 57N 22 35 E
Ayers Rock, Australia 34 F5 25 23S 131 5 E
Ayr, U.K. 7 D4 55 28N 4 38W
Azamgarh, India 23 F9 26 5N 83 13 E
Azerbaijan ■, Asia 15 F8 40 20N 48 0 E
Azores, Atl. Oc. 2 C8 38 44N 29 0W
Azov, Sea of, Europe 15 E6 46 0N 36 30 E
Azuero Pen., Panama 45 F8 7 30N 80 30W

B

Babol, Iran 24 B4 36 40N 52 50 E
Babuyan Chan., Phil. 22 B4 18 40N 121 30 E
Bacău, Romania 11 E14 46 35N 26 55 E
Bacolod, Phil. 22 B4 10 40N 122 57 E
Bad Axe, U.S.A. 42 D6 43 48N 83 0W
Badajoz, Spain 9 C2 38 50N 6 59W
Badalona, Spain 9 B7 41 26N 2 15 E
Baden-Württemberg □, Germany 10 D5 48 20N 8 40 E
Baffin I., Canada 39 B12 68 0N 75 0W
Baghdad, Iraq 24 B3 33 20N 44 30 E
Baguio, Phil. 22 B4 16 26N 120 34 E
Bahamas ■, N. Amer. 45 C10 24 0N 75 0W
Baharampur, India 23 G12 24 2N 88 27 E
Bahawalpur, Pakistan 23 E3 29 24N 71 40 E
Bahía = Salvador, Brazil 46 D6 13 0S 38 30W
Bahía □, Brazil 46 D5 12 0S 42 0W
Bahía Blanca, Argentina 47 F3 38 35S 62 13W
Bahraich, India 23 F8 27 38N 81 37 E
Bahrain ■, Asia 24 C4 26 0N 50 35 E
Baia Mare, Romania 11 E12 47 40N 23 35 E
Baie-St-Paul, Canada 43 B12 47 28N 70 32W
Baikal, L., Russia 18 D12 53 0N 108 0 E
Baja California, Mexico 44 B2 31 10N 115 12W
Bakersfield, U.S.A. 40 C3 35 23N 119 1W
Bakhtaran, Iran 24 B3 34 23N 47 0 E
Baku, Azerbaijan 15 F8 40 29N 49 56 E
Balabac Str., E. Indies 22 C3 7 53N 117 5 E
Balaghat, India 23 J8 21 49N 80 12 E
Balaton, Hungary 11 E9 46 50N 17 40 E
Balboa, Panama 44 H14 8 57N 79 34W
Baldwin, U.S.A. 42 D5 43 54N 85 51W
Balearic Is., Spain 9 C7 39 30N 3 0 E
Baleshwar, India 23 J11 21 35N 87 3 E
Bali, Indonesia 22 D3 8 20S 115 0 E
Balıkeşir, Turkey 13 E12 39 35N 27 58 E
Balikpapan, Indonesia 22 D3 1 10S 116 55 E
Balkan Mts., Bulgaria 13 C10 43 15N 23 0 E
Balkhash, L., Kazakstan 18 E9 46 0N 74 50 E
Ballarat, Australia 34 H7 37 33S 143 50 E
Balqash, Kazakstan 18 E9 46 50N 74 50 E
Balrampur, India 23 F9 27 30N 82 20 E
Balsas →, Mexico 44 D4 17 55N 102 10W
Baltic Sea, Europe 6 G11 57 0N 19 0 E
Baltimore, U.S.A. 42 F9 39 17N 76 37W
Bam, Iran 24 C4 29 7N 58 14 E
Bamako, Mali 28 F3 12 34N 7 55W
Bamberg, Germany 10 D6 49 54N 10 54 E
Bamenda, Cameroon 30 C4 5 57N 10 11 E
Bancroft, Canada 42 C9 45 3N 77 51W
Banda, India 23 G8 25 30N 80 26 E

Place names on the yellow-coded large scale map section are to be found in the index at the end of that section

Place names on the yellow-coded large scale map section are to be found in the index at the end of that section

INDEX TO WORLD MAPS

Place names on the yellow-coded large scale map section are to be found in the index at the end of that section

INDEX TO WORLD MAPS

Place names on the yellow-coded large scale map section are to be found in the index at the end of that section

Place names on the yellow-coded large scale map section are to be found in the index at the end of that section

Place names on the yellow-coded large scale map section are to be found in the index at the end of that section

INDEX TO WORLD MAPS

Kurashiki

Man, I. of

Kurashiki, *Japan* **19 B3** 34 40N 133 50 E
Kurdistan, *Asia* **24 B3** 37 20N 43 30 E
Kure, *Japan* **19 B3** 34 14N 132 32 E
Kurgan, *Russia* **18 D8** 55 26N 65 18 E
Kuril Is., *Russia* **18 E17** 45 0N 150 0 E
Kurnool, *India* **25 D6** 15 45N 78 0 E
Kursk, *Russia* **14 D6** 51 42N 36 11 E
Kuruman, *S. Africa* **31 B3** 27 28S 23 28 E
Kuruman →, *S. Africa* **31 B3** 26 56S 20 39 E
Kurume, *Japan* **19 C2** 33 15N 130 30 E
Kushiro, *Japan* **19 F12** 43 0N 144 25 E
Kushtia, *Bangla.* **23 H12** 23 55N 89 5 E
Kütahya, *Turkey* **15 G5** 39 30N 30 2 E
Kutaisi, *Georgia* **15 F7** 42 19N 42 40 E
Kutch, Gulf of, *India* **23 H2** 22 50N 69 15 E
Kutch, Rann of, *India* **23 G2** 24 0N 70 0 E
Kuwait, *Kuwait* **24 C3** 29 30N 48 0 E
Kuwait ■, *Asia* **24 C3** 29 30N 47 30 E
Kuybyshev = Samara, *Russia* **14 D9** 53 8N 50 6 E
KwaMashu, *S. Africa* **31 B5** 29 45S 30 58 E
Kwangju, *S. Korea* **21 C7** 35 9N 126 54 E
Kyōto, *Japan* **19 B4** 35 0N 135 45 E
Kyrgyzstan ■, *Asia* **18 E9** 42 0N 75 0 E
Kyūshū, *Japan* **19 C2** 33 0N 131 0 E
Kyzyl Kum, *Uzbekistan* **18 E8** 42 30N 65 0 E
Kzyl-Orda, *Kazakstan* **18 E8** 44 48N 65 28 E

L

La Chorrera, *Panama* **44 H14** 8 50N 79 50W
La Coruña, *Spain* **9 A1** 43 20N 8 25W
La Mancha, *Spain* **9 C4** 39 10N 2 54W
La Paz, *Bolivia* **46 D3** 16 20S 68 10W
La Perouse Str., *Asia* **36 C6** 45 40N 142 0 E
La Plata, *Argentina* **47 F4** 35 0S 57 55W
La Porte, *U.S.A.* **42 E4** 41 36N 86 43W
La Rioja □, *Spain* **9 A4** 42 20N 2 20W
La Roche-sur-Yon, *France* **8 C3** 46 40N 1 25W
La Rochelle, *France* **8 C3** 46 10N 1 9W
La Sarre, *Canada* **42 A8** 48 45N 79 15W
La Spézia, *Italy* **12 B3** 44 7N 9 50 E
La Tuque, *Canada* **43 B11** 47 30N 72 50W
Labé, *Guinea* **28 F2** 11 24N 12 16W
Labrador □, *Canada* **39 C13** 53 20N 61 0W
Labuk B., *Malaysia* **22 C3** 6 10N 117 50 E
Lac-Mégantic, *Canada* **43 C12** 45 35N 70 53W
Laccadive Is. = Lakshadweep Is., *Ind. Oc.* **25 D6** 10 0N 72 30 E
Lachine, *Canada* **43 C11** 45 30N 73 40W
Laconia, *U.S.A.* **43 D12** 43 32N 71 28W
Ladakh Ra., *India* **23 B6** 34 0N 78 0 E
Ladoga, L., *Russia* **14 B5** 61 15N 30 30 E
Ladybrand, *S. Africa* **31 B4** 29 9S 27 29 E
Ladysmith, *S. Africa* **31 B4** 28 32S 29 46 E
Lae, *Papua N. G.* **34 B8** 6 40S 147 2 E
Lafayette, *Ind., U.S.A.* **42 E4** 40 25N 86 54W
Lafayette, *La., U.S.A.* **41 D8** 30 14N 92 1W
Lagos, *Nigeria* **30 C2** 6 25N 3 27 E
Lagos, *Portugal* **9 D1** 37 5N 8 41W
Lahn →, *Germany* **10 C4** 50 19N 7 37 E
Lahore, *Pakistan* **23 D5** 31 32N 74 22 E
Lahti, *Finland* **6 F13** 60 58N 25 40 E
Laingsburg, *S. Africa* **31 C3** 33 9S 20 52 E
Lake Charles, *U.S.A.* **41 D8** 30 14N 93 13W
Lakewood, *U.S.A.* **42 E7** 41 29N 81 48W
Lakshadweep Is., *Ind. Oc.* **25 D6** 10 0N 72 30 E
Lamon Bay, *Phil.* **22 B4** 14 30N 122 20 E
Lancaster, *N.H., U.S.A.* **43 C12** 44 29N 71 34W
Lancaster, *Pa., U.S.A.* **42 E9** 40 2N 76 19W
Lancaster Sd., *Canada* **39 A11** 74 13N 84 0W
Landes, *France* **8 D3** 44 0N 1 0W
Land's End, *U.K.* **7 F4** 50 4N 5 44W
Langres, *France* **8 C6** 47 52N 5 20 E
Langres, Plateau de, *France* **8 C6** 47 45N 5 3 E
Languedoc, *France* **8 E5** 43 58N 3 55 E
Lannion, *France* **8 B2** 48 46N 3 29W
L'Annonciation, *Canada* **43 B10** 46 25N 74 55W
L'Anse, *U.S.A.* **42 B3** 46 45N 88 27W
Lansing, *U.S.A.* **42 D5** 42 44N 84 33W
Lanzhou, *China* **20 C5** 36 1N 103 52 E
Laoag, *Phil.* **22 B4** 18 7N 120 34 E
Laon, *France* **8 B5** 49 33N 3 35 E
Laos ■, *Asia* **22 B2** 17 45N 105 0 E
Lapeer, *U.S.A.* **42 D6** 43 3N 83 19W
Lapland, *Europe* **6 E12** 68 7N 24 0 E
Laptev Sea, *Russia* **18 B14** 76 0N 125 0 E
Laredo, *U.S.A.* **40 E7** 27 30N 99 30W
Lárisa, *Greece* **13 E10** 39 36N 22 27 E
Larvik, *Norway* **6 G10** 59 4N 10 0 E
Las Palmas, *Canary Is.* **28 C1** 28 7N 15 26W
Las Vegas, *U.S.A.* **40 C3** 36 10N 115 9W
Lashio, *Burma* **25 C8** 22 56N 97 45 E
Latakia, *Syria* **24 B2** 35 30N 35 45 E
Latina, *Italy* **12 D5** 41 28N 12 52 E
Latvia ■, *Europe* **14 C3** 56 50N 24 0 E
Launceston, *Australia* **34 J8** 41 24S 147 8 E
Laurentian Plateau, *Canada* **39 C13** 52 0N 70 0W
Lausanne, *Switz.* **10 E4** 46 32N 6 38 E
Laut, *Indonesia* **22 C2** 4 45N 108 0 E
Lauzon, *Canada* **43 B12** 46 48N 71 10W
Laval, *France* **8 B3** 48 4N 0 48W
Lawrence, *U.S.A.* **43 D12** 42 43N 71 10W
Layla, *Si. Arabia* **24 C3** 22 10N 46 40 E
Lazio □, *Italy* **12 C5** 42 10N 12 30 E
Le Creusot, *France* **8 C6** 46 48N 4 24 E
Le Havre, *France* **8 B4** 49 30N 0 5 E
Le Mans, *France* **8 C4** 48 0N 0 10 E
Le Puy-en-Velay, *France* **8 D5** 45 3N 3 52 E
Leamington, *Canada* **42 D6** 42 3N 82 36W
Lebanon, *Ind., U.S.A.* **42 E4** 40 3N 86 28W
Lebanon, *Ky., U.S.A.* **42 G5** 37 34N 85 15W
Lebanon, *Pa., U.S.A.* **42 E9** 40 20N 76 26W
Lebanon ■, *Asia* **24 B2** 34 0N 36 0 E
Lecce, *Italy* **13 D8** 40 23N 18 11 E
Leduc, *Canada* **38 C8** 53 15N 113 30W
Leeds, *U.K.* **7 E6** 53 48N 1 33W
Leeuwarden, *Neths.* **10 B3** 53 15N 5 48 E
Leeuwin, C., *Australia* **34 G2** 34 20S 115 9 E
Leeward Is., *Atl. Oc.* **44 L18** 16 30N 63 30W
Leganés, *Spain* **9 B4** 40 19N 3 45W
Legnica, *Poland* **10 C9** 51 12N 16 10 E
Leh, *India* **23 B6** 34 9N 77 35 E
Lehututu, *Botswana* **31 A3** 23 54S 21 55 E
Leicester, *U.K.* **7 E6** 52 38N 1 8W
Leiden, *Neths.* **10 B3** 52 9N 4 30 E
Leine →, *Germany* **10 B5** 52 43N 9 36 E
Leipzig, *Germany* **10 C7** 51 18N 12 22 E
Léman, L., *Europe* **10 E4** 46 26N 6 30 E
Lena →, *Russia* **18 B14** 72 52N 126 40 E
Leningrad = St. Petersburg, *Russia* **14 C5** 59 55N 30 20 E
Leninsk-Kuznetskiy, *Russia* **18 D10** 54 44N 86 10 E
Lens, *France* **8 A5** 50 26N 2 50 E
Leominster, *U.S.A.* **43 D12** 42 32N 71 46W
León, *Mexico* **44 C4** 21 7N 101 40W
León, *Spain* **9 A3** 42 38N 5 34W
Lérida, *Spain* **9 B6** 41 37N 0 39 E
Les Sables-d'Olonne, *France* **8 C3** 46 30N 1 45W
Leskovac, *Serbia, Yug.* **13 C9** 43 0N 21 58 E
Lesotho ■, *Africa* **31 B4** 29 40S 28 0 E
Lésvos, *Greece* **13 E12** 39 10N 26 20 E
Leszno, *Poland* **11 C9** 51 50N 16 30 E
Lethbridge, *Canada* **38 D8** 49 45N 112 45W
Leti Is., *Indonesia* **22 D4** 8 10S 128 0 E
Letiahau →, *Botswana* **31 A3** 21 16S 24 0 E
Leuven, *Belgium* **10 C3** 50 52N 4 42 E
Lévis, *Canada* **43 B12** 46 48N 71 9W
Levkás, *Greece* **13 E9** 38 40N 20 43 E
Lewiston, *U.S.A.* **43 C12** 44 6N 70 13W
Lewistown, *U.S.A.* **42 E9** 40 36N 77 34W
Lexington, *U.S.A.* **42 F5** 38 3N 84 30W
Lexington Park, *U.S.A.* **42 F9** 38 16N 76 27W
Leyte, *Phil.* **22 B4** 11 0N 125 0 E
Lhasa, *China* **20 D4** 29 25N 90 58 E
Liaoning □, *China* **21 B7** 41 40N 122 30 E
Liaoyang, *China* **21 B7** 41 15N 122 58 E
Liaoyuan, *China* **21 B7** 42 58N 125 2 E
Liberec, *Czech Rep.* **10 C8** 50 47N 15 7 E
Liberia ■, *W. Afr.* **28 G3** 6 30N 9 30W
Libourne, *France* **8 D3** 44 55N 0 14W
Libreville, *Gabon* **32 D1** 0 25N 9 26 E
Libya ■, *N. Afr.* **29 C8** 27 0N 17 0 E
Libyan Desert, *Africa* **29 C9** 25 0N 25 0 E
Lichinga, *Mozam.* **33 G7** 13 13S 35 11 E
Lichtenburg, *S. Africa* **31 B4** 26 8S 26 8 E
Liechtenstein ■, *Europe* **10 E5** 47 8N 9 35 E
Liège, *Belgium* **10 C3** 50 38N 5 35 E
Liepāja, *Latvia* **14 C3** 56 30N 21 0 E
Liguria □, *Italy* **12 B3** 44 30N 8 50 E
Ligurian Sea, *Medit. S.* **12 C3** 43 20N 9 0 E
Likasi, *Congo (D.R.)* **32 G5** 10 55S 26 48 E
Lille, *France* **8 A5** 50 38N 3 3 E
Lillehammer, *Norway* **6 F10** 61 8N 10 30 E
Lilongwe, *Malawi* **33 G6** 14 0S 33 48 E
Lim Fjord, *Denmark* **6 G9** 56 55N 9 0 E
Lima, *Peru* **46 D2** 12 0S 77 0W
Lima, *U.S.A.* **42 E5** 40 44N 84 6W
Limerick, *Ireland* **7 E2** 52 40N 8 37W
Limnos, *Greece* **13 E11** 39 50N 25 5 E
Limoges, *France* **8 D4** 45 50N 1 15 E
Limousin, *France* **8 D4** 45 30N 1 30 E
Limoux, *France* **8 E5** 43 4N 2 12 E
Limpopo →, *Africa* **33 K6** 25 5S 33 30 E
Linares, *Spain* **9 C4** 38 10N 3 40W
Lincoln, *Maine, U.S.A.* **43 C13** 45 22N 68 30W
Lincoln, *Nebr., U.S.A.* **41 B7** 40 49N 96 41W
Lincoln Sea, *Arctic* **48 A4** 84 0N 55 0W
Lindsay, *Canada* **42 C8** 44 22N 78 43W
Lingga Arch., *Indonesia* **22 D2** 0 10S 104 30 E
Linhai, *China* **21 D7** 28 50N 121 8 E
Linköping, *Sweden* **6 G11** 58 28N 15 36 E
Linton, *U.S.A.* **42 F4** 39 2N 87 10W
Linxia, *China* **20 C5** 35 36N 103 10 E
Linz, *Austria* **10 D8** 48 18N 14 18 E
Lion, G. du, *France* **8 E6** 43 10N 4 0 E
Lipetsk, *Russia* **14 D6** 52 37N 39 35 E
Lippe →, *Germany* **10 C4** 51 39N 6 36 E
Lisbon, *Portugal* **9 C1** 38 42N 9 10W
Lisieux, *France* **8 B4** 49 10N 0 12 E
Lismore, *Australia* **34 F9** 28 44S 153 21 E
Listowel, *Canada* **42 D7** 43 44N 80 58W
Lithuania ■, *Europe* **14 C3** 55 30N 24 0 E
Little Current, *Canada* **42 C7** 45 55N 82 0W
Little Karoo, *S. Africa* **31 C3** 33 45S 21 0 E
Little Laut Is., *Indonesia* **22 D3** 4 45S 115 40 E
Little Rock, *U.S.A.* **41 D8** 34 45N 92 17W
Liuzhou, *China* **21 D5** 24 22N 109 22 E
Liverpool, *U.K.* **7 E5** 53 25N 3 0W
Livingstone, *Zambia* **33 H5** 17 46S 25 52 E
Livonia, *U.S.A.* **42 D6** 42 23N 83 23W
Livorno, *Italy* **12 C4** 43 33N 10 19 E
Ljubljana, *Slovenia* **10 E8** 46 4N 14 33 E
Ljusnan →, *Sweden* **6 F11** 61 12N 17 8 E
Llanos, *S. Amer.* **46 B2** 5 0N 71 35W
Lloret de Mar, *Spain* **9 B7** 41 41N 2 53 E
Lobatse, *Botswana* **31 B4** 25 12S 25 40 E
Lobito, *Angola* **33 G2** 12 18S 13 35 E
Loches, *France* **8 C4** 47 7N 1 0 E
Lock Haven, *U.S.A.* **42 E9** 41 8N 77 28W
Łódź, *Poland* **11 C10** 51 45N 19 27 E
Lofoten, *Norway* **6 E10** 68 30N 14 0 E
Logan, *Ohio, U.S.A.* **42 F6** 39 32N 82 25W
Logan, *W. Va., U.S.A.* **42 G7** 37 51N 81 59W
Logan, Mt., *Canada* **38 B5** 60 31N 140 22W
Logansport, *U.S.A.* **42 E4** 40 45N 86 22W
Logroño, *Spain* **9 A4** 42 28N 2 27W
Lohardaga, *India* **23 H10** 23 27N 84 45 E
Loir →, *France* **8 C3** 47 33N 0 32W
Loire →, *France* **8 C2** 47 16N 2 10W
Lombárdia □, *Italy* **12 B3** 45 40N 9 30 E
Lomblen, *Indonesia* **22 D4** 8 30S 123 32 E
Lombok, *Indonesia* **22 D3** 8 45S 116 30 E
Lomé, *Togo* **30 C2** 6 9N 1 20 E
Lomond, L., *U.K.* **7 C4** 56 8N 4 38W
Łomza, *Poland* **11 B12** 53 10N 22 2 E
London, *Canada* **42 D7** 42 59N 81 15W
London, *U.K.* **7 F6** 51 30N 0 3W
Londrina, *Brazil* **47 E4** 23 18S 51 10W
Long Beach, *U.S.A.* **40 D3** 33 47N 118 11W
Long Branch, *U.S.A.* **43 E11** 40 18N 74 0W
Long I., *Bahamas* **45 C9** 23 20N 75 10W
Long I., *U.S.A.* **43 E11** 40 45N 73 30W
Long Xuyen, *Vietnam* **22 B2** 10 19N 105 28 E
Longlac, *Canada* **42 A4** 49 45N 86 25W
Lons-le-Saunier, *France* **8 C6** 46 40N 5 31 E
Lop Nor, *China* **20 B4** 40 20N 90 10 E
Lorain, *U.S.A.* **42 E6** 41 28N 82 11W
Loralai, *Pakistan* **23 D2** 30 20N 68 41 E
Lorca, *Spain* **9 D5** 37 41N 1 42W
Lorient, *France* **8 C2** 47 45N 3 23W
Lorraine, *France* **8 B7** 48 53N 6 0 E
Los Angeles, *Chile* **47 F2** 37 28S 72 23W
Los Angeles, *U.S.A.* **40 D3** 34 4N 118 15W
Los Mochis, *Mexico* **44 B3** 25 45N 108 57W
Lot →, *France* **8 D4** 44 18N 0 20 E
Louis Trichardt, *S. Africa* **31 A4** 23 1S 29 43 E
Louisa, *U.S.A.* **42 F6** 38 7N 82 36W
Louiseville, *Canada* **43 B11** 46 20N 72 56W
Louisiana □, *U.S.A.* **41 D8** 30 50N 92 0W
Louisville, *U.S.A.* **42 F5** 38 15N 85 46W
Lourdes, *France* **8 E3** 43 6N 0 3W
Lowell, *U.S.A.* **43 D12** 42 38N 71 19W
Lower Tunguska →, *Russia* **18 C10** 65 48N 88 4 E
Lowville, *U.S.A.* **43 D10** 43 47N 75 29W
Luanda, *Angola* **32 F2** 8 50S 13 15 E
Luanshya, *Zambia* **33 G5** 13 3S 28 28 E
Lubbock, *U.S.A.* **40 D6** 33 35N 101 51W
Lübeck, *Germany* **10 B6** 53 52N 10 40 E
Lublin, *Poland* **11 C12** 51 12N 22 38 E
Lubumbashi, *Congo (D.R.)* **33 G5** 11 40S 27 28 E
Lucknow, *India* **23 F8** 26 50N 81 0 E
Lüda = Dalian, *China* **21 C7** 38 50N 121 40 E
Lüderitz, *Namibia* **31 B2** 26 41S 15 8 E
Ludhiana, *India* **23 D5** 30 57N 75 56 E
Ludington, *U.S.A.* **42 D4** 43 57N 86 27W
Ludwigshafen, *Germany* **10 D5** 49 29N 8 26 E
Lugano, *Switz.* **10 E5** 46 0N 8 57 E
Lugansk, *Ukraine* **15 E6** 48 38N 39 15 E
Lugo, *Spain* **9 A2** 43 2N 7 35W
Lule →, *Sweden* **6 E12** 65 35N 22 10 E
Luleå, *Sweden* **6 E12** 65 35N 22 10 E
Lüneburger Heide, *Germany* **10 B6** 53 10N 10 12 E
Lunéville, *France* **8 B7** 48 36N 6 30 E
Luni →, *India* **23 G3** 24 41N 71 14 E
Luoyang, *China* **21 C6** 34 40N 112 26 E
Luray, *U.S.A.* **42 F8** 38 40N 78 28W
Lusaka, *Zambia* **33 H5** 15 28S 28 16 E
Lutsk, *Ukraine* **11 C13** 50 50N 25 15 E
Luxembourg, *Lux.* **10 D4** 49 37N 6 9 E
Luxembourg ■, *Europe* **10 D4** 49 45N 6 0 E
Luzern, *Switz.* **10 E5** 47 3N 8 18 E
Luzhou, *China* **20 D5** 28 52N 105 20 E
Luzon, *Phil.* **22 B4** 16 0N 121 0 E
Lvov, *Ukraine* **11 D13** 49 50N 24 0 E
Lyakhov Is., *Russia* **18 B16** 73 40N 141 0 E
Lydenburg, *S. Africa* **31 B5** 25 10S 30 29 E
Lynchburg, *U.S.A.* **42 G8** 37 25N 79 9W
Lynn Lake, *Canada* **38 C9** 56 51N 101 3W
Lyonnais, *France* **8 D6** 45 45N 4 15 E
Lyons, *France* **8 D6** 45 46N 4 50 E

M

Ma'an, *Jordan* **24 B2** 30 12N 35 44 E
Maas →, *Neths.* **10 C3** 51 45N 4 32 E
Maastricht, *Neths.* **10 C3** 50 50N 5 40 E
Macapá, *Brazil* **46 B4** 0 5N 51 4W
Macau □, *China* **21 D6** 22 16N 113 35 E
M'Clintock Chan., *Canada* **38 A9** 72 0N 102 0W
MacDonnell Ras., *Australia* **34 E5** 23 40S 133 0 E
Macedonia □, *Greece* **13 D10** 40 39N 22 0 E
Macedonia ■, *Europe* **13 D9** 41 53N 21 40 E
Maceió, *Brazil* **46 C6** 9 40S 35 41W
Mach, *Pakistan* **23 E1** 29 50N 67 20 E
Machakos, *Kenya* **32 E7** 1 30S 37 15 E
Machias, *U.S.A.* **43 C14** 44 43N 67 28W
Machilipatnam, *India* **25 D7** 16 12N 81 8 E
Mackay, *Australia* **34 E8** 21 8S 149 11 E
Mackay, L., *Australia* **34 E4** 22 30S 129 0 E
McKeesport, *U.S.A.* **42 E8** 40 21N 79 52W
Mackenzie →, *Canada* **38 B6** 69 10N 134 20W
Mackenzie Mts., *Canada* **38 B6** 64 0N 130 0W
Mackinaw City, *U.S.A.* **42 C5** 45 47N 84 44W
McKinley, Mt., *U.S.A.* **38 B4** 63 4N 151 0W
McKinley Sea, *Arctic* **48 A6** 82 0N 0 0 E
Maclear, *S. Africa* **31 C4** 31 2S 28 23 E
Mâcon, *France* **8 C6** 46 19N 4 50 E
Macon, *U.S.A.* **41 D10** 32 51N 83 38W
Macquarie Is., *Pac. Oc.* **36 N7** 54 36S 158 55 E
Madadeni, *S. Africa* **31 B5** 27 43S 30 3 E
Madagascar ■, *Africa* **33 J9** 20 0S 47 0 E
Madaripur, *Bangla.* **23 H13** 23 19N 90 15 E
Madeira, *Atl. Oc.* **28 B1** 32 50N 17 0W
Madeira →, *Brazil* **46 C4** 3 22S 58 45W
Madhya Pradesh □, *India* **23 H7** 21 50N 78 0 E
Madison, *Ind., U.S.A.* **42 F5** 38 44N 85 23W
Madison, *Wis., U.S.A.* **41 B9** 43 4N 89 24W
Madisonville, *U.S.A.* **42 G4** 37 20N 87 30W
Madiun, *Indonesia* **22 D3** 7 38S 111 32 E
Madras = Chennai, *India* **25 D7** 13 8N 80 19 E
Madrid, *Spain* **9 B4** 40 25N 3 45W
Madurai, *India* **25 E6** 9 55N 78 10 E
Mafeking, *S. Africa* **31 B4** 25 50S 25 38 E
Mafeteng, *Lesotho* **31 B4** 29 51S 27 15 E
Magadan, *Russia* **18 D17** 59 38N 150 50 E
Magdalen Is., *Canada* **43 B17** 47 30N 61 40W
Magdalena →, *Colombia* **46 A2** 11 6N 74 51W
Magdeburg, *Germany* **10 B6** 52 7N 11 38 E
Magelang, *Indonesia* **22 D3** 7 29S 110 13 E
Magellan's Str., *Chile* **47 H2** 52 30S 75 0W
Maggiore, L., *Italy* **12 B3** 45 57N 8 39 E
Magnetic Pole (North), *Canada* **48 B1** 77 58N 102 8W
Magnetic Pole (South), *Antarctica* **48 D13** 64 8S 138 8 E
Magnitogorsk, *Russia* **14 D10** 53 27N 59 4 E
Magog, *Canada* **43 C11** 45 18N 72 9W
Mahakam →, *Indonesia* **22 D3** 0 35S 117 17 E
Mahalapye, *Botswana* **31 A4** 23 1S 26 51 E
Mahanadi →, *India* **23 J11** 20 20N 86 25 E
Maharashtra □, *India* **23 J5** 20 30N 75 30 E
Mahesana, *India* **23 H4** 23 39N 72 26 E
Maiduguri, *Nigeria* **29 F7** 12 0N 13 20 E
Maijdi, *Bangla.* **23 H13** 22 48N 91 10 E
Maikala Ra., *India* **23 J8** 22 0N 81 0 E
Maimana, *Afghan.* **24 B5** 35 53N 64 38 E
Main →, *Germany* **10 C5** 50 0N 8 18 E
Maine, *France* **8 C3** 47 55N 0 25W
Maine □, *U.S.A.* **43 C13** 45 20N 69 0W
Mainz, *Germany* **10 C5** 50 1N 8 14 E
Majorca = Mallorca, *Spain* **9 C7** 39 30N 3 0 E
Makasar, Str. of, *Indonesia* **22 D3** 1 0S 118 20 E
Makgadikgadi Salt Pans, *Botswana* **31 A4** 20 40S 25 45 E
Makhachkala, *Russia* **15 F8** 43 0N 47 30 E
Makiyivka, *Ukraine* **15 E6** 48 0N 38 0 E
Makkah, *Si. Arabia* **24 C2** 21 30N 39 54 E
Makunda, *Botswana* **31 A3** 22 30S 20 7 E
Malabar Coast, *India* **25 D6** 11 0N 75 0 E
Malacca, Str. of, *Indonesia* **22 C2** 3 0N 101 0 E
Málaga, *Spain* **9 D3** 36 43N 4 23W
Malang, *Indonesia* **22 D3** 7 59S 112 45 E
Malanje, *Angola* **32 F3** 9 36S 16 17 E
Mälaren, *Sweden* **6 G11** 59 30N 17 10 E
Malatya, *Turkey* **15 G6** 38 25N 38 20 E
Malawi ■, *Africa* **33 G6** 11 55S 34 0 E
Malaysia ■, *Asia* **22 C3** 5 0N 110 0 E
Maldives ■, *Ind. Oc.* **25 E6** 5 0N 73 0 E
Malegaon, *India* **23 J5** 20 30N 74 38 E
Mali ■, *Africa* **28 E4** 17 0N 3 0W
Mallorca, *Spain* **9 C7** 39 30N 3 0 E
Malmö, *Sweden* **6 G10** 55 36N 12 59 E
Malone, *U.S.A.* **43 C10** 44 51N 74 18W
Malta ■, *Europe* **12 G6** 35 50N 14 30 E
Malvinas, Is. = Falkland Is. □, *Atl. Oc.* **47 H4** 51 30S 59 0W
Man, I. of, *U.K.* **7 D4** 54 15N 4 30W

Place names on the yellow-coded large scale map section are to be found in the index at the end of that section

INDEX TO WORLD MAPS

Place names on the yellow-coded large scale map section are to be found in the index at the end of that section

Place names on the yellow-coded large scale map section are to be found in the index at the end of that section

Place names on the yellow-coded large scale map section are to be found in the index at the end of that section

Place names on the yellow-coded large scale map section are to be found in the index at the end of that section

Tabas   **Vänern**

T

Place names on the yellow-coded large scale map section are to be found in the index at the end of that section

Vanino, *Russia* ..... **18 E16** 48 50N 140 5 E
Vännäs, *Sweden* . **6 F11** 63 58N 19 48 E
Vannes, *France* ... **8 C2** 47 40N 2 47W
Vanrhynsdorp,
  S. Africa .... **31 C2** 31 36S 18 44 E
Vanua Levu, *Fiji* .. **35 D14** 16 33S 179 15 E
Vanuatu ■, *Pac. Oc.* **35 D12** 15 0S 168 0 E
Varanasi, *India* ... **23 G9** 25 22N 83 0 E
Varanger Fjord,
  Norway .... **6 D13** 70 3N 29 25 E
Varberg, *Sweden* .. **6 G10** 57 6N 12 20 E
Varna, *Bulgaria* .. **13 C12** 43 13N 27 56 E
Västerås, *Sweden* . **6 G11** 59 37N 16 38 E
Västervik, *Sweden* . **6 G11** 57 43N 16 33 E
Vatican City ■, *Europe* **12 D5** 41 54N 12 27 E
Vatnajökull. *Iceland* . **6 B5** 64 30N 16 48W
Vättern, *Sweden* .. **6 G10** 58 25N 14 30 E
Vega, *Norway* .... **6 E10** 65 40N 11 55 E
Vellore, *India* ...... **25 D6** 12 57N 79 10 E
Vendée □, *France* .. **8 C3** 46 50N 1 35W
Vendôme, *France* .. **8 C4** 47 47N 1 3 E
Venezuela ■, *S. Amer.* **46 B3** 8 0N 66 0W
Venice, *Italy* ..... **12 B5** 45 27N 12 21 E
Ventoux, Mt., *France* **8 D6** 44 10N 5 17 E
Veracruz, *Mexico* .. **44 D5** 19 10N 96 10W
Veraval, *India* .... **23 J3** 20 53N 70 27 E
Vercelli, *Italy* ..... **12 B3** 45 19N 8 25 E
Verdun, *France* .... **8 B6** 49 9N 5 24 E
Vereeniging, *S. Africa* **31 B4** 26 38S 27 57 E
Verkhoyansk, *Russia* **18 C15** 67 35N 133 25 E
Verkhoyansk Ra.,
  Russia .... **18 C14** 66 0N 129 0 E
Vermont □, *U.S.A.* . **43 D11** 44 0N 73 0W
Verona, *Italy* ..... **12 B4** 45 27N 11 0 E
Versailles, *France* .. **8 B5** 48 48N 2 8 E
Verviers, *Belgium* . **10 C3** 50 37N 5 52 E
Vesoul, *France* .... **8 C7** 47 40N 6 11 E
Vesterålen, *Norway* . **6 E10** 68 45N 15 0 E
Vesuvio, *Italy* .... **12 D6** 40 49N 14 26 E
Veszprém, *Hungary* . **11 E9** 47 8N 17 57 E
Vicenza, *Italy* .... **12 B4** 45 33N 11 33 E
Vichy, *France* ..... **8 C5** 46 9N 3 26 E
Victoria, *Canada* .. **38 D7** 48 30N 123 25W
Victoria □, *Australia* . **34 H7** 37 0S 144 0 E
Victoria, L., *Africa* ... **32 E6** 1 0S 33 0 E
Victoria de Durango =
  Durango, *Mexico* . **44 C4** 24 3N 104 39W
Victoria Falls,
  Zimbabwe ...... **33 H5** 17 58S 25 52 E
Victoria I., *Canada* . **38 A8** 71 0N 111 0W
Victoria West, *S. Africa* **31 C3** 31 25S 23 4 E
Victoriaville, *Canada* . **43 B12** 46 4N 71 56W
Vienna, *Austria* .... **10 D9** 48 12N 16 22 E
Vienne, *France* .... **8 D6** 45 31N 4 53 E
Vienne →, *France* .. **8 C4** 47 13N 0 5 E
Vientiane, *Laos* ... **22 B2** 17 58N 102 36 E
Vierzon, *France* ... **8 C5** 47 13N 2 5 E
Vietnam ■, *Asia* .. **22 B2** 19 0N 106 0 E
Vigo, *Spain* **9 A1** 42 12N 8 41W
Vijayawada, *India* . **25 D7** 16 31N 80 39 E
Vikna, *Norway* .... **6 F10** 64 55N 10 58 E
Vilaine →, *France* .. **8 C2** 47 30N 2 27W
Vilhelmina, *Sweden* . **6 F11** 64 35N 16 39 E
Villach, *Austria* ... **10 E7** 46 37N 13 51 E
Villahermosa, *Mexico* . **44 D6** 17 59N 92 55W
Ville-Marie, *Canada* . **42 B8** 47 20N 79 30W
Villeneuve-sur-Lot,
  France .... **8 D4** 44 24N 0 42 E
Vilnius, *Lithuania* . **14 D4** 54 38N 25 19 E
Vilyuy →, *Russia* .. **18 C14** 64 24N 126 26 E
Vilyuysk, *Russia* .. **18 C14** 63 40N 121 35 E
Viña del Mar, *Chile* . **47 F2** 33 0S 71 30W
Vincennes, *U.S.A.* . **42 F4** 38 41N 87 32W
Vindhya Ra., *India* . **23 H6** 22 50N 77 0 E
Vineland, *U.S.A.* .. **43 F10** 39 29N 75 2W
Vinnitsa, *Ukraine* . **11 D15** 49 15N 28 30 E
Vire, *France* **8 B3** 48 50N 0 53W
Virgin Is. (British) □,
  W. Indies **45 D12** 18 30N 64 30W
Virgin Is. (U.S.) □,
  W. Indies **45 D12** 18 20N 65 0W
Virginia, *S. Africa* . **31 B4** 28 8S 26 55 E
Virginia □, *U.S.A.* . **42 G8** 37 30N 78 45W
Visby, *Sweden* .... **6 G11** 57 37N 18 18 E
Vishakhapatnam, *India* **25 D7** 17 45N 83 20 E
Vistula →, *Poland* . **11 A10** 54 22N 18 55 E
Viterbo, *Italy* ..... **12 C5** 42 25N 12 6 E
Viti Levu, *Fiji* .... **35 D14** 17 30S 177 30 E
Vitória, *Brazil* **46 E5** 20 20S 40 22W
Vitoria, *Spain* **9 A4** 42 50N 2 41W
Vitsyebsk, *Belarus* . **14 C5** 55 10N 30 15 E
Vladikavkaz, *Russia* . **15 F7** 43 0N 44 35 E
Vladimir, *Russia* .. **14 C7** 56 15N 40 30 E
Vladivostok, *Russia* . **18 E15** 43 10N 131 53 E
Vlissingen, *Neths.* . **10 C2** 51 26N 3 34 E
Vlóra, *Albania* .... **13 D8** 40 32N 19 28 E
Vltava →,
  Czech Rep. ..... **10 D8** 50 21N 14 30 E
Vogelkop, *Indonesia* . **22 D5** 1 25S 133 0 E
Vogelsberg, *Germany* **10 C5** 50 31N 9 12 E
Vojvodina □,
  Serbia, Yug. .... **13 B9** 45 20N 20 0 E
Volga →, *Russia* .. **15 E8** 46 0N 48 30 E
Volga Hts., *Russia* . **15 D8** 51 0N 46 0 E
Volgograd, *Russia* . **15 E7** 48 40N 44 25 E
Volksrust, *S. Africa* . **31 B4** 27 24S 29 53 E
Vologda, *Russia* ... **14 C6** 59 10N 39 45 E
Vólos, *Greece* .... **13 E10** 39 24N 22 59 E
Volta →, *Ghana* ... **30 C2** 5 46N 0 41 E

Volta, L., *Ghana* .. **30 C2** 7 30N 0 15 E
Volzhskiy, *Russia* . **15 E7** 48 56N 44 46 E
Vorkuta, *Russia* ... **14 A11** 67 48N 64 20 E
Voronezh, *Russia* . **14 D6** 51 40N 39 10 E
Vosges □, *France* .. **8 B7** 48 20N 7 10 E
Vrede, *S. Africa* ... **31 B4** 27 24S 29 6 E
Vredenburg, *S. Africa* . **31 C2** 32 56S 18 0 E
Vryburg, *S. Africa* . **31 B3** 26 55S 24 45 E
Vryheid, *S. Africa* . **31 B5** 27 45S 30 47 E
Vyatka →, *Russia* . **14 C9** 55 37N 51 28 E

W

Waal →, *Neths.* ... **10 C3** 51 37N 5 0 E
Wabash, *U.S.A.* ... **42 E5** 40 48N 85 49W
Wabash →, *U.S.A.* . **42 G3** 37 48N 88 2W
Waco, *U.S.A.* **41 D7** 31 33N 97 9W
Wâd Medanî, *Sudan* . **29 F11** 14 28N 33 30 E
Waddington, Mt.,
  Canada **38 C7** 51 23N 125 15W
Wagga Wagga,
  Australia .... **34 H8** 35 7S 147 24 E
Wah, *Pakistan* .... **23 C4** 33 45N 72 40 E
Waigeo, *Indonesia* . **22 D5** 0 20S 130 40 E
Wainganga →, *India* **23 K7** 18 50N 79 55 E
Waingapu, *Indonesia* **22 D4** 9 35S 120 11 E
Wakayama, *Japan* . **19 B4** 34 15N 135 15 E
Wałbrzych, *Poland* . **10 C9** 50 45N 16 18 E
Wales □, *U.K.* **7 E5** 52 19N 4 43W
Walgett, *Australia* . **34 F8** 30 0S 148 5 E
Wallaceburg, *Canada* . **42 D6** 42 34N 82 23W
Wallachia = Valahia,
  Romania .... **11 F13** 44 35N 25 0 E
Wallis & Futuna, Is.,
  Pac. Oc. **35 C15** 13 18S 176 10W
Walvis Bay, *Namibia* . **31 A1** 23 0S 14 28 E
Wanganui, *N.Z.* ... **35 H14** 39 56S 175 3 E
Wapakoneta, *U.S.A.* . **42 E5** 40 34N 84 12W
Warangal, *India* ... **25 D6** 17 58N 79 35 E
Wardha →, *India* .. **23 K7** 19 57N 79 11 E
Warrego →, *Australia* **34 G8** 30 24S 145 21 E
Warren, *Mich., U.S.A.* . **42 D6** 42 30N 83 0W
Warren, *Ohio, U.S.A.* . **42 E7** 41 14N 80 49W
Warren, *Pa., U.S.A.* . **42 E8** 41 51N 79 9W
Warrenton, *S. Africa* . **31 B3** 28 9S 24 47 E
Warrnambool,
  Australia .... **34 H7** 38 25S 142 30 E
Warsaw, *Poland* ... **11 B11** 52 13N 21 0 E
Warsaw, *U.S.A.* ... **42 E5** 41 14N 85 51W
Warta →, *Poland* .. **10 B8** 52 35N 14 39 E
Warwick, *U.S.A.* .. **43 E12** 41 42N 71 28W
Wasatch Ra., *U.S.A.* . **40 B4** 40 30N 111 15W
Washington, D.C.,
  U.S.A. **42 F9** 38 54N 77 2W
Washington, Ind.,
  U.S.A. **42 F4** 38 40N 87 10W
Washington, Pa.,
  U.S.A. **42 E7** 40 10N 80 15W
Washington □, *U.S.A.* . **40 A2** 47 30N 120 30W
Washington, Mt.,
  U.S.A. **43 C12** 44 16N 71 18W
Washington I., *U.S.A.* . **42 C4** 45 23N 86 54W
Waterbury, *U.S.A.* . **43 E11** 41 33N 73 3W
Waterford, *Ireland* . **7 E3** 52 15N 7 8W
Waterloo, *Canada* . **42 D7** 43 30N 80 32W
Watertown, *U.S.A.* . **43 D10** 43 59N 75 55W
Waterval-Boven,
  S. Africa .... **31 B5** 25 40S 30 18 E
Waterville, *U.S.A.* . **43 C13** 44 33N 69 38W
Watseka, *U.S.A.* ... **42 E4** 40 47N 87 44W
Watubela Is.,
  Indonesia ...... **22 D5** 4 28S 131 35 E
Waukegan, *U.S.A.* . **42 D4** 42 22N 87 50W
Waukesha, *U.S.A.* . **42 D3** 43 1N 88 14W
Wauwatosa, *U.S.A.* . **42 D4** 43 3N 88 0W
Wawa, *Canada* **42 B5** 47 59N 84 47W
Wayne, *U.S.A.* **42 F6** 38 13N 82 27W
Waynesboro, *U.S.A.* . **42 F8** 38 4N 78 53W
Waynesburg, *U.S.A.* . **42 F7** 39 54N 80 11W
Wazirabad, *Pakistan* . **23 C5** 32 30N 74 8 E
Webster Springs,
  U.S.A. **42 F7** 38 29N 80 25W
Weddell Sea,
  Antarctica **48 E5** 72 30S 40 0W
Weifang, *China* .... **21 C6** 36 44N 119 7 E
Welch, *U.S.A.* **42 G7** 37 26N 81 35W
Welkom, *S. Africa* . **31 B4** 28 0S 26 46 E
Welland, *Canada* .. **42 D8** 43 0N 79 15W
Wellesley Is., *Australia* **34 D6** 16 42S 139 30 E
Wellington, *N.Z.* .. **35 J13** 41 19S 174 46 E
Wellsboro, *U.S.A.* . **42 E9** 41 45N 77 18W
Wellsville, *U.S.A.* . **42 D9** 42 7N 77 57W
Wels, *Austria* ..... **10 D8** 48 9N 14 1 E
Wenzhou, *China* ... **21 D7** 28 0N 120 38 E
Wepener, *S. Africa* . **31 B4** 29 42S 27 3 E
Weser →, *Germany* . **10 B5** 53 36N 8 28 E
West Bend, *U.S.A.* . **42 D3** 43 25N 88 11W
West Bengal □, *India* . **23 H11** 23 0N 88 0 E
West Beskids, *Europe* . **11 D10** 49 30N 19 0 E
West Fjord, *Norway* . **6 E10** 67 55N 14 0 E
West Point, *U.S.A.* . **42 G9** 37 32N 76 48W
West Pt., *Canada* .. **43 A15** 49 52N 64 40W
West Virginia □,
  U.S.A. **42 F7** 38 45N 80 30W
Westbrook, *U.S.A.* . **43 D12** 43 41N 70 22W

Western Australia □,
  Australia .... **34 F3** 25 0S 118 0 E
Western Ghats, *India* . **25 D6** 14 0N 75 0 E
Western Sahara ■,
  Africa **28 D2** 25 0N 13 0W
Western Samoa =
  Samoa ■, *Pac. Oc.* **35 C16** 14 0S 172 0W
Westerwald, *Germany* . **10 C4** 50 38N 7 56 E
Westminster, *U.S.A.* . **42 F9** 39 34N 76 59W
Weston, *U.S.A.* ... **42 F7** 39 2N 80 28W
Wetar, *Indonesia* .. **22 D4** 7 30S 126 30 E
Whangarei, *N.Z.* ... **35 H13** 35 43S 174 21 E
Wheeling, *U.S.A.* .. **42 E7** 40 4N 80 43W
White →, *U.S.A.* .. **42 F4** 38 25N 87 45W
White Nile →, *Sudan* . **29 E11** 15 38N 32 31 E
White Sea, *Russia* . **14 A6** 66 30N 38 0 E
Whitefish Point, *U.S.A.* **42 B5** 46 45N 84 59W
Whitehorse, *Canada* . **38 B6** 60 43N 135 3W
Whitewater, *U.S.A.* . **42 D3** 42 50N 88 44W
Whitney, Mt., *U.S.A.* . **40 C3** 36 35N 118 18W
Whyalla, *Australia* . **34 G6** 33 2S 137 30 E
Wiarton, *Canada* .. **42 C7** 44 40N 81 10W
Wichita, *U.S.A.* ... **41 C7** 37 42N 97 20W
Wichita Falls, *U.S.A.* . **40 D7** 33 54N 98 30W
Wiener Neustadt,
  Austria .... **10 E9** 47 49N 16 16 E
Wiesbaden, *Germany* . **10 C5** 50 4N 8 14 E
Wilge →, *S. Africa* . **31 B4** 27 3S 28 20 E
Wilhelmshaven,
  Germany .... **10 B5** 53 31N 8 7 E
Wilkes-Barre, *U.S.A.* . **43 E10** 41 15N 75 53W
Willemstad, *Neth. Ant.* **45 E11** 12 5N 69 0W
Williamsburg, *U.S.A.* . **42 G9** 37 17N 76 44W
Williamson, *U.S.A.* . **42 G6** 37 41N 82 17W
Williamsport, *U.S.A.* . **42 E9** 41 15N 77 0W
Williston, *S. Africa* . **31 C3** 31 20S 20 53 E
Willowmore, *S. Africa* . **31 C3** 33 15S 23 30 E
Wilmington, Del.,
  U.S.A. **43 F10** 39 45N 75 33W
Wilmington, Ohio,
  U.S.A. **42 F6** 39 27N 83 50W
Winchester, Ky.,
  U.S.A. **42 G6** 38 0N 84 11W
Winchester, Va.,
  U.S.A. **42 F8** 39 11N 78 10W
Windhoek, *Namibia* . **31 A2** 22 35S 17 4 E
Windsor, *Canada* .. **42 D6** 42 18N 83 0W
Windward Is.,
  W. Indies **44 P20** 13 0N 61 0W
Winnebago, L., *U.S.A.* . **42 D3** 44 0N 88 26W
Winnipeg, *Canada* . **38 D10** 49 54N 97 9W
Winnipeg, L., *Canada* . **38 C10** 52 0N 97 0W
Winooski, *U.S.A.* .. **43 C11** 44 29N 73 11W
Winston-Salem, *U.S.A.* **41 C10** 36 6N 80 15W
Winterthur, *Switz.* . **10 E5** 47 30N 8 44 E
Wisconsin □, *U.S.A.* . **41 B9** 44 45N 89 30W
Witbank, *S. Africa* . **31 B4** 25 51S 29 14 E
Witdraai, *S. Africa* . **31 B3** 26 58S 20 48 E
Wkra →, *Poland* .. **11 B11** 52 27N 20 44 E
Włocławek, *Poland* . **11 B10** 52 40N 19 3 E
Wokam, *Indonesia* . **22 D5** 5 45S 134 28 E
Wolfsburg, *Germany* . **10 B6** 52 25N 10 48 E
Wollongong, *Australia* . **34 G9** 34 25S 150 54 E
Wolverhampton, *U.K.* . **7 E5** 52 35N 2 7W
Wönsan, *N. Korea* . **21 C7** 39 11N 127 27 E
Woods, L. of the,
  Canada **38 D10** 49 15N 94 45W
Woodstock, *Canada* . **42 D7** 43 10N 80 45W
Woonsocket, *U.S.A.* . **43 E11** 42 0N 71 31W
Worcester, *S. Africa* . **31 C2** 33 39S 19 27 E
Worcester, *U.S.A.* . **43 D12** 42 16N 71 48W
Worms, *Germany* .. **10 D5** 49 37N 8 21 E
Wrangel I., *Russia* . **18 B19** 71 0N 180 0 E
Wrocław, *Poland* .. **11 C9** 51 5N 17 5 E
Wuhan, *China* .... **21 C6** 30 31N 114 18 E
Wuhu, *China* ..... **21 C6** 31 22N 118 21 E
Wuppertal, *Germany* . **10 C4** 51 16N 7 12 E
Würzburg, *Germany* . **10 D5** 49 46N 9 55 E
Wutongqiao, *China* . **20 D5** 29 22N 103 50 E
Wuxi, *China* ...... **21 C7** 31 33N 120 18 E
Wuzhou, *China* .... **21 D6** 23 30N 111 18 E
Wyndham, *Australia* . **34 D4** 15 33S 128 3 E
Wyoming □, *U.S.A.* . **40 B5** 43 0N 107 30W

X

Xau, L., *Botswana* . **31 A3** 21 15S 24 44 E
Xenia, *U.S.A.* **42 F6** 39 41N 83 56W
Xiaguan, *China* ... **20 D5** 25 32N 100 16 E
Xiamen, *China* .... **21 D6** 24 25N 118 4 E
Xi'an, *China* ...... **21 C5** 34 15N 109 0 E
Xiangfan, *China* ... **21 C6** 32 2N 112 8 E
Xiangtan, *China* ... **21 D6** 27 51N 112 54 E
Xingu →, *Brazil* .. **46 C4** 1 30S 51 53W
Xining, *China* ..... **20 C5** 36 34N 101 40 E
Xuzhou, *China* .... **21 C6** 34 18N 117 10 E

Y

Yablonovyy Ra.,
  Russia .... **18 D13** 53 0N 114 0 E
Yakutsk, *Russia* ... **18 C14** 62 5N 129 50 E
Yamagata, *Japan* .. **19 A7** 38 15N 140 15 E
Yambol, *Bulgaria* .. **13 C12** 42 30N 26 36 E

Yamdena, *Indonesia* . **22 D5** 7 45S 131 20 E
Yamethin, *Burma* .. **25 C8** 20 29N 96 18 E
Yamuna →, *India* .. **23 G8** 25 30N 81 53 E
Yangtze Kiang →,
  China .... **21 C7** 31 48N 121 10 E
Yanji, *China* ...... **21 B7** 42 59N 129 30 E
Yantai, *China* ..... **21 C7** 37 34N 121 22 E
Yaoundé, *Cameroon* . **30 D4** 3 50N 11 35 E
Yapen, *Indonesia* .. **22 D5** 1 50S 136 0 E
Yarkhun →, *Pakistan* . **23 A4** 36 17N 72 30 E
Yarmouth, *Canada* . **43 D14** 43 50N 66 7W
Yaroslavl, *Russia* .. **14 C6** 57 35N 39 55 E
Yatsushiro, *Japan* . **19 C2** 32 30N 130 40 E
Yazd, *Iran* .... **24 B4** 31 55N 54 27 E
Yekaterinburg, *Russia* . **14 C11** 56 50N 60 30 E
Yellow Sea, *China* . **21 C7** 35 0N 123 0 E
Yellowknife, *Canada* . **38 B8** 62 27N 114 29W
Yellowstone →,
  U.S.A. **40 A6** 47 59N 103 59W
Yellowstone National
  Park, *U.S.A.* **40 B5** 44 40N 110 30W
Yemen ■, *Asia* ... **24 D3** 15 0N 44 0 E
Yenbo, *Si. Arabia* . **24 C2** 24 0N 38 5 E
Yenisey →, *Russia* . **18 B10** 71 50N 82 40 E
Yeniseysk, *Russia* . **18 D11** 58 27N 92 13 E
Yeola, *India* ...... **23 J5** 20 2N 74 30 E
Yerevan, *Armenia* . **15 F7** 40 10N 44 31 E
Yeu, I. d', *France* .. **8 C2** 46 42N 2 20W
Yibin, *China* ...... **20 D5** 28 45N 104 32 E
Yichang, *China* .... **21 C6** 30 40N 111 20 E
Yining, *China* ..... **20 B3** 43 58N 81 10 E
Yogyakarta, *Indonesia* . **22 D3** 7 49S 110 22 E
Yokkaichi, *Japan* .. **19 B5** 34 55N 136 38 E
Yokohama, *Japan* . **19 B6** 35 27N 139 28 E
Yokosuka, *Japan* .. **19 B6** 35 20N 139 40 E
Yonkers, *U.S.A.* ... **43 E11** 40 56N 73 54W
Yonne →, *France* .. **8 B5** 48 23N 2 58 E
York, *U.K.* **7 E6** 53 58N 1 6W
York, *U.S.A.* **42 F9** 39 58N 76 44W
Yosemite National
  Park, *U.S.A.* **40 C3** 37 45N 119 40W
Yoshkar Ola, *Russia* . **14 C8** 56 38N 47 55 E
Youngstown, *U.S.A.* . **42 E7** 41 6N 80 39W
Yuan Jiang →, *China* . **21 D6** 28 55N 111 50 E
Yucatán, *Mexico* .. **44 D7** 19 30N 89 0W
Yucatan Str.,
  Caribbean **44 C7** 22 0N 86 30W
Yugoslavia ■, *Europe* **13 B9** 44 0N 20 0 E
Yukon →, *U.S.A.* .. **38 B3** 62 32N 163 54W
Yukon Territory □,
  Canada **38 B6** 63 0N 135 0W
Yunnan □, *China* .. **20 D5** 25 0N 102 0 E
Yuzhno-Sakhalinsk,
  Russia .... **18 E16** 46 58N 142 45 E
Yvetot, *France* .... **8 B4** 49 37N 0 44 E

Z

Zabrze, *Poland* .... **11 C10** 50 18N 18 50 E
Zagreb, *Croatia* ... **10 F9** 45 50N 16 0 E
Zagros Mts., *Iran* .. **24 B3** 33 45N 48 5 E
Zahedan, *Iran* .... **24 C5** 29 30N 60 50 E
Zaïre = Congo →,
  Africa .... **32 F2** 6 4S 12 24 E
Zaïre = Congo, Dem.
  Rep. of the ■, *Africa* **32 E4** 3 0S 23 0 E
Zákinthos, *Greece* . **13 F9** 37 47N 20 57 E
Zambezi →, *Africa* . **33 H7** 18 35S 36 20 E
Zambia ■, *Africa* .. **33 G5** 15 0S 28 0 E
Zamboanga, *Phil.* .. **22 C4** 6 59N 122 3 E
Zamora, *Spain* **9 B3** 41 30N 5 45W
Zamość, *Poland* ... **11 C12** 50 43N 23 15 E
Zanesville, *U.S.A.* . **42 F6** 39 56N 82 1W
Zanjan, *Iran* ...... **24 B3** 36 40N 48 35 E
Zanzibar, *Tanzania* . **32 F7** 6 12S 39 12 E
Zaporozhye, *Ukraine* . **15 E6** 47 50N 35 10 E
Zaragoza, *Spain* .. **9 B5** 41 39N 0 53W
Zaria, *Nigeria* .... **30 B3** 11 0N 7 40 E
Zaskar Mts., *India* . **23 C6** 33 15N 77 30 E
Zeebrugge, *Belgium* . **10 C2** 51 19N 3 12 E
Zeerust, *S. Africa* . **31 B4** 25 31S 26 4 E
Zenica, *Bos.-H.* ... **13 B7** 44 10N 17 57 E
Zhangjiakou, *China* . **21 B6** 40 48N 114 55 E
Zhangzhou, *China* . **21 D6** 24 30N 117 35 E
Zhanjiang, *China* .. **21 D6** 21 15N 110 20 E
Zhejiang □, *China* . **21 D7** 29 0N 120 0 E
Zhengzhou, *China* . **21 C6** 34 45N 113 34 E
Zhigansk, *Russia* .. **18 C14** 66 48N 123 27 E
Zhitomir, *Ukraine* . **11 C15** 50 20N 28 40 E
Zibo, *China* ...... **21 C6** 36 47N 118 3 E
Zielona Góra, *Poland* . **10 C8** 51 57N 15 31 E
Zigong, *China* .... **20 D5** 29 15N 104 48 E
Ziguinchor, *Senegal* . **28 F1** 12 35N 16 20W
Žilina, *Slovak Rep.* . **11 D10** 49 12N 18 42 E
Zimbabwe ■, *Africa* . **33 H5** 19 0S 30 0 E
Zion National Park,
  U.S.A. **40 C4** 37 15N 113 5W
Zlatoust, *Russia* .. **14 C10** 55 10N 59 40 E
Zlín, *Czech Rep.* .. **11 D9** 49 14N 17 40 E
Zonguldak, *Turkey* . **15 F5** 41 28N 31 50 E
Zrenjanin, *Serbia, Yug.* **13 B9** 45 22N 20 23 E
Zug, *Switz.* .... **10 E5** 47 10N 8 31 E
Zunyi, *China* ...... **20 D5** 27 42N 106 53 E
Zürich, *Switz.* .... **10 E5** 47 22N 8 32 E
Zwickau, *Germany* . **10 C7** 50 44N 12 30 E
Zwolle, *Neths.* .... **10 B4** 52 31N 6 6 E

Place names on the yellow-coded large scale map section are to be found in the index at the end of that section